MW00980582

Using Norton Utilities

Alan C. Elliott

Using Norton Utilities

Copyright © 1990 by Que® Corporation.

All rights reserved. Printed in the United States of America. No part of this book may be used or reproduced in any form or by any means, or stored in a database or retrieval system, without prior written permission of the publisher except in the case of brief quotations embodied in critical articles and reviews. Making copies of any part of this book for any purpose other than your own personal use is a violation of United States copyright laws. For information, address Que Corporation, 11711 N. College Ave., Carmel, IN 46032.

Library of Congress Catalog No.: 90-61529

ISBN: 0-88022-580-7

This book is sold *as is*, without warranty of any kind, either express or implied, respecting the contents of this book, including but not limited to implied warranties for the book's quality, performance, merchantability, or fitness for any particular purpose. Neither Que Corporation nor its dealers or distributors shall be liable to the purchaser or any other person or entity with respect to any liability, loss, or damage caused or alleged to be caused directly or indirectly by this book.

93 92 91 4 3

Interpretation of the printing code: the rightmost double-digit number is the year of the book's printing; the rightmost single-digit number, the number of the book's printing. For example, a printing code of 90-1 shows that the first printing of the book occurred in 1990.

Using Norton Utilities is based on Norton Utilities 5.0, Norton Commander 3.0, and Norton Backup 1.1.

DEDICATION

To the next generation...

Amy
Elizabeth
John
Laura
Lisa
Marcie
Mary
Thomas
Valarie
William

Publishing Director

Lloyd J. Short

Acquisitions Editor

Karen A. Bluestein

Product Director

Shelley O'Hara

Project Manager

Paul Boger

Production Editor

Fran Blauw

Editor

Kelly Currie

Technical Editors

Jim Karney
Dan Schnake

Indexer

Sherry Massey

Editorial Assistant

Patricia J. Brooks

Book Design and Production

Hilary Adams
Dan Armstrong
Bill Basham
Claudia Bell
Jill D. Bomaster
Brad Chinn
Don Clemons
Sally Copenhaver
Travia Davis
Tom Emrick
Dennis Hager
Susan Hill
Tami Hughes
Bill Hurley
Betty Kish
Bob LaRoche
Larry Lynch
Diana Moore
Cindy L. Phipps
Joe Ramon
Dennis Sheehan
Louise Shinault
Bruce Steed
Mary Beth Wakefield

Composed in Garamond by Que Corporation.

About the Author

Alan C. Elliott

Alan C. Elliott, M.A.S., is Assistant Director of Academic Computing Services at the University of Texas Southwestern Medical Center in Dallas. He is the author of several books, including *Introduction to Microcomputing with Applications*, *A Daily Dose of the American Dream*, and *PC Programming Techniques*. He is coauthor of the 1985 and 1988 editions of the *Directory of Statistical Microcomputing Software*. His programming credits include Kwikstat (statistical data analysis) and PC-CAI (a computer-assisted instruction language), published by TexaSoft. His articles have appeared in professional and popular periodicals, including *PC Week*, *Collegiate Microcomputer Journal*, and *Communications in Statistics*.

CONTENTS AT A GLANCE

Table of Contents

IV Using Norton Backup

ACKNOWLEDGMENTS

I want to thank Karen Bluestein for the opportunity to work on this book. The entire staff at Que was very helpful and supportive throughout this project. Special thanks go to Shelley O'Hara, Fran Blauw, and Paul Boger for their help in editing the manuscript, asking insightful questions to make the presentation better, and for their encouragement. Jim Karney and Dan Schnake deserve thanks for their careful technical review of the manuscript.

This project could not have been finished without the support of my wife, Annette, and without some patience from my kids, Mary and William.

TRADEMARK ACKNOWLEDGMENTS

Que Corporation has made every effort to supply trademark information about company names, products, and services mentioned in this book. Trademarks indicated below were derived from various sources. Que Corporation cannot attest to the accuracy of this information.

1-2-3 is a registered trademark of Lotus Development Corporation.

Bernoulli Box is a registered trademark of Iomega Corporation.

Clipper is a trademark of Nantucket, Inc.

COMPAQ 386 is a trademark, and COMPAQ is a registered trademark of COMPAQ Computer Corporation.

Crosstalk is a registered trademark of Digital Communications Associates, Inc.

dBASE III PLUS and dBASE IV are trademarks, and dBASE II, dBASE III, and MultiMate are registered trademarks of Ashton-Tate Corporation.

MCI Mail is a registered servicemark of MCI Communications Corporation.

Microsoft Windows, Microsoft Windows Write, Microsoft Works, MS-DOS, and Multiplan are registered trademarks of Microsoft Corporation.

Novell is a registered trademark of Novell, Inc.

PageMaker is a registered trademark of Aldus Corporation.

Paradox is a trademark of Ansa Corporation.

ProComm is a registered trademark of Datastorm Technologies, Inc.

PS/2 and IBM PCjr are trademarks, and IBM is a registered trademark of International Business Machines Corporation.

Quattro is a registered trademark of Borland International, Inc.

R:BASE, WordStar Professional, and WordStar 2000 are registered trademarks of Microrim, Inc.

SpinRite is a trademark of Gibson Research Corporation.

Ventura Publisher is a registered trademark of Ventura Software, Inc.

VP-Planner is a registered trademark of Paperback Software International.

WordPerfect is a registered trademark of WordPerfect Corporation.

XyWrite is a trademark of XyQuest, Inc.

Conventions Used in This Book

The conventions used in this book have been established to help you learn to use the program quickly and easily. As much as possible, the conventions correspond with those used in the Norton Utilities documentation.

Screen names, menu names, and menu options appear in headline-style format. For example, select Time and Date.

Words or commands that you must type appear in italics. For example, type *prompt*. Or, they appear on a separate line. For example, type

COPY REPORT.TXT C:REPORT.TXT

Prompts or messages that appear on-screen are in digital type. For example, `Do you wish to continue or stop? (Y/N)`

In the command syntax, items enclosed in [brackets] are optional. For example, type

BE BEEP [*filespec*][/E]

Items that appear in *italics* are command variables. You should replace the *filespec* variable with a real file specification when you enter the command at the DOS prompt. For example, the file specification for a file named MYFILE.TXT in the \WP50 directory is \WP50\MYFILE.TXT.

The [*d:*] option is a designation for the disk drive name, such as drive A, B, C, or D.

Who Should Read *Using Norton Utilities*?

Using Norton Utilities is for anyone who uses an IBM or compatible personal computer with the PC DOS or MS-DOS operating system. Norton Utilities 5.0 and the companion programs, Norton Commander 3.0 and Norton Backup, give you capabilities to protect, recover, and manage your computer's resources beyond what is available from standard DOS commands. This book will help you get the most out of your computer and the Norton programs.

Norton Utilities, Commander, and Backup are known as the premier data recovery and disk management programs available for IBM PC and compatible computers. The goals of this book are to

- Help beginning computer users understand and learn how to use these programs.
- Help new and seasoned users gain insights into making information storage more reliable, safer, and better organized.

Computer users with some experience will tell you "It's not *if* you will lose information on your computer—it's *when*!" You are reading this book because you want to prevent that inevitable *when*, or you already have experienced it and are looking for a way to make sure that it doesn't happen again. Perhaps you are in the middle of a crisis and are looking for some way to recover information that may be lost. This book contains the information that, along with Norton Utilities, can give you the best chance of data recovery and can help you prevent many kinds of data loss in the future.

Hard disks can be a blessing and a curse. They are a blessing because they can store a great deal of information. They are a curse when you have hundreds of unorganized files and you can't find the one you need. The file-management commands in Norton Utilities and the organizational features in Norton Commander can help you manage your hard disk. This book will show you how to use these programs to organize your disk, find lost files, navigate through a maze of directories, and be more productive in the use of your hard disk.

What Is Covered in this Book?

This book covers Norton Utilities 5.0, with references to Norton Advanced Utilities 4.5 when Version 4.5 commands have been changed or integrated into different 5.0 commands. This book also covers Norton Commander Version 3.0 and Norton Backup, Versions 1.0 and 1.1.

This book is divided into four parts and five appendixes. The following sections discuss the contents in more detail.

Part I: Taking Charge of Your Computer

Part I of this book provides an overview of Norton Utilities and Norton Commander. Because you may be using one or both of these programs, the overviews are separated into two brief chapters. If you are interested only in Norton Utilities, for example, you easily can skip the information concerning Commander. The book will at times explain how the two programs can work together to enhance your control and use of your computer, however.

Part II: A Closer Look at Norton Utilities

Part II begins by introducing the most commonly used features of Norton Utilities. This part groups the various Norton commands into four major topics based on how you use the program. Chapter 3 describes ways to protect your information on disk—how to prevent accidental formatting, how to restore formatted disks, how to protect files from erasure, and how to get rid of important information safely. Chapter 4 discusses ways to recover lost information—information that you have erased or lost because of damage to your disk.

Chapter 5 is devoted to showing you how the utilities can help take good care of your hard disk—increasing safety, speed, and efficiency. Chapter 6 brings together a number of other Norton commands to help you better manage the information on your computer. Part II concludes with Chapter 7, a reference section that lists Norton Utilities commands alphabetically and gives a brief summary of the use of each command. This reference section will be helpful if you are comfortable with a command, but simply need a reminder about its syntax or options.

Part III: A Closer Look at Norton Commander

Part III begins with an explanation of how you can use Norton Commander as a supplement to DOS. Even if you are well versed in DOS, you can benefit from the enhanced power provided by Norton Commander. Commander operates like a super-DOS that is always available when you are at a DOS prompt. From the DOS prompt you still can enter a normal DOS command, or you can access a Commander feature. If you use a mouse, you can access Commander's features by pointing to an option on-screen and clicking the mouse button—just point and shoot.

Chapter 8 describes the basic DOS-enhancing features of Norton Commander. The disk-management features enable you to use menus and on-screen graphics which assist you in copying, renaming, erasing, finding files, and so on. With the directory-management features, you can make, remove, and change directories. The viewing feature enables you to examine Lotus 1-2-3 files, dBASE files, and a variety of other popular kinds of spreadsheet, database, word processing, graphics, or text files at any time—without having to use the program that created these special files.

Chapter 9 describes how you can create and use menus to make access to programs easier and more intuitive. With Commander and a modem you can link to MCI Mail, which enables you to send and receive electronic mail and send paper mail and faxes. You can access other electronic messaging networks by using MCI Mail.

Part IV: Using Norton Backup

Part IV, consisting of Chapter 10, covers the use of the Norton Backup program. This program enables you to copy information from your hard disk to a number of floppy disks. Then, if your hard disk is damaged or you lose files that cannot be recovered, you can use the backup copies of your hard disk to retrieve that information. Chapter 10 covers Versions 1.0 and 1.1 of Norton Backup. The differences in these versions are minor. Version 1.1 is an update to provide compatibility with a larger number of computers than Version 1.0 provided.

The Appendixes

The several appendixes give you additional information and tips about using Norton Utilities and Commander. If you are a computer beginner, you will want to read the brief introduction to PC DOS and MS-DOS (Appendix A). This appendix contains information about the basic DOS commands that are referred to in this book.

Appendix B provides a comparison of DOS and Norton commands. If you already know and use some of these DOS commands, this comparison will show you which Norton commands you can substitute for DOS commands and what additional features the Norton commands offer.

Appendix C includes installation instructions for Norton Utilities, Norton Commander, and Norton Backup. You already may have installed these programs using the information in the original program manual. If not, Appendix C will lead you through the installation process. It also will give you some additional information not covered in the Norton program manuals.

If you have a problem with your disk and don't know which Norton command to use, see Appendix D. This troubleshooting guide is divided into two parts. The first part deals with common disk problems and solutions, including the following kinds of situations:

- The computer no longer boots from the hard disk.
- The hard disk will not format as a system disk.
- The computer has a virus infection.
- You have continuing read-and-write problems on your hard disk that you can solve only with a low-level format.

The second part of Appendix D discusses responses to common DOS error messages that deal with disk problems. The appendix refers to DOS and Norton commands that can help you solve the problem.

Appendix E contains a listing of the ASCII codes used on IBM and compatible computers. These codes may be helpful in deciphering information when you directly edit information on disk.

What You Need To Use this Book

To use this book you need to have an IBM PC compatible computer that uses the MS-DOS or PC DOS operating system Version 2.0 or higher. Although many of the commands covered in this book will work on floppy disk systems, a significant amount of the book discusses hard disk management. You need copies of Norton Utilities, Norton Commander, or Norton Backup. Because the book contains three major sections covering these programs separately, you can use this book for information on one, two, or all three programs. Some examples require you to attach a printer to your computer. Also, you may need a blank diskette for some examples.

Before you read this book, you should familiarize yourself with a text editing program such as DOS's Edlin editor. Edlin is briefly described in the introduction to DOS (Appendix A). Any editor or word processor that can save files in Text mode will do. If you already use a text editing or word processing program that can save files in Text mode, you can use that program for the small amount of editing used in the examples in this book. Most of the tutorials in the book do not require text editing. Even if you do not know how to use a text editor, most examples in this book include alternative ways of creating needed files.

How To Use this Book

This book explains how to use Norton Utilities from a topical viewpoint and on a command-by-command basis. If you are a new user of Norton Utilities (or want to refresh your knowledge of the programs), you will want to read Chapters 3 through 6 carefully. These chapters cover the use of Norton commands.

If you already know how to use a Norton command, but you need a refresher about the command syntax or options, refer to Chapter 7. This chapter lists the commands alphabetically and briefly explains all options. You may want to refer to Chapter 7 often, even after you learn the basics of Norton commands.

If you have a problem with a diskette or hard disk and don't know which commands are appropriate to fix the problem, refer to the troubleshooting guide in Appendix D. This appendix also is useful when you encounter a disk-related DOS error message. Appendix D contains a selection of alphabetically listed DOS error messages. Each message is described with possible causes and solutions.

What Is Not Covered in this Book

Some problems related to information on your computer are beyond the scope of this book. If you lose information by accidentally erasing a range of cells in a Lotus 1-2-3 worksheet before saving it, for example, this book (and Norton Utilities) cannot help you recover from the mistake. Also, if you turn off the computer or lose power before saving a file to disk, the information is lost. These are instances when information is stored in the electronic memory of the computer and has not been placed on disk.

At times, software programs may contain bugs that make the information in a file useless. The logical nature of the file may be fine—that is, the file is okay according to DOS, but the information in the file has been scrambled or overwritten by the program. This kind of problem cannot be solved with the Norton programs. If you overwrite a file on disk with a file having the same name, the original file cannot be recovered because its space on disk is now being used by different information. These are cases where the file is stored properly on disk, but the information in the file is wrong.

Although Norton Utilities may be helpful for recovering from damage caused by some computer virus programs, these dangerous programs are getting more and more sophisticated in their capability to destroy data on a computer. There are simply too many ways that a virus can destroy data to be covered in this book. Appendix D gives you some help on this topic, however.

Physical damage to a hard disk or diskette can make data unrecoverable by the methods covered in this book. In some cases, professional disk repair technicians can extract information from a physically damaged disk. Mechanical problems with a disk drive also can cause loss of information. This problem must be corrected by a technician before you can recover any information.

Part I

Taking Charge of Your Computer

Includes

An Overview of Norton Utilities 5.0

An Overview of Norton Commander 3.0

1

An Overview of Norton Utilities 5.0

Norton Utilities 5.0 consists of a number of programs (often called Norton commands) that provide you with tools to manage information on disk. These tools include programs to protect information, recover information, make your hard disk work more efficiently, and manage your computer resources. The syntax for many of the Norton commands is similar to the PC DOS (or MS-DOS) command syntax that you already may be using.

Although PC DOS and MS-DOS have a number of useful commands, they lack some of the elements necessary to give you vital control over the safety of your files. One of the purposes of Norton Utilities is to fill this gap left by DOS.

If you are familiar with how to use DOS commands, you will find that many of the Norton commands use a similar syntax and therefore will be simple to learn and use. You can use some of the Norton commands as replacements for DOS commands. The replacement commands generally contain significant improvements over the normal DOS commands. The Norton Safe Format command, for example, not only formats a disk, but also is designed to prevent you from *accidentally* formatting a disk.

If you have been using Norton Utilities 4.5, you will find that some of the Version 4.5 commands have been incorporated into new Version 5.0 commands. Thus, Norton Utilities 5.0 has fewer commands to learn, but those commands have more options and features than the old 4.5 commands. Chapter 7, which gives an alphabetical listing of Norton commands, lists both 4.5 and 5.0 commands. When a 4.5 command has been incorporated into a 5.0 command, this is indicated in the description of the command.

The Norton Utilities commands fall into four basic categories:

- *Group 1:* Protects the information on your disk.
- *Group 2:* Helps you recover lost information.
- *Group 3:* Helps you fine-tune and manage the resources on your hard disk.
- *Group 4:* Helps you manage the information on your hard disk to make your work more efficient and productive.

This chapter provides an overview of the Norton Utilities commands and refers you to the chapters in which you can find more specific information about the commands.

Protecting Your Files

The Norton Utilities programs probably are most famous for helping you to recover lost information. These programs also are useful in preventing the loss of information to begin with. In fact, the old adage "a stitch in time saves nine" has relevance here. If you can safeguard your information on disk from the beginning, so much the better. Specific details on protecting the information on your disk are provided in Chapter 3, "Protecting Your Files."

A number of bad things can happen to information on your disk. *Physical problems* have to do with damage to the storage media and the mechanics of the disk drive. *Logical damage* involves the loss of magnetically stored information on disk.

Physical damage to a floppy diskette can be the result of a coffee spill, a bent diskette, a diskette left in a car on a hot summer day, or any number of other misuses of the diskette. You should always store a floppy diskette in its protective envelope and never expose it to heat, dust, or liquids.

A hard disk can sustain physical damage if you move the computer or bump it while it is operating. Even if you drop the computer only an inch, you can damage the hard disk. Usually, only a technician can repair physical damage to a disk—and then not always. Problems related to misaligned disk drives also require technical help.

Because information on a disk is stored as a magnetic image, this image can weaken until information is difficult or impossible to read. Loss of information on disk often results from accidental deletion of files or accidental formatting of the disk. Logical damage to a disk occurs when DOS loses information about where the data is stored—that is, DOS "forgets" where a file is located on disk. With Norton Utilities, you may be able to fix (or prevent) damage related to logical problems, magnetic weaknesses, or accidental erasure or formatting of the disk.

Preventing Problems

One of the strengths of Norton Utilities is its capability to help you prevent problems. Probably the first thing you should do with Norton Utilities is to make sure that you are safe from the prospect of someone accidentally formatting your hard disk. Otherwise, you could lose weeks, months, or years of work in a matter of minutes. Prevent this disaster by using the Safe Format command, a Norton replacement for the DOS FORMAT command. Safe Format gives you an added layer of protection against accidental formatting because the user must go through a few more steps to initiate a format.

If you load Norton Utilities with the Install program that comes on disk, you can replace the DOS FORMAT command with the Norton Safe Format command (see Appendix C). If you do not choose this option during the installation, you still can perform that task manually (see Chapter 3). Even if you manage to format a disk accidentally, you still can recover all information by using the Norton Format Recover command (unlike DOS's FORMAT command).

Restoring Formatted Disks

Implementing the IMAGE (Format Recovery) procedure protects you from the accidental formatting of your disk. Each time you boot your computer, the Image program stores information about your files (a duplicate copy of DOS directory information) on disk. Then, if your disk accidentally is formatted, the Unformat program can use this duplicate information to restore the formatted disk. When a disk is formatted, the actual data on the disk is not disturbed. The format clears out the file information in the disk's directory. With a duplicate copy of the information on disk, the Unformat program can reconstruct the information needed to unformat the disk and get all the files back.

Preventing Files from Being Changed or Erased

Individual files on disk can be lost if you accidentally overwrite them with another file or erase them. You also may have files that you want to protect from being used by the wrong person. The Norton Disk Monitor enables you to protect information on your disk from unauthorized use. If you have a number of files that you want to protect from accidental change or use, the Disk Monitor program can help.

Keeping Erased Information out of the Wrong Hands

Another way to protect information is to make sure that it does not fall into the wrong hands. As mentioned before, formatting a disk does not destroy the information on the disk but simply erases some of the information in the disk's directory. If you erase a file or format a disk, someone with a program such as Norton Utilities can recover that information, so the data is not safely destroyed. This problem is a potential one for anyone who places financial, personal, corporate, or other secret or valuable information on a disk. Norton provides alternatives to the DOS ERASE (DELETE) and FORMAT commands. You can use the Wipe Info command to completely destroy information on a disk.

Recovering Damaged or Lost Files

Chapter 4, "Recovering Files," covers techniques of recovering information from lost or damaged files. No matter how many precautions you take, you still have a good chance of losing some information on your computer disk. For example, you may enter the command DEL *.DAT rather than DIR *.DAT. This simple typographical error can mean the erasure of important information. Perhaps you erase a file because you think you have another copy of it elsewhere—only to find that the erased file was your only copy after all. Also, you may intentionally format your disk because you have a backup and then discover that the backup is no good. Before Norton Utilities arrived on the scene, you had little hope of recovering any of that information. Now you have a number of tools to give you more than a fighting chance to recover lost data.

Losing or Damaging Files

Files can be lost or damaged in a number of ways. You can format your disk accidentally. You can inadvertently or incorrectly enter the DEL or ERASE command and erase a whole batch of important files. Loss of information also can occur when the power shuts off for some reason before you save a file to your disk. Perhaps your program freezes, forcing you to perform a warm boot (Ctrl-Alt-Del) before all information is written to a file. Your disk may become too full so that DOS loses information about where the contents of a file are located. Bugs in software, hardware failures, and human errors are all potential causes of damaged files.

Recovering or Fixing Files

In many cases, Norton Utilities can help you recover all or portions of damaged or lost files. The primary programs for recovery include the Unerase, Unformat, Norton Disk Doctor II (NDD), and Norton Disk Edit commands.

The Unerase command is useful for recovering files that you have erased. Norton Disk Doctor II is a powerful program that attempts to diagnose problems with your disk (such as those caused by fragmented files, unclosed files from power outages, and so on) and correct these problems automatically.

The Norton Disk Edit program enables you to "perform surgery" on the information on disk. By directly editing the logical inner workings of the disk, you can remove or replace bad or damaged information with good information. If the disk information that contains the addresses of files on disk is damaged, for example, you may be able to transplant a new copy of this information to disk—making the information usable again. The Disk Edit program is powerful and dangerous. Like the knife of a surgeon, it can be helpful in the hands of someone who carefully and knowledgeably uses it. If you accidentally change important disk information, however, you can destroy access to all the data on your disk.

Taking Good Care of Your Hard Disk

Keeping information on your disk safe is vital. As with an automobile, a few maintenance tasks can keep your machine running smoothly and at top speed. Chapter 5, "Making Your Hard Disk Work Efficiently," covers several Norton Utilities commands that you can use to perform these maintenance procedures.

Testing Your Computer for Problems

Problems relating to your hard disk can mount before you even realize that a problem exists. Norton Utilities includes commands that enable you to keep track of how your computer system and hard disk are performing. The Norton Disk Doctor II closely examines all the information on your disk and determines whether problems exist that could cause information in a file to become lost. NDD II optionally attempts to correct such problems when they are found.

Making Your Disk Run Smoother and Faster

One of the problems with disks is that, after much use, files become entangled or fragmented. When DOS runs out of enough space to store a file in one contiguous area on the disk, the operating system resorts to storing a part of a file here, a part there, and so on. This problem can get bad enough to cause DOS to lose information on some files. Also, because DOS must look here and there to find a file, your access to the hard disk can be slowed considerably. The Norton Speed Disk (SD) command can rearrange the files on your hard disk in such a way as to remove fragmentation and restore maximum speed to the disk. If you hear your disk grinding when a file is being read or saved, or if your disk seems to be slowing down, you may be able to regain speed by using the Speed Disk command.

Another command that can help your hard disk work more efficiently is the Calibrate command. You can use this command to adjust how much information DOS reads from your hard disk in one pass. Fine tuning this adjustment can give your hard disk more speed. Calibrate also can perform a nondestructive low-level format of your hard disk to check the disk for reliability without disturbing the information already on disk.

Have you ever spent time looking through a directory listing to find a particular file? Being able to list the files by the date they were created—or by size, name, or extension—would undoubtedly be helpful. With the Norton Directory Sort command, you can list files in a number of ways, making the search for files easier and faster.

Another Norton command that can make your disk more efficient is File Find. You can use File Find to determine how much of the disk is being used to store files and how much of the space is allocated for use but is not used.

Managing Your Computer's Resources

A number of commands in Norton Utilities can give you more control over your computer than you can have by using DOS commands alone. These Norton commands help you manage your hard disk more efficiently and enable you to choose certain setup parameters for your computer.

Because a hard disk can store many files, just keeping track of potentially thousands of files easily can become a management nightmare. Suppose you created a report last month but now cannot remember which directory contains table 1.A, or where that graphic about sales on the East Coast is located. Norton has the commands to enable you to find information quickly.

Are you tired of working on a monitor that displays black and white (or black and amber, or black and green) when you are using DOS—even though you are using a color monitor? Would you like to display more that 25 lines on your EGA monitor? Would you like to create your own custom program menu? Chapter 6, "Managing the Resources of Your Computer," describes how to control these items by using Norton Utilities.

Navigating Directories

As newer and more advanced hard disks come on the market, users must deal with keeping track of more information on disk. The Norton Change Directory (NCD) command enables you to navigate between directories much more easily than having to remember the full names of each directory on disk. The NCD command replaces the functions of the DOS commands Change Directory, Remove Directory, and Make Directory—and offers more. With NCD, you can display the directory on-screen in a tree-like graph that shows various relationships among the directories. Using the arrow keys, you can highlight the directory you want to access. Not only can you make, change to, and remove directories as in DOS—in NCD, you also can rename directories.

Finding Information on Your Hard Disk

Within each directory on disk, you may have hundreds of files. Finding a particular file can be a nightmare. Often you know you have a file on disk but you cannot remember where you saw it. The Norton File Find command enables you to find a specific file no matter which directory holds it. File Find also can perform a text search to find a file by searching the text inside the file. The File Find command even can search files that you have erased.

Controlling Your Computer's Settings

The Norton Control Center is a utility that enables you to make your computer do things you may never have thought possible. You can change the size of your cursor, for example. If you use a laptop with a hard-to-read monitor, making the cursor bigger makes it easier to find on-screen. Some PCs require that you use the DOS Setup program on the diagnostic disk to set the date and time on the computer permanently. You now can do that with the Norton Control Center. Other settings available include monitor colors, how fast characters repeat when you hold down a key for more than a few seconds, how many lines are displayed on-screen, and settings for serial ports.

Creating Better Batch Files

Batch files contain series of commands that you use repetitively. DOS has a number of commands that are used in batch files, such as the PAUSE command and the ECHO command. Norton Utilities supplies some additional commands, called the Batch Enhancer commands, that enable you to create more sophisticated batch files. Using these commands, you can draw boxes, prompt the user for input, branch according to the user's answer, and so on.

Using Norton Utilities 5.0

You should be convinced by now that Norton Utilities has a myriad of commands that can help you use your computer more safely and more productively. This program has other helpful features, however. Unlike most DOS commands, which you can use only from the DOS prompt, Norton gives you two ways to use commands. First, if you are familiar with a command, you can type it at the DOS prompt just as you would use any DOS command. Second, you can access Norton commands from a menu—one that reminds you of the purpose of the command and the options that are available. The following sections discuss how to use Norton Utilities.

Giving Norton Commands from the DOS Prompt

You can use Norton Utilities commands as if they were DOS commands. In fact, Norton designed commands so that they operate with a syntax similar to DOS commands. To format a disk in drive A with the system switch (make the disk a bootable disk), for example, you could enter the familiar DOS command

```
FORMAT A:/S
```

To format a disk in drive A with the Norton Safe Format command and the same option, enter this command:

```
SFORMAT A:/S
```

Notice that the syntax of the two commands is identical; only the names of the commands are different. Also notice that a command consists of distinct parts—the command (SFORMAT, in this example), any parameters (the disk drive), and switches. In the discussion of each command, the appropriate syntax is explained.

Using the Norton Menu

If you do not remember how to enter a Norton command at the DOS prompt, you have another option. Norton Utilities provides you with an easy-to-use menu interface with which you can access the Norton commands. This interface is called the *Norton Menu*. To use the Norton Menu, you need to remember only one command: NORTON. After you type this command at the DOS prompt, you see a screen similar to the one in figure 1.1.

The Norton Menu screen consists of two parts. On the left side of the screen is a box containing a list of the available Norton commands. In figure 1.1, the Disk Doctor II command is highlighted on the list. At the bottom of the screen, notice the command NDD. NDD is the command

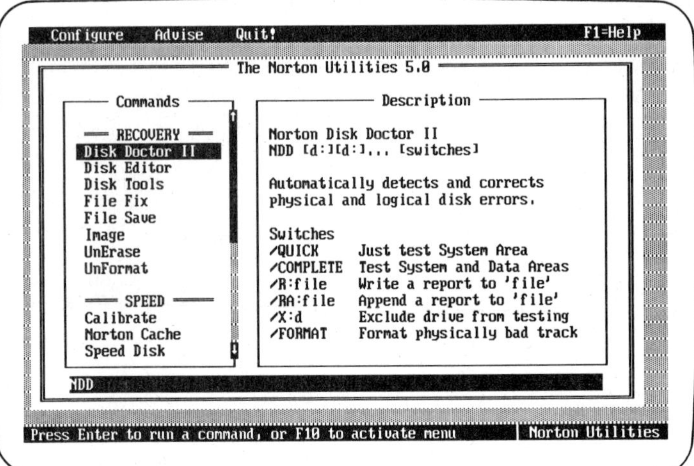

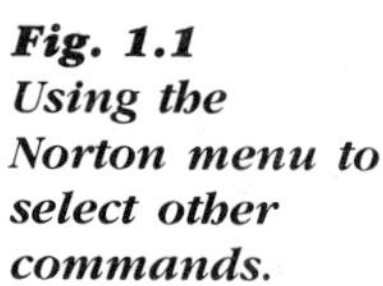
***Fig. 1.1** Using the Norton menu to select other commands.*

name of the Norton Disk Doctor II. To the right of the command list is a brief description of the highlighted command. In this case, a description of Norton Disk Doctor II is given, including the syntax of the NDD command and available switches. Not all commands are visible at one time in the command list. In a list box such as this, you can use the up- and down-arrow keys to display the remaining commands. You can press Home to go to the top of the list and End to go to the bottom of the list.

You can list the commands in the Norton Menu list by topic or alphabetically. See "Accessing the Configure Pull-Down Menu," later in this chapter, for more information.

Press Esc to end the Norton Menu program and to return to the DOS prompt.

Choosing Commands with the Point-and-Shoot Method

With the Norton menu, you can point to the name of the command you want to use by using the arrow keys on the cursor keypad to move the highlight up or down in the command list. After you highlight (*point* to) the command you want to use, you can press Enter to run (*shoot*) the command. This point-and-shoot method enables you to choose and run a command easily without having to remember the exact command name or options.

At the bottom of the Norton Menu screen is an input line that displays the selected command—the one to which you are pointing. Your cursor is positioned after the command on the input line. Here, you can type any options or switches before you press Enter to activate the command.

To run a command and enter switches, follow these steps:

1. Point to the command to use.

2. Type the appropriate switches or options.

3. Press Enter.

Using a Mouse

If your computer has a mouse attached, you also can use the mouse to point and shoot. When you move the mouse, you will see a pointer (a block or an arrow) on the Norton screen. To choose a command, point to the command and click the mouse button once. The command appears at the bottom of the screen and you then can type any appropriate switches or options and press Enter to run the command.

To reveal commands that are not shown on the list, place the mouse pointer on the up or down arrow at the top or bottom right of the command box. You then can press the mouse key to move the command list up or down.

On a two-button mouse, pressing both buttons together is the same as pressing Esc on the keyboard.

Using Norton Menu's Command-Line Editing Keys

Some command lines get complicated, and you may get to the end of a line before you realize that you have made an error at the beginning. You can use the Backspace key to erase all your work and start over, of course. If you use the built-in WordStar-like editing keys, however, you can save yourself some work. Table 1.1 lists these editing keys.

Table 1.1
Norton Menu Editing Keys

Key	*Effect*
→	Moves cursor to the right
←	Moves cursor to the left
Ctrl-D	Moves cursor right one character
Ctrl-S	Moves cursor left one character
Ctrl-→ or Ctrl-F	Moves cursor right one word
Ctrl-← or Ctrl-A	Moves cursor left one word
Ctrl-Home	Moves cursor to beginning of line
Ctrl-End	Moves cursor to end of line
Backspace	Deletes character to the left
Del or Ctrl-G	Deletes character at cursor
Ctrl-T	Deletes word to the right
Ctrl-W	Deletes word to the left
Ctrl-Y	Deletes the line

Viewing the Norton Menu Help Screens

At the top right of the Norton Menu screen, `F1=Help` is displayed. This reminds you that you can press F1 to bring up a series of Norton Help screens that function like a mini-manual for the Norton Utilities. You also can select Help by pointing to F1 = Help with your mouse pointer and clicking once.

Using the Configure Menu

On the top line (menu bar) of the Norton menu, the menu items Configure, Advise, and Quit appear. Configure and Advise are pull-down menus. The Quit option ends the Norton Menu program. To open up one of these menus, press F10 or point to the menu item with the mouse pointer and click once. After you extend a pull-down menu, you can move to one of the other menus by pressing the right- or left-arrow key or by pointing to the menu bar, pressing and holding the mouse button, and dragging the mouse to the left or right. Figure 1.2 shows the Configure menu.

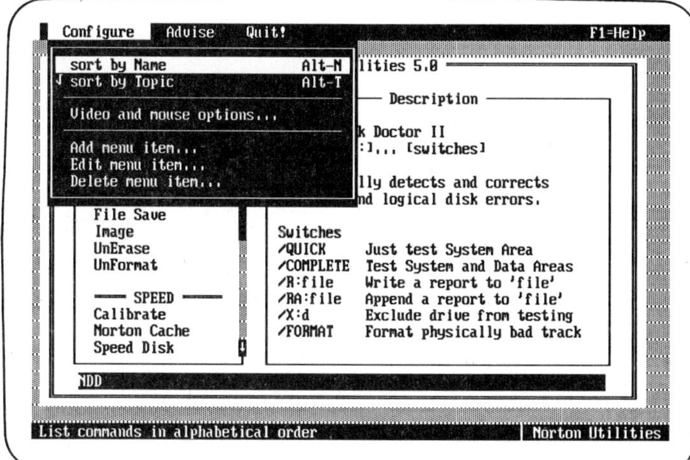

***Fig. 1.2** Accessing the Pull-down menus on the Norton menu screen.*

The Configure menu has three parts. The top part contains the first two options and enables you to choose how the commands are listed in the Norton menu. In figure 1.1, the commands are listed by topic. The topics are Recovery, Speed, Security, and Tools. Within the topics, the commands are listed alphabetically. If you choose the Sort by Name option, all commands will be listed alphabetically. The second part of the Configure menu sets video options; the third part of the Configure menu enables you to add, delete, or edit the contents of the menu.

To choose an item on a pull-down menu you can use the up- and down-arrow keys to highlight your choice and then press Enter. Alternatively, you can point to your choice with the mouse cursor and click. Notice that the Sort topics have Alt commands listed across from them, which you can use as shortcuts. The shortcut for Sort by Name is Alt-N, and the shortcut for Sort by Topic is Alt-T. When you see commands like these listed in a pull-down menu, it means that you can access these commands without pulling down the menu by entering the command listed. Therefore, to sort commands by name even when the Configure menu is *not* pulled down, you can enter the command Alt-N. (Hold down the Alt key and press the N key.)

Another way to choose an option from a pull-down menu is to press a hot key. A *hot key* enables you to use a shortcut to perform a function. Often, a hot key is the first letter of the menu choice. However, if there are two menu options that begin with the same letter, the hot key is the capitalized letter in the option. For the two Sort options, for example, the hot keys are N for `sort by Name` and T for `sort by Topic`. After you extend the Configure menu, you can press N to choose the Sort by Name option, V to choose the Video option, and so on.

Setting Video and Mouse Options

The Video and Mouse option on the Configure menu enables you to choose how the Norton menu (and other Norton menus) appear on your monitor. After you choose this option, a screen similar to the one in figure 1.3 appears. There are four types of settings in this dialog box: Screen Colors, Graphics Options, Screen Options, and Mouse Options.

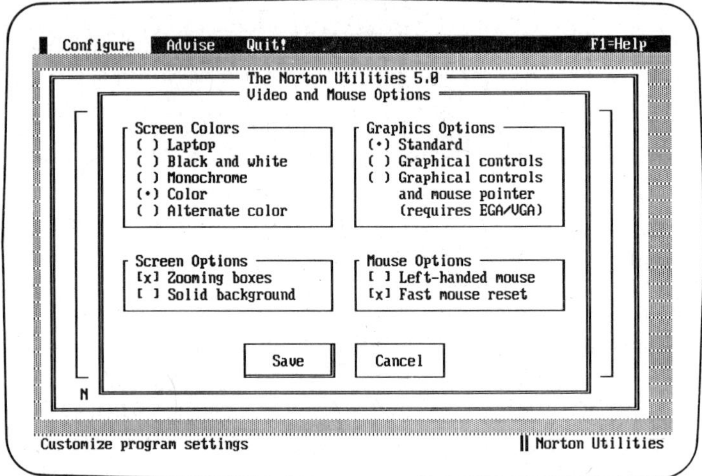

Fig. 1.3 ***Setting video and mouse options in the Norton menu.***

Selecting Options with Radio Buttons

The Screen Colors and Graphics Options boxes contain radio buttons. These buttons are represented by parentheses (or circles on EGA or VGA monitors) with a dot in the middle of only one of the options per box. The term *radio button* comes from being able to choose only one radio station on your car radio by choosing one button. When you choose one button, all other buttons on the radio are turned off. In the same way, when you see a dialog box that contains radio buttons, you know that you can choose only one option in that box. To select a radio button, use the arrow keys to highlight the button you want to choose, and then press the space bar to choose the button. This will turn off any other radio button in the box. If you have a mouse, point to the button you want to choose and click once. You also can select buttons by pressing the appropriate hot key. The hot key is the first letter of the option name or the capitalized letter of an option. You would press L, for example, to select the Laptop Screen Colors button.

In the Screen Colors box, you can choose between five color combinations: Laptop, Black and White, Monochrome, Color, and Alternate Color. The Laptop, Black and White, and Monochrome options use combinations of black and different intensities of white. The Color and Alternate Color options use mostly blue, green, black, and white. Choose any of the color options that suit your taste.

In the Graphics Options box, the Standard option displays a square cursor-like mouse pointer and nongraphics radio and check buttons. The Graphical Control option displays round radio buttons but the mouse cursor is in the standard mode. For the Graphics Controls and Mouse Pointer option (available only for EGA and VGA), the mouse pointer is an arrow.

Selecting Options with Check Boxes

The two boxes in figure 1.3, Screen Options and Mouse Options, contain check boxes. Unlike radio buttons, you can choose any number of check boxes in an option box. Use arrow keys to point to the box you want and press the space bar to turn the option on or off (an X means the option is turned on). If you are using a mouse, point to an option and click. Also, you can press the option's hot key to choose an item.

In the Screen Options box, you can select the Zooming Boxes option so that when dialog boxes appear on-screen, they look like they zoom into place—the boxes grow from a small square to the final size. The Solid Background option enables you to choose a solid or textured background on Norton menu screens.

In the Mouse Options box, the Left-Handed Mouse option enables you to choose your mouse for left-handed or right-handed use. This simply changes the meanings of the buttons on a two-button mouse. You should turn on the Fast Mouse Reset option if you are using PS/2 or COMPAQ mouse ports.

After you set all of the options you want on the Video and Mouse Options menu, choose Save to save this information to disk. To choose Save, press Enter, press the S hot key, or point to the Save box with your mouse pointer and press Enter.

Adding, Editing, or Deleting Menu Items

The Norton menu enables you to customize its contents. You can add your own commands to the list, edit how the commands are presented, or delete items from the menu. See Chapter 6 for information on how to change items on the Norton menu.

Using the Advise Menu

When you choose Advise on the top menu bar, three menu items are revealed:

- Common Disk Problems
- DOS Error Messages
- CHKDSK Error Messages

These items give you advice on solutions to problems you may encounter. The Common Disk Problems option covers problems such as when your computer will no longer boot from a disk, what to do if you have formatted your hard disk, problems in copying files, and other topics related to accessing information on your disk. The DOS Error Messages option gives explanations for DOS messages that you get when you use a DOS command and it does not work properly (for example, `Abort, Retry, or Fail`). The CHKDSK Error Messages option advises you what to do if the DOS CHKDSK command finds problems on your disk such as problems in the File Allocation Table (FAT). For more information on the Advise menu topics, see Appendix D.

Accessing the Norton Menu from Any Directory

To begin the Norton menu, you simply type the command *norton* at the DOS prompt. If you are not in the Norton directory, however, DOS cannot execute this command unless you have given a PATH command that includes the Norton directory (usually \NORTON) in the DOS search path. The DOS search path typically is set up in the AUTOEXEC.BAT file, in a line similar to this one:

```
PATH C:;\C:\DOS;C:\NORTON
```

With the \NORTON directory included in the path (in this example, the directory is on drive C), you can access the Norton menu (and all Norton commands) from any directory and drive on your computer.

Examine the AUTOEXEC.BAT file in your root directory to see whether the file contains the \NORTON directory in a PATH command. If Norton Utilities is stored in a directory with another name, that name should be in the PATH statement. If the \NORTON directory is not included in your PATH statement, you should add the directory to the statement in order to make the best use of the program. Remember that if you change your AUTOEXEC.BAT file, the changes do not take effect until you reboot your computer. If you need more information on setting up your AUTOEXEC.BAT file, refer to Appendix A, "An Introduction to DOS."

Getting Instant Help

In addition to the information provided about commands on the Norton Menu screen, you have another way to get on-screen help about Norton commands. If you enter at the DOS prompt a Norton command followed by a question mark, a Help screen appears. This screen lists the command's possible options and switches and may give some sample uses of the command. To get information on the BE (Batch Enhancer) command, for example, enter the following at the DOS prompt:

```
BE ?
```

Figure 1.4 shows the help information that appears on-screen.

```
C:\NORTON>be ?
Batch Enhancer, Norton Utilities v2.0, (C) Copyright 1990 by Peter Norton

    BE command [parameters]
          or
    BE filespec

Commands available:

      ASK
      BEEP
      BOX
      CLS
      DELAY
      GOTO
      PRINTCHAR
      ROWCOL
      SA
      WINDOW

For more help on a specific command type:
      BE command ?

C:\NORTON>
```

Fig. 1.4 ***A help screen for the Norton Batch Enhancer (BE) command.***

Summary

The information on your computer disk may not be safe. Things that can compromise your data are problems such as accidental erasures, unintentional disk formatting, problems with computer programs, power outages, and other difficulties. Although DOS has a few options that can help you protect your data, more are needed. Norton Utilities gives you additional ways to build in preventive measures and protect the information on your computer disk. Then, if a loss occurs, you still may be able to recover some or all of your information by using Norton Utilities recovery techniques.

Norton Utilities programs are not only for protection and recovery. The program also includes a number of commands that help you manage the information on your computer and make your disk run faster and safer.

This book helps you get the most out of Norton Utilities. It groups and explains the commands by the four basic ways you will use them: protection, recovery, maintenance, and management of information on your hard disk.

2

An Overview of Norton Commander 3.0

Norton Commander 3.0 is a program that makes your personal computer easier to use and gives you more control over your computer than you have with DOS alone. The features that Commander offers can be categorized into several areas:

- An easier way to perform many common DOS commands such as COPY, RENAME, DELETE, and others. Rather than you having to remember DOS syntax for these commands, Commander leads you through the command process with a series of menus and prompts.
- Commands that perform tasks that DOS cannot do. Commander enables you to rename directories, view sorted directories, compare directories, control hidden file attributes, and so on.
- A way to view spreadsheet, database, and word processing files without having to use the application program.
- A communication program for sending and receiving MCI mail.
- A communication link for sending information between two computers.
- The option to choose between entering commands at the DOS prompt or accessing commands from a menu structure. You also can use a mouse to access menus in Commander.

This list of features is not exhaustive, but should give you an idea of the kinds of tasks you can perform with Commander. Using Norton Commander is like adding a "power package" to a plain automobile. DOS is that plain automobile that generally gets you where you want to go. With

Commander added onto DOS, however, you have power windows (pull-down menus), extra horsepower (commands that can do more than DOS commands), a car phone (MCI Mail), and more. Commander makes using your computer more fun, and the program's array of features also can make you more productive.

This book guides you through the setup and use of Norton Commander to show you how to take advantage of its numerous features. You learn why you would use a Commander feature, when you would want to use a feature, and how to use the feature. This overview chapter introduces you to Commander's capabilities and menu structure and tells you how to access menu choices. Details of the menu items are covered in Chapters 8 and 9.

Working with Basic Commander Features

Chapter 8 covers the basic features of Norton Commander. These include the ability to perform commands such as Copy, Rename, and Move from a menu interface. You also can view WordPerfect and other word processor files, Lotus 1-2-3 and other spreadsheet files, and dBASE and other database files directly from Commander without having to access another program. Chapter 8 also covers Commander's version of the Norton Change Directory command which is more extensive than the similar command in Norton Utilities.

Working with Advanced Commander Features

Chapter 9 covers several advanced features of Norton Commander. These include creating your own menus, specifying file extension meanings, and using Commander Mail and Commander Link.

Creating Menus

One of the ways you can customize Commander so that your computer works intuitively for you is to create and use your own menus. You can create menus to automate series of commands that you perform regularly.

You may create a menu that enables you to choose which application program to begin (WordPerfect, Lotus 1-2-3, Excel, and so on), for example. If you are familiar with batch files, you will find that these menus are created similarly and perform similar tasks. Rather than just use DOS batch commands, however, you can access Commander menu commands.

Specifying File Extensions

If Commander knows which application is associated with a file in a directory listing, you can choose that file and have Commander automatically load the application, using the file name you have highlighted on-screen. You first must define the file types you plan to use, however. You can specify that all files with the WP extension are WordPerfect files, for example. Then if you choose a file with a WP extension by selecting the file name on-screen, Commander loads WordPerfect with that file being edited.

Using Commander Mail

With Commander, you can access MCI Mail. To do so, you must have a modem attached to your computer and a phone line. You also must have an MCI account number and password. When you use MCI Mail, you can send and receive electronic mail, faxes, telexes, and paper mail.

Tip: If you do not have an MCI Mail account, you can arrange to get one by calling 1-800-444-6245. Normally, a fee is required to set up the account, but sometimes MCI waives the fee. (At the writing of this book, the fee was $25.) Ask the service representative whether MCI will waive the fee because you are using Norton Commander.

Using Commander Link

Commander Link enables you to move information quickly between two computers. To use Commander Link, you must have a serial cable connecting the two computers and Commander Link must be running on both computers. The cable between the two computers must be a *null modem cable*—a special serial cable that acts as a modem link between two computers (for more information, see Chapter 8). You can purchase such a cable from your local computer shop. Commander Link is helpful for moving large numbers of files from one computer to another. You can use Link to copy your WordPerfect directory from one computer to another, for example.

Using Norton Commander

This book assumes that you already have installed Norton Commander on your hard disk. If you have not, refer to Appendix C for installation instructions. Be sure that you choose to place the \NC directory name in the PATH statement in your AUTOEXEC.BAT file (an option during installation). If you already have installed Commander but did not place \NC in your PATH statement, refer to Appendix A on how to use the DOS PATH command and how to edit an AUTOEXEC.BAT file.

To begin the Norton Commander program, type *nc* at the DOS prompt.

A screen similar to the one in figure 2.1 appears. As you learn in Chapter 8, you can customize the way that Commander looks on your screen. Generally, the screen includes four areas of interest: a right panel, a left panel (not visible in fig. 2.1), a menu of function key commands at the bottom of the screen, and a menu bar at the top of the screen (not visible in fig. 2.1). You can control the visibility of the panels on-screen by pressing Ctrl-F1 for the left panel or Ctrl-F2 for the right panel. Notice also that the normal DOS prompt appears just above the function key menu.

C:\NC

Name		Size	Date	Time
..		▸UP--DIR◂	1-29-90	1:34p
IN		▸SUB-DIR◂	1-29-90	1:58p
OUT		▸SUB-DIR◂	1-29-90	1:58p
SENT		▸SUB-DIR◂	1-29-90	1:58p
inread	me	1312	10-23-89	3:00p
mci	exe	103396	10-23-89	3:00p
nc	exe	3100	10-23-89	3:00p
nc	hlp	45727	10-23-89	3:00p
ncmain	exe	139274	10-23-89	3:00p
read	me	974	10-23-89	3:00p
123view	exe	52464	10-23-89	3:00p
chkmail	bat	342	10-23-89	3:00p
dbview	exe	61026	10-23-89	3:00p
mci	hlp	27050	10-23-89	3:00p
mcidrivr	exe	71272	10-23-89	3:00p
paraview	exe	62596	10-23-89	3:00p
pcxview	exe	46094	10-23-89	3:00p
rbview	exe	67966	10-23-89	3:00p
refview	exe	63492	10-23-89	3:00p
ser-test	exe	4400	10-23-89	3:00p

```
C:\NC>
1Help  2Menu  3View  4Edit  5Copy  6RenMov  7Mkdir  8Delete  9PullDn  10Quit
```

Fig. 2.1
The Norton Commander opening screen.

Using Menus and Commands

Commander gives you a choice in how you can access computer commands. You can enter a command at the DOS prompt or choose a command from one of Commander's menus. When Commander is running, the DOS prompt always appears on-screen. If you enter a DOS command, it works as it always has worked (although pressing F3 will not recall the command). When the command's action is finished, you are returned to the Commander screen. If you enter at the DOS prompt a command to begin an application program—such as a word processor—the application runs normally, and you return to the Commander screen when you exit that program. If you want to access a Commander command rather than a DOS command, you must choose the command from a Commander menu or by using a hot key combination. (On the initial Commander screen, only one menu is present—the function key menu. See Chapter 8 for information on how to control which menus are displayed.)

Understanding the Selection Methods

To access Commander features such as menu commands, you may use a technique called *point and shoot*. When the Commander screen is displayed, for example, and you press the up- or down-arrow key on the cursor keypad, a highlight moves up or down in the list of files in the right panel of the screen. If you want to select a file to be used in some actions (such as when you're copying, renaming, and so on), you point to the file by highlighting it. Then, to choose what you want to do to the file (shoot), you press Enter or a menu key (such as one of the function keys). In many cases when using Commander, you point to an item by highlighting it and you choose it by pressing Enter.

If you are using a mouse, a small square cursor appears on-screen. You can move this cursor by moving the mouse. The point-and-shoot technique with a mouse is to move the mouse pointer to some menu item or file name (point) and then choose the item (shoot) by clicking the left or right mouse button. If you have a mouse, you can use the mouse or the arrow keys to point to a selection.

In most menus and dialog boxes, you also can choose an option by pressing the first letter of the option. When you press the F10 (Quit) function key to end Commander, for example, the dialog box in figure 2.2 appears. You have several ways to choose Yes or No:

- Use the right- and left-arrow keys to move the highlight to Yes or No, and press Enter to select the highlighted choice.

- Press the first letter of your choice—press the N key to choose No or press Y to choose Yes.
- Using the mouse, move the pointer on top of your choice and click the mouse button.

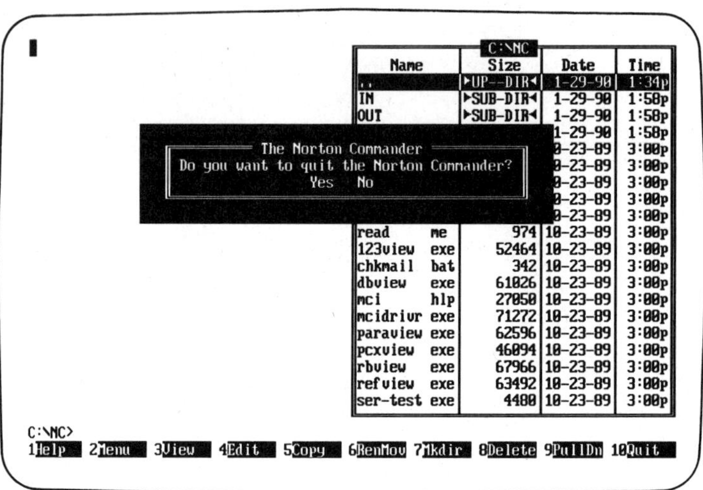

Fig. 2.2
The Quit dialog box.

In some menus, more than one option starts with the same letter. In that case, an option's name may have all lowercase letters except one character. To choose that option, you type the option's uppercase character, even if it is not the first character of the name. If you see the menu selection `tiMe` in a menu, for example, press M to choose that option.

Accessing the Function Key Menu and the Menu Bar

You access Commander's features through two types of menus: the Function Key menu and the menu bar.

The Function Key menu appears along the bottom of the Commander screen. To access the function key commands, you press the appropriate function key on the keyboard or point to the function key name on-screen and click the mouse button. Chapter 8 explains how to use the function keys. The F2 (Menu) function key, however, is covered in Chapter 9.

The menu bar consists of five menus: Left, Files, Commands, Options, and Right. To make the menu bar at the top of the screen visible, press F9

(PullDn). Then, to pull down one of the five menus, press the left- or right-arrow key to highlight the menu name and press Enter. If you are using a mouse, point to the menu you want and click the mouse button. When you select a menu, it appears on-screen. Figure 2.3 shows the Left menu selected.

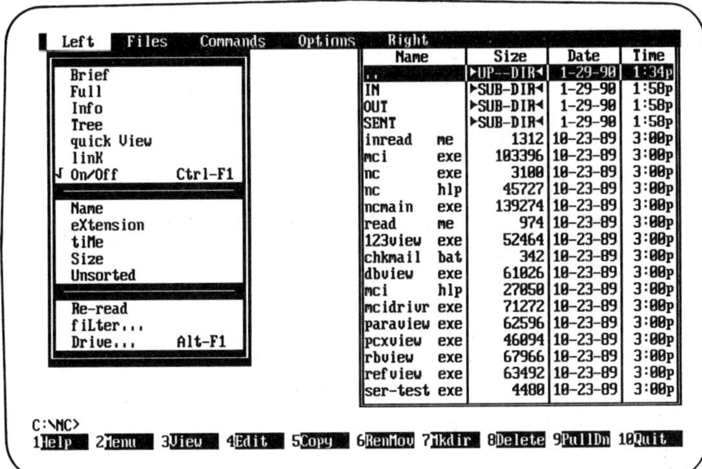

Fig. 2.3 Displaying the Left menu.

To choose one of the options from a selected pull-down menu, use the up- and down-arrow keys to point to an option and then press Enter, press the uppercase letter associated with your menu choice, or point to a selection with the mouse. After one of the pull-down menus is in view, you also can use the right- and left-arrow keys to move between the five menu bar menus to choose other commands. With the mouse, you can point to the menu bar, click and hold the button, and drag the mouse pointer left or right to make one of the other menus appear. To close a pull-down menu, press Esc or click the mouse button while pointing outside the menu box. See Chapter 8 to learn more about using menu options.

Getting Help

The Norton Help system is like a miniature manual on disk. After you choose the Help option by pressing F1 or choosing Help from the Files menu, you see the menu shown in figure 2.4. Choosing any of these menu options displays helpful information. If you want to know about the program's Find Files option, for example, you can choose Find Files from the

Help menu to display information about how to use that option. Choose one of the Help menu options by using the arrow keys to highlight the option and then pressing Enter, or by pointing and clicking with the mouse. To exit the Help menu, press Esc or choose the Cancel option at the bottom of the screen.

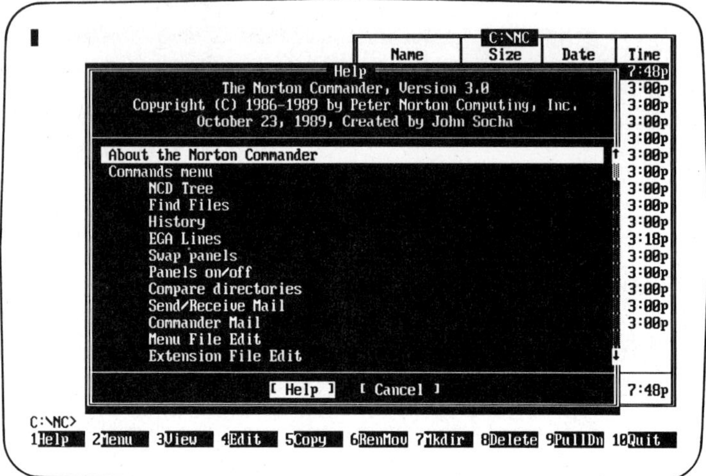

Fig. 2.4
The Help menu.

Summary

Norton Commander gives you power beyond DOS and gives you a more user-friendly environment for your computer. With Commander, you still can access DOS commands in the normal way, but you also can perform some DOS functions (and more) from menus. Commander enables you to pick and choose how to manage your files and how to control your computer setup. As a bonus, you also have access to PC-to-PC communications and MCI Mail.

Part II

A Closer Look at Norton Utilities

Includes

Protecting Your Files

Recovering Files

Making Your Hard Disk Work Efficiently

Managing the Resources of Your Computer

Using Norton Utilities Commands

3

Protecting Your Files

The information stored on your disk is subject to many potential dangers. As the computer operator and systems manager, you must protect your information in the following ways:

- Prevent information from being lost as a result of accidental formatting
- Prepare for possible accidental formatting
- Prevent important files from being erased or overwritten
- Permanently dispose of valuable or secret information

This chapter discusses the Norton Utilities commands that can help you protect the information on your disk in these ways. The Safe Format (SFORMAT) command gives you protection against accidental formatting and provides other features not available with the DOS FORMAT command. Just in case your disk *is* accidentally formatted, Norton provides the Image and Unformat commands. Using the Image command, you can prepare for an accidental format so that you can recover your files after the format by using the Unformat command. The File Save command protects erased files by preserving the unerased information for a certain amount of time so that you can unerase files if you need to. The Disk Monitor command protects your files from being overwritten or erased. The Diskreet command protects files from being used by an unauthorized person. The Wipe Info command enables you to get rid of secret or valuable information safely so that no program can recover it.

Preventing Accidental Formats

Formatting is the procedure that prepares a disk (a floppy diskette or a hard disk) to store information. If you format a disk that contains information (files), the information on the disk is erased. This loss can be devastating if the disk contained important data that is hard to recover.

Computer users commonly call in their company's computer support people, for example, to help recover accidentally formatted hard disks. Sometimes the hard disk contained important research, financial, or organizational information and was not regularly backed up. In many cases, these people must reconstruct the information that had been on disk from letters, papers, and records dating back several years—costing thousands of dollars in personnel time. In some cases, the original source of the information cannot be recovered. Few of these people are prepared in any way for this expensive problem.

Note: Although Norton Utilities does not provide a backup procedure, backing up information on disk should be a standard practice. DOS provides a process for making backup copies of your hard disk using the BACKUP command. You can buy a backup program called Norton Backup. A number of other software programs also enable you to back up your hard disk onto floppy diskettes, tapes, or other media. Using the DOS BACKUP procedure is covered in Appendix A. See Chapter 10 for more information on using the Norton Backup program.

Depending on the version of DOS you are using, it is very easy to format a disk accidentally. Versions of DOS before 3.3 enable you to format the hard disk (drive C) simply by entering the following command:

```
FORMAT C:
```

(If you are at the C> prompt, you just use FORMAT.) Then press Enter in response to a prompt asking whether you are sure that your disk is in place. Beginning with DOS Version 3.3, you also must give a volume name to the disk before the format proceeds.

Whatever the cause, accidental formatting is a problem that continues to occur, even with the recent DOS safeguard of requiring a volume label in the FORMAT command. The Norton Utilities Safe Format command gives you additional levels of protection against accidental formatting. Safe Format displays information on-screen about the impending format, for example. Even after entering the Safe Format command, you must choose to begin the process by selecting an item from the Safe Format menu. The menu also gives you easy access to a number of formatting options. If the disk already contains data, Safe Format gives you a warning message.

Also, even if you choose to proceed with the format, Safe Format saves a copy of the old file information to a place on disk that can be recovered. Because the formatting procedure essentially just wipes out all information about where files are stored on disk, you can use the old file information to recover the information on disk. Refer to "Restoring Formatted Disks," later in this chapter, for a discussion of how recovery works.

Installing Safe Format

You can install Safe Format in one of two ways. One method is to use the Norton command SFORMAT rather than the DOS command FORMAT. You may sometimes forget to type *sformat* in place of FORMAT, however, or someone who does not know the Norton command may be using your computer. The second—and better—way to install Safe Format is to substitute the SFORMAT command for the DOS FORMAT command on disk. When you use the Norton installation program, you are given the option of replacing the old DOS FORMAT command with the Norton command. The SFORMAT command is renamed FORMAT and placed in the directory that contained the old FORMAT.COM command. The old DOS FORMAT.COM command file is renamed XXFORMAT.COM. Therefore, whenever you enter the FORMAT command at the DOS prompt, you actually are using the Safe Format command.

If you did not load Norton Utilities with the installation program, or if you did so but did not replace DOS FORMAT with SFORMAT during the installation, you can do so now. Suppose that your DOS commands are in a directory named C:\DOS and the Norton commands are in a directory named C:\NORTON. To replace DOS FORMAT with SFORMAT, follow these steps:

1. Rename the old DOS FORMAT.COM command by using this command:

   RENAME C:\DOS\FORMAT.COM XXFORMAT.COM

2. Copy the Safe Format command (SFORMAT.EXE) from the \NORTON directory to the \DOS directory with this command:

   COPY C:\NORTON\SFORMAT.EXE C:\DOS\FORMAT.EXE

Your RENAME and COPY commands may differ slightly. If your DOS commands are in a directory other than the \DOS directory, substitute that directory name for \DOS in the preceding examples. Similarly, if your

Norton commands are in a directory other than \NORTON, substitute that directory name for \NORTON. If your directories are on a drive other than drive C, substitute your drive name for C.

Renaming the old FORMAT.COM file as XXFORMAT.COM is important. If the FORMAT.COM (DOS version) and FORMAT.EXE (Norton version) files exist on disk, the FORMAT command accesses the COM version (old DOS), because DOS always chooses to run a COM-type program rather than an EXE-type program if both programs exist. Also, make sure that you do not have another FORMAT.COM located somewhere on your disk in a directory that is accessed (according to your path) before your DOS directory. If your path statement in your AUTOEXEC.BAT file is PATH C:\;C:\DOS etc., DOS will access the root directory (\) before the \DOS directory when looking for a command file. Otherwise, DOS uses that version of FORMAT and not the Norton Safe Format command.

Using Safe Format

The syntax of the SFORMAT command is

SFORMAT [*d:*][*switches*]

or

FORMAT [*d:*][*switches*]

where *d:* is the letter of the drive you want to format and *switches* are the available switches you can use with Safe Format.

When the syntax of a command is described throughout this book, options are listed in [brackets]. In the FORMAT command, therefore, the drive letter described as [*d:*] is an optional parameter. It does not have to appear when you use the command. When you use items listed in brackets in the description, do not actually use the brackets on the DOS command line. If there are parameters in the description of a command that are *not* surrounded by brackets, those options are required.

You use switches in the command to select formatting options. Safe Format has the same switches as the DOS FORMAT command, in addition to a few added by Norton.

The Norton Safe Format switches similar to DOS FORMAT switches follow:

Switch	*Effect*
/B	Leaves space for system files
/S	Places system files on disk
/V:*label*	Places a volume *label* on disk
/1	Formats as single-sided
/4	Formats as 360K (in 1.2M drive)
/8	Formats 8 sectors per track
/N:*n*	Specifies number of sectors per track (*n*=8, 9, 15, or 18)
/T:*n*	Specifies number of tracks (*n*=40 or 80)
/F:*size*	Specifies size of diskette (*size* = 360K or 720K)

The Norton Safe Format switches particular to Norton's Safe Format switches follow:

Switch	*Effect*
/A	Uses Automatic mode (useful in batch files)
/*size*	Specifies size of diskette (*size* = 360K or 720K)
/Q	Uses Quick Format mode
/D	Uses DOS FORMAT mode
/C	Uses Complete Format mode (diskette only)

To format a disk in drive B as a system disk (copy system files to the disk) and place the volume label MYDISK on the disk, for example, use this command:

```
FORMAT B:/S/V:MYDISK
```

Notice in the command that the drive name is represented as a single letter followed by a colon. If no drive name is given, Safe Format prompts you to select the drive to format (see fig. 3.1). Using the up- and down-arrow keys, you can move the highlight to the drive of your choice and press Enter. Alternatively, you can type the letter of the drive containing the disk you want to format. To select drive B, for example, press B on the keyboard. If you are using a mouse, you can point to the drive letter and click. When the OK box is highlighted, you can press Enter to choose the drive letter and continue the format. To choose Cancel, press Tab or the arrow keys to move the highlight to the Cancel box and press Enter. If you are using a mouse, point to the Cancel box and click to cancel the format.

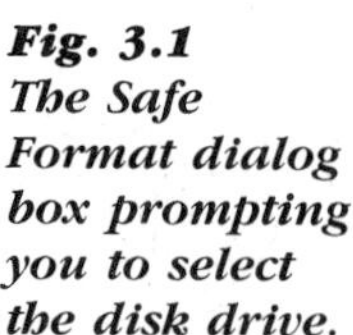

Fig. 3.1
The Safe Format dialog box prompting you to select the disk drive.

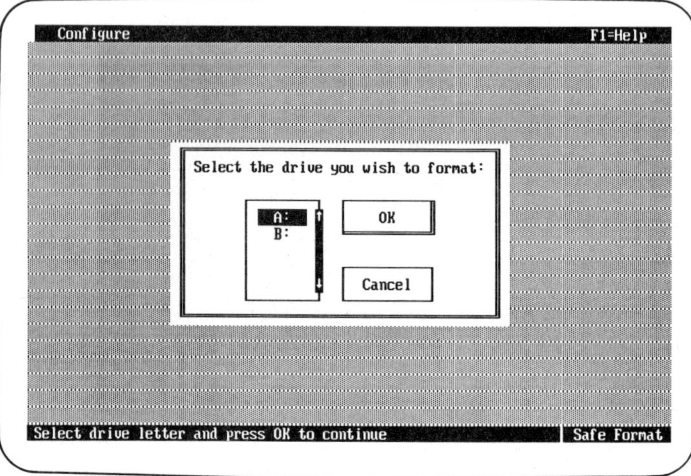

The switches used by both Format and Safe Format are described in Appendix A in the discussion of the DOS Format command. The following switches are those peculiar to the Safe Format command:

- */A:* Enables you to bypass choosing Begin Format from the Norton Safe Format menu. The format automatically begins without any response required from you. This switch is primarily for use in batch files, where you perform the same kind of format repetitively and want to avoid having to answer prompts. You need to be careful when using this switch because it defeats some of the purposes of the Safe Format command. If you are sure that the format you want to perform is selected properly, however, the /A switch can save you some time.

- */Q:* Enables you to perform a quick format. This switch is useful for formatting disks that you have formatted previously. Rather than check the entire disk for bad sectors, as in a normal format, the command in the Quick Format mode merely replaces the system area of the disk with a new system area. This process is essentially the same as erasing all the files on the disk.

- */D:* Enables you to revert to the DOS FORMAT procedure. With this switch, the format is performed as if it were performed by the DOS FORMAT command—the system information is not saved for possible recovery. You may want to use the DOS version of FORMAT if there are files on the disk that you do not want to be recovered easily (for example, personnel records).

- */C:* Uses all the Safe Format functions and reformats any bad sectors of the diskette to make the disk more reliable. Use this switch only on floppy diskettes.

Selecting Options from the Safe Format Menu

After you issue the Safe Format command (and, if necessary, indicate the drive to format), the Safe Format menu appears on-screen (unless you used the /A switch). This screen enables you to choose from menus the same options that are available with switches (see fig. 3.2).

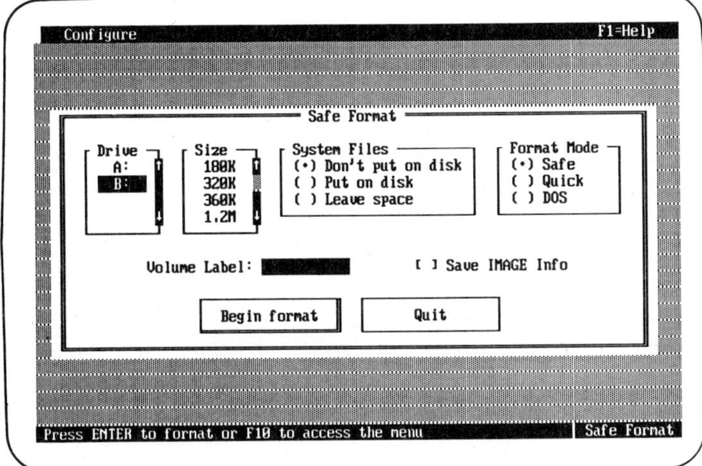

Fig. 3.2* *The Safe Format screen with menu selections.

The Safe Format menu screen consists of several option boxes and fields. If all options are set as you want them, press Enter to begin the format. You can use the arrow keys, the Tab key, or your mouse to highlight the Quit box and then press Enter (or press Q) to end Safe Format.

To change some of the settings on the Safe Format menu, use the arrow keys or Tab to move from one option to another and select your choices. The Safe Format menu contains four boxes:

- *Drive:* Tells you which disk is to be formatted. Depending on how you installed Norton Utilities, hard disk names may not appear in the list of drives to format.

- *Size:* Tells you the size of the disk—360K, 1.2M, and so on—about to be formatted.

- *System Files:* Tells you whether the disk to be formatted will contain the system files, or whether space will be reserved for system files. (These settings relate to the /S and /B switches.) Notice that the System Files options are radio buttons, so you can choose only one option in the box at a time: Don't Put on Disk, Put on Disk, or Leave Space.
- *Format:* Tells you which format mode will be used—Safe, Quick, or DOS. (These settings are radio buttons, and relate to the /Q and /D switches. See table 3.1.)

The Volume Label option tells you which, if any, label will be given to the disk. (You also can set this option by using the /V:*label* switch.)

The Save Image Info option causes Safe Format to take a "snapshot" of the disk's system area so that you can unformat the disk if you discover that you formatted the wrong disk.

Table 3.1
Format Modes

Mode	*Effect*
Safe	Formats the disk, but keeps file information on disk so that you can recover files.
Quick	Creates a new system area and does not overwrite any data area. This mode is useful for formatting previously formatted diskettes. By erasing the system area that contains the addresses of all files and directories on disk, this format is simply a quick way to erase all files and remove all directories from a disk.
DOS	Formats a disk, using the regular DOS procedure. No recovery information is written to disk, and Format Recover may not be able to recover any files.

Using Begin Format

The Begin Format option on the Safe Format menu initiates formatting with all the option settings that you chose on the Safe Format screen. To choose Begin Format, press Enter or point to the Begin Format box with your mouse and click. After you select this option, the Safe Format command attempts to read the disk to see whether you are attempting to format a disk that already contains data. Figure 3.3 shows the warning that is given if information is found on a disk to be formatted. This safeguard prevents you from formatting a disk that contains important data. If the disk to be formatted contains information, you are given an option to stop the procedure before the formatting begins. If you choose not to proceed, you are returned to the Safe Format screen. If you choose to proceed, the format process begins.

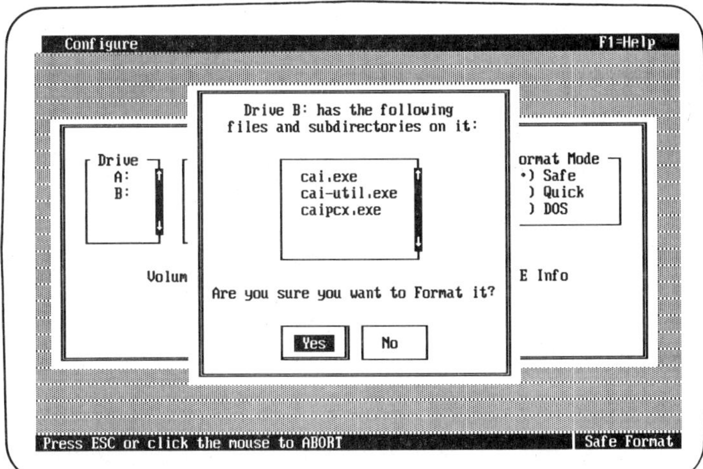

Fig. 3.3 The Safe Format warning screen.

After the format process begins, statistics and a display of progress appear on the Safe Format screen (see fig. 3.4). The graph tells you how much of the disk has been formatted. Next to the graph are statistics with which you can track the progress of the format. The Safe Format screen also shows you how much space is available on the disk and whether any bad sectors were found.

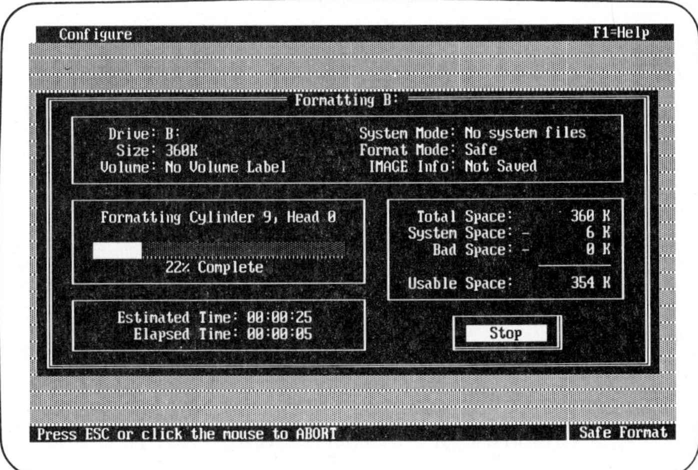

Fig. 3.4 Safe Format in progress.

If you press Esc during the format process, a dialog box appears, asking

```
Do you wish to cancel the current operation?
```

If you are using the Save Image Info option or the Safe Format mode, you may as well let the format finish, even if you mistakenly format the wrong disk. Then you can recover the information with the Unformat command. If you used the DOS or Complete Format mode and discover that you are formatting the wrong disk, interrupt the format immediately and attempt to recover the original information on disk with the Unerase, Unformat command (see Chapter 4 and "Restoring Formatted Disks," later in this chapter).

Restoring Formatted Disks

No matter how many precautions you take, you (or someone else) still may find a way to accidentally format a disk that contains important information. With a little preventive medicine, however, you can handle this problem. The medicine is the Norton Utilities Unformat command. This powerful command has two aspects. First, you can use it to plan for the possibility of an accidental format—you have the Image command store file information to a safe location on disk each time you boot. Second, if you ever need to recover a formatted disk, you can use the Unformat command to access that file information to reconstruct your disk directories.

Preparing for an Accidental Format

Norton Utilities does its best to help you recover from what used to be a complete and total disaster. The work that Norton Utilities can do, however, depends on how well you prepare for the potential problem. The best two ways you can protect yourself are to use the Safe Format and Image commands. Keeping periodic backups of your disks also is extremely important.

The syntax for the Image command is

IMAGE [*switch*]

This command creates a file named IMAGE.DAT that contains information about the files currently existing on your disk. If IMAGE.DAT already exists, the old IMAGE.DAT is renamed IMAGE.BAK. If you use the

/NOBACK switch, the file IMAGE.BAK, which contains information from the preceding use of the IMAGE command, is not created.

When a disk is formatted, the only thing that changes is the information on disk that tells DOS where to find files (your directory). IMAGE.DAT is an alternative copy of that information. Therefore, if a disk accidentally is formatted, the information in IMAGE.DAT can help recover all files that were present on disk when the Image command was last executed.

Because Unformat can help recover only the files that were present the last time the Image command was run, you need to use Image periodically. For most people, a convenient method is to issue the command each time the computer is booted. The next section describes how to do that.

Running Image from the AUTOEXEC.BAT File

To run the Image command each time you boot your computer, place the command in your AUTOEXEC.BAT file. (The AUTOEXEC.BAT file is a batch file that contains a series of commands that execute each time you boot your computer.) You would place the following command, for example, in your AUTOEXEC.BAT file:

```
IMAGE
```

If you are familiar with the AUTOEXEC.BAT file and are comfortable using an ASCII editor (such as the Edlin editor), you simply can add the preceding line to your existing AUTOEXEC.BAT file. If you stored Norton Utilities in a directory other than the root directory (usually \NORTON), make sure that a Path command precedes the Image command in the AUTOEXEC.BAT file. Your AUTOEXEC.BAT file, for example, may contain the following lines:

```
PATH C:\;C:\DOS;C:\NORTON
IMAGE
```

The first command (PATH) sets up the DOS search path to look for commands first in the root directory, then in the DOS directory, and finally in the \NORTON directory. The next line issues the Norton Image command, which DOS now is able to find in the \NORTON directory.

If you are not familiar with your AUTOEXEC.BAT file or do not know how to use an ASCII editor to change the file, you can use the following alternative procedure. This example assumes that your Norton Utilities commands are in a directory named \NORTON, that you are booting from drive C, and that you already have an AUTOEXEC.BAT file in the root directory. Follow these steps to add the Image command to AUTOEXEC.BAT:

1. Make sure that you are in the root directory by typing this command:

   CD\

2. Rename the current AUTOEXEC.BAT file by using this command:

   RENAME AUTOEXEC.BAT AUTOEXEC.OLD

3. Create a temporary file that contains the Format Recover command. First type the following line:

   COPY CON TMP

   Then press Enter. The cursor moves to the next line at the left margin, with no prompt displayed.

4. Enter the following line and press Enter:

   \NORTON\IMAGE

5. Press Ctrl-Z.

   You have created a file named TMP. The regular DOS prompt now reappears.

6. Enter the following command at the DOS prompt:

   COPY TMP+AUTOEXEC.OLD AUTOEXEC.BAT

This command places the Image command from the file named TMP in the first line of your AUTOEXEC.BAT file.

Now when you boot your computer, Norton issues the Image command and creates the file IMAGE.DAT. You can erase the TMP file. The AUTOEXEC.OLD file contains your old version of AUTOEXEC.BAT, in case you need it again.

If the IMAGE.DAT file is present, other Norton commands (Disk Edit and Unerase, for example) use that file automatically. These programs do not need the IMAGE.DAT file to work, but if the file is there, the programs work faster and better.

Running Image from the DOS Prompt

You do not have to run the Image command from the AUTOEXEC.BAT file. You can run the Image command at any time by entering the command at the DOS prompt. If you enter the command

```
IMAGE
```

the IMAGE program creates a new copy of the IMAGE.DAT file on disk.

Tip: As an added safety measure, in case you accidentally format your hard disk, make sure that you have a bootable floppy diskette that contains the Unformat program. Format a floppy diskette in drive A, using the /S (System) switch. Place a copy of the UNFORMAT.EXE program from your \NORTON directory onto the diskette in drive A. Also keep important files such as AUTOEXEC.BAT, CONFIG.SYS, and any other files needed to boot your computer on this diskette. Other commands to place on this diskette for emergency use include the DOS command DEBUG and the Norton commands NDD (Norton Disk Doctor II), Disk Edit, and Safe Format. Keep the diskette nearby, in case you need to use it.

Recovering a Formatted Disk

You will have a much easier time recovering your data if you planned ahead and issued the Image command recently. Even if you formatted your hard disk and do not have a IMAGE.DAT file, however, you may be able to recover data.

If your hard disk has just been formatted, you need to proceed with some care. Do not write new information to the hard disk before attempting to perform a recovery. First, boot the computer from a floppy diskette, using the same version of DOS that was on the hard disk before it was formatted.

If your boot diskette does not contain the Unformat command, place a diskette containing the Unformat command into the floppy disk drive. From the diskette containing the Unformat command (drive A, for example), enter this command:

```
UNFORMAT
```

An explanation of the Unformat procedure appears on-screen (see fig. 3.5). If you choose to continue, you are prompted to select the drive to unformat (see fig. 3.6). Use the arrow keys or your mouse to select the drive to format and choose OK to continue.

You then are asked if the disk to be unformatted had the IMAGE.DAT file saved (see figure 3.7). Choose Yes if you know that the IMAGE.DAT file was saved or if you are not sure. Choose No if you know for sure that

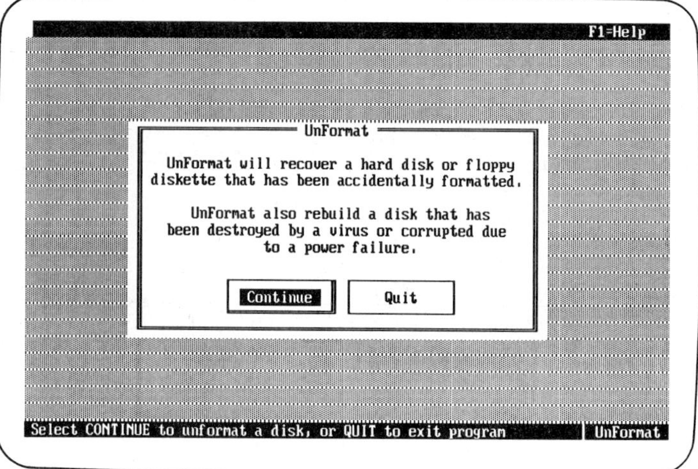

Fig. 3.5* *The Unformat explanation screen.

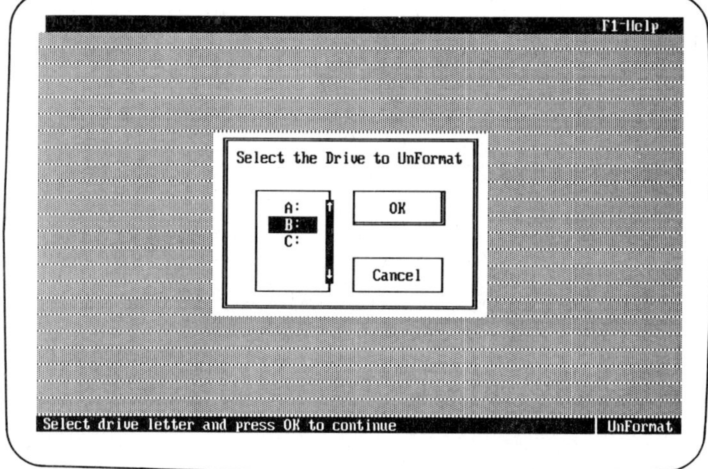

Fig. 3.6* *Selecting the disk to unformat.

there is no IMAGE.DAT file on the disk. If you choose No, refer to the next section, "Unformatting a Disk without IMAGE.DAT."

Norton gives you one more chance to cancel the Unformat command (see fig. 3.8). If you answer Yes in this dialog box, the unformatting process begins. The Unformat program begins looking for the IMAGE.DAT and IMAGE.BAK information on the disk. A graphic appears on-screen with a `Searching for IMAGE info...` message. When the Image information is found, a screen like the one in figure 3.9 appears. If two versions of the

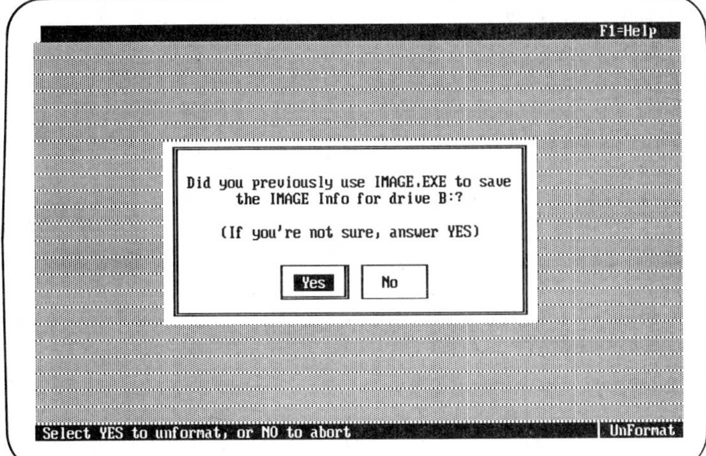

Fig. 3.7
The Unformat command prompt to search for IMAGE.DAT.

IMAGE information (one named IMAGE.BAK) are found, a message tells you that two versions have been found, and you may choose from the most recent version or the previous version. If the most recent IMAGE.DAT information is not usable (perhaps you ran the Image program *after* the disk had been formatted, for example) you may want to use the previous version—the IMAGE.BAK information.

After you select the Image version you want, you are prompted with an `Are you sure you want to restore . . .?` message. Answer Yes to continue. You then are prompted to choose between a full or partial restore.

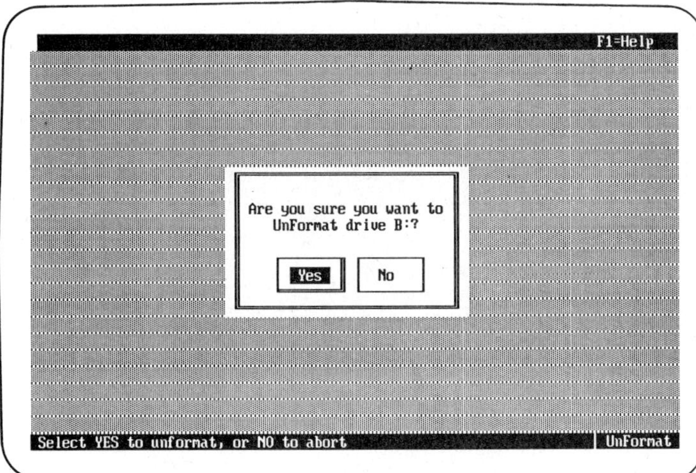

Fig. 3.8
The Unformat warning screen.

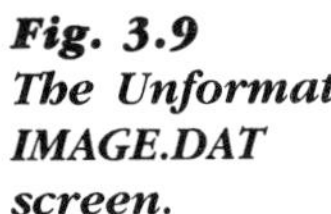

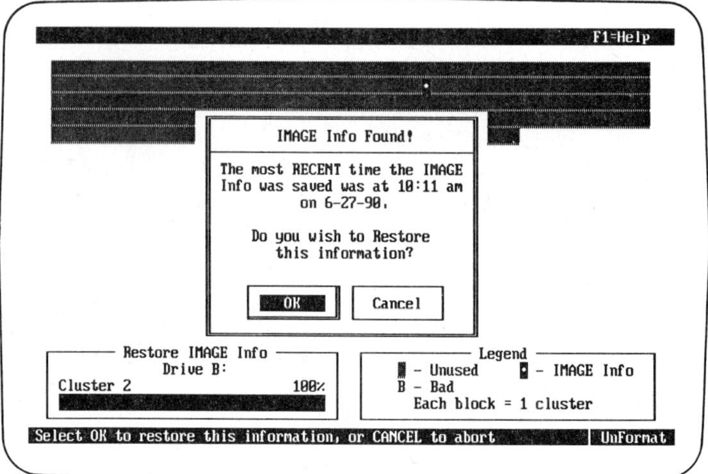

Fig. 3.9
The Unformat IMAGE.DAT screen.

A partial restore restores only parts of the system area, including the boot record and the file allocation table. Usually, you will choose a full restore (see fig. 3.10). Finally, the restoration begins. You will hear the drive churning as the information is recovered. The recovery process generally takes only a few minutes. When the recovery is finished, you get a message telling you that the drive has been restored successfully to its previous state.

After the recovery finishes, you still may have some problems with a few files—those that were changed since you gave the last Image command.

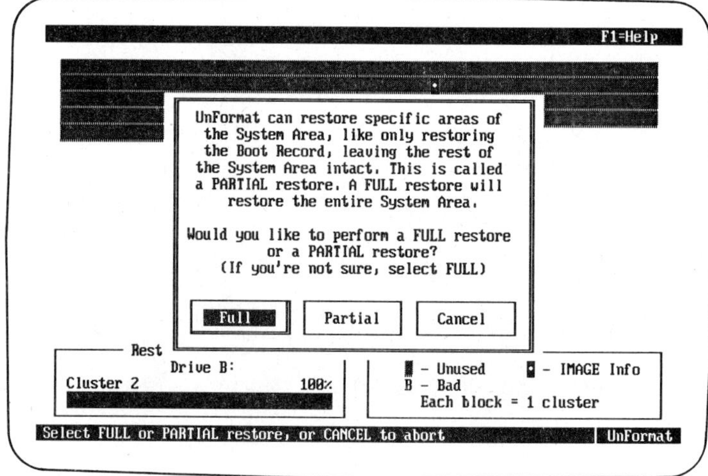

Fig. 3.10
Selecting a full or partial unformat.

Run the Norton Disk Doctor (the NDD command) to clear up any problems that may remain. These problems may be sectors that remain unallocated to files. The NDD command often can sort out these problems and recover the remaining files. See Chapter 4 for more information on the NDD (Norton Disk Doctor II) command.

Tip: The best way to learn how to use Unformat is on a practice disk—when all you have to lose is some time. Format a disk and place several files on it. You even may want to include a few subdirectories. Now format the disk using the Save Image Info option from the Safe Format screen. After you format the test disk, run the Unformat program and see how it can restore the disk. This procedure gives you some experience and confidence for the time when you may need to restore your disk in a real situation.

Unformatting Disks without IMAGE.DAT

If you did not prepare for the disk being formatted—you did not use the Image or Safe Format command—Norton Utilities may be able to help, but the recovery will take more work. The Unformat command often can help you recover some files from a hard disk that has been formatted. You cannot restore a floppy diskette that has been reformatted using regular DOS format, however, by using Unformat. When a hard disk is reformatted, only the system area is overwritten—not the entire disk. When a floppy diskette is formatted using DOS format, the entire disk is overwritten.

Begin the Unformat command, as described in "Restoring Formatted Disks," earlier in this chapter. If there is any chance that the IMAGE.DAT file is on disk, allow the Unformat command to search for it. If you cannot find IMAGE.DAT, you must attempt to recover your data without it.

The Unformat command attempts to recover as many files as possible. First, the program must search the disk, looking for directory and file names. This search may take some time.

Unformat usually is able to recover all directories and files in those directories except for the files in the root directory. Some versions of DOS (COMPAQ 3.1 and AT&T 2.11) overwrite information thoroughly with a format, and recovery is not possible.

When the Unformat command finishes what it can do, your disk should contain directories named DIR0000, DIR0001, DIR0002, and so on. The original names of the directories are lost, but files are grouped in the new directories as they were in the original directories. All 1-2-3 files will be in one directory, for example, and all WordPerfect files will be in another directory.

You can retrieve the original names of the directories in one of two ways. If you are using a version of DOS earlier than 3.0, you need to make new directories, copy the files from each recovered directory into each new directory, and then delete the old directories and files.

You can use a second, much easier, method if you are working with DOS 3.0 or later. This technique uses the Norton Change Directory command. To rename a directory, enter the command

```
NCD /N
```

The /N switch tells NCD not to update the directory name information stored on disk in the TREEINFO.NCD file, because you do not want to keep the names DIR0000, DIR0001, and so on.

The NCD command brings up the Norton Change Directory screen. The screen includes a list of all the directories that have been recovered (DIR0000, DIR0001, and so on). To find out what the directories contain, you must examine the names of some of the files. If the directory DIR0001 contains your WKS files, for example, it must be your Lotus 1-2-3 directory.

After you decide what the names of the directories should be (for example, DIR0000 is \WP50; DIR0001 is \LOTUS, and so on), you can change the directory names. Using the arrow keys, highlight the name of one of the directories. Press F6 (Rename) and type a new name for the directory. Continue this process until you have renamed all the directories. To exit the Norton Change Directory screen, press F10 (Quit).

After renaming the upper-level directories on your disk, run the Norton Disk Doctor (NDD) program to clear up any problems with recovered files. These problems usually are *unallocated sectors*—portions of the disk that have not been assigned properly to a file or free space. The command to run the NDD program is

```
NDD C:/QUICK
```

The /Quick switch tells NDD to test the system area of the disk only—not the entire disk. (The system area is where the unallocated sectors' information will be located.)

If your disk is supposed to be bootable, but is not, use the Norton Disk Doctor command to make a disk bootable to restore this capability to your disk. The Norton Change Directory (NCD) and Norton Disk Doctor (NDD) commands are covered in Chapter 4.

The Unformat command is not perfect, but it restores all the information that was not erased during the Format process. One of the major problems is that all the files in the root directory—AUTOEXEC.BAT, CONFIG.SYS, and others, for example—are lost. You must reconstruct these files. If you do not have backup copies of the files, you must rebuild them in a text editor.

Using Unformat To Recover from a Virus Attack

The Unformat command also may help you recover from some versions of destruction brought about by a computer virus. If your disk has become unusable because of a virus attack, use the Unformat command to attempt recovery, just as if the disk had been formatted. If you have a recent copy of IMAGE.DAT on your disk, your chances of recovery are good.

Protecting Files by Setting Attributes

One way of protecting your important files is to prevent them from being erased or overwritten. Suppose that you have a valuable Lotus 1-2-3 worksheet named ABLE.WKS. Overwriting that file from Lotus is possible (and sometimes easy). If you overwrite the file, you cannot recover it with an Unerase command. Files that are particularly important to protect from erasure or change are COMMAND.COM, AUTOEXEC.BAT, and CONFIG.SYS.

When you create a file on disk, DOS stores the name of the file, as well as other pieces of vital information. You see some of that information when you enter the DOS DIR command—the size of the file, the date and time the file was created, and so on. DOS also stores four other pieces of information that you usually do not see. You can toggle these four pieces of information, called *attributes*, on or off to set or turn off the attributes.

Attributes	*Description*
Archive	When the Archive attribute is set (on), the file has not been backed up. When you create a file, DOS sets the Archive bit on. When you perform the backup procedure, the Archive attribute is turned off.

Hidden — When the Hidden attribute is set, the file does not appear in a directory when you perform the DIR command. On a bootable disk, the DOS files named IBMBIO.COM and IBMDOS.COM usually are hidden files. When you perform a CHKDSK command, you may notice a report of hidden files.

System — System files are similar to hidden files. When the System attribute is on, DOS considers the file a system file and does not display it in a directory when you issue a DIR command.

Read-only — When the Read-only attribute is set, the information in a file can be read or used by a program, but DOS prevents the file from being changed or erased.

With the Norton Utilities File Find command, you can control these attributes and protect important files from accidental change or erasure.

A common problem occurs, for example, when one person gives a friend a diskette containing a program. The friend copies the program from the diskette to the hard disk with a command such as

```
COPY A:*.* C:
```

The problem with this command is that some files on the floppy diskette may overwrite files on the hard disk, particularly COMMAND.COM. When you reboot the computer, the version of COMMAND.COM that was copied from the diskette may conflict with the other system files, and the computer therefore may refuse to reboot. Other important files such as AUTOEXEC.BAT and CONFIG.SYS also may have been overwritten.

Of course, copying a diskette onto the root directory of your hard disk without knowing much about what is on the diskette would be ill-advised. To protect against this kind of problem, you can set the Read-only attribute for important files in the root directory on the hard disk. Then, if you copy a diskette that you do not know much about, you will not overwrite your original files.

Other benefits derive from setting certain attributes. Hiding files, for example, can prevent other people from accessing your secret information. (This method is not foolproof—if other users know about the File Find command, they can change the attribute back.) Also, if you want a file to be backed up more than once, you can turn the Archive attribute on after a backup procedure. For additional methods of protecting files, see the sections on the Norton Disk Monitor (DISKMON) and the Diskreet commands, later in this chapter.

You also can use the File Find command to search for files (see Chapter 6). The syntax for the File Find command is

FILEFIND [*filespec*][*attributes*][*switches*]

where *filespec* represents the specified files you want to examine, *attributes* represents the attributes you want to change, and *switches* represents the other available switches you can use with file attributes. The attribute switches follow:

/A	Archive
/HID	Hidden
/R	Read-only
/SYS	System
/CLEAR	Clear (remove) all attributes

To use the File Find command to set an attribute, you follow the attribute switch with a plus (+) or minus (−) sign. A plus sign turns on the attribute and a minus sign turns off the attribute.

You can use DOS global file specifications to select the files on which to work. When you use the File Find command from the DOS prompt, it reports on files from the entire disk (all directories) unless you tell it otherwise. File specification prefixes you can use follow:

Filespec Prefix	*Meaning*
None	Search entire drive
.\	Search current directory
:.*	Search all drives

To set the Read-only attribute of all COM files in the current directory, for example, use

FILEFIND .*.COM/R+

To set the Read-only *and* Hidden attributes on the entire disk, use

FILEFIND *.COM/R+/HID+

To see a list of the attributes of a certain group of files within the current directory, use this syntax:

FILEFIND .\[*filespec*]

To list attributes of all COM files, use this command:

FILEFIND .*.COM

Figure 3.11 shows the preceding command when the root directory is the current directory. The files that match *.COM are included in a list box at the bottom right of the screen. Notice that the letters ARSH follow the file name IBMBIO.COM. This means that this file has all attributes set. You can see that some of the files have only the Archive attribute set. If there are more files listed than will fit in the list box, you can use the up- and down-arrow keys to bring other file names into view. If you are using a mouse, you can click on the up and down arrows on the right side of the list box to move the list up and down in the box.

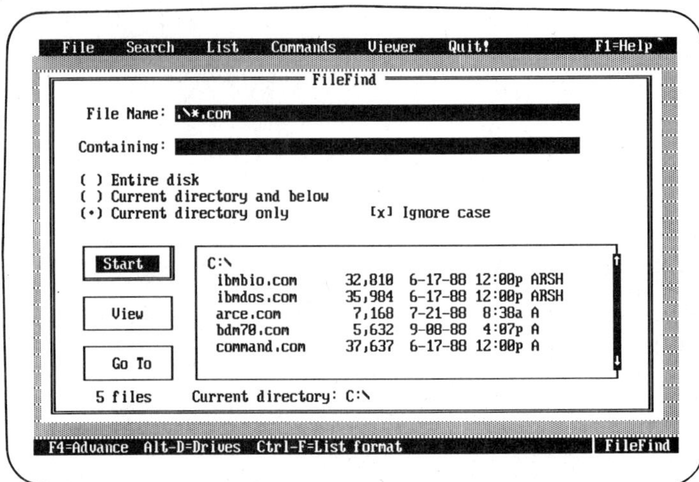

Fig. 3.11
The File Find selection screen.

Using File Find Interactively To View Attributes

You also may use the File Find command interactively. If you enter the command without any switches, a screen similar to figure 3.11 appears. Using the arrow keys or Tab to move to the fields on-screen, you then can use the File Find command by doing the following:

1. Enter the file specification of the files you want to list in the File Name field.

2. Choose one of the radio buttons indicating what File Find should list: Entire Disk, Current Directory and Below, or Current Directory Only.

3. Choose Start.

   This begins the search, and the resulting list appears in the list box.

Using File Find To Set File Attributes

After you list certain files, you can change the attributes of a file. Notice the menu bar at the top of the File Find screen in figure 3.11. The Commands menu option contains a selection—Set Attributes—which enables you to set the attributes of a particular file. To set the Read-only attribute of the file COMMAND.COM, for example, you would do the following:

1. Highlight the file name COMMAND.COM on the list. Use the arrow keys to highlight the file, or point to the file with a mouse and click.
2. Press F10 to display the pull-down menus and use the right- or left-arrow keys to pull down the Commands menu. Alternatively, point to the word `Commands` with the mouse pointer and click.
3. Choose Attributes. You should see a screen similar to fig. 3.12.
4. Using your arrow keys and the space bar or a mouse, choose to set the Read-only option. (An X should appear, indicating that Read-only is on).
5. Press Enter to accept this setting.

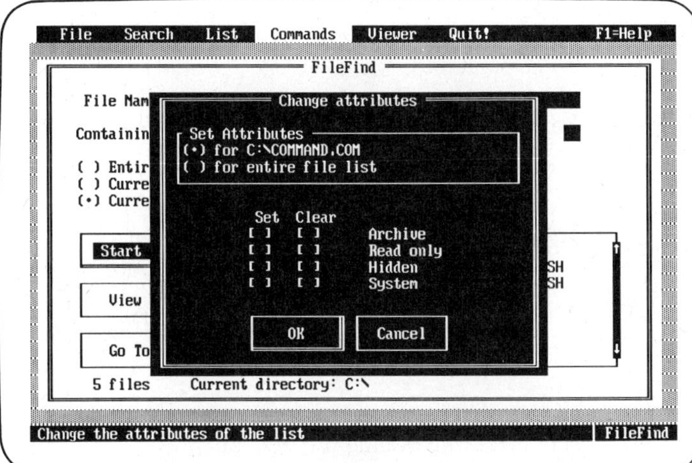

Fig. 3.12
Changing file attributes by using File Find.

The Read-only attribute for the COMMAND.COM file now will be on, and if someone tries to erase or copy over that file, DOS will prevent it.

Summarizing the File-Protection Features of File Find

To summarize, one of the features of the File Find command is its capability to protect your files in several ways:

- You can make all important files Read-only.

  Be aware, however, that some files to which programs write cannot be set to Read-only. You should make at least the important files in the root directory (including COMMAND.COM, AUTOEXEC.BAT, and CONFIG.SYS) Read-only. You can turn off Read-only temporarily if you need to change any of these files.

- You can hide valuable files.

  As mentioned before, using the Hidden attribute is not a fail-safe method of protection. People easily can get by this precaution. If you hide files, however, you can prevent someone from accidentally displaying information while borrowing your computer to do a quick 1-2-3 spreadsheet.

- You can turn the Archive attribute off for some important files for extra protection.

  If you regularly back up your computer with incremental backups, the files that have been backed up already do not get backed up again. If you turn on the Archive attribute for certain files, however, those files are included in the next backup, even if they have not changed since the last backup. You may want to do this so that you will have a duplicate copy of the backup in case one copy is damaged or lost.

You should have noticed that there are a number of other features of the File Find command not covered in this chapter. See Chapter 6, "Managing the Resources of Your Computer," for more information.

Using File Save To Keep Erased Files Safe Longer

When you erase a file, DOS does not actually erase the contents of the file. DOS erases only the directory information about the file; this is why Norton can unerase a file. When you erase a file, however, DOS gets the message that the space on disk that the file used now is available for other files. After another file has written over the "erased" space, you no longer can unerase the erased file that occupied that space.

The File Save command moves the contents of unerased files to a part of the disk that is not used as much. This makes the files less likely to be overwritten, and the files will remain unerasable longer. File Save is able to manage this "erased" space on disk, and you can tell it to stop protecting files after a certain number of days or when a certain amount of space is being used for the erased information.

File Save is a memory-resident program; when you begin the program it stays in the computer's memory, monitoring what is going on while you run other programs. You can run the File Save program interactively or as a DOS-type command. You will want to run the program interactively at first to set your options for which drives you want to protect, how long you want to save files, and so on. Then, you can activate the File Save command by placing it in your AUTOEXEC.BAT file so that the protection is turned on each time you boot your computer.

Using File Save Interactively

To use File Save interactively, choose the File Save option from the Norton menu or enter

```
FILESAVE
```

at the DOS prompt. The File Save screen appears (see fig. 3.13). On this screen, you can specify the following:

Option	*Effect*
Choose Drives	Specifies which drives to protect
File Protection	Specifies which files to protect
Purge Files	Removes files from protection

The Choose Drives option enables you to specify on which drives files will be protected when you erase them. If you select Choose Drives, you are prompted to choose the disk drives that you want to protect. File Save will monitor only files being erased on the disks you specify.

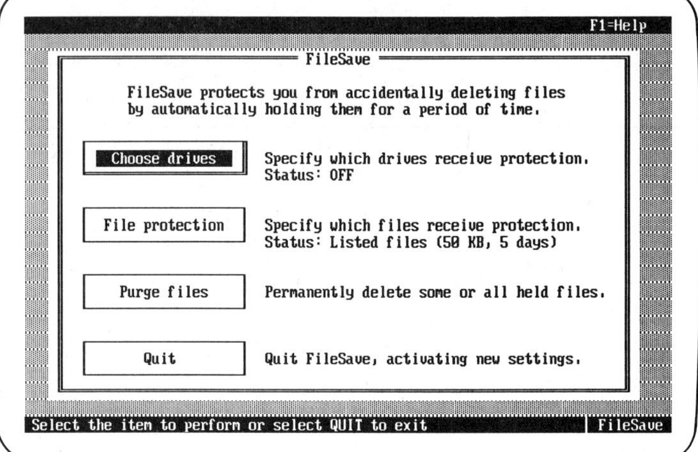

Fig. 3.13
The File Save menu.

The File Protection option enables you to choose which files to protect when you erase them. From the File Protection screen, you can instruct File Save to monitor all files, a list of files, or all files except those on a list (see fig. 3.14). You also can choose to monitor or not monitor archived files. Files that are archived—files that have the Archive attribute off—already have been backed up, and you should have a copy of those files to recover if needed. Therefore, you may choose *not* to protect these files.

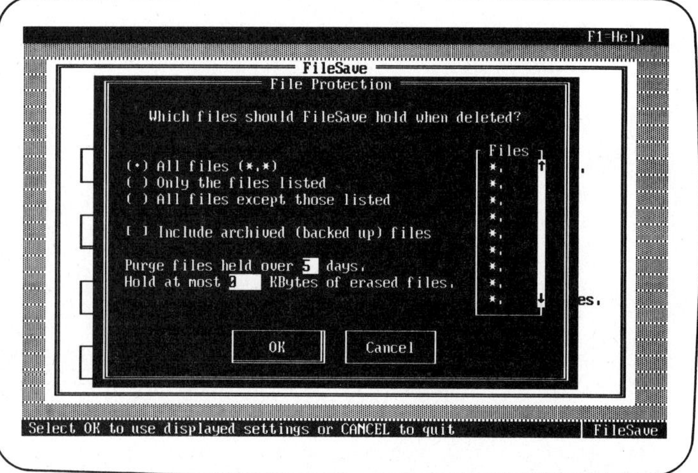

Fig. 3.14
The File Save File Protection screen.

If you choose to protect files on a list or to exclude files on a list, you must make a list first, of course. The Files box at the right of the File Protection screen is where you enter your list. Notice that the Files list has *. listed (no file names) a number of times. To place file specifications in this list, use the arrow keys, Tab, or the mouse to move to the Files list box. Then, enter extensions of those files to include or exclude. You may choose to exclude *.EXE and *.COM files, for example, because you probably have copies of these files on original disks. On the other hand, you may want to include *.DBF and *.WK1 files because these are important data files. You can choose to include *or* exclude; you cannot do both.

The Purge Files option enables you to choose how long a file will be held before it is no longer protected. The default is five days. The Hold at Most option enables you to specify how much space on disk to use to protect erased files.

When you quit File Save, the options you chose are saved. Then, regardless of whether you begin the program from the DOS prompt or from your AUTOEXEC.BAT file, these settings are used.

Using File Save from the DOS Prompt

The File Save command usually is included in the AUTOEXEC.BAT file so that it is in effect when any files are deleted. The syntax of this command is

FILESAVE [*switches*]

The available switches for the File Save command follow:

Switch	*Effect*
/STATUS	Displays the status of the File Save command.
/ON	Enables the File Save command to move deleted files to a safe area.
/OFF	Disables the File Save command, so that deleted files are not affected. The File Save command remains in memory, but does not function unless it is turned back on by the /ON switch.
/UNINSTALL	If the File Save command was the last memory-resident (TSR) command loaded, this switch removes the command from memory.

Using Disk Monitor To Protect Information Against Destruction

You can use the Disk Monitor command to protect your information on disk from accidental or unauthorized destruction. Although setting attributes provides some protection, Norton's Disk Monitor command can give you an additional level of control over the use of files. Disk Monitor's file protection also can give you more safety against a virus infection.

Before you can access a file (write to a file, change a file, or erase a file), the Disk Monitor command protects files by checking to see whether you have given permission for the file to be altered in this way. If the file is protected from change, Disk Monitor will not enable you to alter the file. When a program is running that tries to alter a protected file—a spreadsheet program, for example—a message appears telling you that a protected file is about to be altered. You then can choose to allow the change to proceed, to stop the change from happening, or to cancel the protection altogether.

Having such protection of important files can protect you from virus programs that may try to alter critical files such as your COMMAND.COM, AUTOEXEC.BAT, or CONFIG.SYS file.

Setting Up Disk Monitor Interactively To Protect Files

The Disk Monitor program is a memory-resident program. This means that when you begin the program, it stays in the computer's memory to monitor what is going on while you run other programs. You can use the Disk Monitor program interactively, or from the DOS prompt. The first time you use Disk Monitor, however, you must use it interactively to select its initial settings. To begin Disk Monitor, choose Disk Monitor from the Norton menu or enter the command

```
DISKMON
```

at the DOS prompt. A screen similar to the one in figure 3.15 appears. On the Disk Monitor menu screen there are four options:

Option	*Effect*
Disk Protect	Enables or disables protection
Disk Light	Turns on and off access light on-screen
Disk Park	Parks disk heads for moving computer
Quit	Quits and saves new settings

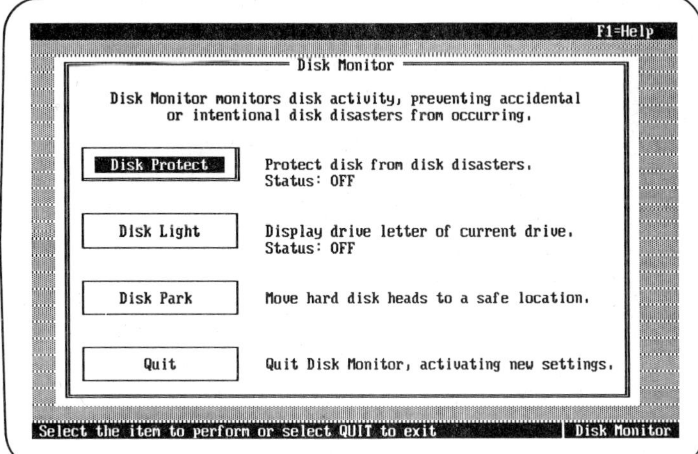

Fig. 3.15 The Disk Monitor menu screen.

By using the arrow keys and Enter or the mouse pointer, you can choose one of these four selections. The Disk Protect option enables you to turn protection on and off and to specify which files you want to protect. After you choose the Disk Protect option, a screen similar to the one in figure 3.16 appears. From the Disk Protection screen, you can choose the following options:

- *System Files:* Specifies protection for the system area on your disk. This includes the partition table, the boot record, and the system files.
- *Files:* Specifies protection for files listed in the Files box, excluding all files listed in the Exceptions box.
- *System Area and Files:* Specifies both kinds of protection.
- *Entire Disk:* Ensures that no program writes to any portion of the disk without your permission.

Another option on the Disk Protect screen is the Allow Floppy Format option. If you check this option, Disk Monitor enables you (or a program) to format floppy disks without asking for your permission.

When you choose Quit, the settings you chose are stored in a file named DM.INI. If you use Disk Monitor as a command from the DOS prompt, the settings in DM.INI are used.

From the Disk Monitor screen, you can use the Disk Light option to enable a blinking light on your monitor to tell you when your disk is being accessed. This is helpful if you cannot easily see the disk light on

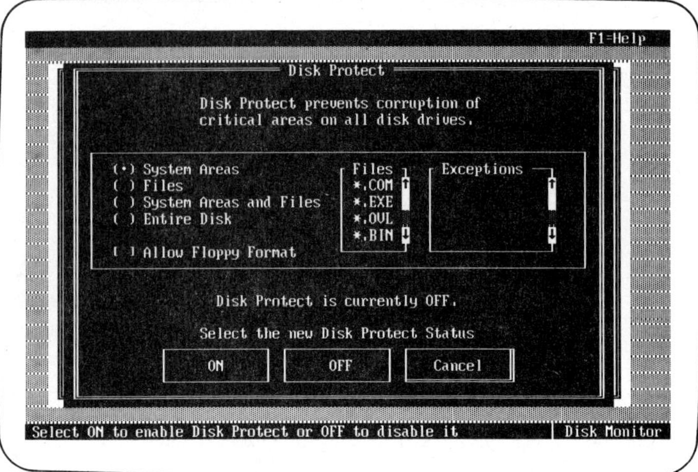

Fig. 3.16
The Disk Monitor Disk Protect screen.

your hard disk. It also is important to be able to see when your disk is being accessed so that you can monitor this activity visually. If you notice a program accessing a disk when it should not be using it, you may want to test that program for possible virus infection.

The Disk Park option enables you to move the heads on your disk drive to a safe place so that you can move the computer without destroying data. On many new computers, the heads park automatically when you turn off the computer. If you do not know whether the heads park automatically, you should use Disk Park before you move your computer.

Using Disk Monitor from the DOS Prompt

The syntax for using the Disk Monitor command from the DOS prompt is

DISKMON [*switches*]

The available switches for the Disk Monitor command follow:

Switch	*Effect*
/STATUS	Tells Disk Monitor to display a summary of the Disk Monitor status on-screen.

/PROTECT– or /PROTECT+	Tells Disk Monitor to turn the protect feature on (+) or off (–). When this feature is turned on, protection is set to your selections that were stored in DM.INI when you selected these items by running the command interactively.
/LIGHT+ or /LIGHT–	Tells Disk Monitor to turn the disk light feature on (+) or off (–).
/PARK	Tells Disk Monitor to park all drives.
/UNINSTALL	Uninstalls the Disk Monitor program from memory, if it was the last TSR loaded into memory.

Using Diskreet To Prevent Unauthorized Access to Files

The Norton Diskreet command enables you to protect files so that users cannot access the files unless they have permission (they must know a password). This provides much more protection than the Disk Monitor protection or protection by setting file attributes. Files stored by Diskreet are encrypted so that they are unreadable, even by the Disk Edit program. You can protect files individually or by group by using a pseudo-disk on your disk that is called an ndisk. An *ndisk* operates like a disk drive, but files stored on this drive are encrypted automatically by Diskreet, and only users who know the password can access the files. If you try to access an ndisk, you are prompted to enter a password. If you do not know the password, you cannot successfully type, read, or otherwise access the files on that "disk." After you "open" an ndisk by supplying the correct password, you may access these files, and they are decrypted as you access them. When you close the ndisk, the files again become inaccessible.

You can regulate access to ndisk interactively or from a DOS prompt command. You can regulate automatic closing of an ndisk after it has been inactive for a certain period or create a hot key that quickly closes an ndisk. Also, you can audit access to an ndisk to determine if someone has been trying to access your information without your permission.

You can choose two versions of ndisk encrypting called *quick encryption* (a Norton proprietary method) and *DES* (data encryption standard). The Quick option is fast and effective but not quite as secure as the DES method. The DES method is slow but very secure, and you probably will want to use it only if your information being protected is akin to the "Manhattan Project" (top secret).

When you store information in an ndisk, it is very secure. If you forget your password, not even Norton can help you unscramble your files.

See "Setting Up a Diskreet Ndisk," later in this chapter, for more information.

Installing Diskreet

The Diskreet program is a memory-resident program (TSR), which means that when you load the program, it stays in memory and monitors the computer while you run other programs.

Before you use the Diskreet program, however, you must include the following line in your CONFIG.SYS file:

DEVICE=*path*\DISKREET.SYS

where *path* is the name of the directory where your Norton files are stored. If Norton Utilities is stored in the directory named \NORTON, for example, you would use this command:

DEVICE=\NORTON\DISKREET.SYS

When you boot the computer, this tells DOS to make the Diskreet driver available for use. The first time you boot with the Diskreet device driver installed, you see information on-screen similar to figure 3.17. This screen gives you information about the Diskreet program, including all of the default settings. Diskreet creates a file named DISKREET.INI that contains the settings for the program. When you boot again, you will see only the copyright notice for Diskreet.

The Diskreet driver takes up some of the RAM memory in your computer. If your computer has extended memory (over 640K), you can save some space for use by your programs by placing the HIMEM.SYS driver (or PCSHADOW.SYS for COMPAQ computers) in your CONFIG.SYS file. To place the HIMEM.SYS driver (in the \Norton directory) into the CONFIG.SYS file, for example, you would use the command

DEVICE=\NORTON\HIMEM.SYS

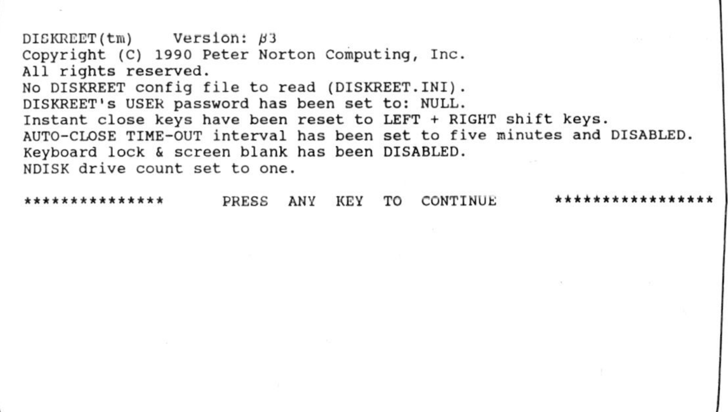

DISKREET(tm) Version: β3
Copyright (C) 1990 Peter Norton Computing, Inc.
All rights reserved.
No DISKREET config file to read (DISKREET.INI).
DISKREET's USER password has been set to: NULL.
Instant close keys have been reset to LEFT + RIGHT shift keys.
AUTO-CLOSE TIME-OUT interval has been set to five minutes and DISABLED.
Keyboard lock & screen blank has been DISABLED.
NDISK drive count set to one.
*************** PRESS ANY KEY TO CONTINUE *****************

Fig. 3.17
The first-time Diskreet screen when booting.

Place the DEVICE command *before* the DEVICE=\NORTON\DISKREET.SYS command in your CONFIG.SYS file.

Using Passwords

Information stored with Diskreet is kept only as safe as your password. You should choose your password with care. The more important your information, the more careful you should be about choosing and protecting your password. Diskreet requires passwords of six or more characters.

Some ideas of passwords *not* to use are your name, names of relatives, pets, license plate numbers, or any other kind of name or number associated with you or with your company. These are the first things someone will try when attempting to get at your information.

The most effective passwords are random characters such as ZTLFEWBDD. However, these are hard to remember. You could pick a strange word out of the dictionary, but a real hacker even may use some method of trying every word in the dictionary (spelled forward and backward) to get to your files. A compromise would be to combine two words that are easy to remember but have no real meaning. Examples are LAUGH.BOOK, TREE/COMPUTER and WHITE:RING. If you choose to write down your password, place it in a protected area—a safe or a locked drawer, for example.

There are three kinds of passwords used in Diskreet. The main password is used to protect the Diskreet settings, and affect all ndisks. The disk password protects a specific ndisk, or group of files. The file password protects an individual file. You will see these passwords referred to in the remaining discussion about Diskreet.

Setting Up a Diskreet Ndisk

To create a Diskreet ndisk, you must travel through a series of setup screens that will prompt you for information about how you want your ndisk to work. You will answer questions about where to store information, which password to use, how much space to allocate to the disk, which method of encryption to use, and so on. The following information walks you through this setup procedure and explains the screens you will see as you set up your Diskreet disks.

To enter the Diskreet command, choose Diskreet from the Norton menu or enter the command DISKREET at the DOS prompt. The first screen you see is shown in figure 3.18. From this screen, you can choose to work with individual files or with a protected disk (an ndisk).

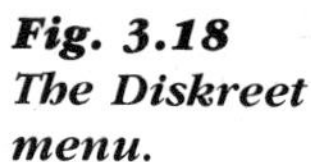

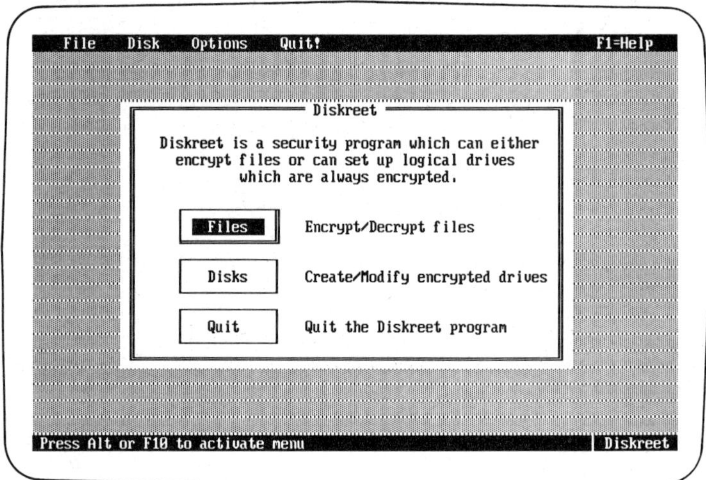

Fig. 3.18
The Diskreet menu.

Encrypting and Decrypting Individual Files

If you choose the Files option on the Diskreet menu, a menu appears, enabling you to select from the following:

- Encrypt
- Decrypt
- File Options

If you choose Encrypt, a screen like figure 3.19 appears. From this screen you can choose which file to encrypt. Notice that there the prompt `File name:` appears, where you can enter the name of the file to encrypt. Using the three list boxes—Files, Dirs, and Drives—you can highlight the name of the specific file you want to encrypt. Use your arrow keys or Tab to move to the different prompts or list boxes on-screen or point to a prompt or list box with your mouse and click to choose the file name to encrypt. After you choose the file to encrypt, choose OK to continue (press Enter or point and click).

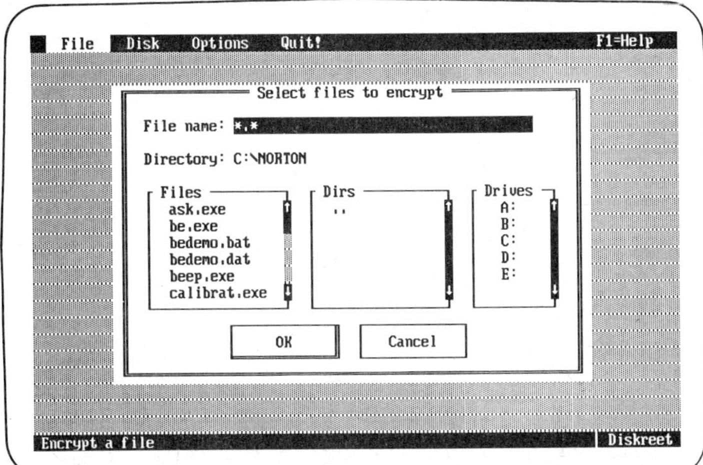

Fig. 3.19
The Diskreet menu to choose files to encrypt.

After you choose a file to encrypt, you are prompted to verify the file name. The encryption will create the encrypted file with a different extension. If you encrypt the file named REPORT.WKS, for example, the file may be saved encrypted as REPORT.SEC (Secret). You are prompted to enter a password to use; remember it.

After the file is encrypted, it looks like gibberish if you try to read it. To get the file back to normal, you must decrypt it. To decrypt a file, choose the Files option from the Diskreet menu, and then choose Decrypt. You see a file selection screen like the one you used to choose a file to encrypt. After you choose the file to decrypt, you are asked for a password and the file is decrypted.

To change the options for file encryption, choose File Options after you choose File from the Diskreet menu. A screen like the one in figure 3.20 appears. From this screen, you can choose to encrypt by using the proprietary or DES method. You can tell Diskreet to get rid of an original file after it has been encrypted. If you *do not* do this, your old file remains unprotected on disk. You can set the attributes for the encrypted file to Hidden and/or Read-only and you can choose to use the same password for as long as you are in Diskreet to prevent you from having to enter a password each time to encrypt or decrypt a file. After you choose settings on this menu, choose the Save option to save this information to disk. Exit this option by choosing OK.

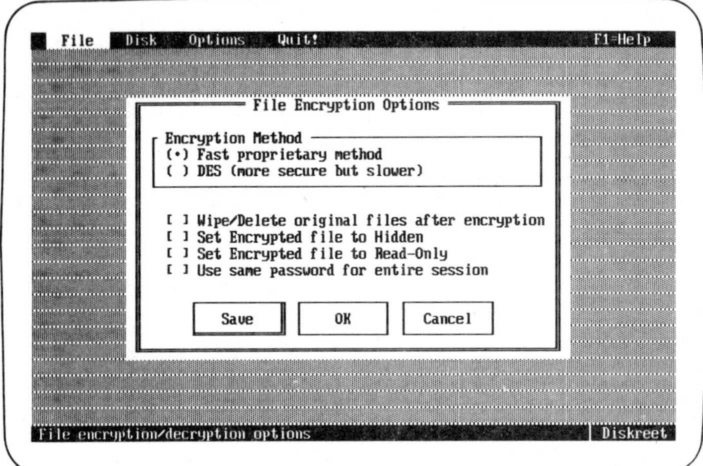

Fig. 3.20
The Diskreet menu to choose file-encryption options.

Creating a Diskreet Ndisk

Unlike encrypting individual files, a Diskreet ndisk provides a method for automatically encrypting and decrypting all files that are written to or read. These files are stored in a pseudo-disk called an ndisk. It behaves much like any other disk drive except for its encrypting and decrypting features. The following information leads you through the creation of a ndisk:

1. Begin Diskreet by choosing the Diskreet option from the Norton menu or by entering the command DISKREET at the DOS prompt. You see the menu shown in figure 3.18. From this menu, choose the Disks option.

2. The first time you use Diskreet, you see a screen like the one shown in figure 3.21. From this screen, choose Yes—you do want to create a new ndisk drive. The next screen you see asks you where you want the ndisk information stored. Usually, you will choose your hard disk, although it is possible to place an ndisk on a floppy disk.

3. The next screen (which appears automatically) is shown in figure 3.22. It asks questions about how the disk is named, which

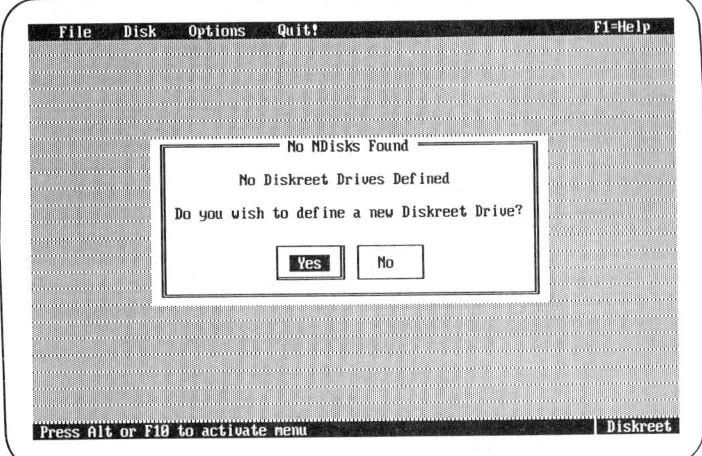

Fig. 3.21 The Diskreet menu.

encryption to use, and which method of prompting for a password will be used. Also, you can check if you want audit information shown when an ndisk is opened. This shows you how many successful and unsuccessful attempts have been made to open your disk. Use your arrow keys and the space bar to choose the options you want, or point and click with a mouse. Choose between the proprietary or DES encryption method and whether to display the audit information.

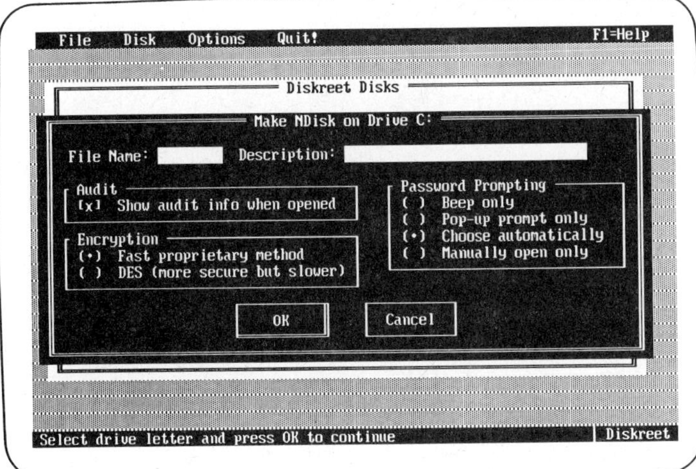

Fig. 3.22 The Diskreet menu for selecting options to create an ndisk.

There are four password-prompting methods available. The Beep Only option causes a beep to occur when you try to access a file on an ndisk. No prompt appears on-screen. You then must enter the password for the access to be successful. The Pop-up Prompt option causes a window to pop-up on-screen and you are prompted to enter the password. This method may not work in some programs that use high resolution graphics screens. The Choose Automatically option enables Diskreet to choose the method of prompting that it thinks will work for the particular program being run. If you choose Manual Open Only, then the only way to access the information is by first running the Diskreet program to open the disk.

After you choose your settings, choose OK (press Enter) or click on OK to end this screen. If you choose Cancel, all of the settings revert to their previous states and the screen closes.

4. The next screen that automatically appears is shown in figure 3.23. This screen enables you to select the size of your ndisk. The All Available Space option uses all unused space on the disk. You probably will use this only if you are making an entire floppy disk an ndisk. Usually, you will enter some amount in the Specific Size option. Choose a reasonable amount according to how much information you expect to store on the disk. You can make the disk larger or smaller later. After you make your selection, choose OK.

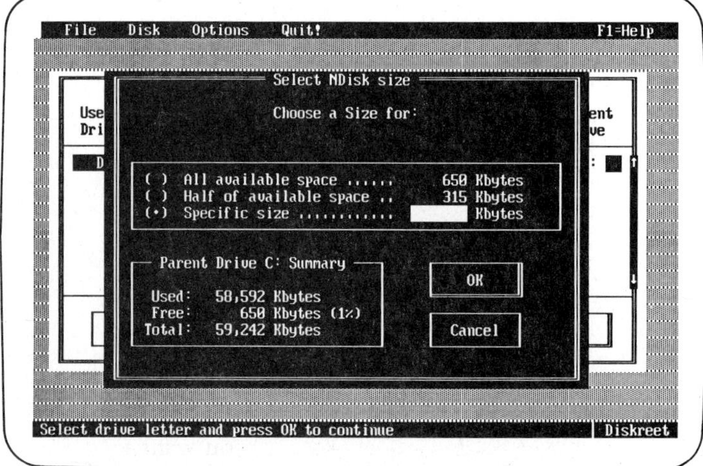

Fig. 3.23 The Diskreet menu for choosing the size of an ndisk.

5. After you define your ndisk, you are prompted twice to enter your password. (You enter the same password twice as a verification). The password does not appear on-screen as you type it. Instead, a series of asterisks appears. Your password must contain at least six characters. The next screen warns you that you need to remember the password you just entered (see fig. 3.24). Information stored in an ndisk is worthless unless you know the password.

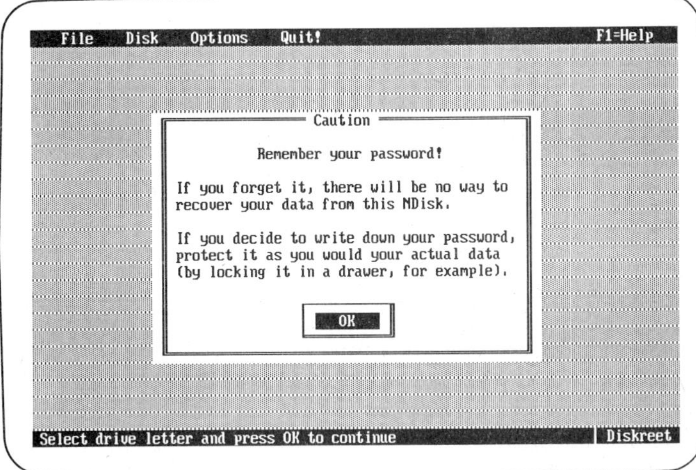

Fig. 3.24 ***The Diskreet caution screen about the importance of remembering your password.***

6. After you define your password, you are prompted to choose (or verify) the drive name of your new disk. Norton will assign an unused drive name (such as D or E) to your disk. Eventually, you may have more than one ndisk, and you will have to indicate which one you are working with. Choose OK to verify that this drive name is okay. If you chose the Audit Info option earlier, an audit screen appears, giving you information on when this disk was last opened, when the password was last changed, how many attempts have been made to open the disk, and how many of those attempts failed.

7. The creation of your ndisk is complete. Diskreet now shows a screen like the one in figure 3.25. This screen lists the one or more ndisks that are available to you. Using the arrow keys or mouse, you can select the disk you want to use or modify.

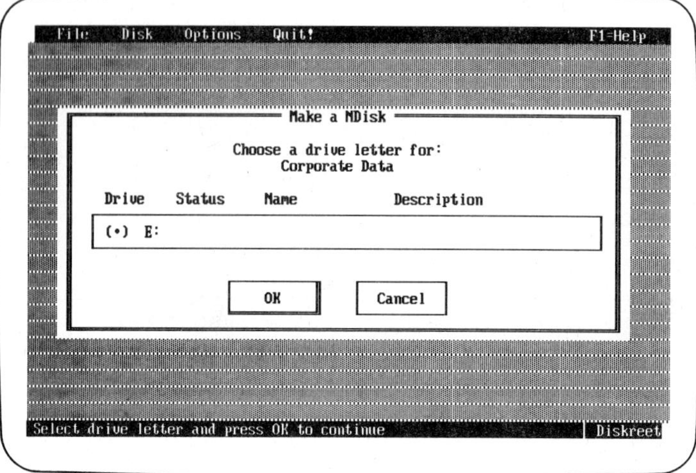

Fig. 3.25
The Diskreet selection screen for choosing the drive letter of an ndisk.

Modifying Diskreet Ndisk Options

After you begin the Diskreet program and choose the Disk option, you see a screen similar to the one in figure 3.26. From this screen, you can use the menu bar at the top of the screen to work with individual files (File), change selections concerning the ndisk (Disk), or change options related to how the ndisk works (Options).

Fig. 3.26
The Diskreet main menu with menu bar.

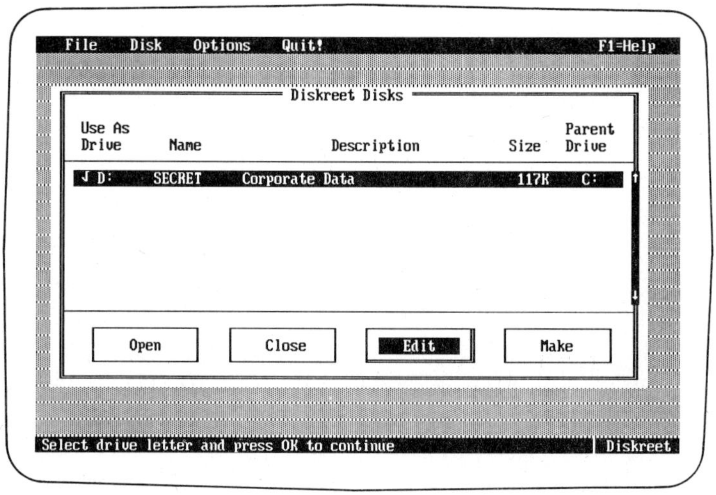

Using File Options

The File menu option enables you to encrypt or decrypt a file or change file options, as was discussed earlier in the "Encrypting and Decrypting Individual Files" section.

Using Disk Options

The Diskreet Disk menu enables you to access, close, or delete ndisks and to modify their sizes and change disk passwords. After you choose the Disk menu, you see the following selections:

- *Search Floppies (Alt-S):* Tells ndisk to search the floppy drives for ndisks. If you have just placed a floppy disk in a disk drive, Diskreet will not know it is there until you choose the Search Floppies option. Notice that you can enter Alt-S anytime the Diskreet program is running to choose this option.
- *Close All (Alt-C):* Closes all ndisks. This is a fast way to close down access to your ndisk drives. Notice that the command Alt-C also performs this task.
- *Adjust Size:* Enables you to make your ndisk larger or smaller. You are prompted to enter the new size for your disk.
- *Delete:* Enables you to delete an entire ndisk from your disk.
- *Change Disk Password:* Enables you to change the password used to access your ndisk.

Using the Options Menu To Change Ndisk Settings

After you choose the Options menu, you see the following selections:

- *System Settings:* Displays a screen like the one in figure 3.27. This screen enables you to select the number of drives to allocate as ndisks and enables you to take the Ndisk Manager out of memory. The Ndisk Manager, which is loaded as a result of the DISKREET.SYS device driver in your CONFIG.SYS file, takes up about 50K of RAM memory. If you need that memory to run a program, you must choose the Do Not Load the Ndisk Manager option and reboot your computer to reclaim that memory. With the Ndisk Manager not in memory, your ndisks will not function. To make your ndisks work again, you have to come back to this option, turn it off, and reboot.

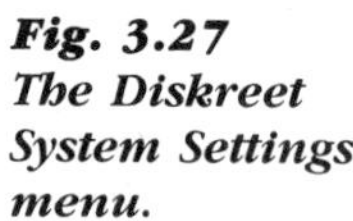

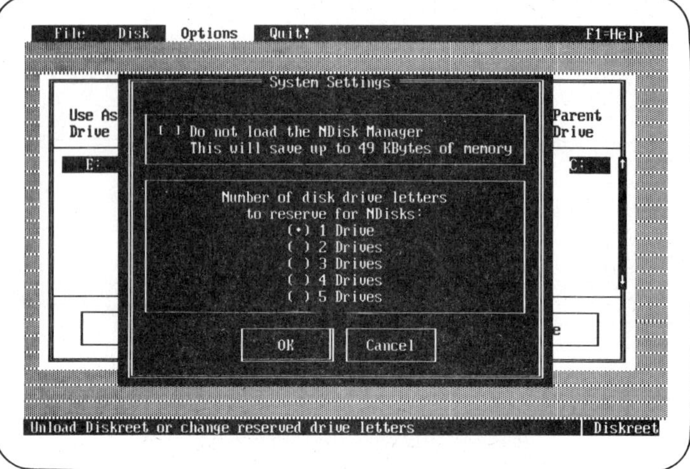

Fig. 3.27
The Diskreet System Settings menu.

- *Startup Disks:* Displays a screen like the one shown in figure 3.28. This screen enables you to indicate which disks are opened for use when your computer is booted. To choose a disk for automatic opening, choose the Edit option. A list of available ndisks appears. Choose which ndisk to start up automatically, and then choose whether it will open as soon as the computer is booted or the first time it is accessed. If you choose to have an ndisk start automatically, you still are prompted to enter the password when the disk is first opened. After you open the disk, the files in the disk are available until you close the disk.

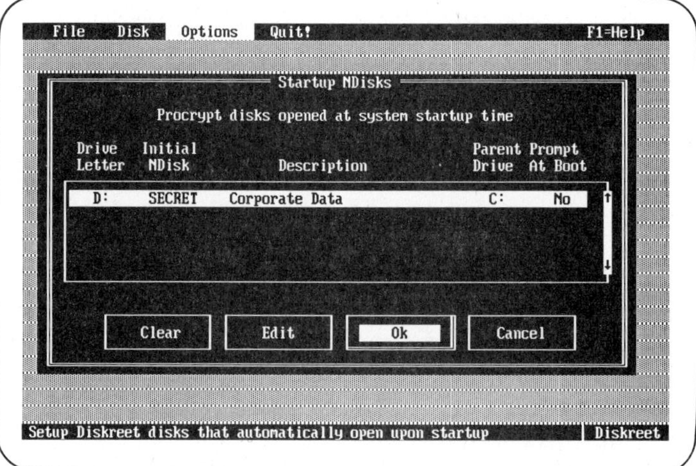

Fig. 3.28
The Diskreet Modify Startup NDisks screen.

- *Auto-Close Timeouts:* Displays a screen like the one in figure 3.29. This setting tells Diskreet to close an ndisk if it has not been accessed for a certain amount of time. The default time is 5 minutes. To set this value, make sure the Enable Auto Close setting is marked and enter the number of minutes to use. Choose OK to save this setting and exit this screen.

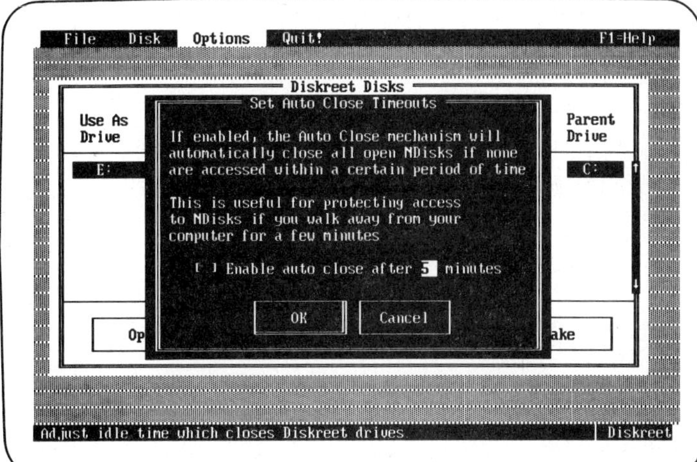

Fig. 3.29
The Diskreet Set Auto-Close Timeouts screen.

- *Keyboard and Screen Lock:* Displays a screen similar to the one shown in figure 3.30. This screen enables you to choose a Quick-Close hot key and keyboard locking. To choose the hot key, make sure the Enable Quick-Close option is checked and then choose one of the hot-key combinations. A Quick-Close hot key enables you to close quickly all ndisks. The Enable Locking option causes the screen to clear and the keyboard to lock until the main password is entered. If you choose the Enable Locking option, choose a hot key to cause the locking to take place. If you select both Quick-Close and Enable Locking, the same hot key will make both take place at once.

- *Security:* Displays a screen similar to the one in figure 3.31. This screen enables you to choose what to do when an ndisk is modified. The Quick Clear option does not remove encrypted data on the disk. Therefore, the information can be restored and read (if someone knows the password). The Overwrite option writes over the data one time on the disk. This usually is sufficient to destroy the data. If you really want security, however, choose the Security Wipe option, which writes over the data many times, using a Department of Defense procedure.

- *Change Main Password:* Specifies a new main password. This is the password needed to alter auto-close timeouts and keyboard locking.

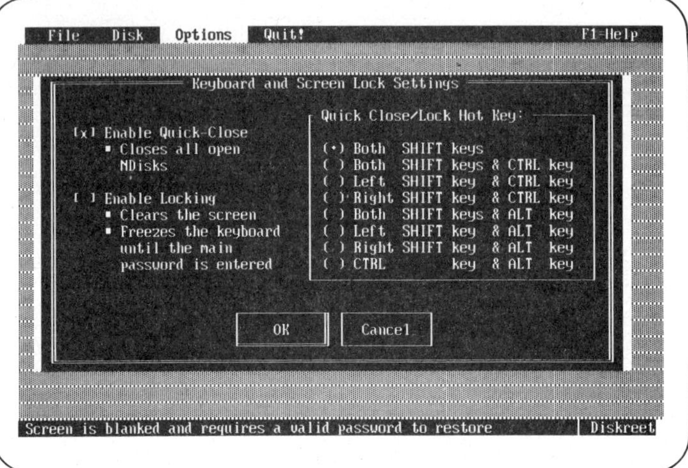

Fig. 3.30
The Diskreet Keyboard Lock screen.

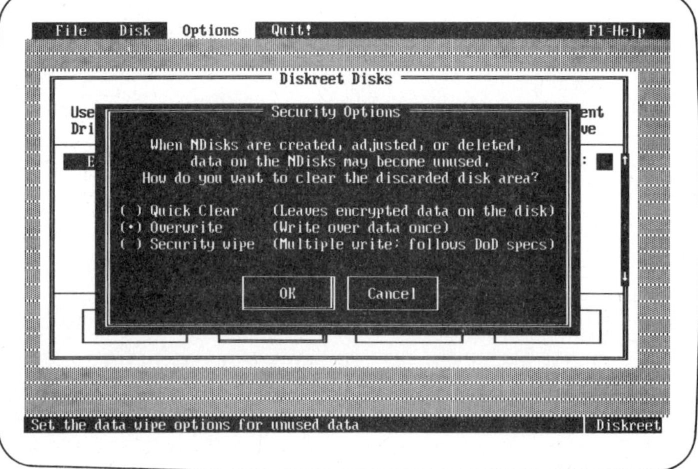

Fig. 3.31
The Diskreet Security Option screen.

Controlling Diskreet from the DOS Prompt

Many of the items you can control through the Diskreet menu also can be controlled by using the Diskreet command at the DOS prompt. The syntax for using Diskreet from the DOS prompt is

DISKREET [*switches*]

The available switches for the Diskreet command follow:

Switch	*Effect*
/ENCRYPT:*filespec*	Encrypts the specified file.
/DECRYPT:*filename*	Decrypts the specified file.
/PASSWORD:*your password*	Tells the Diskreet command which password to use for encryption or decryption of a file.
/SHOW[:*d*]	Instructs the command to show the hidden drives (ndisks) being used to store files.
/HIDE[:*d*]	Instructs the command to hide the specified drive (ndisk).
/CLOSE	Instructs the command to close all ndisks.
/ON	Instructs the command to enable the Diskreet driver.
/OFF	Instructs the command to disable use of the Diskreet driver.

Getting Rid of Files Permanently

With all this discussion about how to bring back files after disks have been formatted, you may be concerned about how to get rid of files permanently. The fact that some people do not even think about this problem (or did not know about it) is amazing. In a recent magazine story, a Fortune 100 company (a computer company, no less) auctioned off thousands of outdated PCs. Some were purchased by reporters who were able to unformat the hard disks and find out a great deal of important information.

After you erase a file by using the DOS ERASE or DELETE command, only one character in the disk directory is changed. This character tells DOS that the file is deleted. The actual contents of the file have not changed, and most of the information about the file still is intact. When you format a disk, the system information is erased, and information in the root directory is erased, but the actual contents of many files may be intact.

To give users a better way to prevent important information from getting into the wrong hands, Norton Utilities provides the Wipe Info command. This command permanently deletes files and disks. If you have information that should not fall into the wrong hands, the Wipe Info command should be an essential part of your information-protection plan.

Warning: It is important that you thoroughly understand Wipe Info and how files are erased before using it to delete important files permanently.

Wipe Info overwrites the information on disk with several writes of random data. Wipe Info includes a government option that overwrites the information on a disk according to governmental Department of Defense (DoD) specifications. These specifications call for a 1/0 pattern (a pattern of 1s and 0s) to be written to the disk three times, a random number to be written to the disk, and then the last number written to the disk to be read back from the disk for verification (DoD 5220.22-M). The government has adopted these specifications because a single erasure of magnetic information may not be enough. A faint magnetic "fingerprint" may remain on a disk after a single erasure.

Using Wipe Info Interactively

Use the Wipe Info command to overwrite all information in a file on disk so that no information can be recovered. You can use Wipe Info interactively or as a command from the DOS prompt. To use Wipe Info interactively, enter the command WIPEINFO at the DOS prompt. A screen similar to the one in figure 3.32 appears.

The Wipe Info menu screen gives you three options:

- *Files:* Displays a screen similar to the one in figure 3.33. On this screen, you can enter the names of the files to be wiped. Use the global characters * and ? to specify multiple files. By

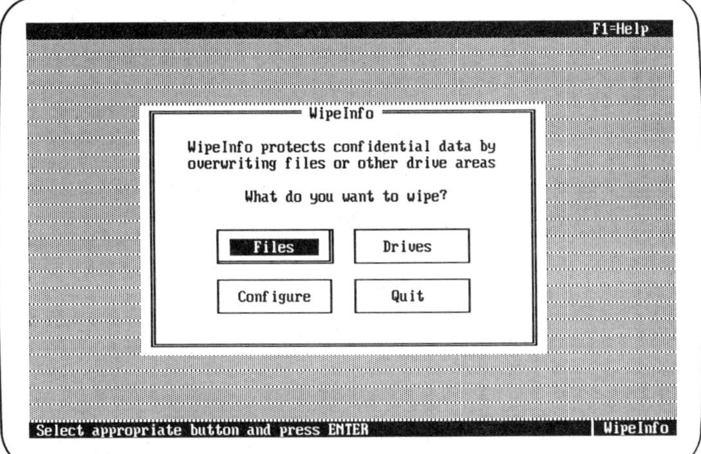

Fig. 3.32
The Wipe Info menu.

checking the appropriate boxes, you can choose to wipe files with matching filespecs in subdirectories, to have the program prompt you before wiping each file (confirm each file), and to wipe Hidden files and/or Read-only files that match the file specification. Also, you can choose to wipe the file or delete the file (like a regular DOS DELETE command). The Wipe Unused File Slack Only option causes Wipe Info to wipe only any portion of the disk that is allocated to a file, but unused. This does not affect the file itself—it only wipes out information that is in the slack space of the file. After you select your options, choose Wipe to begin the wiping procedure, or choose Cancel to cancel the wipe.

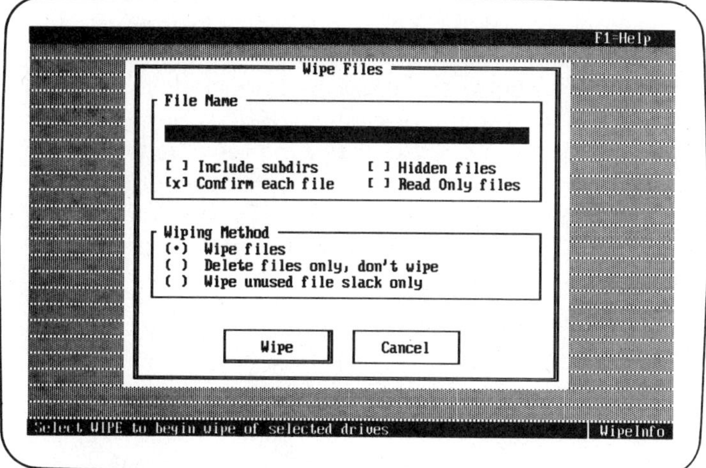

Fig. 3.33
The Wipe Files menu.

- *Drives:* Displays a screen like the one in figure 3.34. On this screen you can select which drives to wipe. Also, you can choose to wipe the entire disk or only the unused portions of the disk. Wiping the unused portion of the disk gets rid of any erased files that someone could restore to see important information. After you select the options on this menu, choose Wipe to begin wiping, or choose Cancel to cancel the wipe.

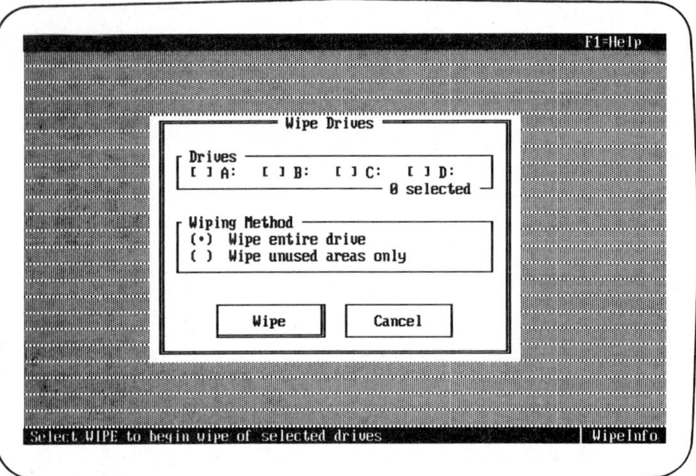

Fig. 3.34
The Wipe Drives menu.

- *Configure:* Enables you to choose how information is wiped from the disk. Figure 3.35 shows the Wipe Configuration screen. From this screen, choose the Fast Wipe or Government Wipe options. You can change several of the numbers within the options. You use the arrow keys, Tab, or the mouse pointer to move to those fields to change the numbers. For the Fast Wipe option, you can change the write value from 0 to another number (from 1 to 255). For the Government Wipe option, you can change the number of times the write is repeated and the final value written (default is 246). Also, you can change the repeat count from 1 to another number. After you set these settings, choose the Save Settings selection, and then choose OK to return to the Wipe Info menu.

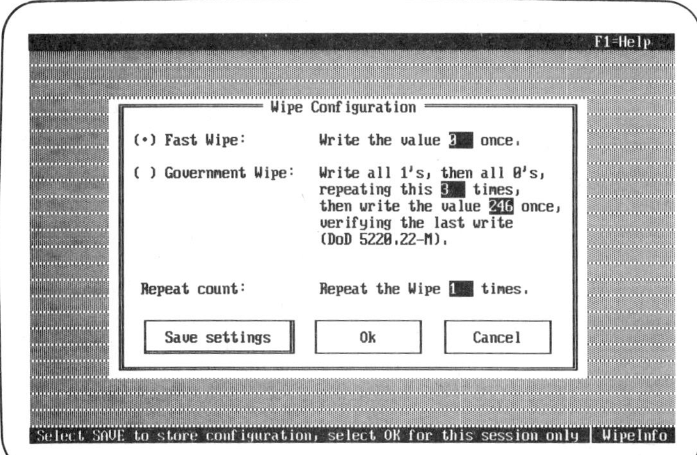

Fig. 3.35 The Wipe Configuration menu.

Using Wipe Info From the DOS Prompt

The Wipe Info command overwrites information on disk so that it cannot be recovered. This includes wiping files or the entire disk. The syntax for the Wipe Info command is

WIPEINFO *d:*[*disk or file switches*] [*common switches*]

The disk switch available for the Wipe Info command follows:

Switch	*Effect*
/E	Causes the command to overwrite information only that currently is unused or that is in "erased" files—files marked for erase by the DOS ERASE command, but otherwise recoverable.

The file switches available for the Wipe Info command follow:

Switch	*Effect*
/N	Uses "No-wipe" mode, which causes the Wipe File command to behave like the ERASE command. The file is marked as erased, but is not overwritten.
/K	Also wipes any slack space allocated to a file.

/S	Wipes out files that match the *filespec* in subdirectories also.

The common switches available for the Wipe Info command follow:

Switch	*Effect*
/G*n*	Uses a government-standard overwriting procedure. The default for *n* (number of overwrites) is 3. Value written to disk is ASCII value 246.
/R*n*	Overwrites the disk *n* times. The default is 1.
/V*n*	Selects the value that is to be used to overwrite information on the disk. The value can be from 0 to 255. Although the default is 0, the /G switch overrides this default.

To wipe disk D using the governmental standard, for example, enter the command

```
WIPEINFO D:/G
```

When you begin Wipe Info from the DOS prompt with a file specification and switches, you will skip the interactive Wipe Info menu and see the Wipe Files or Wipe Drives screen. From this screen, you can set or change options as described in "Using Wipe Info Interactively," earlier in this chapter.

Even if you go ahead and begin Wipe Info and suddenly have a change of heart or discover that you are wiping out the wrong disk, you can interrupt the process by pressing Ctrl-Break. Some information on the disk still may be recoverable if the operation has not proceeded too far. In fact, Norton has designed Wipe Info to destroy the most unused part of the disk first, so that if you stop the procedure quickly, you have a good chance of being able to use some of the information on disk.

Use Wipe Info when a computer with a hard disk is given to another person and that computer contained information that should not be made available to the recipient. If you want to wipe out only data files but leave programs intact on a computer, first erase all the confidential files and then use Wipe Info with the /E switch to wipe out all the erased files. The programs are left intact.

Summary

Norton Utilities 5.0 offers you a number of ways to protect your information on disk. Most of these safety measures, however, require that you do a little planning. Make sure that you set up your AUTOEXEC.BAT file to issue the Image command each time you boot. Also make sure that you are using the Safe Format command rather than the original DOS FORMAT command. If you accidentally do format a disk, you will be able to recover it if you have taken these precautions.

Other safety precautions you can use include setting file attributes to Read-only or Hidden. Use File Save, Disk Monitor, and Diskreet to monitor which files are used and changed on your disk. Finally, when protecting information means making sure that it does not get into the wrong hands, you can use Wipe Info to do a more thorough job of getting rid of information on disk than the DOS ERASE, DELETE, and FORMAT commands provide.

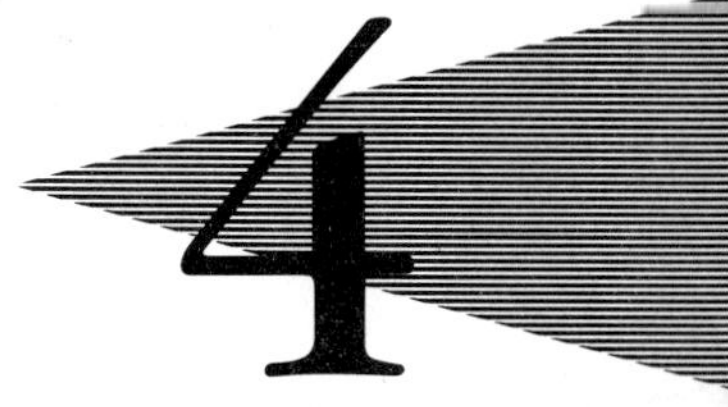

Recovering Files

Chapter 3 covers techniques for protecting the information on your disk by using preventive measures. At times, however, the best prevention does not work. You accidentally may use the command DEL when you mean to use DIR, for example. The consequences of these commands are quite different. The DIR command displays a list of files, and the DEL command erases (deletes) files. Accidental erasure is one of many ways—and probably the most common way—that files can be lost. Accidental formatting is another common cause of information loss. Some losses of information, however, are hard to control. You can lose files through excessive fragmentation on disk, for example. Also, the magnetic image on your disk can be damaged by a weakening of the magnetic signal. This chapter deals with ways of recovering lost information and describes the Norton Unerase command (unerases files or directories), the Norton Disk Doctor II (searches for and corrects file problems on disk), Disk Tools (fixes a variety of disk problems), File Fix (fixes dBASE, 1-2-3, and Symphony files) and Disk Editor (examines and edits disk contents directly).

Before you learn how to use these Norton data-recovery commands, however, you need to understand the basics of how disks work—knowledge that is valuable if you want to manage disks. If you already are familiar with how disks store information, you may want to skip the next section.

Understanding How Disks Work

This section describes how disks store information, how disks operate, and how DOS manages the information on disk. This information can give you a better understanding of what is happening in your computer. Knowing how disks handle data can be of particular help if you use the Norton Disk Editor command to edit information on disk or to recover erased files.

Computers have a binary thought process. That is, the memory of a computer consists of 0s (zeros) and 1s (ones). Information in the computer's RAM (random-access memory) is stored on the memory chip as an on or off signal, with the on signal being a 1, and the off signal a 0. Each RAM chip stores thousands of these 0s and 1s. When you create a word processing document, for example, RAM stores the entire document as a series of 0s and 1s.

Therefore, to store computer information, you must have a way to store these 0s and 1s. Early computers used punch cards. A hole punched in the card was interpreted as a 1; no hole meant 0. Today, the popular way to store computer information is on magnetic-sensitive media.

In your earlier years in elementary school, you may recall your science teacher placing some steel shavings on a sheet of paper and placing a magnet under the paper. The shavings all pointed in one direction or another, according to the poles of the magnet. Magnetic-sensitive media, such as that on a cassette recorder tape, a VCR tape, or a floppy diskette, is covered with a coat of iron oxide. The iron oxide reacts to magnetism in a way similar to those steel shavings on the paper. On a cassette recorder, the recording head is an electric magnet that magnetizes the iron oxide on the tape as it goes by. The stronger the signal, the more the iron oxide reacts. To store computer information to magnetic media, only two signals are needed: a strong signal and a weak signal. The computer interprets a strong magnetic signal as a 1 and a weak signal as a 0. Thus, a pattern of 1s and 0s can be written to and then read from magnetic media.

A computer disk is sort of a cross between a record and a cassette tape. Information on the disk is stored on magnetic tracks (like the magnetic coating on the cassette tape), and is similar to the grooves on a record (except that you cannot see the magnetic tracks).

On the disk (a floppy diskette or a hard disk), the magnetic media is coated on the top and bottom of the disk. A small head similar to the recording head on a tape recorder rides just above the surface of the disk. This head places magnetic signals on the disk (patterns of 0s and 1s) and reads them back. The work of reading and writing to disk, however, is not done haphazardly—it is, in fact, a precise bit of mechanical and software engineering.

Studying the Evolution of Floppy and Hard Disks

Disk media has improved over time. When the IBM PC first arrived on the scene in 1981, its only disk media was a single-sided floppy diskette. The disk drive had a read/write head on only one side of the diskette in the drive. Soon, double-sided diskettes appeared, in which the drive had a read/write head on both sides of the diskette. This improvement to the drive was relatively straightforward. No new housing or motor was needed. The addition of a second head and some electronics doubled the storage capacity of the disk.

One of the problems with reading and writing information to a floppy diskette is dust particles. Dust in the air limits the precision (smallness) of the information storage area on the disk. Another problem with floppy diskettes is that they are just that—floppy. When they are spinning around in the disk drive, some up and down movement occurs. Because of this movement, keeping the read/write head close enough to work but not close enough to scratch the surface of the disk is difficult. In fact, some diskettes wear out because of contact with the read/write head.

The solution to the problems of dust and movement, as well as the problem of not having enough room on a disk to store information was the development of the hard disk. First, a hard disk is housed in a dust-free compartment, so dust is not a problem. Second, the magnetic media is coated on a hard platter (thus, the name hard disk). These two improvements enable the read/write head to be placed closer to the disk, to read and write with more precision, and to rotate faster, enabling data to be stored and retrieved more quickly than on a floppy disk. Third, the hard disk has a greater storage capacity than the floppy diskette.

Most improvements to disk storage have involved the storage of more information with more precision on the magnetic surface of the disk. The mechanical and electrical improvements have given the disks this capability, and DOS has responded with the capability to handle the added capacity.

Understanding How Disks Are Organized

DOS keeps track of the information stored on disk. When a disk is formatted—whether it is a floppy diskette or a hard disk—circular areas called *tracks* are written (magnetically) on the disk. A standard 360K floppy diskette has 40 tracks, numbered 0 to 39. High density floppy disks (1.2M) use 80 tracks. Each track consists of a number of pieces called *sectors*. On a 360K diskette, each track has 9 sectors, numbered 1 through 9. Figure 4.1 illustrates the tracks and sectors on a typical 360K disk.

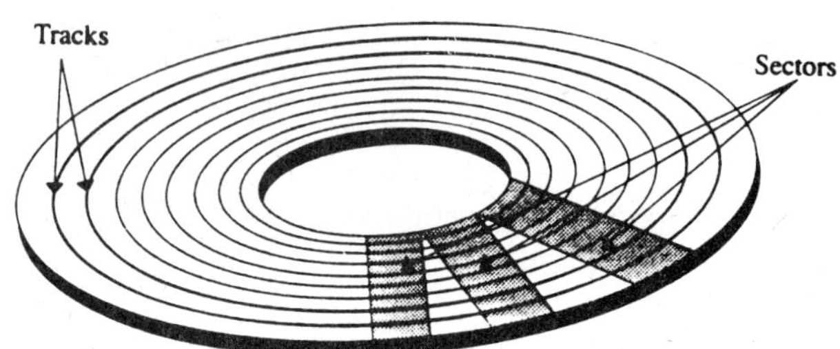

Fig. 4.1
A disk's tracks and sectors.

Because disks are two-sided (numbered 0 and 1), the top and bottom of the disks contain tracks. A pair of matching tracks on a disk is called a *cylinder*. Some hard disks have more than one platter or disk. When two disks are included, sides are numbered 0 and 1 on the first disk and 2 and 3 on the second disk. The set of four matching tracks on the two disks is the cylinder.

After a disk is organized into tracks and sectors by the formatting process, DOS knows how to read and write information to the disk. The operating system now knows where to place the read/write head so that it reads information from a particular track. In fact, DOS reads and writes information to the disk in a specific amount of bytes, called a *cluster*. A *byte* is eight 0 and 1 signals. Usually, each character stored on disk requires one byte of space. Thus, a byte often is referred to as one character of information. The number of sectors of information contained in a cluster depends on how many sectors per track are stored on disk. DOS uses two-sector clusters (1024 bytes) on 360K and 720K diskettes, one-sector clusters (512 bytes) on 1.2M and 1.44M diskettes, and 4-, 8-, or 16-sector clusters on most hard disks.

Understanding How DOS Manages Information

Specific areas on a formatted disk hold particular kinds of information. The *system area* contains the boot record, the FAT (file allocation table), and the root directory. The system area is stored on track 0—the outermost track of the disk. Whenever DOS needs to know information about the files stored on a disk, DOS reads this information from the system area of the disk. When you enter a DIR command, for example, DOS first looks at the root directory to get information on the files and then displays this information on-screen.

The *data area* on disk immediately follows the system information on disk. This area is where the actual information in files is stored. The contents of this data area and how DOS knows how to read and write the data are controlled by the information in the system area—the boot record, the FAT, and the root directory.

The Boot Record

DOS reserves the first sector of the first track of a disk as the DOS *boot record*. The boot record contains characteristics about the disk such as the version of DOS used to format the disk, the number of bytes per sector on disk, the number of heads, and other information. The boot record is written to every formatted disk, even if the disk is not a bootable disk.

The File Allocation Table

The *file allocation table* (FAT) contains information about disk storage. The FAT tells DOS which clusters on the disk are in use, are available for use, or are bad and should not be used. When you need to write a file to disk, DOS consults the FAT to find out where to store the information. If a file is large and cannot fit in one contiguous space on disk, DOS uses the FAT to find the next available space. The result is a file that is stored in pieces on disk—a fragmented file.

In addition, because the FAT deals in clusters, it may allocate a file to a cluster that is not fully used. For example, if a cluster is 512 bytes, and a 200-byte file is stored, 312 bytes of unused space remain on disk. This unused disk space is called *slack*. (You can determine the amount of slack on disk by using the Norton File Size command. See Chapter 5.) Cluster sizes differ, so the slack space for a particular file on a floppy diskette may be different from the slack for the same file on a hard disk. Although a floppy diskette may have a 512-byte cluster, for example, many hard disks have 2048-byte clusters. The same 200-byte file would have a slack space of 1848 bytes on such a hard disk.

The Root Directory

The third part of the system information on disk is the *root directory*, which is the main directory (\) on any formatted disk. This space on disk is allocated for storing information about the files in the root directory. Any subdirectories have their own areas where file information is stored. Subdirectories are similar to files, because they can be stored in the data area in no particular location except where DOS has room to store them. Table 4.1 shows the information that the root directory reports for each file contained within it.

Table 4.1
File Information Stored in the Root Directory

Item	*Size in Bytes*	*How Stored*
File name	8	ASCII characters
Extension	3	ASCII characters
Attributes	1	Bit values
Time	2	Coded time
Date	2	Coded date
Starting FAT entry	2	Word
File size	4	Long integer

The root directory reserves 10 bytes for future use in case something else about a file needs to be stored.

Notice that the file name storage is eight characters—the maximum length for a file name. The extension is allocated three characters. Attributes include Read-only, Archive, Hidden, and System. (You can control the attributes with the Norton File Find command. See Chapter 3.) The starting FAT entry tells DOS where to look in the FAT to find where the file is stored on disk. The date and time entries tell DOS when this file was last changed, and the length entry tells DOS how much space the file takes in bytes. The information in the How Stored column specifies the method used to store this information.

Understanding How Files Are Erased

When a file is stored on disk, the information contained in the file is written to the data area of the disk. The information about where this information is stored is in the directory (the root directory or a similar subdirectory area) and in the FAT. When you erase a file by using the DOS ERASE or DEL command, the first character of the entry in the directory that contains the file name is replaced with the ASCII character number 229 (ς), and related entries in the FAT are zeroed out. The information in the file is not overwritten (unless you use Wipe Info) or removed by DOS. The ASCII sigma character number 229 that DOS adds to the erased file's directory tells DOS that the file and file space it occupied are now free to be used by other files. If you have erased a file named MYFILE, for example, its "erased" name will be σYFILE in the DOS directory. It will not appear when you use the DIR command, but you can view this erased name by using the Norton Utilities Unerase command.

Because the ERASE or DEL command does not touch the real information in the file, you may be able to recover an erased file if you have written no other files (or few files) to disk since the file was erased. The rest of this chapter discusses ways to recover files.

Retrieving Erased Files and Directories

If the file space used by an erased file has not been used by a subsequent write to the disk, you can recover the file by using the Unerase command. Because an erased file can have its contents overwritten at any time, you must decide as soon as possible that a file needs to be unerased. If you unerase a file immediately after it has been erased, you should have no problem at all. If you create one or more files after erasing a file, however, the original file may no longer be unerasable.

To issue the Unerase command, select the Unerase option from the Norton menu or type UNERASE at the DOS prompt.

When you begin Unerase, the program searches for all unerasable files in the current directory. If the program finds erased files, the file names (as far as Unerase can figure out, without the first character) are displayed. If the file MARY.TXT had been erased, for example, the Unerase program reports that the file ?ARY.TXT can be recovered. Figure 4.2 shows a screen where a number of files are listed as candidates for unerasing. Unerase will provide a prognosis of the likelihood that these files can be successfully unerased. The possible prognoses are excellent, good, average and poor. To choose which file to unerase, use the arrow keys to highlight the file name and press Enter to choose Unerase, or point to a file name and click twice. If you choose to unerase the file ?ARY.TXT, for example, you will see the screen in figure 4.3, which asks you for the first letter in the file's name.

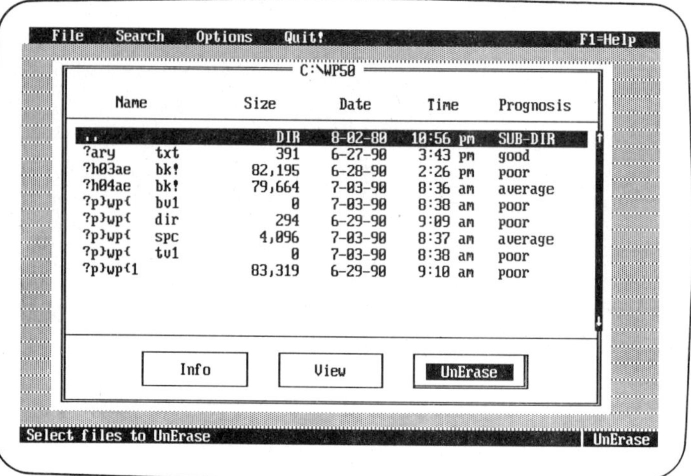

Fig. 4.2 Viewing potential files to unerase on the Unerase screen.

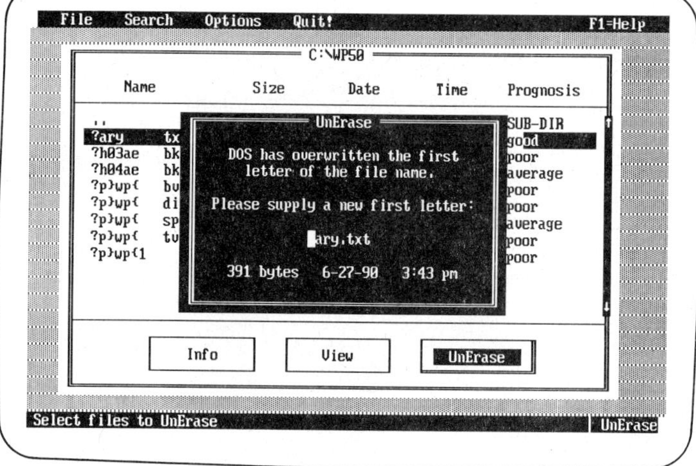

Fig. 4.3 Supplying the first letter of an erased file name on the Unerase screen.

To complete the unerasing, press M to unerase the file MARY.TXT. You return to the screen shown in figure 4.2, where you can choose other files to unerase.

If a file cannot be unerased automatically, you see a message like the one in figure 4.4. In this case, you may use the Search for Lost Names option (see "Searching for Lost Names," later in this chapter), or you may need to use the Manual Unerase procedure discussed in "Using the Manual Unerase Procedure."

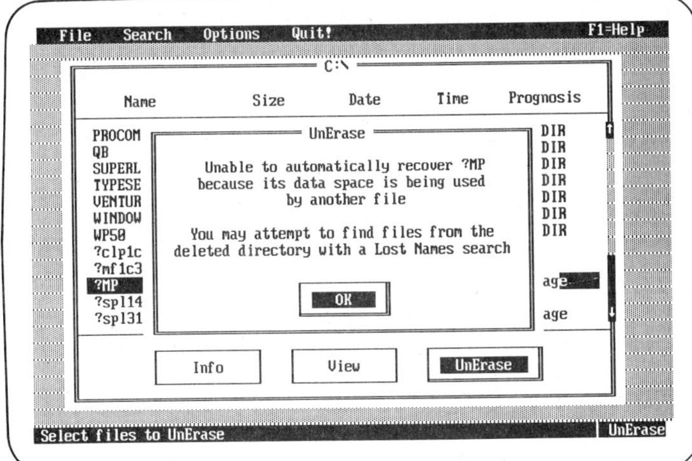

Fig. 4.4
An Unerase message telling you that a directory cannot be unerased because its space has been used by another file.

To locate files in other directories, you can go to another directory from the current directory by using the following procedure. The top file name in figure 4.2 is `..`, which is actually the indication of the subdirectory information. If you highlight `..` and press Enter (or point and click twice), you go to the previous directory—in this example, the root directory—where a list of all directories appears on the list. Then you highlight another directory name, press Enter, and go to another directory to look for more files to unerase. As you will see later, you also can use the Unerase menu bar to change directories.

If you erase (remove) a directory, it appears in the list with other erased files, but the indicator `DIR` appears in the Size column instead of a number. Figure 4.5, for example, contains information about an erased directory named TMP. Its name in the list is ?MP, and under the Size column it is listed as a DIR. To unerase this directory, you highlight its name and press Enter to choose the Unerase option. Alternatively, you can point to the entry with the mouse and click twice. If the directory can be unerased, you are prompted to enter the first letter of its name. After the directory is unerased, you can go to that directory by clicking on the directory name to see if it contains any files that can be unerased.

If a file or directory cannot be unerased or is unerased only partially, you still may be able to recover portions of the file or directory by using the Norton Disk Editor (see "Using the Norton Disk Editor," later in this chapter for more information). However, you always should try to use Unerase to erase files and directories before resorting to the more complicated Disk Edit command.

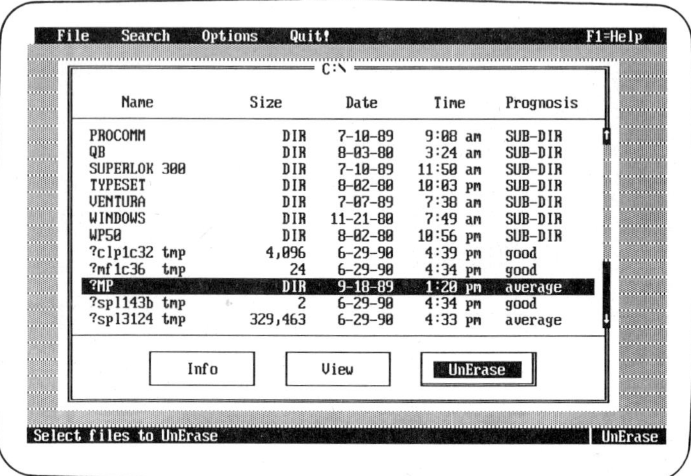

Fig. 4.5 Selecting a directory to unerase.

Notice the menu bar at the top of the Unerase screen. These menu items—File, Search, and Options—provide other choices for unerasing files. The Quit selection ends the Unerase program. The selections for each of these options are described in the following section.

Using the Unerase File Menu

The File menu at the top of the Unerase screen enables you to specify selections for the listing, selecting, and naming of files (see fig. 4.6). Notice the Alt commands beside some of the options. You can choose the corresponding option from the Unerase screen without opening the File menu. To choose the View Current Directory option, for example, press Alt-C. You cannot choose the options that are in parentheses. The Rename option, for example, is in parentheses, which means that you currently cannot choose that option. If you point to (highlight) a file name for an unerased file, this option becomes available, and it appears on the list without parentheses.

The File menu options follow:

- *View Current Directory:* Causes the Unerase screen to list all files in the current directory that are erased. This includes the file name (with a question mark as the first character), date, time, and prognosis for recovery. Use this option when you want to find a file in the directory to unerase.

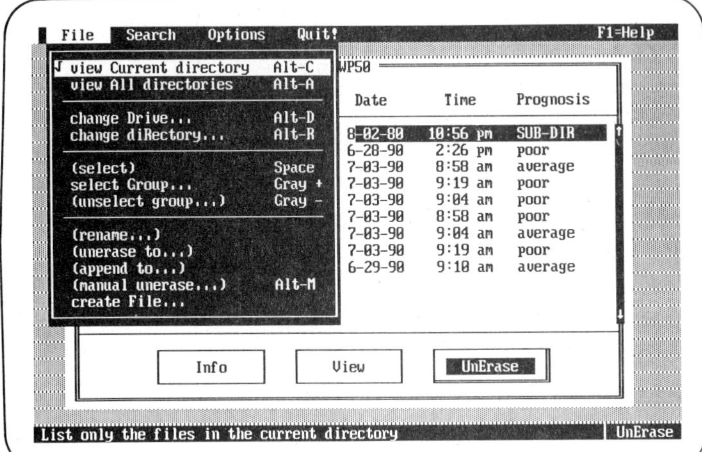

Fig. 4.6 The Unerase program's File pull-down menu.

- *View All Directories:* Enables you to look at erased files in all directories on the current disk. Erased files are listed by directory in the Unerase list box. You can highlight and unerase files in this list. Use this option if you want to unerase files in a number of directories, or when you are not sure which directory contains the files you want to unerase.

- *Change Drive:* Enables you to tell Unerase to display erased files on another drive. Displays a list of available drives, from which you can choose the drive to view.

- *Change Directory:* Enables you to tell Unerase to display erased files on another directory. Displays a list of directories, from which you can choose the directory you want to view.

- *Select:* Enables you to select an individual file. Highlight that file name and choose the Select option from the File menu. You can choose the Select option only if a file name is highlighted in the Unerase list. Otherwise, the file name is in parentheses, which means that you cannot choose the file at that time. Another way to select an individual file is to point to the file name and press the space bar. After you select a file, arrowheads appear on both sides of the file name in the Unerase list of files.

- *Select Group:* Enables you to select a group of files, choose the Select Group option from the File menu. You are prompted to enter a file specification for the files to select. If you type **.g**, for example, you select all files with extensions beginning with the letter g. Arrows appear on each side of each selected file name. You also may press the gray + key (on your cursor pad) to invoke the Select Group option. After you select the files to unerase, choose the Unerase option. You then are prompted to enter the first character of each file name in your selection list.

- *Unselect Group:* Enables you to unselect the list of files to unerase.

  To unselect a group, choose Unselect Group from the File menu or press the gray – key. You then are prompted to enter a file specification. If you type **.gbk*, for example, all files currently selected that have the extension GBK are unselected, and the arrows at the sides of those names disappear.

- *Rename:* Renames files. If a file in the Unerase list is recovered, you can rename a file by highlighting the file name and choosing the Rename option. You are prompted to enter a new name for the file.

- *Unerase To:* Unerases and saves files to another disk drive. Choose Unerase. You are prompted to choose the drive name where you want the file to be copied as it is unerased. For the Unerase To option to be active, you must be pointing to a file name that can be unerased.

- *Append To:* Enables you to append the contents of the highlighted file to another file. You are prompted to enter the name of the file to which you want to append the highlighted file.

- *Manual Unerase:* Enables you to unerase a file that you could not unerase with the Unerase program. Usually, files with a poor prognosis cannot be recovered automatically. See "Using the Manual Unerase Procedure," later in this chapter.

- *Create File:* Enables you to create a file by searching for erased clusters and building a file from unerased material on disk. This is similar to a manual unerase. See "Using the Manual Unerase Procedure," later in this chapter.

Using the Unerase Search Menu

The Unerase Search menu bar selection enables you to search for erased files, using certain criteria. Figure 4.7 shows the Search menu. You can search for the kind of file (Text, dBASE, 1-2-3, Symphony, and so on), for files containing a text string, or for file names that may not appear on the

Unerase list (files in erased subdirectories). You also may specify searches within a range of clusters on the disk.

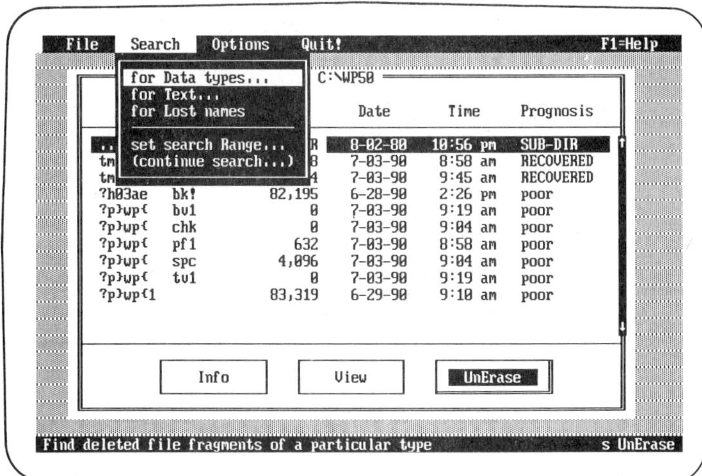

Fig. 4.7
The Unerase program's Search pull-down menu.

The Unerase Search menu options follow:

- *Data Types:* Enables you to search the disk for files that are normal ASCII text files, dBASE-type files, Lotus 1-2-3-type files, or Symphony-type files. After you choose the Data Type option, you can select which types of files to search for. After you finish the search, the files listed in the Unerase file list will be those types you selected.

- *Search for Text:* Enables you to search for erased files that contain a certain string of text. If you choose this option, you are prompted to enter the text for which you want to search. If you are looking for files that contain information about the 1991 budget, for example, you may specify the text "1991 Budget" as your text string. After you finish the search, the files listed in the Unerase file list will be those types you selected.

- *Lost Names:* Enables you to search for file names that usually will not appear in the Unerase file list. These are erased files that were a part of an erased directory. If these lost file names are listed in the Unerase file list, you can unerase them like any other files.

- *Set Search Range:* Enables you to tell Unerase which clusters to search, by specifying the Set Search Range criteria. You are asked to enter the beginning and ending cluster number. This may save time if you have a large disk. During a search, you can interrupt the search by pressing Esc. If you want to continue the search from the point where it stopped, choose the Continue Search option.

Using the Unerase Options Menu

The Options menu enables you to choose a sort order to be used when listing file names in the Unerase file list. You also may choose to list non-erased (all) files in the list. Figure 4.8 shows the Options menu.

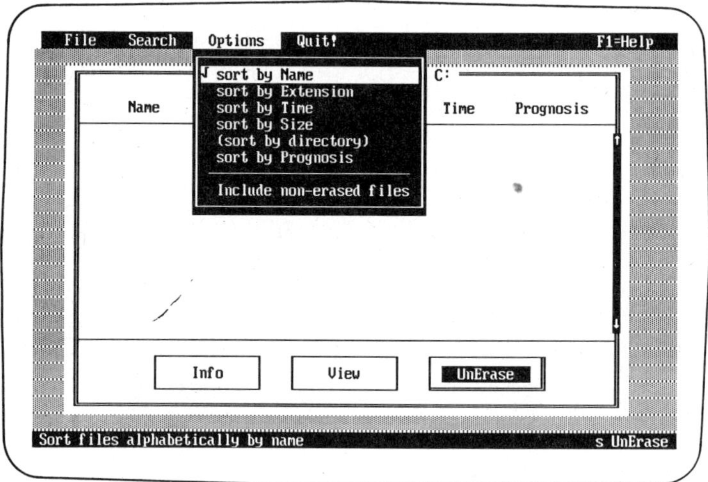

Fig. 4.8 The Unerase program's Options pull-down menu.

From the list of options, you may choose to list files in sorted order, by file name, extension, time, size, or prognosis. The Sort by Directory option is available if you previously chose the View All Directories option from the File menu. From this options menu, you also may choose to include nonerased files in the list box. You may want to have these files listed to use the File menu Rename or Append options.

Using the Manual Unerase and Create File Options

Descriptions of the Manual Unerase and Create File options in the Unerase File menu were skipped earlier in this chapter, because these options require more knowledge about the way files are stored on disk. The descriptions here assume that you know how clusters are used to store files on disk.

When a file cannot be unerased automatically with Unerase, you have the option of trying to put the file together manually, by using the Manual Unerase procedure. The Create File procedure is the same as the Manual Unerase procedure, except that you start with a new file name instead of resurrecting an erased file name. If you start with an erased file name, the initial Manual Unerase screen contains information about the attributes of the file, its size, the first cluster in the file, the file size, and other information (see fig. 4.9). If you are beginning with a new file name, the screen will be similar, but there will be no attributes, no first cluster, and no known size for the file.

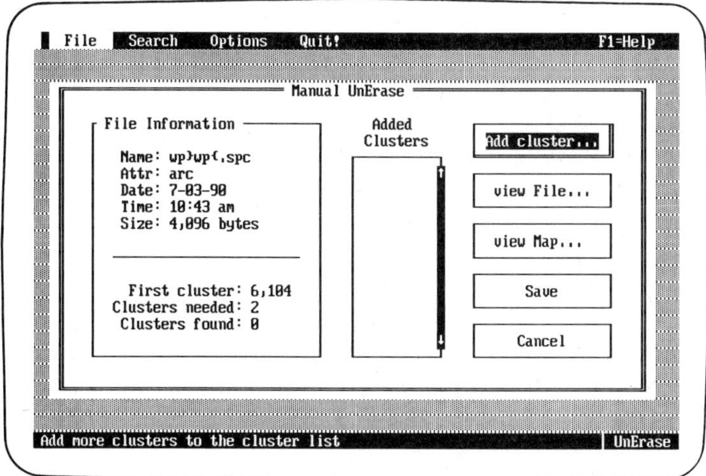

Fig. 4.9
The Unerase program's Manual Unerase screen.

You use the options on the right side of the Manual Unerase screen to help you piece together the file to unerase. The Added Clusters box shows you which clusters you used to make up the file. If you know how many clusters it takes to make up the file (clusters needed), you will know when you have completed the task of finding all of a file's cluster. Then you can save the file and end the Manual Unerase procedure. You use the View File option to look at the contents of the clusters that have been added to the list. The View Map option enables you to see a map of your hard disk and to see where the found clusters are located relative to one another.

Using Manual Unerase

To manually unerase a file, follow these steps:

1. Choose the file name of the file that you want to unerase from the Unerase screen. If Unerase cannot unerase this file automatically, choose the Manual Unerase option from the File menu.

2. Choose the Add Clusters option from the Manual Unerase screen. Add clusters using the All Clusters, Next Probable, Data Search, or Cluster Number options.

3. Verify that the clusters you added belong to the file by using the View File option. Move clusters, if necessary, so that the clusters are in the right order.

4. If all clusters have been found, stop and save the file to disk. If all clusters have not been found, return to Step 2 and continue.

   If you cannot recover the file by using Manual Unerase, you still may be able to recover all or parts of the file by using the Norton Disk Editor. See "Using the Norton Disk Editor," later in this chapter, for more information.

Adding Clusters to the File

If you choose the Add Cluster option from the Manual Unerase screen, you see the screen in figure 4.10.

This screen lists four options that help you locate clusters for the file you are trying to unerase:

- *All Clusters:* Pieces together all of the most likely clusters that make up the erased file. When the All Clusters option cannot determine the next cluster, it stops. The found clusters are listed in the Added Clusters list on the Manual Unerase main screen. If you locate all of the clusters required to put together the erased file, you can choose the Save option to save the unerased file to disk as an unerased file. If all of the clusters have not been found, you need to try one of the other three options.

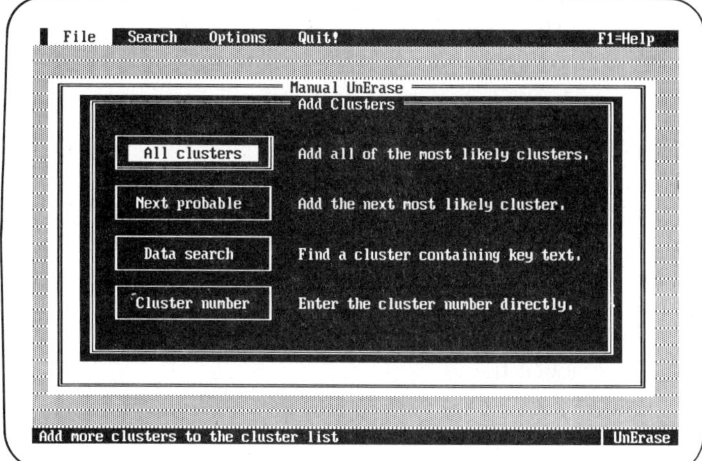

Fig. 4.10
The Manual Unerase menu.

- *Next Probable:* Adds the cluster to the file that the program determines is the next probable cluster to the file. After you add such a cluster, you should then choose the View File option to look at the contents of the file. If the file is a text file, you should be able to determine if the pieces of the file are fitting together. If the cluster you added belongs to the file but is in the wrong order, you can change the order of the clusters. To move a cluster to another location in the cluster list, use the arrow keys or your mouse to highlight the cluster you want to move. Press the space bar to pick up that cluster, and then use the up- and down-arrow keys to move that cluster to a new location in the list. Press the space bar again to anchor the cluster to the list. If you add a cluster and then determine that the cluster does not belong to the file you are trying to unerase, you can use the arrow keys (or mouse) and the space bar to select that cluster. Then, press the Del key to delete that cluster from the Added Clusters list.

- *Data Search:* Helps you find the next cluster in your file (use this if Next Probable could not locate the next cluster). First, you need to view the file and determine what will be next in the file. Suppose that you are unerasing a report. You find sections in the report labeled I through VI. Therefore, you may want to search for the text "VII" to find the next cluster. If you choose to search for text, you see a screen like the one shown in figure 4.11. You can enter the text in ASCII or Hex

(Hexadecimal code). Usually, you will enter ASCII. If you enter search text in ASCII, it also appears in Hex. If you want the search to be case-sensitive, unselect the Ignore Case option. After you enter your search text and select Find, a search for the text begins. If the search text is found, a few lines of the cluster found are shown on-screen. You can choose to do the following:

Option	*Effect*
Add Cluster	Adds this cluster to the list
Find Next	Continues search for next matching text
Hex	Displays the find in hexadecimal format (if Text mode)
Text	Displays the find in Text mode (if Hex mode)
Done	Stops the search

The Hex and Text mode alternate. If the find is displayed in Text mode, you optionally can choose Hex mode. If the find is displayed in Hex mode, you can change to Text mode. Continue the search until you find the right cluster to add.

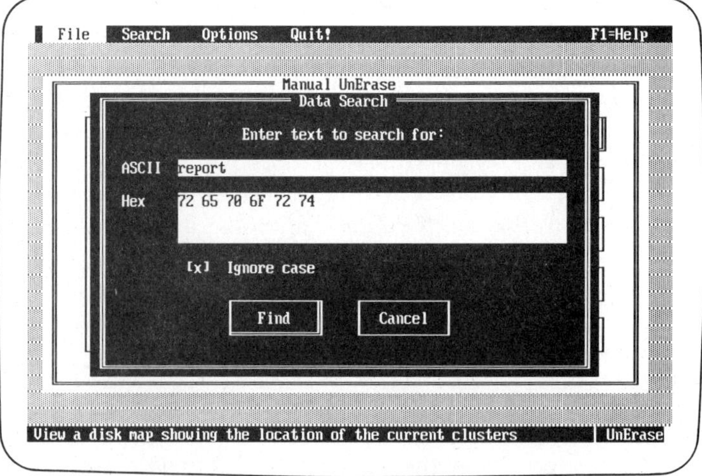

Fig. 4.11 Using the Manual Unerase screen to specify a search text string.

- *Cluster Number:* Adds one or more clusters to the list. In some instances, you may know the cluster number of the cluster you want to add to your file. You may have intentionally placed clusters on the disk in particular locations, for example, to hide them for a special reason. Or, you may have located a cluster using a technique other than Unerase.

Doctoring Your Hard Disk with Norton Disk Doctor

In addition to losing information by erasing files and removing directories, you may lose information from flaws on the disk. Norton also provides a way to address this problem.

One of the most powerful programs in the Norton Utilities arsenal is the Norton Disk Doctor II. Using detailed knowledge about the boot record, the file allocation table (FAT), and the system area, the Norton Disk Doctor often is able to figure out where problems exist on a disk and what can be done to eliminate the problems. Not all problems can be solved, but the Disk Doctor tries.

The syntax of the Norton Disk Doctor II (NDD) command is

NDD [*d:*][*d:*][*switches*]

The *d:* designations are disk drive names; you can specify more than one drive (Norton does not mention any limit).

The available switches for the NDD command follow:

Switch	*Effect*
/QUICK	Omits the test for bad cylinders, but tests the partition table, boot record, root directory, and lost clusters.
/COMPLETE	Tests for bad cylinders on the disk, as well as the partition table, boot record, root directory, and lost clusters.
/R:*file*	Instructs NDD to output a report about the results of its testing to the file named. Use with /QUICK or /COMPLETE.
/RA:*file*	Same as /R, but appends the report to the file instead of making a new file. Use with /QUICK or /COMPLETE.
/X:*d*	Excludes drive *d* from examination.

If you enter the NDD command with no switches, the command operates in interactive mode—you choose the options you want from a menu.

The Norton Disk Doctor II main menu is shown in figure 4.12. This menu contains four choices:

- *Diagnose Disk:* Tells NDD to examine your disk to check the integrity of the information stored on the disk.
- *Undo Changes:* Undos any changes made by NDD and returns your disk to its original state.
- *Options:* Sets certain options for the program.
- *Quit:* Ends the NDD program.

Details about the first three NDD options in this list are covered in the next few sections.

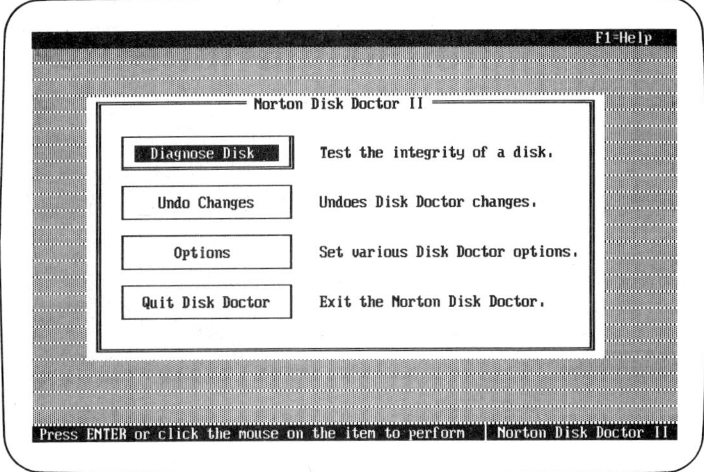

Fig. 4.12 The Norton Disk Doctor II main menu.

Diagnosing a Disk

The Norton Disk Doctor II Diagnose Disk option performs a variety of tests on your disk to verify that the information stored on the disk can be accessed properly. You should use the Diagnose Disk option on occasion as preventive maintenance on your hard disk. Also, if your disk access becomes erratic—for example, you experience trouble trying to read a file or your computer no longer boots properly—use NDD to diagnose the problem.

If you never have used NDD on your hard disk, it is a good idea to perform a full test so that you can find and resolve any problems or potential problems. Afterward, using the Quick test may be sufficient to locate most file problems. NDD Diagnose Disk performs more than 100 tests to analyze your disk. Under normal disk operation, you probably need to use the NDD diagnosis about once a month.

Problems on a disk usually are the result of corrupted information being placed on disk or bad spots on the disk that cause information to be unreadable. A bad spot, for example, can be caused by loss of the magnetic signal. NDD attempts to read information from all parts of the disk. If a part of the disk cannot be read and no file currently is using the bad part, the problem is simple to fix. NDD marks that area as bad, and DOS knows from now on not to use it. If the bad spot is in a location where a file is stored, however, NDD must try to read as much of the file as possible and move it to another, safe location on disk. Then the command marks the bad area so that area is never used again.

Note: Often, when NDD finds a problem on disk, a prompt asks whether you want the problem to be fixed or ignored. Unless you have a specific reason *not* to fix a problem, you should allow NDD to try to correct the problem on the disk.

After you choose the Diagnose Disk option from the NDD menu, you see a list of possible disks to test (see fig. 4.13). You specify the disk or disks to test by using the arrow keys to highlight the first disk of your choice and then press the space bar. A check mark appears next to your choice. You then can choose any other disk to test. After you make your selections, press Enter to begin the test procedures.

Figure 4.14 shows the first test screen (in this example, you have decided to test the hard disk). Notice the seven-part test list at the top of the screen, titled `Diagnosing Drive C:`. As each part of the test progresses, the corresponding description for that test area is highlighted on-screen and a blinking dot appears before the description name. When a test for an area is complete, a check mark appears next to the test description.

Information about the progress of the current test being performed is presented at the bottom of the screen. In figure 4.14, a test of the file allocation tables is in progress.

The Norton Disk Doctor tests to see whether bad information is located in the system areas or data areas of the disk. If your hard disk is partitioned into several disks (C and D, for example), the NDD partition table test checks to see if the allocation of space is properly accounted for. The tests of the boot record, file allocation tables, and directory structure, test

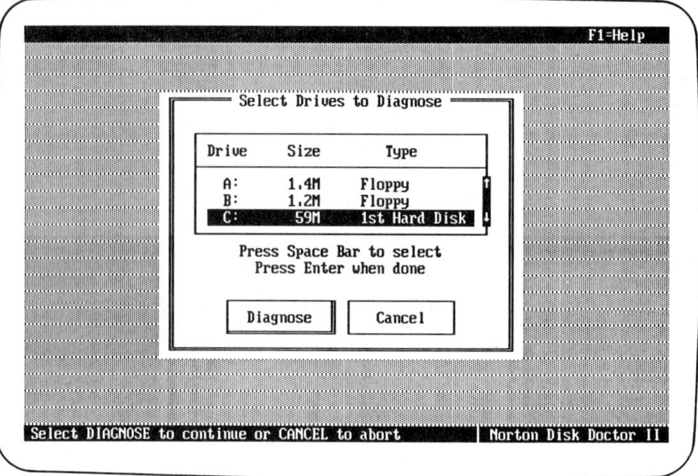

***Fig. 4.13* The Norton Disk Doctor list of drives to diagnose.**

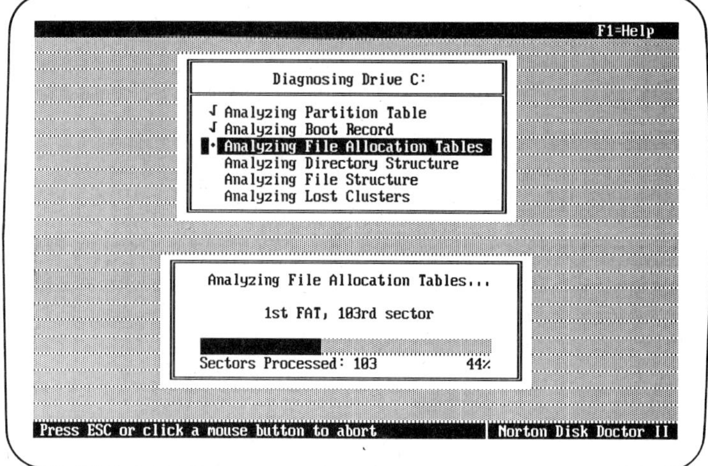

***Fig. 4.14* The Norton Disk Doctor lists tests in progress.**

the integrity of the system information on disk. That is, NDD determines whether the system information can be read from disk and whether the system information makes sense. In the system area of the disk, NDD reads the information and compares what it read from disk to what should be on the disk, just as you look at a manuscript to see whether all the parts—the title, the contents, the body, and the index—are there. If NDD finds that something is missing, is wrong or out of place, the program usually knows how to fix it.

Figure 4.15 shows a dialog box that appears if an error is found in testing the disk. In this example, the boot record was bad. You are given the choice to correct the problem or to cancel the testing. When you see a dialog box like this, read the description of the problem carefully. Then, read the recommendation. In most cases, you should follow the recommendation. In this example, if you choose Yes, NDD makes this disk bootable.

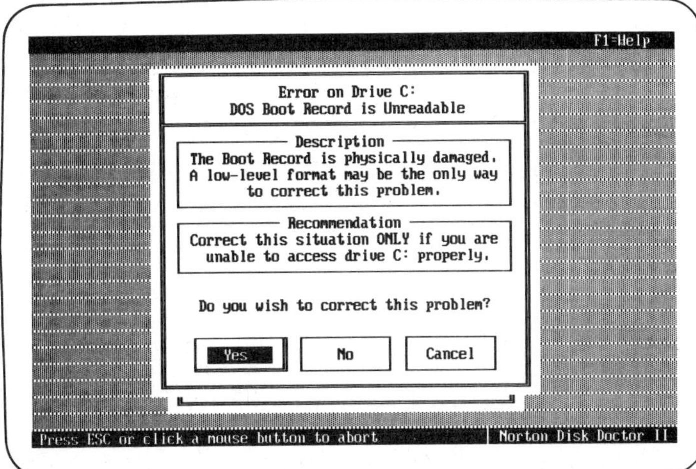

Fig. 4.15
A Disk Doctor error message telling you that the boot record is unreadable.

When NDD tests the file allocation table, it analyzes the FAT to see if available space on disk is accounted for as space being used by a file, sectors marked as bad spots on the disk, or free space. Space on a disk may be unaccounted for when a file is not properly saved to disk. This unaccounted space appears in the FAT as a lost cluster—a place on disk that was reserved for use by a file, but was never used. Lost clusters can occur when you turn off the computer, reboot the computer, or when the power fails while a file is open. A series of lost clusters related to one file is called a *chain*.

The File Structure test examines how your files are stored on disk to make sure that the file allocation is okay. The Lost Clusters test looks for information about files that were not stored properly—this is sometimes caused by programs that are abruptly stopped, as in a power outage. The Surface test checks for physical defects on your disk. Before NDD performs the Surface test, you see a screen like the one shown in figure 4.16.

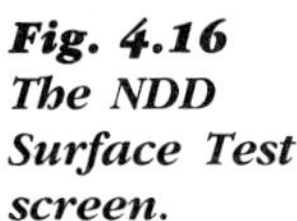

Fig. 4.16 The NDD Surface Test screen.

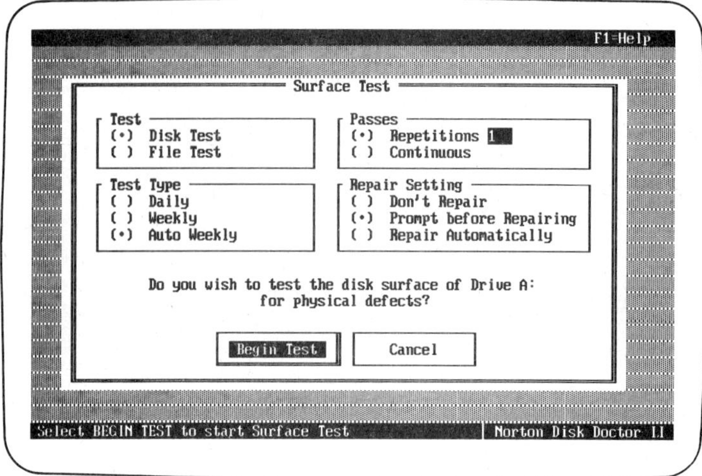

From the Surface Test screen, you can choose several options about how the test will be performed. This screen contains four boxes:

- *Test:* Tells the test to look at the surface of the entire disk (Disk Test), or to test only the portions of the disk occupied by files (File Test). File Test is faster, but Disk Test is more thorough.

- *Passes:* Enables you to specify a certain number of repetitions of the test (the default is 1, but you can change it to repeat up to 999 times), or to perform the test until you interrupt it by pressing Esc. Usually, one repetition is sufficient. If there are intermittent problems, however, you may want to run the test for a number of repetitions or continuously to try to locate the problem.

- *Test Type:* Enables you to select from three tests:

Daily	Performs a quick scan of the disk.
Weekly	Tests the disk more thoroughly than the daily test, but takes twice the time.
Auto Weekly	Provides the most thorough test.

  The names of these options may be confusing. You do not *have* to perform the Daily test daily, or the Weekly test weekly. The names are only meant as a guide. The default test is the Auto Weekly test, which Norton recommends that you do every Friday.

- *Repair Setting:* Tells NDD what to do if a problem is found during the Surface test. You can select from three options:

Don't Repair	Tells NDD not to attempt to repair the disk if a problem is located. Use if you want a report about your disk's problems, but do not want to repair the disk.
Prompt Before Repairing	Tells NDD to ask you if you want a problem solved before trying to fix a disk problem. (Prompt Before Repairing is the default setting.) Usually, you will want NDD to tell you whether a problem has been found so that you can decide whether you want to fix it.
Repair Automatically	Tells NDD to try to repair each problem as it is found, without prompting.

You probably still will want to create a report to document any fixes. If the same fixes occur time after time, you may want to consider performing a low-level format of the disk (see Chapter 5).

Figure 4.17 shows a problem screen that could appear during a Surface test. In this case, cluster 166 was found to contain a bad sector. You can choose to mark this cluster as bad, in which case it will no longer be used. Notice the message that says

```
This cluster is not used.
```

If this cluster had been part of a file, NDD would have *moved* it rather than *marked* it. Moving the cluster places the file information in a cluster that is good, which enables you to try to save the file information. If you choose Skip, the cluster is not affected. If you choose Auto, this and all subsequent bad sectors are marked or moved. Choose Cancel to end the test.

When the disk analysis is complete, a brief summary appears on-screen (see fig. 4.18). You may want to produce a report about the disk test, particularly if disk problems were found. Figure 4.19 is a sample report. Keep these reports as a record of your disk problems.

The header on the report provides information about the date and time of the analysis. The Disk Totals section gives you information about the storage capacity of the disk. The *total disk space* is the number of bytes of information that the disk can hold. *Bad sectors* are places on disk that have been found (usually, by the format procedure) to be unsuitable for

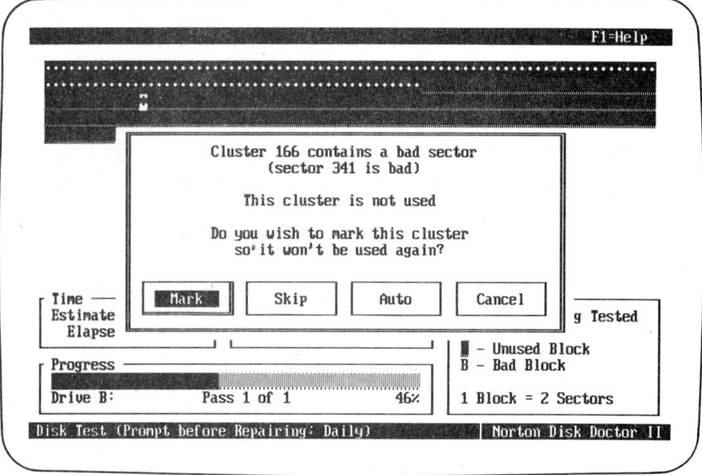

***Fig. 4.17* The NDD Surface Test error message when a bad sector is found.**

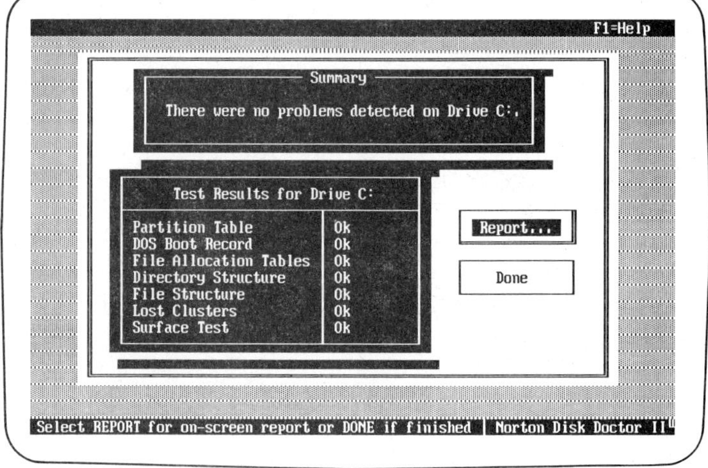

***Fig. 4.18* The NDD summary screen after tests are complete.**

storing information. If you subtract the number of bytes taken up by the user files and bad sectors from the total, you get the number of *bytes available on the disk.*

The Logical Disk Information section of the report describes the logical parameters used to store information on the disk. The Media Descriptor gives you a code for what kind of disk is being used. These codes are listed in table 4.2. In figure 4.19, the analyzed disk is a 360K diskette. The small `h` following the `FD` beside `Media Descriptor` means that `FD` is in hexadecimal. The Physical Disk Information section includes information about

```
          Norton Disk Doctor II
         Norton Utilities,  5.0
     Thursday, July  5, 1990 9:04 am

        *************************
        *  Report for Drive B:  *
        *************************

               DISK TOTALS
  -----------------------------------------
      362,496 bytes Total Disk Space
       10,240 bytes in Bad Sectors
      352,256 bytes Available on the Disk


          LOGICAL DISK INFORMATION
  -----------------------------------------
            Media Descriptor:  FD
             Large Partition:  No
                    FAT Type:  12-bit
               Total Sectors:  720
              Total Clusters:  354
            Bytes Per Sector:  512
         Sectors Per Cluster:  2
           Bytes Per Cluster:  1,024
              Number of FATs:  2
         First Sector of FAT:  1
   Number of Sectors Per FAT:  2
    First Sector of Root Dir:  5
Number of Sectors in Root Dir:  7
Maximum Root Dir File Entries:  112
    First Sector of Data Area:  12


          PHYSICAL DISK INFORMATION
  -----------------------------------------
                Drive Number:  1
                       Heads:  2
                   Cylinders:  40
            Sectors Per Track:  9
               Starting Head:  0
           Starting Cylinder:  0
             Starting Sector:  1
                 Ending Head:  1
             Ending Cylinder:  39
               Ending Sector:  9


             SYSTEM AREA STATUS
  -----------------------------------------

       DOS Boot Record is Unreadable
            Status: Corrected


            FILE STRUCTURE STATUS
  -----------------------------------------
      No Errors in the File Structure
```

Fig. 4.19
A summary report of Norton Disk Doctor's tests.

Fig. 4.19 (continued)

```
               SURFACE TEST STATUS
-----------------------------------------
                  Test Settings
             -----------------------
                      Test:  Disk Test
                 Test Type:  Daily
            Repair Setting:  Repair Automatically
          Passes Requested:  1
          Passes Completed:  1
              Elapsed Time:  00:02:56

 Error reading Sector 15 in Cluster 3
    Cluster 3 currently not in use
 Status: Corrected; Marked as Unusable

 Error reading Sector 17 in Cluster 4
    Cluster 4 currently not in use
 Status: Corrected; Marked as Unusable

 Error reading Sector 31 in Cluster 11
    Cluster 11 currently not in use
 Status: Corrected; Marked as Unusable

 Error reading Sector 55 in Cluster 23
    Cluster 23 currently not in use
 Status: Corrected; Marked as Unusable

 Error reading Sector 61 in Cluster 26
    Cluster 26 currently not in use
 Status: Corrected; Marked as Unusable

 Error reading Sector 62 in Cluster 27
    Cluster 27 currently not in use
 Status: Corrected; Marked as Unusable

 Error reading Sector 66 in Cluster 29
    Cluster 29 currently not in use
 Status: Corrected; Marked as Unusable

 Error reading Sector 68 in Cluster 30
    Cluster 30 currently not in use
 Status: Corrected; Marked as Unusable

Error reading Sector 396 in Cluster 194
   Cluster 194 currently not in use
 Status: Corrected; Marked as Unusable

Error reading Sector 696 in Cluster 344
   Cluster 344 currently not in use
 Status: Corrected; Marked as Unusable
```

how the data is physically on disk. The drive number tells you which drive the disk was in when it was analyzed. Drive numbers 0, 1, 2, and so on, refer to drives A, B, C, and so on. In figure 4.19, therefore, the disk was analyzed in drive B (drive number 1).

Table 4.2
System ID Codes Reported

Code	*Meaning*
F0	A 1.4M, 3 1/2-inch diskette
F8	A hard disk
F9	A 1.2M, 5 1/4-inch diskette or a 720K, 3 1/2-inch diskette
FD	A 360K, 5 1/4-inch diskette
FE	A 160K, 5 1/4-inch diskette
FF	A 320K, 5 1/4-inch diskette

The Norton Disk Doctor reports any problems found in the system area or in the file structure, giving information about what the problems were and how (and if) they were fixed. In the System Area Status section of the report, figure 4.19 shows that the DOS boot record was found to be unreadable, and that the problem was corrected.

Notice the material provided under the Surface Test Status section at the bottom of the report in figure 4.19. The first item gives the following information:

```
Error reading Sector 15 in Cluster 3
   Cluster 3 currently not in use
 Status: Corrected; Marked as Unusable
```

In this case, a bad cluster was located, but no information was currently residing in that area. Therefore, the cluster was marked as bad, and no file information was damaged. If the cluster had contained information, NDD would have tried to move as much good information as possible to a good cluster and would have reported that the files were moved, but that they may not be fully recovered or usable.

If you discover by reading the report that NDD moved some of your files, you should examine those files to see whether they contain any damaged areas. You can examine word processing files in your word processor. If NDD moved program files, you probably should recopy them from the original source to the disk to guarantee that the contents of the file are okay.

Undoing Changes

After you run the NDD program and make changes to your disk, you may want to reverse those changes—perhaps a moved file is no longer usable, for example, and you want to try some other way to recover it, such as using the Norton Disk Editor. As NDD makes changes to your disk, it stores the information about those changes to a file called NDDUNDO.DAT. If you choose the UnDo Changes option from the NDD menu, the disk is restored to its original condition.

Setting Options

If you choose the Options selection from the NDD menu, you see another menu (see fig. 4.20). This menu enables you to select settings for the Surface test, to select a custom error message, and to choose tests to skip.

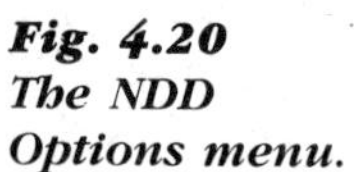

Fig. 4.20
The NDD Options menu.

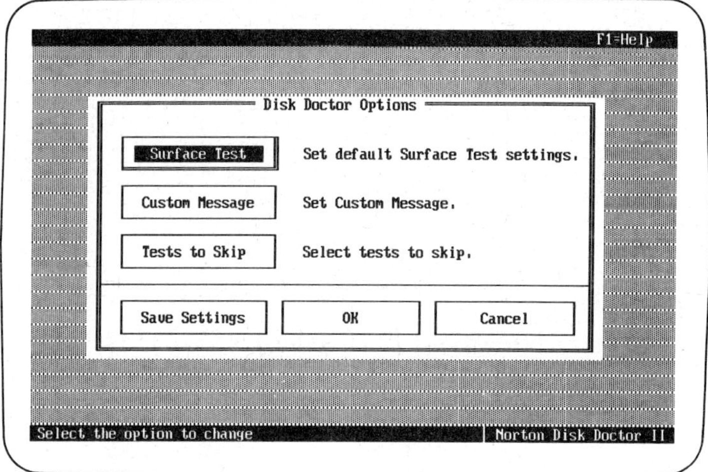

The options on the Disk Doctor Options screen follow:

- *Surface Test:* Displays a screen like the one in figure 4.16. You can choose options other than the normal defaults, and then save this information to disk. When NDD is used again, either interactively or as a command from the DOS prompt, your new defaults are used.

- *Custom Message:* Enables you to customize the message that appears on-screen when an error is encountered in the system area test. Figure 4.21 shows this screen. Suppose you have placed the NDD command on a number of computers in your company, but you do not want inexperienced users to make corrections on their disks without the company computer-support team knowing about the problem. In this case, you could create a custom message like the one in figure 4.21:

```
Please Contact USER Support at . . .
```

If NDD finds a system area problem, this message appears on-screen.

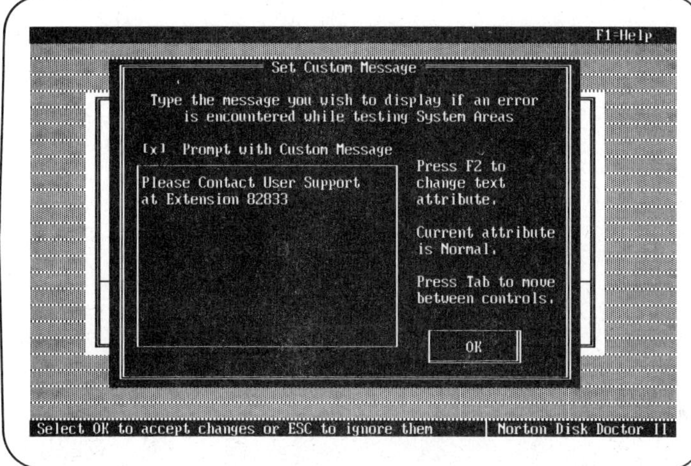

Fig. 4.21
The NDD Set Custom Message screen.

- *Tests to Skip:* Enables you to choose tests for NDD to skip. You usually need this option if your computer is not 100-percent IBM PC-standard compatible. You may choose from four skip options, as shown in figure 4.22.

After you make selections in the Surface Test, Custom Message, and Tests to Skip screens, you should choose the Save Settings option from the Options menu to save this information to disk. Then, when the NDD program begins, your chosen options are in effect.

Using Disk Tools

Several options included in Norton Disk Doctor 4.5 now are incorporated into Disk Tools for Version 5.0, including the following:

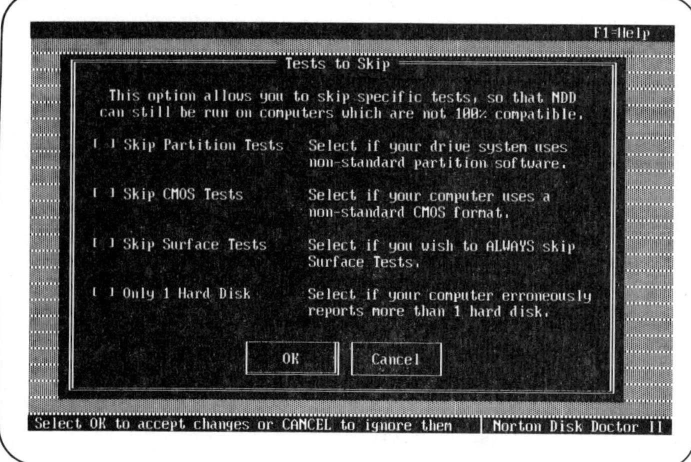

Fig. 4.22
The NDD Tests to Skip screen.

- Make a Disk Bootable
- Recover from DOS's Recover
- Revive a Defective Diskette

The new Disk Tools command also contains the following options:

- Mark a Cluster
- Create Rescue Diskette
- Restore Rescue Diskette

To begin Disk Tools, choose the Disk Tools option from the Norton menu or enter the command

```
DISKTOOL
```

at the DOS prompt. A screen like the one in figure 4.23 appears, which contains the six menu options just mentioned. These options are described in the following sections.

Making a Bootable Disk

Sometimes you may want to make an unbootable disk a bootable disk. This feature may be of particular importance for a hard disk. A disk can lose its capability to boot if the magnetic signal on the boot record becomes weak or if the low-level format loses alignment with the read/

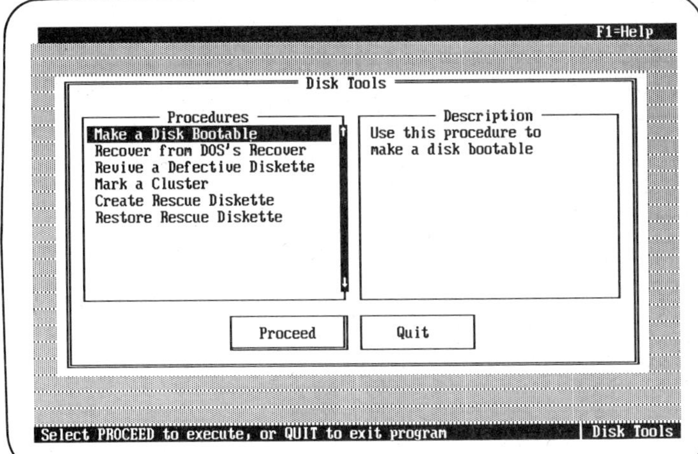

Fig. 4.23
The Disk Tools main menu.

write head. Also, software programs accidentally may overwrite important system information required for booting. The NDD command can place a fresh copy of the system information on the disk, making it bootable again.

Sometimes a disk may not have been set up properly as a bootable disk. If the disk was formatted originally as a nonbootable disk, DOS cannot make it into a bootable disk. Even though DOS has a SYS command that should copy the system files to a nonbootable disk, the command works only if you told the format procedure to leave room on the disk to receive the system files. Otherwise, DOS writes data onto the area of the disk reserved for the system, making it impossible for the SYS command to work for that disk. Disk Tools, however, can move files around, copy system information to the disk, and make the disk bootable. Using Disk Tools to make a disk bootable can save you a great deal of time. Without the Disk Tool command, you would have to copy all files off the disk, reformat the disk by using the /S switch, and copy files back to the disk. This process could take hours; the Disk Tool procedure takes only a few minutes.

If you choose the Make a Disk Bootable option from the Disk Tools menu, the program first prompts you to make sure that the correct disk is in the drive. Then it moves any information that is in the system area to a free area and copies the appropriate system files and COMMAND.COM onto the disk. In PC-DOS, two system files that contain part of DOS are stored on the disk as hidden files (they do not appear when you use the DIR command). If the disk does not have enough room to accept the system files, you see an error message. If you want to make this disk bootable, erase some files and try the procedure again.

Recovering from DOS's RECOVER Command

The DOS RECOVER command is poorly named. Many people see this command and assume that it can recover lost files or turn bad files into good files. Actually, you use the DOS RECOVER command to recover files that have a defective sector. This DOS command is primitive, however, compared with what you can do in Norton Utilities. The DOS manual states that the RECOVER command "recovers a disk with a bad sector." The recovery process used by DOS, however, eliminates all subdirectories on your disk and renames all your files to obscure names. Trying to find the contents of each file could take hours, and for some files the task may be nearly impossible. If you are using Norton Utilities, you should never have a reason to use the DOS RECOVER command.

If you have used the RECOVER command accidentally or because you thought it would recover damaged files, you can use the Norton Disk Doctor to place files back into their proper directories—as long as you have not written other files to the disk. You have to rename files in the root directory and directories. If you choose Recover from DOS's RECOVER from the Disk Tools menu, you are warned that you should use this procedure only if you have run the DOS RECOVER program or if the root directory on the disk has been destroyed. If you continue, you are prompted to choose the disk to recover. Select the drive name of the disk you want to recover.

If you choose to have the program proceed, a screen appears, showing you the progress of the recovery. You are advised that Disk Tools has been able to recover the directories but has named them DIR0000, DIR0001, and so on. All the files in the root directory are named FILE0000._DD, FILE0001._DD, and so on. Any files in directories other than the root directory are recovered with their full names intact.

Figure 4.24 summarizes what happens to a disk when you use Disk Tools to recover from the RECOVER command. The first part of the screen, listing (1), shows you the directory structure for a sample diskette. The root directory contains three directories and two files. Each of the three directories (\WP, \123, and \DB3) contains two files. After the DOS RECOVER program is run, the result is listing (2). Now all directories are gone, and all files are in the root directory. All files have been renamed FILE0001.REC, FILE0002.REC, and so on. As noted in listing (3), the Recover from the RECOVER option recovers the directories (although it does not recover their names) and the files in the directories.

```
--------------------------------------------------------------------------
RECOVERING FROM THE DOS RECOVER COMMAND
--------------------------------------------------------------------------
(1) THE ORIGINAL DISK - Three directories each containing 2 files

COMMAND  COM      37637 06-17-88  12:00p
AUTOEXEC BAT        294 10-23-89  10:43a
WP            <DIR>     01-02-90  12:10p
├── LETTER   WP          294 10-23-89  10:43a
└── REPORT   WP          158 09-18-89  12:50p

123           <DIR>     01-02-90  12:10p
├── SALES    WK1         294 11-23-89  10:41a
└── BUDGET   WK2         158 05-16-89  12:20p

DB3           <DIR>     01-02-90  12:10p
├── SALES    DBF         298 11-23-89  10:47a
└── CUSTOM   DBF         158 11-18-89  12:33p

(2) After the DOS RECOVER program has been run - all files in root directory

FILE0001 REC       1024 01-01-80   4:17a
FILE0002 REC       1024 01-01-80   4:17a
FILE0003 REC       1024 01-01-80   4:17a
FILE0004 REC       1024 01-01-80   4:17a
FILE0005 REC       1024 01-01-80   4:17a
FILE0006 REC       1024 01-01-80   4:17a
FILE0007 REC       1024 01-01-80   4:17a
FILE0008 REC       1024 01-01-80   4:17a
FILE0009 REC       1024 01-01-80   4:17a
FILE0010 REC       1024 01-01-80   4:17a
FILE0011 REC      37888 01-01-80   4:17a

(3) After Recover from Recover has been run, 3 directories, two files each

DIR0000       <DIR>     01-02-90  12:10p
├── LETTER   WP          294 10-23-89  10:43a
└── REPORT   WP          158 09-18-89  12:50p
DIR0001       <DIR>     01-02-90  12:10p
├── SALES    WK1         294 11-23-89  10:41a
└── BUDGET   WK2         158 05-16-89  12:20p
DIR0002       <DIR>     01-02-90  12:10p
├── SALES    DBF         298 11-23-89  10:47a
└── CUSTOM   DBF         158 11-18-89  12:33p
FILE0003 _DD       1024 01-02-90  12:15p
FILE0004 COM      37888 01-02-90  12:15p
-----------------------------------------------------------------
```

Fig. 4.24. Using Disk Tools to recover from DOS's RECOVER command.

To make all directory and file names what they were before you used RECOVER, you need to rename the files FILE0003._DD and FILE0004.COM, using the DOS RENAME command. You also need to rename the directories by using the Norton Change Directory (NCD) command.

Reviving a Defective Disk

The next selection on the Disk Tools menu is the Revive a Defective Diskette option. The main task of this option is to put fresh format information on the disk. This procedure can be helpful if a diskette has become difficult or impossible to read, which may happen if you are using a floppy diskette often. Sometimes the diskette begins to wear out, the software program overwrites the system area, the disk becomes scratched, or other problems cause the diskette to lose some of its information. If you have accessed the FAT so many times that its information has begun to wear thin, the Revive process can place a new copy on disk.

During a normal format procedure, a disk is checked for bad spots. If found, these spots are marked and are not used to store information. A disk, however, can develop bad places *after* the original format has taken place. At times, the magnetic signal that stores information on disk may become weak and unreadable.

Also, on some parts of a hard disk, the magnetic coating may be thin in spots and may wear out over an extended period of use. If this problem occurs, you can use NDD to mark bad spots and move data to safe areas of the disk.

These bad areas in the magnetic media can limit access to data in a particular file or can sometimes make a disk completely unreadable. These problems often show up as *read errors* when you are trying to access information on a disk. You may get the message `Abort, Retry, Ignore, Fail?` when trying to read a disk that you know was readable previously.

The Disk Tools program can attempt to recover information from this kind of disk. Disk Tools may perform a type of reformatting of certain areas of the disk. This formatting does not destroy information like a normal formatting does, but instead recreates certain vital parts of the disk to make it readable again. Disk Tools performs a variety of tests on the disk to see whether it can recover questionable information and rework defective areas of the disk to become usable again.

After you choose the Revive a Defective Diskette option, the program first asks you to choose which floppy diskette to analyze. A screen reports the progress of the procedure, and when the revival is finished, you see a message that the diskette has been revived. You should diagnose the disk to verify that the system information was not lost.

If you are having problems with a floppy diskette and have revived or recovered the disk by using Disk Tools, you should copy information from the original diskette to another diskette. If the first diskette is one that you have used frequently and may be wearing out, copy the information to a new diskette and use the new one. If you are having problems with a hard disk, make sure that you keep backups. In fact, you always should keep backup copies of all important files even before you have problems with a hard disk.

Marking a Cluster

The Mark a Cluster option enables you to mark any cluster on a disk as bad or good. You may want to mark a cluster as bad if you have discovered that a cluster has intermittent problems. Marking the cluster as bad means that it will no longer be used to store file information. You also can mark a cluster as bad to hide and protect information; the information in that cluster will not be overwritten as long as the cluster is marked as bad. If you mark a cluster as bad that is used currently by a file, the information in that cluster is copied to a safe location on disk so that the information in the file still is intact. Marking a cluster as good means that the cluster now is available for use to store file information. You can use Mark a Cluster to bring back clusters that you have marked as bad.

After you choose Mark a Cluster, you are prompted to indicate which disk you will be using (drive A, B, C, and so on). Then, you are prompted to enter the number of the cluster to mark, and whether you want to mark it as bad or good.

Creating and Using a Rescue Disk

Options 5 and 6 on the Disk Tools menu are Create Rescue Diskette and Restore Rescue Diskette. After you choose Create Rescue Diskette, you see a screen like the one shown in figure 4.25. A rescue disk contains information about your disk, including information about your partition tables, your boot records, and your setup (CMOS) values. When you create a rescue disk, this information is written to a disk (usually a floppy disk), and is stored in three files: PARTINFO.DAT, BOOTINFO.DAT, and CMOSINFO.DAT.

The partition information tells you how your hard disk was set up originally when you used the FDISK command to tell DOS how your disk was to be used (for example, one drive, two drives, the size of the drives, and so on). The boot information tells you how your disk was formatted (under which version of DOS) and other system information. The CMOS setup information is stored in RAM and kept active by a battery. The PC-AT was the first to use this kind of setup. Many new computers no longer store information in CMOS. If you have to run the Setup program to configure your computer, then your computer has CMOS. If your battery goes dead, your computer will lose its CMOS settings.

If your hard disk has lost the partition, boot, or CMOS information, you can restore that information (except for date and time) to your disk by using the Restore Rescue Disk option. After you choose this option, you

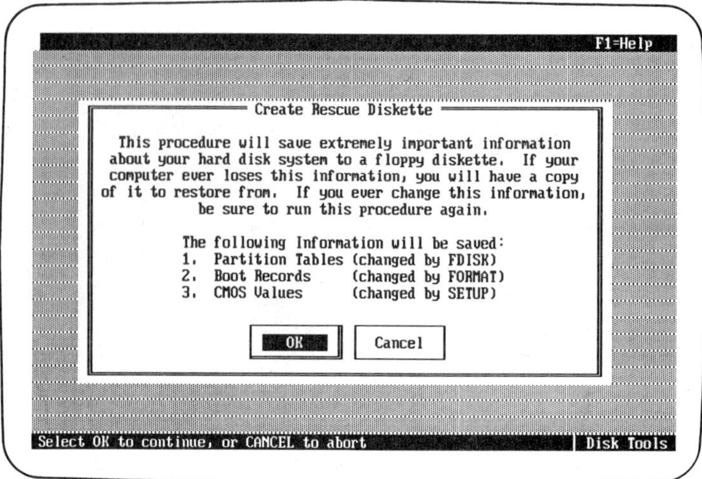

Fig. 4.25
The Disk Tools Create a Rescue Diskette screen.

can choose which of the three pieces of information to restore. You must have your floppy disk with the information on it to complete the restore successfully.

Using File Fix

You use the File Fix command to recover corrupted dBASE, Lotus 1-2-3, or Symphony files. These files can become corrupted when the power is turned off abruptly, when a program accesses the file incorrectly, or when the information stored on disk is damaged because of a bad spot on the disk. If you have erased all records in a dBASE database, the File Fix command often can recover those records. File Fix uses knowledge about how these files are created to attempt to recover the information in the file. If all of the information cannot be recovered, File Fix may be able to recover some of the information in the file.

You begin File Fix by choosing the File Fix option from the Norton menu or entering the command

```
FILEFIX
```

at the DOS prompt. The initial File Fix menu is shown in figure 4.26. From this menu, you can choose to fix Lotus 1-2-3, Symphony, or dBASE-type files.

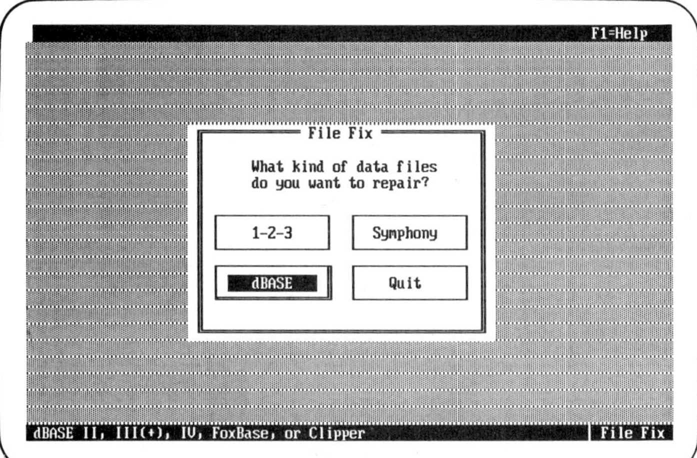

Fig. 4.26
The File Fix main menu.

Fixing dBASE Files

After you choose the dBASE option from the File Fix menu, you see the Choose File to Repair screen (see fig. 4.27). You can use the dBASE option to fix files that were created by programs that create and use dBASE-type files. These programs include dBASE II, III PLUS, and IV; Fox-BASE; Clipper; Wampum; Kwikstat; and others. From this menu, you can choose the file to fix. Use the arrow keys to highlight the file to fix and press Enter. Alternatively, point to the file with a mouse and click.

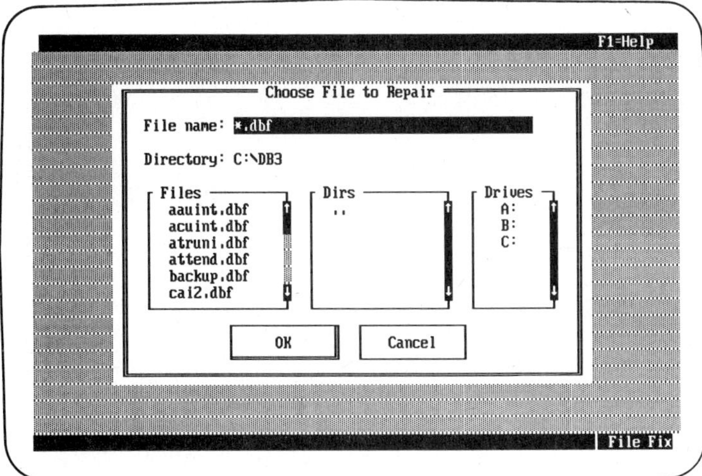

Fig. 4.27
Using the File Fix menu to select which file to fix.

The repair screen gives you several options about how to attempt the repair (see fig. 4.28). Usually, you will choose Fully Automatic. If this does not work, you then can try Review Damaged Records or Review All Records. If the file was created by Clipper, choose the Use Clipper Field Limits options. Sometimes when dBASE files are damaged, the information in the database is shifted, and data is not aligned properly in the fields. In this case, choose Fix Shifted Data Automatically. If this does not work, you can correct the shifting manually. The Strict Character Checking option means that only characters that usually are allowed should be allowed in records. A few programs, such as the SBT Accounting series, enable special graphics characters in the record. If you are using such a program, unselect the Strict Character Checking option. After you set all of the selections, choose Begin.

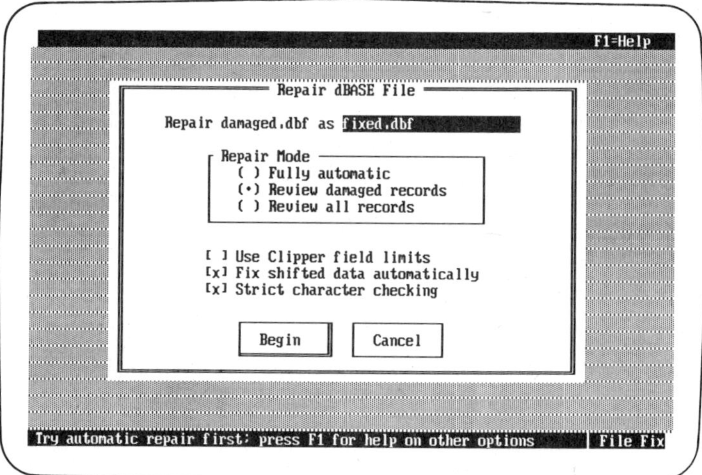

Fig. 4.28 Selecting dBASE fix options from the File Fix menu.

If you choose to review the dBASE file, you see a screen like the one shown in figure 4.29. This screen lists the structure of the database as far as File Fix can determine. If this data has been corrupted, you can revise this information by choosing the Revise option. Otherwise, choose Accept.

Another screen you will see if you choose to review the information is shown in figure 4.30. This screen displays the contents of a record. If the record looks okay, choose the Accept option, and the next record is displayed. If the data does not line up in the fields, you can shift the data by choosing the Shift option. If you want to reject a record, choose the Reject option. If you want to return to Automatic mode for the rest of the records, choose the Mode option, and then Automatic. Select the Cancel option to cancel the fix.

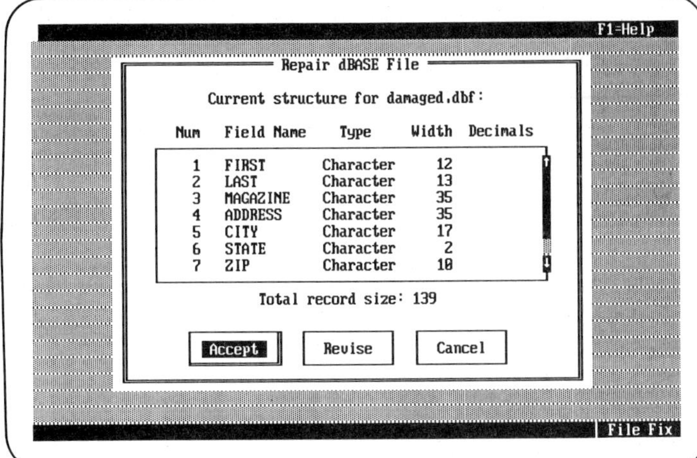

***Fig. 4.29* Using File Fix to display a dBASE database structure.**

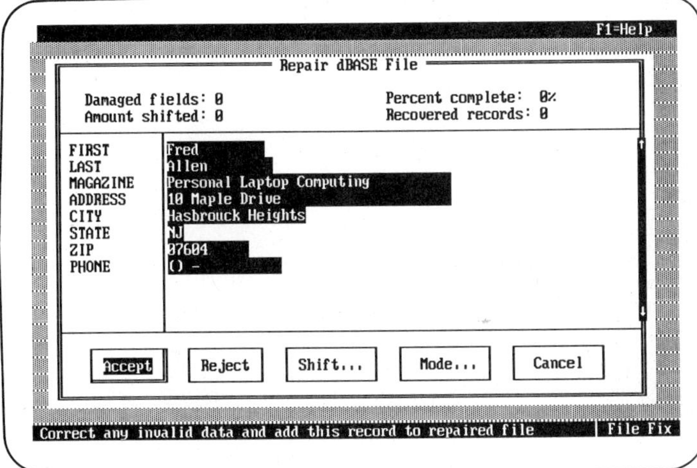

***Fig. 4.30* Viewing a dBASE record in File Fix.**

After a file is fixed, a summary screen tells you how much of the file was accepted and how much was rejected. Always carefully examine the file in the program for which it is intended before making a decision to fully recover the information.

Fixing 1-2-3 and Symphony Files

The 1-2-3 option enables you to fix spreadsheet files from the Lotus 1-2-3 program or similar programs, such as Twin. The Symphony option enables you to fix Symphony files. The procedure for fixing 1-2-3 and Symphony files is similar. After you choose the 1-2-3 or Symphony option, you see a file list. Choose the file you want to fix. The next screen that appears is similar to the one shown in figure 4.31. You may choose Attempt Recovery of All Data (this includes formulas, macros, and so on) or Recover Cell Data Only. Usually, you will choose to recover all data. If this does not work, choose to recover cell data only. After the recovery process is complete, File Fix gives you a summary screen listing how much of the file it recovered.

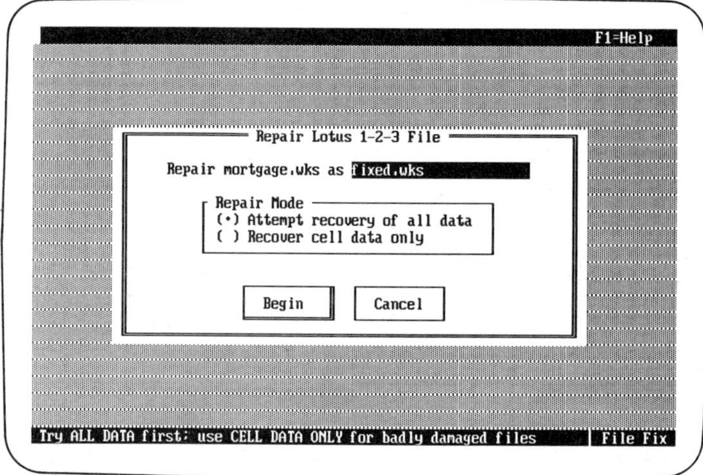

Fig. 4.31 ***Selecting a 1-2-3 repair mode from the File Fix menu.***

Using the Norton Disk Editor

Unerase and the Norton Disk Doctor are powerful programs, but sometimes even these programs cannot solve your problem. If you first tried Unerase and NDD to recover some information from a disk, but you still have important things to recover, your next step is the Norton Disk Editor option.

Disk Editor is a set of routines that enables you to explore the information on the disk down to the level of examining each individual byte. With Disk Editor, you can display and directly edit information on a disk, including system areas. You can search for lost data, attempt to fix problems in programs, and recover some or all portions of erased files. Data recovery at this level is beyond the scope of this book. Only the essentials of the Disk Editor program are explained here.

Warning: Unless you are very knowledgeable about the structure of a disk, using Disk Editor for all but simple fixes could run the risk of making a disk unusable and unrecoverable. The discussion about Disk Editor assumes that you know disk storage terms such as cluster, sector, partition table, FAT, and so on.

Using the Disk Editor program takes more knowledge about how the disk works and how information is stored than was required for using the NDD and Unerase commands. The Disk Editor program is not as easy to use or as automated as Unerase and NDD. Learning and using the Disk Editor program effectively may take a significant amount of time. If you are trying to recover some information that would take you only an hour to recreate, trying to use Disk Editor to get the data back may not be worth the trouble—you may just want to retype the information.

Also, be aware that the Disk Editor program gives you the capability to do good *and* bad. It is powerful enough for you to destroy your entire disk.

The syntax of the Disk Editor command follows:

DISKEDIT [*d:*] [*path*] [*filespec*][*switches*]

The available switches for the Disk Editor program follow:

Switch	*Effect*
/X:*d*	Excludes certain drives from absolute sector processing. Use this switch if you have nonexistent drives allocated. *d* represents the list of drives to exclude. For example, *DEF* excludes drives D, E, and F from the absolute sector processing.
/M	Selects Maintenance mode, which means that NU bypasses the DOS logical organization. You may need to use this mode if a disk is badly damaged. If NU does not begin to analyze a disk when you run the command, you may want to try the /M switch to see whether that helps. You cannot work with files or unerase files in Maintenance mode.

Begin Disk Editor by choosing the Disk Editor option from the Norton menu or by entering the command

DISKEDIT

at the DOS prompt. When the Disk Editor program begins, it informs you that you are in Read-only mode. This means that you safely can explore your disk without worrying about changing important information on your disk. As you will see, you can change out of Read-only mode by selecting the Configuration option from the Tools menu. The first screen that appears is shown in figure 4.32.

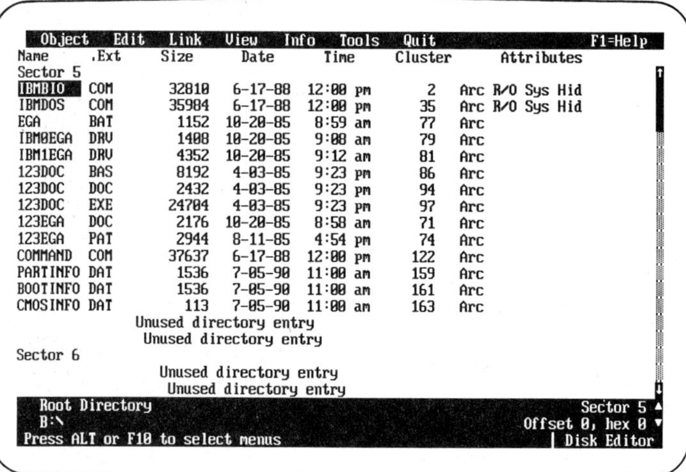

Object Edit Link View Info Tools Quit F1=Help
Name .Ext Size Date Time Cluster Attributes
Sector 5
IBMBIO COM 32810 6-17-88 12:00 pm 2 Arc R/O Sys Hid
IBMDOS COM 35984 6-17-88 12:00 pm 35 Arc R/O Sys Hid
EGA BAT 1152 10-20-85 8:59 am 77 Arc
IBM0EGA DRV 1408 10-20-85 9:00 am 79 Arc
IBM1EGA DRV 4352 10-20-85 9:12 am 81 Arc
123DOC BAS 8192 4-03-85 9:23 pm 86 Arc
123DOC DOC 2432 4-03-85 9:23 pm 94 Arc
123DOC EXE 24704 4-03-85 9:23 pm 97 Arc
123EGA DOC 2176 10-20-85 8:58 am 71 Arc
123EGA PAT 2944 8-11-85 4:54 pm 74 Arc
COMMAND COM 37637 6-17-88 12:00 pm 122 Arc
PARTINFO DAT 1536 7-05-90 11:00 am 159 Arc
BOOTINFO DAT 1536 7-05-90 11:00 am 161 Arc
CMOSINFO DAT 113 7-05-90 11:00 am 163 Arc
Unused directory entry
Unused directory entry
Sector 6
Unused directory entry
Unused directory entry
Root Directory
B:\
Sector 5
Offset 0, hex 0
Press ALT or F10 to select menus
Disk Editor

Fig. 4.32 Viewing files in the current directory on the Norton Disk Editor screen.

This screen is a display of the files found on the disk, listing file specification, size, date, time, the cluster where the file begins, and attributes currently set. On the top bar of the screen is the Disk Editor menu bar containing seven menu selections: Object, Edit, Link, View, Info, Tools, and Quit. To open the pull-down menus, press F10, and then use the arrow keys to select menus or items within menus. If you are using a mouse, point to a menu name and click.

Generally, the way you use the options on this menu is to locate something on disk that you want to change, change it, and then write the change back to disk. Suppose that you have a directory that cannot be erased with the DOS or Norton Remove Directory command. This situation can occur if a file or subdirectory has been corrupted and does not erase properly. DOS refuses to erase the directory because the operating system thinks the directory still contains information. You can erase this directory manually by replacing the first character of its name with the hexadecimal number E5. Using Disk Edit, therefore, you would locate the name of the directory, make the change to the first character, and then write the change back to disk. (In this example, you also would run the CHKDSK/F command or NDD to clean up any lost clusters caused by the change.)

Using the Object Menu

You can choose the object that you want to edit by using the Object menu (see fig. 4.33). The objects that you can choose to use include the drive, the directory, the file, the cluster, the sector, or the physical sector. You select what you want to examine or edit on the disk. The next group of objects are the partition table, the boot record, and copies of the FAT. In this case, the Partition Table option is in parentheses because the floppy disk does not have partitions—therefore you cannot choose Partition Table at this time. The Clipboard option enables you to store a block of information from disk and to place it elsewhere on disk. Generally, before you do any editing on the disk, you choose which object you will edit.

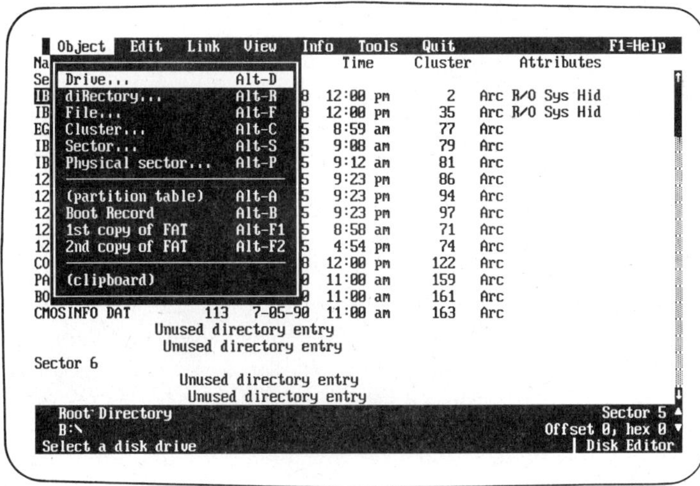

Fig. 4.33 The Norton Disk Editor Object pull-down menu.

Using the Edit Menu

The Edit menu enables you to edit information on the disk (see fig. 4.34). The Undo command in the menu enables you to undo the last items you edited. Undo remembers 512 bytes of information and will undo items in the reverse order of how they were done. However, Undo only undos items within a sector boundary. If you have moved to another sector, Undo only undos things in the current sector. If the Undo command is in parentheses, it means that there is nothing to undo.

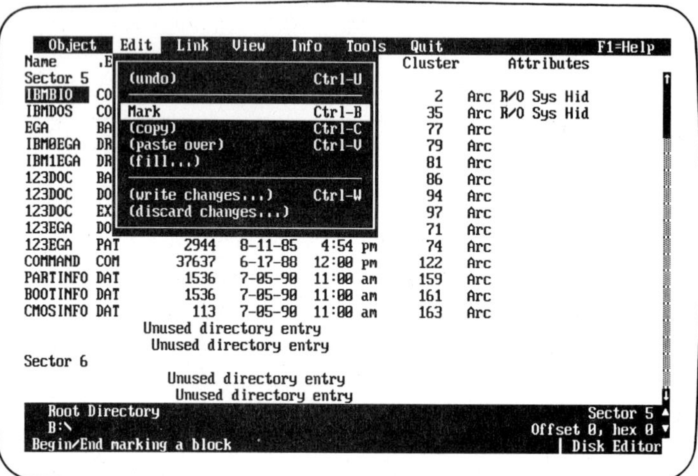

Fig. 4.34 The Norton Disk Editor Edit pull-down menu.

The Mark, Copy, Paste Over, and Fill options enable you to manipulate information on the disk. You use the Mark option to capture information from the disk and to place it in the clipboard for copying elsewhere. To copy information, place your cursor at the beginning of the block you want to copy. Choose Mark from the Edit menu and move your cursor to the end of the block. The information between the beginning and end of the block will be highlighted. If you are using a mouse, point to the beginning of the block, press the button on the mouse, and drag the mouse pointer to the end of the block. To place the information in the clipboard, select Copy from the Edit menu. The clipboard can hold up to 4,096 bytes (characters) of information.

The information remains in the clipboard until you replace it with other information. To copy the information from the clipboard to somewhere else on the disk, go to that location, place your cursor where you want the information to begin, and choose Paste Over from the Edit menu. Note that this overwrites information that is currently in that location—there is no Insert mode.

You use the Fill option to fill a block of space with a single character. Mark a block, as described in the copy procedure. After you choose the

Fill option from the Edit menu, you are prompted to select the character with which to fill the block. You can choose an ASCII character from a list box, and the entire marked region will be filled with that character. This is a method of erasing sensitive information from disk.

After you make changes to a disk by copying or filling, these changes actually are not written to the disk until you choose the Write Changes option from the Edit menu. To choose not to make these changes, select Disregard Changes.

Using the Link Menu

The Link menu enables you to travel back and forth to areas related on a particular file (see fig. 4.35). If you are editing a part of the disk that contains the contents of a file, for example, and you choose the Cluster Chain option from the Link menu, you are taken to the place on disk in the FAT where information about that file is stored. If you are in the FAT, you can link to the file or directory associated with the part of the FAT you are editing. If you are editing a partition, the link enables you to link to the partition table associated with that partition. In each case, allowable links are noted by options in the Link menu *not* surrounded by parentheses.

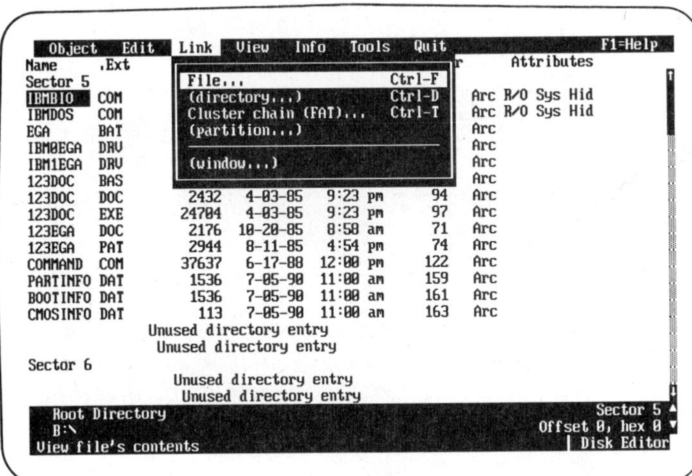

Fig. 4.35
The Norton Disk Editor Link pull-down menu.

Using the View Menu

The View menu enables you to choose various options when viewing information on disk (fig. 4.36). The Hex and Text options enable you to see the information on-screen as ASCII text or in hexadecimal code. Text files usually are viewed in Text mode. Programs or coded files may be viewed in Hex format. The other modes enable you to view data appropriate to what you are looking at. If you are looking at the FAT, for example, you usually would choose to view data in the FAT viewer. The Window options in the View menu enable you to split the screen and view two items simultaneously. You can split the screen by using the Split Window (Shift-F5) option, switch from window to window by using the Switch Window (Shift-F8) option, and adjust the size of the window by using the Grow Window or Shrink Window options.

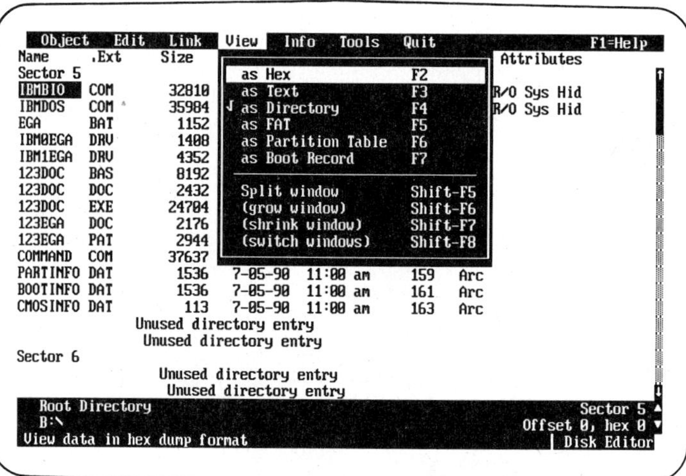

Fig. 4.36
The Norton Disk Editor View pull-down menu.

Using the Info Menu

The Info menu enables you to display information about the object or drive you are viewing, or to look at a map (a graphic display) of the object in relation to all of the clusters on disk. The Info menu is shown in figure 4.37.

Using the Tools Menu

The Tools menu gives you several tools for exploring the contents of a disk (see fig. 4.38):

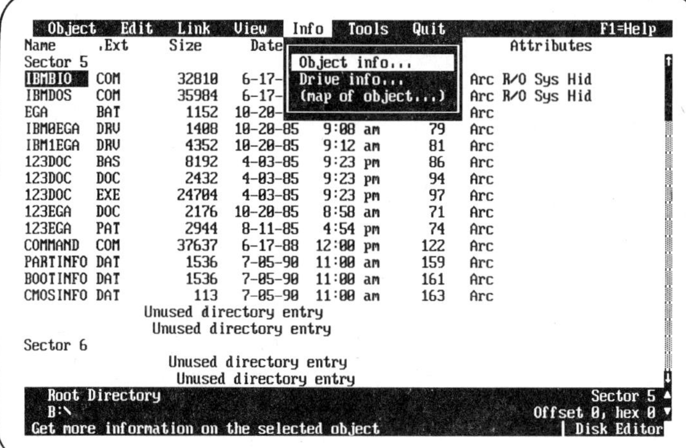

Fig. 4.37
The Norton Disk Editor Info pull-down menu.

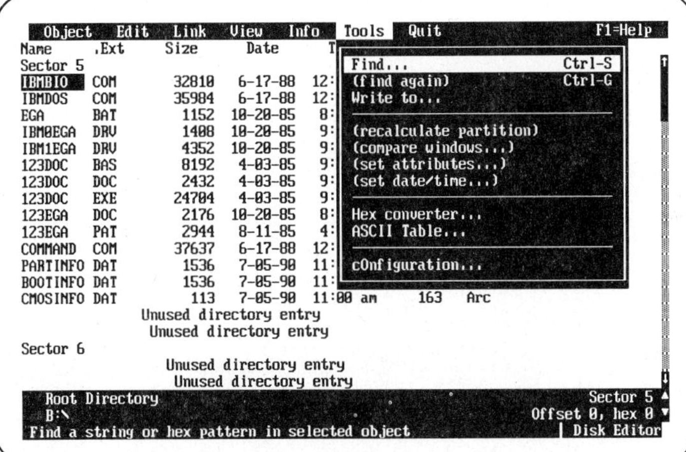

Fig. 4.38
The Norton Disk Editor Tools pull-down menu.

- *Find:* Enables you to search for a string of text on a disk. Find can be helpful if you are looking for information on disk, but you do not know which file (or erased space) contains the information.
- *Find Again:* Repeats the last Find command.
- *Write To:* Writes the current object you are editing to disk. You are asked to specify a file name, starting cluster number, or sector number for the Write To option. Using Write To, you can

find pieces of an erased file and write out the information to disk. The Write To option is a way to recover information that you were not able to recover by using Unerase or Disk Tools.

- *Recalculate Partition:* Calculates two items (available when you are in Partition Table View mode):

  The relative sector number from the starting sector coordinates

  The number of sectors from the starting and ending sector coordinates

- *Compare Windows:* Compares two windows and places the cursor at the first point where the information in the windows disagrees.

- *Set Attributes:* Enables you to change the attributes for a group of files (available when you are in Directory View mode).

- *Set Date/Time:* Enables you to change the date and time for a group of files (available when you are in Directory mode).

- *Hex Converter:* Enables you to convert a hexadecimal value to a decimal value, or vice versa. It also displays the ASCII character associated with the decimal value.

- *ASCII Table:* Displays the ASCII character set and gives the decimal and hex value for each character.

- *Configuration:* Enables you to set several options for using the Disk Editor (see fig. 4.39).

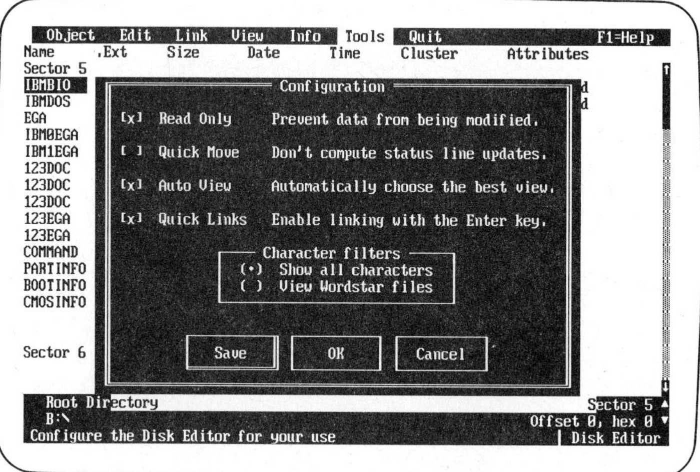

***Fig. 4.39** The Norton Disk Editor Configuration box.*

The Configuration options that you can set follow:

Read-only	Prevents you from writing changed information to disk. You can change the default setting for Read-only to enable users to write changed information to disk.
Quick Move	Enables you to speed up response time by omitting the rewriting of file names in the status bar.
Auto View	Tells Disk Editor to choose automatically the most appropriate view to be used.
Quick Links	Enables you to link from one object to a related object by pressing Enter or clicking the mouse button.
Show All Characters View WordStar Files	Enables you to specify that the text being viewed is stored in WordStar format.
Save	Saves configuration selections to the file NU.INI.
OK	Ends the selection, but does not save changes to disk.
Cancel	Ends the Configuration option menu.

Summary

This chapter covered the core of Norton Utilities' file-recovery options. It began with the easiest and quickest way to unerase a file—the Unerase command. This command always should be your first choice in attempting to unerase a file. If your disk has other problems—such as not enabling you to read files from a disk that used to work—you should try the Norton Disk Doctor to cure what ails the disk. To recover a defective disk or to make a disk bootable, use Disk Tools. To recover a dBASE, Lotus 1-2-3, or Symphony file, use the File Fix command. Finally, if you want to do some real surgery, you can resort to the Norton Disk Editor program and explore and edit the disk or manually unerase files. Try to use the most automated recovery programs first and then progress to those commands in which you can do it all yourself. Be warned, however, that the more power you are given, the more potential you have to mess things up. Practice on a floppy disk where your results do not matter before doing surgery on a "live" disk.

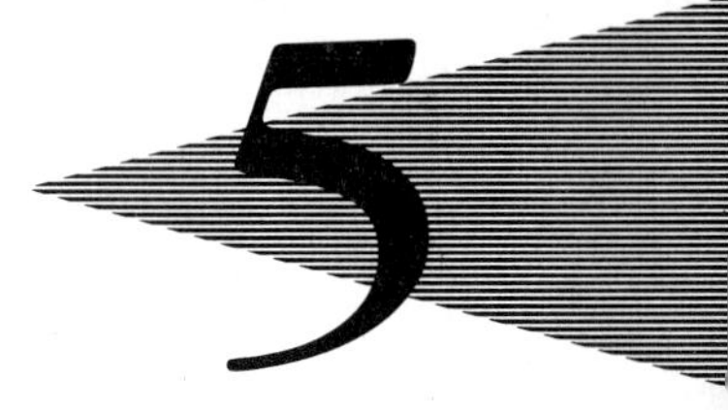

Making Your Hard Disk Work Efficiently

Previous chapters discuss using Norton Utilities to protect and recover files. You should perform other maintenance tasks on your hard disk to help prevent disk problems and to make your disk run smoothly and at top speed.

Just as an automobile needs occasional tuning, a hard disk needs to be adjusted to keep it running at its full potential. A little preventive maintenance goes a long way toward keeping your hard disk running well. When your hard disk gets out of shape (is too full, has too many fragmented files, develops unreadable sectors), it has to work harder to get information, which puts a strain on the hard disk's mechanisms and may cause them to wear out sooner. If the disk fails mechanically, you must have an expert rebuild it in a dust-free, clean room (a hospital operating room, for example) to get your information off the disk. If the plate of your hard disk is damaged, the potential for data recovery is slim. Disk maintenance also is a productivity issue. When the disk is not running well, it slows down, which means that your work on the computer slows down.

Many computer users are in such a hurry that they do not take the time to do preventive maintenance. Spending a little time now, however, can save you from spending a great deal of time later. Norton Utilities gives you some easy-to-use tools that make the disk-maintenance chore as simple and efficient as possible.

Four Norton utilities that deal with making your hard disk work more efficiently are covered in this chapter (three Speed utilities and one Tool utility), as follows:

- *System Information:* Gives you information about your hard disk and produces important information about the current condition of your disk.
- *Speed Disk:* Enables you to rearrange the files on your disk so that you can read and write to them faster.
- *Calibrate:* Enables you to tune the way that you read and write information to and from your hard disk.
- *Norton Cache:* Enables you to adjust how information is read and written to and from your hard disk.

You can use all of these commands to make your hard disk access faster and more efficient. This not only gives you faster working programs; it also reduces wear and tear on your hard disk and may prolong its life.

Examining System Information

With the System Information (SYSINFO) command, you can compare your computer system with other computers in terms of processing and disk speeds. You also can examine the current status and use of the space on your hard disk and learn how your hard disk and RAM memory is being used. The System Information test compares the performance of your computer with that of a standard IBM PC XT, using the Intel 8088 microprocessor, running at 4.77 MHz; the IBM PC AT, using the Intel 80286 microprocessor, running at 8 MHz; and the Compaq 386 computer, using the Intel 80386 microprocessor, running at 33 MHz. The System Information command also is a good way to learn vital information about a computer quickly. If you help other people with their computers (as a user support technician, for example), the System Information command can help you discover information about a computer you have never used before. You may be interested in the existence of a math coprocessor, the type of video display being used, the existence of parallel and serial ports, the amount of memory available and used, and other items described by the System Information command.

When you run the System Information command from the Norton menu or from the DOS prompt with no switches, the program presents about 15 different screens, one following the other, of information about your computer. These screens and their contents are described briefly in this chapter.

Viewing Information on the System Summary Screen

A System Information test on drive C of an IBM PS/2 Model 70 with a 60M hard disk was used to create these screens. The first screen reported—the System Summary screen—is shown in figure 5.1. Notice the four option boxes at the bottom of the screen: Next, Previous, Print, and Cancel. To scroll through the screens, you can use your mouse or arrow keys to choose Next or Previous. Choose Print to print a summary of the screen to the printer. Choose Cancel to end the current screen and go to the pull-down menu mode.

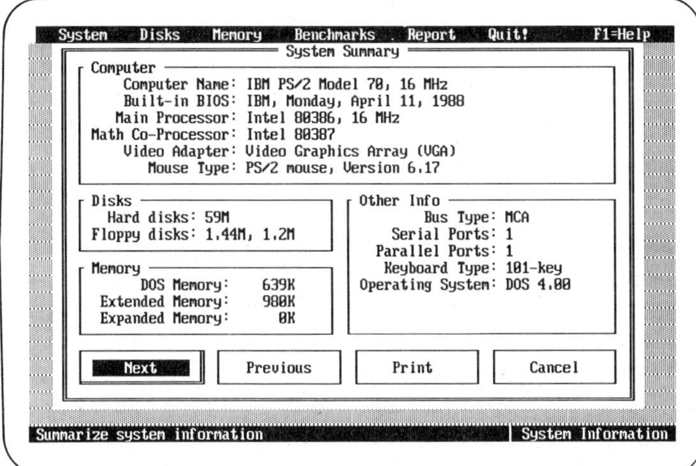

Fig. 5.1
The System Summary screen for an IBM PS/2 Model 70.

The System Summary screen contains system information about the computer being tested. The report tells you the date of the BIOS (basic input/output system). This date can be important because some new programs will not run on older versions of the BIOS—your software should tell you if this is a problem.

Also reported in the System summary are the microprocessors being used (in this case, an Intel 80386 running at 16 MHz) and an math co-processor (Intel 80387). The various Intel microprocessors that can be reported are listed in table 5.1. Also reported in this list is the mouse type (if any) being used. The Disk box tells you the size of your hard disk(s) and floppy disk(s). The Memory box tells you how much DOS memory you have, and how much (if any) extended or expanded memory you have (the various kinds of memory are discussed in "Viewing the Memory Summary Screen," later in this chapter). Other information reported is the bus type, the number of serial and parallel ports, the keyboard being used, and the version of DOS being used. The bus type refers to one of the following busses:

- *ISA:* Standard bus for IBM PC and AT-type computers
- *MCA:* Microchannel bus used on most IBM PS/2s
- *EISA:* EISA bus

The type of bus used determines what kind of expansion cards you can use for your computer. The ISA bus accepts only standard PC/AT-type expansion cards. The MCA bus accepts only MCA cards. The EISA bus accepts EISA or ISA cards.

The serial ports generally are used for communications—for example, a hookup to a modem. You usually use parallel ports to communicate with a printer.

Table 5.1
Intel Microprocessor Chips and Math Coprocessors

Chip Name	*Computer*	*Math Coprocessor*
8088	Original IBM PC	8087
80C88	Usually Laptops	8087
80286	IBM AT class computer	80287
80C286	Usually Laptops	80C287
80386	Wide variety	80387
80386SX	Wide Variety	80387SX
80486	Wide variety	80487

Viewing Information on the Video Summary Screen

The Video Summary screen in System Information gives you information about the type of monitor you are using (see fig. 5.2). This screen tells you which type of display adapter is attached to the computer, the monitor type, and the current video mode. A summary of several kinds of video adapters is given in table 5.2. The resolution column lists the number of dots, or *pixels*, that are on-screen. The larger the number of pixels, the greater the clarity of the screen's image.

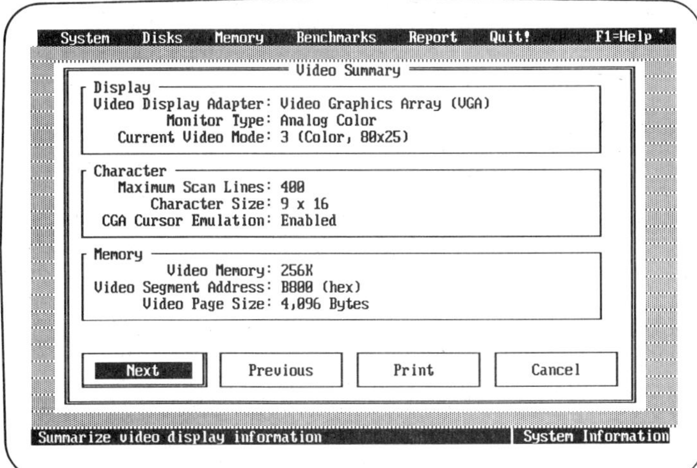

Fig. 5.2 ***The System Information Video Summary screen.***

Table 5.2
Common Video Adapters for IBM-Compatible Computers

Adapter Type	*Resolution*
Monochrome (text only)	640 x 350
CGA Composite	620 x 200
CGA Color	320 x 200 color mode 640 x 200 B&W mode
Enhanced Graphics (EGA)	640 x 350
Multicolor Graphics (MGA)	640 x 480, 16 colors
Vector Graphics (VGA)	640 x 480, 256 colors
Super VGA	800 x 600

The character information tells you the number of scan lines on-screen and the number of pixels used to create a character on-screen (in this case 9 x 16 pixels). The more scan lines, the better the clarity of the picture. The larger the number of pixels used to display a character on-screen, the better the clarity of text. The Memory box contains information about how much memory is allocated to your display and how that memory is used. This information may be important if you are programming to a video adapter or if you have a program that requires a particular level of video features.

Viewing the Hardware Interrupts Screen

The Hardware Interrupts screen tells you the "owner" of the interrupts in your system (see fig. 5.3). A hardware interrupt is a way for hardware devices to request service from the computer. Notice on the list of names on-screen there are items such as the keyboard, communication ports, disks, and so on. When one of these items wants to convey information to the computer, it sends an interrupt signal to the computer. Each device is assigned a unique interrupt signal, so the computer knows who is "talking." Occasionally, when you add a new device to the computer, you are asked to set its interrupt to one that is currently unused. Use this screen to find out which interrupt is unused. Look under the Number, Name, and Owner columns, and you can see which interrupts are unused. These columns are available for use for new devices that you add to your computer.

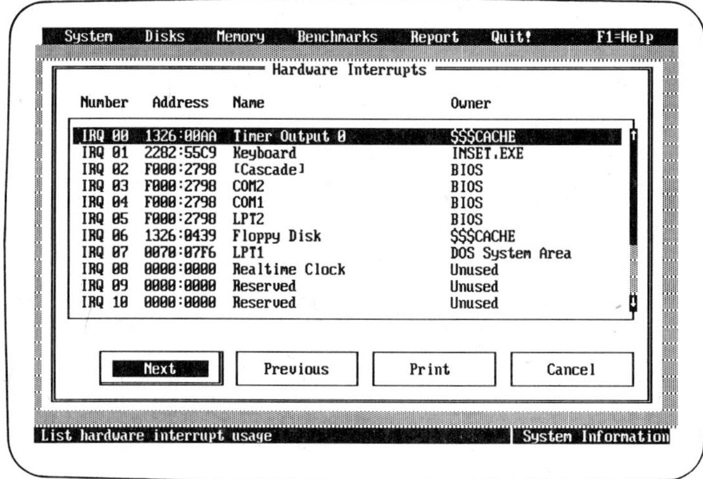

Fig. 5.3
The System Information Hardware Interrupts screen.

Viewing the Software Interrupts Screen

Software interrupts are similar to hardware interrupts, except that instead of a hardware device requesting action from the computer, a software program requests action (see fig. 5.4). The interrupts listed on this screen may be useful for persons writing software programs that must take advantage of these interrupts.

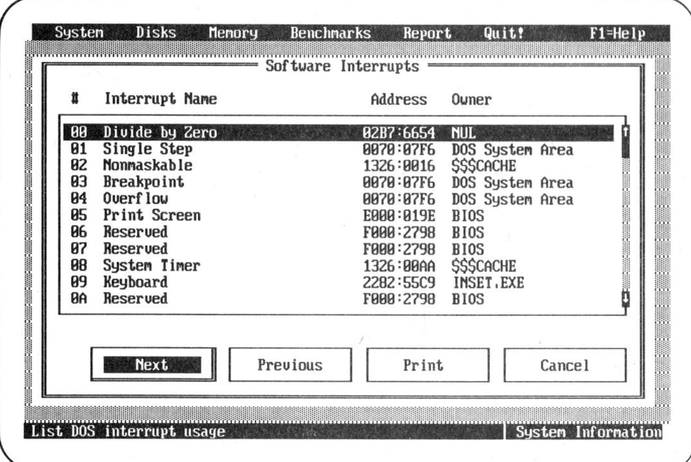

Fig. 5.4
The System Information Software Interrupts screen.

Viewing the CMOS Values Screen

CMOS values contain information about how your computer is configured. The CMOS screen reports on the status of these values (see fig. 5.5). An important piece of information on this screen is the CMOS battery report. If your computer begins to operate erratically, losing time and date information and having problems finding your disks, you can check this screen to see if the battery is operational. If the battery is not operational, the computer may have lost information about its configuration. (See Chapter 4 for information on the Disk Tools Rescue Disk option.)

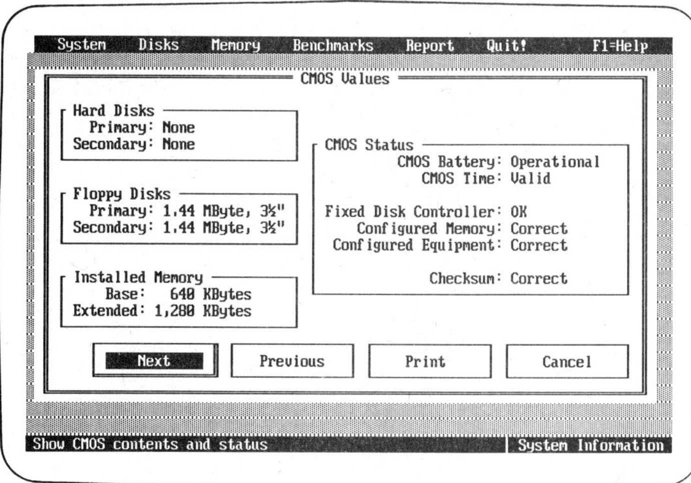

Fig. 5.5
The System Information CMOS Values screen.

Viewing the Disk Summary Screen

The Disk Summary screen tells you how many and which disk drives the computer has available for use. In figure 5.6, drives A, B, C, and D are available for use. Drives A, B, and C are floppy disk drives, and drive D is a hard disk. The hard disk drive D currently is using the directory \NORTON. The other disks, listed as Available, currently are not being used.

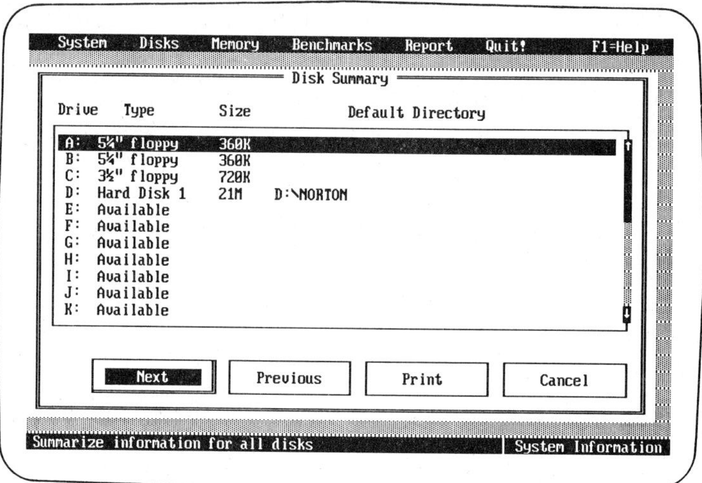

Fig. 5.6 ***A System Information screen showing disk summary information.***

Viewing the Disk Characteristics Screen

The Disk Characteristics screen gives you information about the current disk (see fig. 5.7). A list of available disks are located in the box at the upper right of the screen. You can change to another disk to see information about that disk.

The Logical Characteristics box contains information about how the magnetic information is stored on the disk. As discussed in Chapter 4, the number of bytes per sector usually is 512. That is, when a track on a disk is broken up into sectors, each sector holds 512 bytes of information. This number may change, however, with newer versions of DOS.

When reading information from a disk, DOS reads a certain minimum amount of information at a time. That amount is called a *cluster*. The number of sectors per cluster usually is two for floppy diskettes and four or

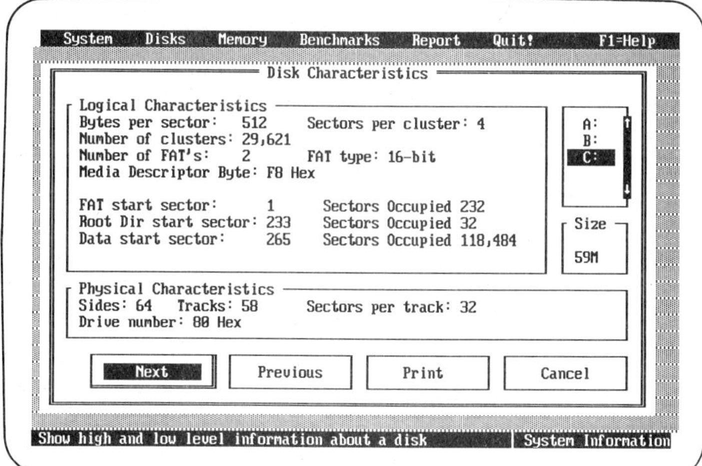

Fig. 5.7
A System Information screen showing disk characteristics information.

more for hard disks. The size of the cluster often determines how much wasted space (slack space) is on disk, as discussed in Chapter 3. The Disk Characteristics screen also reports the number of file allocation tables on the disk. This usually is two, except in the case of RAM disks (memory disks), which may have only one copy of the FAT.

The media descriptor tells you what kind or size of disk has been formatted. Table 5.3 interprets the media descriptor codes displayed on the report. Thus, the disk shown here is a hard disk (code F8).

Table 5.3
Media Descriptor Codes Reported

Code	*Disk Represented*
F0	A 1.4M, 3 1/2-inch diskette
F8	A hard disk
F9	A 1.2M, 5 1/4-inch diskette or a 720K, 3 1/2-inch diskette
FD	A 360K, 5 1/4-inch diskette
FE	A 160K, 5 1/4-inch diskette
FF	A 320K, 5 1/4-inch diskette

The remaining technical information given on the report is of little real use to most computer users. To a technical support person, however, some of this data can be helpful in editing the system information on a disk, using the Norton Disk Editor.

Viewing the Partition Tables Screen

The Partition Tables screen gives you information about the partitions on your hard disk (see fig. 5.8). In this case, there is only one hard disk. If you have partitioned your hard disk into more than one drive using the FDISK command (for example, drives C and D), each drive will show up as a partition.

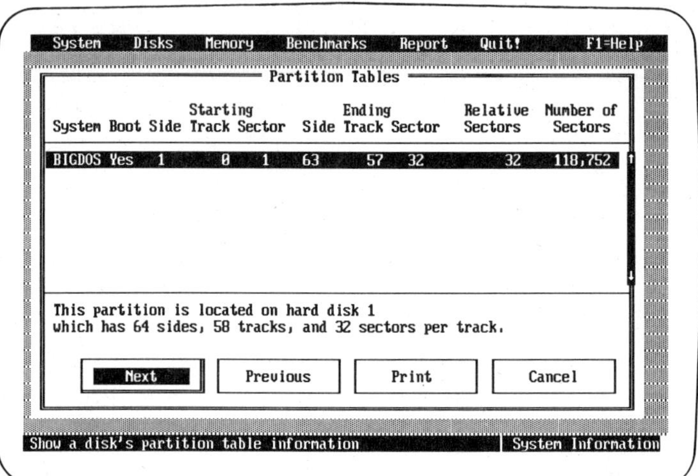

Fig. 5.8
A System Information screen showing partition tables information.

Viewing the Memory Summary Screen

The Memory Summary screen reports information about how your RAM memory is being used by your computer (see fig. 5.9). The Norton SYS-INFO command looks at the computer's RAM (random-access memory) in two ways. The first report is from DOS, called Dos Usage. On the Memory Summary screen, DOS reports 639K of available RAM memory, which is broken down into two parts. 238K of the memory is reportedly being used by DOS and resident programs. The rest is available for use by application programs. The reason for the split is that when your computer boots, it reads DOS information on the boot disk and moves some of that information into RAM so that the information is ready when needed. DOS information therefore takes up some of your RAM. If you have loaded any RAM-resident programs (pop-up, terminate-and-stay resident, and so on), they, too, are loaded into a portion of the RAM, like DOS. If too much of your RAM is taken up with memory-resident programs, you may have a hard time running large application programs such as Microsoft Windows or Aldus PageMaker.

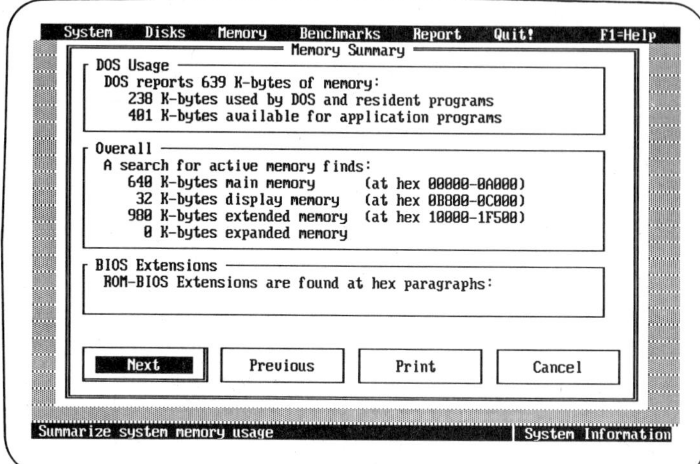

Fig. 5.9 A System Information screen showing memory summary information.

The second method that Norton's System Information command uses to find memory is an overall report of the computer's memory locations. System Information is able to locate four kinds of memory, as follows:

- *Main memory:* This figure should be about the same as the total memory reported by the DOS method.

- *Display memory:* This is RAM located on the monitor display adapter card and used by the monitor.

- *Extended memory:* This is memory above the 640K normal DOS limit.

  Notice that in figure 5.9, more memory was found by SYSINFO's search for memory than by the DOS method because DOS only "sees" the first 640K.

- *Expanded memory:* This is add-on memory that can be accessed by certain programs that subscribe to a special way of using memory developed by Lotus, Microsoft, Intel, and AST companies. Many programs, such as Lotus 1-2-3, use this memory to be able to work with larger amounts of data (spreadsheets, databases, and so on) at one time.

The *ROM-BIOS extended memory*, if present, is memory located on add-in boards such as video display boards or hard disks, but is not a part of the normal RAM memory.

Viewing the TSR Programs Screen

TSR programs (terminate-and-stay resident)—also called memory-resident programs—are programs that, when begun, stay in the computer's RAM memory while other programs are running. By staying in memory, these programs are using some of the RAM memory, making it unusable for other programs. Therefore, you may need to be aware of how much space is being used by these programs. The TSR Programs screen lists the TSR programs and their sizes (see fig. 5.10).

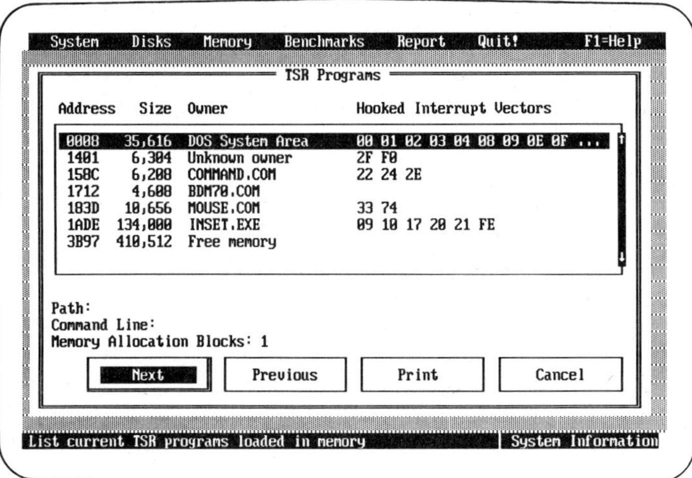

Fig. 5.10
A System Information screen showing TSR programs in memory.

You also may be interested in the order of these memory-resident programs because some programs can be uninstalled only if they are the last program loaded into memory. With the /TSR switch, you can see which programs are in memory, as well as the order of the programs.

If you use the Norton Disk Monitor command, for example, which is a TSR program, and then want to uninstall the program, you can enter the Norton Command

DISKMON/UNINSTALL

This takes the program out of memory only if it is the last TSR program in the list, however. Therefore, you would need to uninstall these programs in the reverse order from how they were listed. (See Chapter 3 for more information.)

Another reason to be interested in TSRs is how much RAM they are using. Some large programs may require almost all of your available RAM to run. You may have to uninstall some TSR programs in order to run large application programs. Most TSR programs enable you to uninstall them—you must check each program's documentation. If you load a TSR program as a result of a command in your AUTOEXEC.BAT file, you also can remove that program from this batch file and reboot.

Viewing the DOS Memory Blocks and Device Drivers Screens

The DOS Memory Blocks and Device Drivers screens are shown in figures 5.11 and 5.12. These screens display the addresses in memory-resident programs and device drivers. This information may be useful to programmers or technicians.

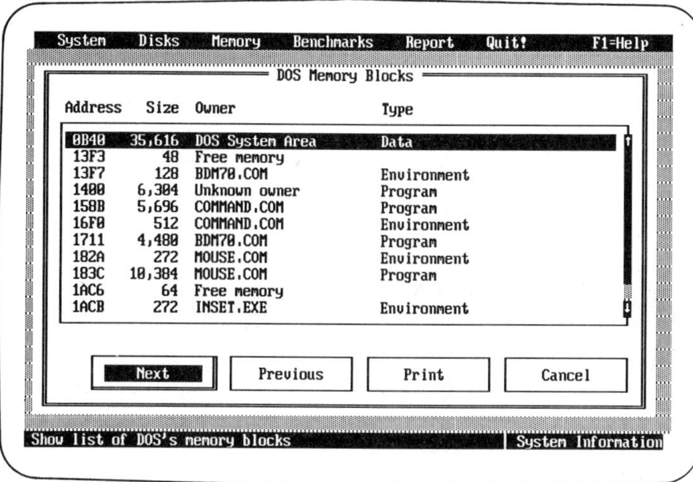

***Fig. 5.11* A System Information screen showing DOS memory blocks.**

Viewing the CPU Speed Screen

The CPU Speed screen shows a graphic comparison of the speed of the current computer—`This computer`—with three other popular computers (see fig. 5.13). This screen gives you an idea of how fast your microprocessor works when compared to these other machines. The original IBM/XT running at 4.77 MHz is used as the base (1.0). The microprocessor in this computer is running about 11 times faster than in an XT computer. Keep in mind that this test may be somewhat misleading because the processing speed of a computer has much to do with what you are processing. One computer may be better at processing numbers, for example, while another is adept at processing text fields.

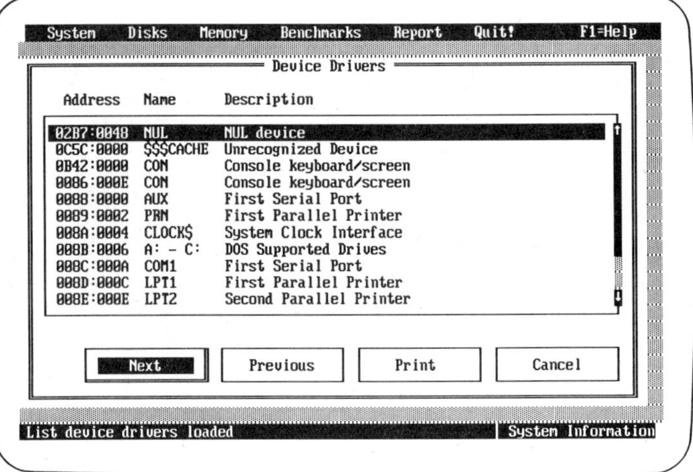

Fig. 5.12
A System Information screen showing device drivers loaded in memory.

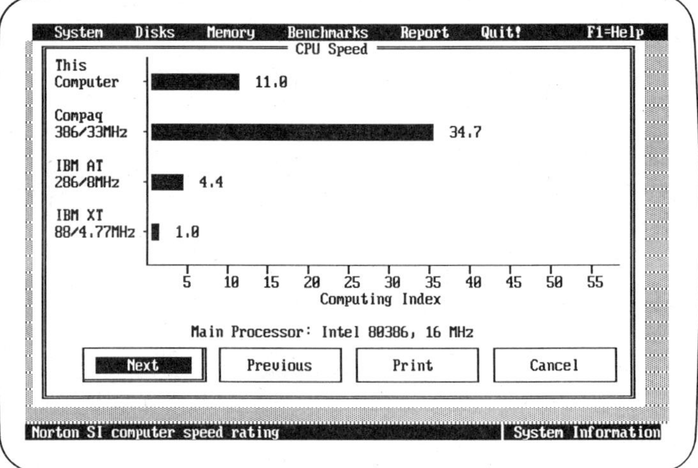

Fig. 5.13
A System Information screen comparing CPU speed with other popular computers.

Viewing the Disk Speed Screen

The Disk Speed screen displays a graphic comparison of the speed of your hard disk when compared to three other popular computers (see fig. 5.14). The hard disk in an IBM/XT computer is used as the base line value (1.0). The hard disk in this computer can access information about 4 1/2 times as fast as the hard disk in the XT computer. You should note, however, that hard disk access also is affected by how much information is on the disk and whether the files on disk are fragmented. Cache programs such as Norton Cache and Norton Calibrate can affect the efficiency of data access on your hard disk (this is discussed later in this chapter).

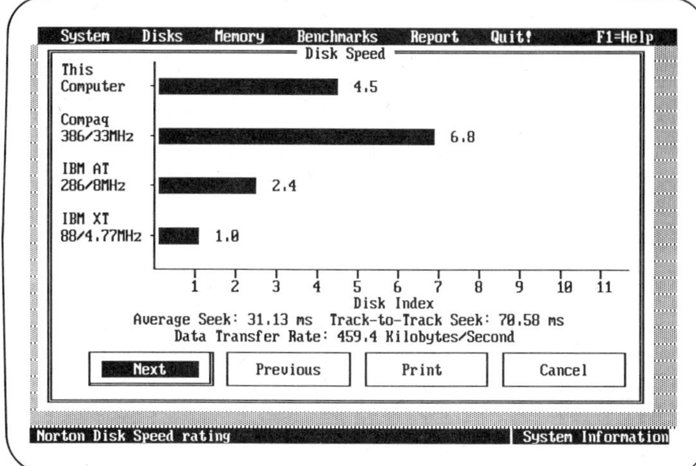

***Fig. 5.14* A System Information screen comparing disk speed with other popular computers.**

Viewing the Overall Performance Index Screen

The Overall Performance Index screen is a weighted combination of disk and CPU indexes, and gives you an overall comparison of your computer with an IBM XT (see fig. 5.15). You should look at these indexes in the same way that you look at the reported miles per gallon on automobiles. The numbers are for comparison only, and your actual "mileage" may vary.

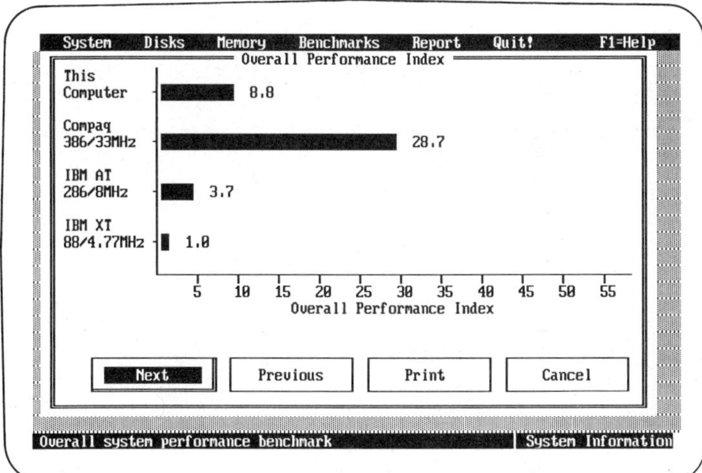

***Fig. 5.15* A System Information screen comparing an overall performance index to other popular computers.**

Viewing Your CONFIG.SYS and AUTOEXEC.BAT Files

The last two screens shown in the System Information report are listings of your CONFIG.SYS and AUTOEXEC.BAT files. You may want to look at the CONFIG.SYS file screen to check which device drivers you have installed; you can check the AUTOEXEC.BAT screen to see which TSR programs you begin at boot time.

Using the System Information Menu Bar

You can view all of the screens described in the previous sections one at a time by choosing the appropriate option from the menu bar at the top of the System Information screen. The options on the menu are System, Disks, Memory, Benchmarks, Report, and Quit. To open these pull-down menus, press F10 or point to a menu with the mouse and click. After you extend the menus, you can use the right- and left-arrow keys to move from menu to menu and the up- and down-arrow keys to select options within the menus.

From the System menu, you can choose any one of the following screens to view:

- System Summary
- Video Summary
- Hardware Interrupts
- Software Interrupts
- Network Information CMOS Values (if available)

From the Disk menu, you can choose any one of the following screens to view:

- Disk Summary
- Disk Characteristics
- Partition Tables

From the Memory menu, you can choose any one of the following screens to view:

- Memory Usage Summary

- TSR Programs
- Memory Block List
- Device Drivers

From the Benchmarks menu, you can choose any of the following screens to view:

- CPU Speed
- Hard Disk Speed
- Overall Performance Index
- Network Performance Speed (if available)

From the Report menu, you can choose any of the following screens to view:

- View CONFIG.SYS
- View AUTOEXEC.BAT
- Print Report

Choose quit to end the System Information program.

Using System Information from the DOS Prompt

You may begin the System Information command by choosing it from the Norton menu or by entering the command SYSINFO at the DOS prompt. The syntax for using the System Information command at the DOS prompt follows:

SYSINFO [*d:*][*switches*]

Where *d:* is the letter of the hard disk drive you want to test. The available switches for the System Infomation command follow:

Switch	*Effect*
/AUTO:*n*	Tells the command to operate in automatic mode. The *n* parameter specifies a delay of *n* seconds between screens.
/DEMO	Tells the command to operate in Demo mode.
/TSR	Tells the command to show all TSR (terminate-and-stay resident) programs in memory.

/N Tells the command to skip the live memory probe. On some computers, the live memory probe forces you to reboot after the SI test. Use the /N switch to get around this problem.

The /AUTO:*n* switch tells the System Infomation command to run in Automatic mode. In this mode, the system information is shown screen by screen with a pause of *n* seconds between screens. The *n* is specified in the switch. If you do not specify an *n* in the switch, the pause between screens is 5 seconds.

The /DEMO switch causes System Information to scroll continuously through four screens: System Summary, CPU Benchmarks, Disk Speed Benchmarks, and Overall Performance. You can use this switch to see how the performance of the computer measures up to other well-known computers (the XT, the AT, and the COMPAQ 386/33, for example).

The /TSR switch causes the System Information command to list TSR programs.

The /N switch tells System Information to bypass the live memory probe when performing its tests. This is a necessary switch on some computers that are not 100-percent compatible clone computers. If the System Information command causes your computer to *freeze* (it does not respond to the keyboard anymore), use the /N switch to prevent this problem.

Making Your Disk Run Faster with Speed Disk

Much already has been said about problems that can arise when the information in files stored on disk is fragmented. As you may recall from discussions in previous chapters, when DOS looks for a place to store a file, the system uses the first available cluster. If the file is too large to be stored in one cluster, DOS places part of the file in the first cluster and the next part of the file in the next available cluster. If a contiguous cluster is not available, DOS finds the next free cluster. Thus, one part of the file may be stored in one cluster, the next part stored in a cluster on another part of the disk, and so on. When many files begin to be fragmented, as will happen over time, your disk access time may increase, because DOS must look in several places to read or write to a file. If the problem becomes too severe, you may even lose some information. Because the problem is so common, Norton Utilities offers a solution: the Speed Disk (SPEEDISK) command.

The Speed Disk command can rearrange the files on your disk so that each file is stored contiguously. You can use Speed Disk, for example, to enable DOS to save a word processing file to an optimized disk in five seconds, rather than in 30 seconds on a fragmented disk.

Trimming the time necessary to save files is not the Speed Disk command's only contribution. A number of programs access your disk many times while you are using them—Aldus PageMaker and Ventura Publisher, for example. The use of these programs can be slowed to a crawl if you have a slow hard disk. The Speed Disk command can have some beneficial productivity advantages when you use it periodically.

Speed Disk physically rearranges the files on your disk. You can use Speed Disk periodically to eliminate any file fragmentation that may have accumulated by repeated use of your disk, particularly a hard disk. You also can run Speed Disk whenever you notice that your disk has been slower than usual.

Because of the drastic reorganization of your disk that occurs, you should take some precautions. First of all, make sure that no memory-resident programs are running. (You can use the System Information command to check this out.) Some programs may be accessing particular places on disk that will be moved by the disk reorganization. If you have a complicated AUTOEXEC.BAT file that loads several programs into memory, you may want to boot from a floppy diskette that contains only DOS and the Speed Disk program. This way, you ensure that no memory-resident programs are being used. Second, although the Speed Disk command generally is safe, having a backup of your hard disk always is advisable before you do anything that alters your disk significantly.

Before running the command, another task you can do to help speed up your disk is to get rid of unnecessary files, such as unneeded backup (BAK) files. The fuller your disk is, the greater the likelihood of disk fragmentation. One way to eliminate unneeded files is to use the Wipe Info command in "nonwiping" or DOS Erase mode across directories (use the /N switch). For example, if you want to erase all BAK files on disk, use the command

```
WIPEINFO C:\*.BAK /N/S
```

The /N switch tells the command to erase files like a DOS ERASE command does, and the /S command tells the command to search for all files that match the *.BAK specification in all subdirectories. Because your initial search is in the root directory, this command erases all *.BAK files on disk.

Optimizing Your Disk Using Speed Disk's Recommendation

Although there are a number of choices you can make when using the Speed Disk program, the easiest way to use the program is to enable it to make a recommendation about how to optimize your disk and then follow that recommendation. The following sections tell you how to use Speed Disk, how to follow its recommendations and how to choose options to optimize your disk.

You can begin the Speed Disk program by choosing it from the Norton menu or by entering the command SPEEDISK at the DOS prompt. When you first begin the Speed Disk program, the program will read information from system memory. Then, you will see a screen like the one in figure 5.16. The drives that appear on your computer may be different, according to what drives you have available on your computer. From this menu, you may choose which disk to optimize. Highlight the drive name of the disk you want to optimize and press Enter or point to the drive with your mouse and click.

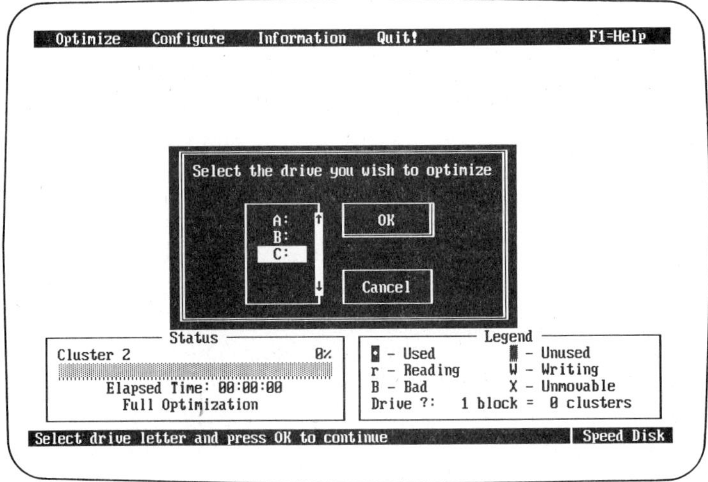

Fig. 5.16
The Speed Disk screen to choose disk drive to optimize.

After you choose the drive to optimize, Speed Disk analyzes the information on the drive and produces a Recommendation dialog box (see fig. 5.17). This box contains a recommended course of action. On this screen, for example, Full Optimization is recommended. To accept this recommendation, press Enter to choose the Optimize option. To manually choose another optimization method, choose Configure. To end the program, press Esc.

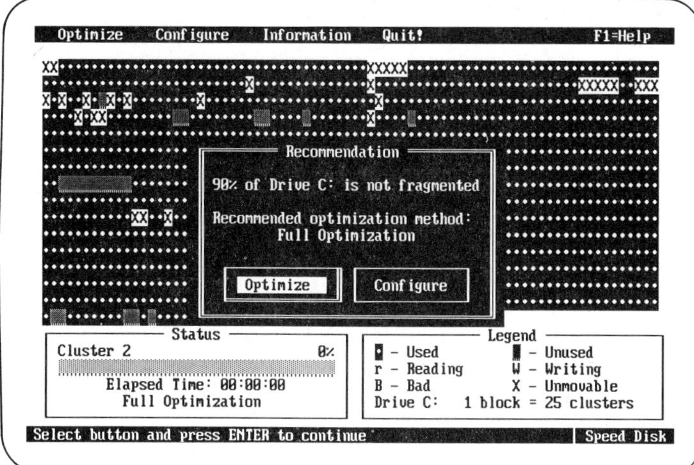

Fig. 5.17
The Speed Disk Recommendation dialog box.

After you choose to accept the recommended optimization method, the optimization begins immediately. Once optimization has begun, do not turn off your computer. If you need to stop the program, press Esc.

If you have never optimized your disk, it is likely that full optimization will be recommended the first time you use Speed Disk. This method is the most thorough, and takes the longest time—maybe an hour, depending on your hard disk size. After you have fully optimized your disk, you may want to use continue to accept the recommended approach on a weekly basis. Subsequent recommended optimization methods may be one of the faster approaches that takes only a few minutes. The various optimization methods are described in table 5.3. If you want to choose manually one of these optimization methods, or you want to choose other Speed Disk options, use the pull-down menus on the menu bar, as described in subsequent sections.

Choosing Speed Disk Options Manually

When you begin the Speed Disk program, you may want to choose *not* to accept the recommended optimization method. If this is the case, choose the Configure option from the Recommendation dialog box. This places you in the pull-down menu mode. The pull-down menus enable you to specify manually Speed Disk options. The menu bar choices are Optimize, Configure, Information, and Quit. Use the right- and left-arrow keys to highlight the menu you want, and then press Enter. Alternatively, point to the menu with the mouse pointer and click. This extends the pull-down menu so that you can choose an option from the menu.

Table 5.3
Speed Disk Optimization Methods

Method	*Meaning*
Full	Gets rid of all file fragmentation, places all files at the beginning portion of the disk so they can be accessed faster.
Files Only	Tries to unfragment as may files as possible, but does not move all files to the beginning of the disk.
Free Space	Moves data forward on the disk to fill in free space.
Directory	Moves directories to front of disk for faster access.
File Sort	Sorts files in directories by filename, extension date and time, ascending order, or descending order. Choose sort order by using the Configure menu.

Using the Speed Disk Optimize Menu

The Speed Disk Optimize menu is shown in figure 5.18. The options in this menu follow:

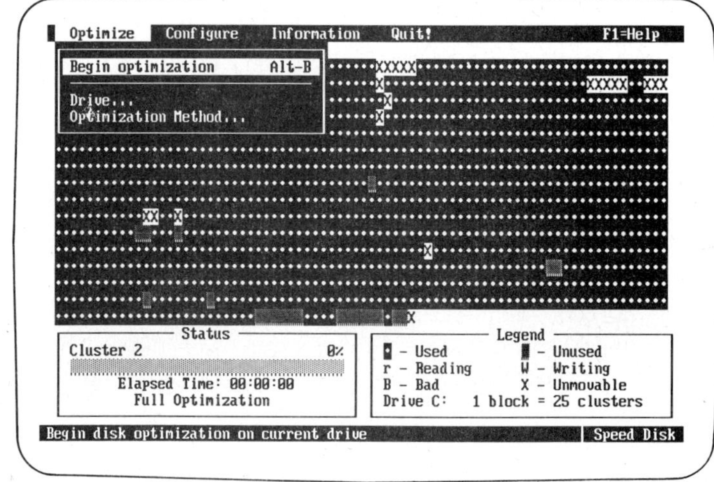

Fig. 5.18
The Speed Disk Optimize pull-down menu.

- *Begin Optimization:* Begins the optimization process. Before you choose this item, you should set all of the options on the other menus to your choice. Notice that you also can press Alt-B to begin optimization, even if you are not in this menu.
- *Drive:* Enables you to choose which drive to optimize.
- *Optimization Method:* Brings up the Select Optimization Method menu (see fig. 5.19). From this menu, you can choose which of the five optimization methods to use. Use the up- and down-arrow keys to highlight the radio button of the method you want, and then press the space bar to select the option. Press Enter to lock in the option or Esc to cancel this menu.

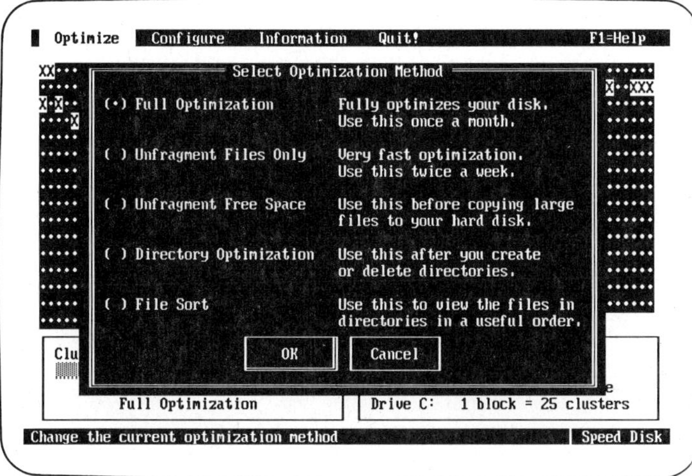

***Fig. 5.19** The Select Optimization Method screen.*

Using the Speed Disk Configure Menu

The Configure menu enables you to choose options concerning how files and directories are ordered in the optimization process (see fig. 5.20). The options in this menu follow:

- Directory Order
- File Sort
- Files To Place First
- Unmovable Files
- Other Options
- Save Options To Disk

The following sections describe these options.

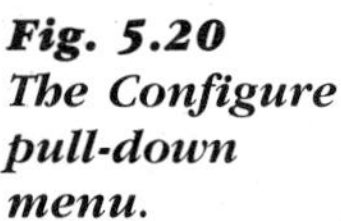

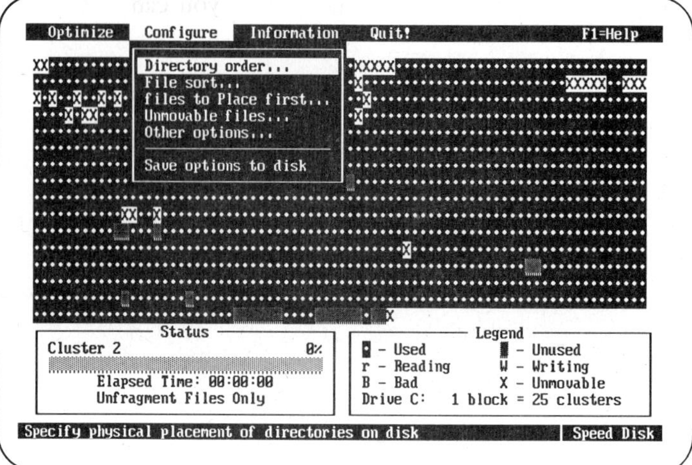

Fig. 5.20
The Configure pull-down menu.

Changing Directory Order

The Directory Order option accesses the Select Directory Order screen, which enables you to specify the order in which directories are placed on the disk (see fig. 5.21). The directories at the beginning of the disk will have the fastest access time. The order that Speed Disk uses by default is the order you specified in your PATH statement, which usually is found in your AUTOEXEC.BAT file. The Directory Order list box contains the list of directories that are ordered on your disk during optimization.

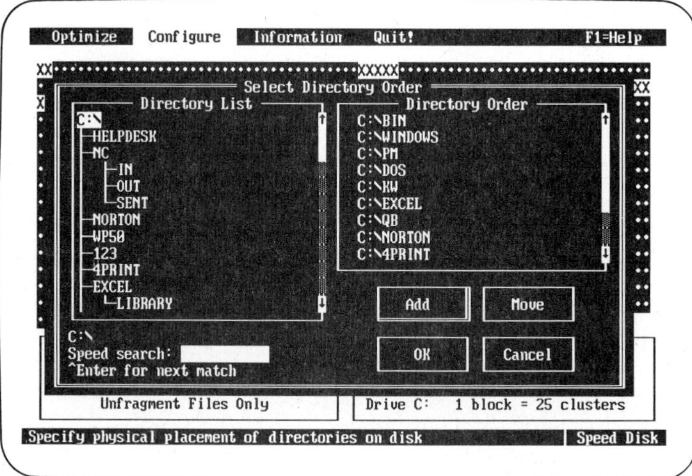

Fig. 5.21
The Speed Disk Select Directory Order screen.

To specify a customized directory order, you can perform any of the following three tasks:

- Move the files already in the list to new locations in the list.
- Add new directories to the Directory Order list.
- Delete directories from the Directory Order list.

To move a name in the Directory Order list, follow these steps:

1. If your cursor is not in the Directory Order box, press Tab to move it there.
2. Use your arrow keys or mouse to point to a directory name in the Directory Order list (*not* the directory list). Press M or the space bar, or double-click the mouse button to select the directory name to move.
3. Using the up- and down-arrow keys, move the directory name to its new place in the list. Anchor the directory name in the list by pressing Enter (or double-clicking again).

If you have no more changes to make, use the right- and left-arrow keys to highlight the OK option and then press Enter.

To add a new name to the Directory Order list, you must copy the name of a directory from the Directory List on the left side of the screen to the right side of the screen, labeled Directory Order. You move back and forth between the right and left sides by pressing the Tab key.

To add a directory to the list on the right side, perform these steps:

1. If your cursor is not in the Directory List box, press the Tab key to place it there.
2. In the Directory List box, highlight the directory you want by using the up- and down-arrow keys.
3. Press Enter to add the selected directory to the end of the list on the right side in the Directory Order box. (Alternatively, double-click the mouse button.)
4. If you want to move the directory name to another location in the list, refer to "Moving a Directory Name in the Directory Order," earlier in the chapter.

To add other directories, repeat the procedure. If you have no more changes to make, use the right- and left-arrow keys to highlight the OK option and then press Enter.

To delete a file from the Directory Order list on the right, follow these steps:

1. Use the Tab key to make sure that your cursor is in the Directory Order list box.
2. In the Directory Order list box, highlight the directory name to delete, or point to it with the mouse pointer.
3. Use the right- and left-arrow keys to highlight the Delete option in the lower right corner of the screen. (When the cursor is in the Directory Order list box, the Add option changes to Delete.) Then press Enter, or double-click with the mouse. (This step *does not* delete the directory from the disk.)

To delete additional directories, repeat this procedure. If you have no more changes to make, use the right- and left-arrow keys to highlight the Finished option and then press Enter.

Selecting File Sort

The File Sort option enables you to specify how files are sorted within directories (see fig. 5.22). Choose Sort Criterion and Sort Order options from the File Sort box. A benefit to sorting files is that this reorganizes file names so that *you* can find the files quickly in a directory of names. When you create a file, DOS locates an empty spot in the disk directory and places the name and information about that file in the directory. Usually, but not always, files in the directory are listed in the order in which they were created. Sorting enables you to place these files in the order that you choose. This feature can help you find certain files faster and determine easily which files are smallest or largest, which files were created last or first, and so on.

Selecting which Files To Place at the Beginning of the Disk

Files placed at the beginning of the disk are accessed faster than those placed later on the disk. Therefore, you may want to place your most commonly used files at the beginning of the disk. Usually, this includes program files—files with the EXE or COM extension. Figure 5.23 shows the Files To Place First list box, where you can place the file specifications for those files that you want to place at the beginning of the disk during optimization. To add a new file to the end of the list, use the up- and down-arrow keys to move the highlight to a blank line and enter a new file specification. You can use the global file characters ? and * in your filespec. To insert a new file within the list, move the cursor to a filespec and choose the Insert option from the Files To Place First box. Insert inserts a blank line above the highlighted filespec. Then, enter a new filespec. To move a file specification, highlight the filespec you want to move, and then press Tab to place the cursor on the Move option. (Alternatively, point with a mouse to Move and click). Then move the filespec up or down by using the arrow keys, or by dragging it with the mouse. To delete a file from the list, highlight the filespec and then choose Delete from the Files To Place First options.

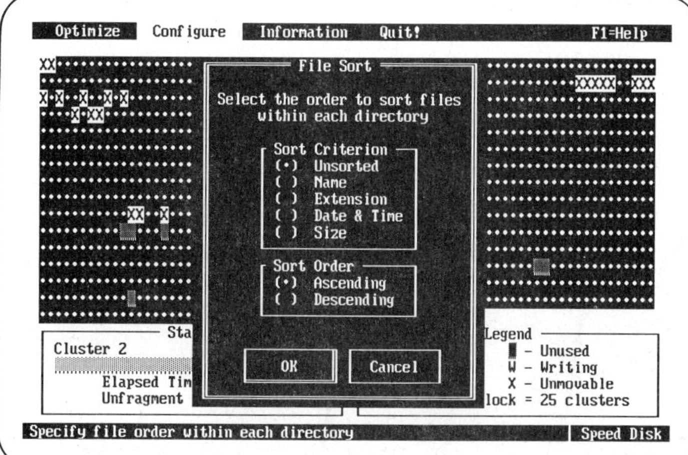

Fig. 5.22
The Speed Disk File Sort screen.

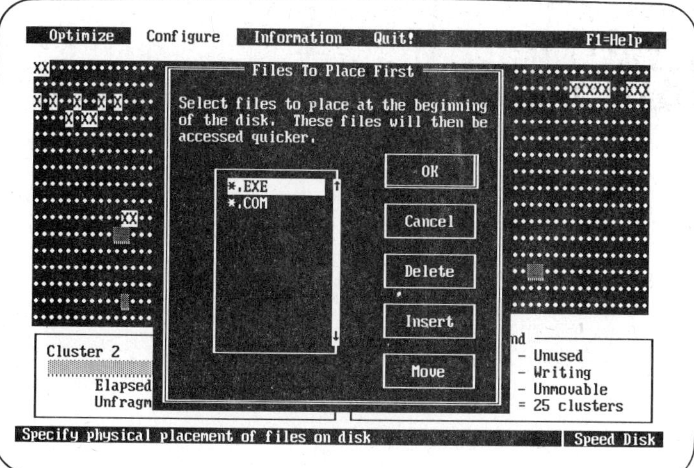

Fig. 5.23
The Speed Disk screen to select files to place first on disk.

Selecting Unmovable Files

Unmovable files will not be physically moved on disk during an optimization. Speed Disk will analyze your disk and mark all hidden files and files related to copy-protection schemes as unmovable. However, if you have other files that are not recognized by Norton as needing to remain unmovable, you can specify the file names manually in the Unmovable Files list box (see fig. 5.24). To add a new file to this list, press the down arrow to go to a blank line and enter the new name. To delete a file from the Unmovable Files list, highlight the file name and choose Delete from the list box menu.

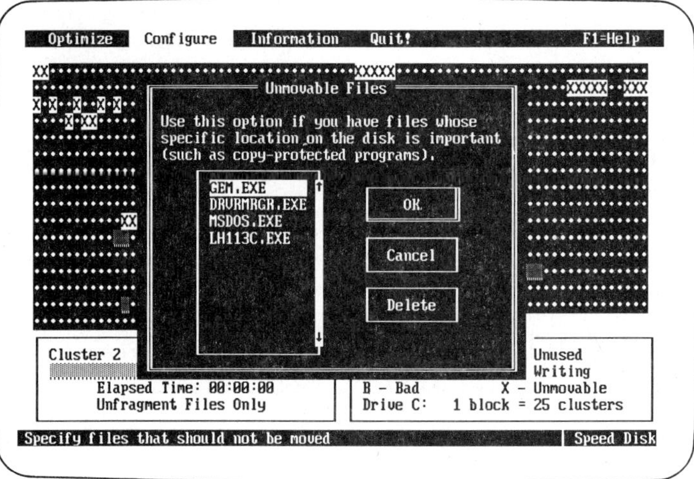

Fig. 5.24 The Speed Disk Unmovable Files screen.

Selecting Other Options

The Other Options item on the Configure menu brings up the screen shown in figure 5.25. The Read-after-Write option and Use DOS Verify option are two ways you can verify that information moved to different locations on the disk during optimization matches the original information. The Read-after-Write option is the best verification, but takes more time than the less accurate Use DOS Verify option. Unless you are pressed for time, always use the Read-after-Write option. You can choose both verification techniques for added protection, or turn both off for no verification. You also can choose the Clear Unused Space option. This option blanks out unused file space on disk so that old file information cannot be recovered from the disk. Use Clear Unused Space if you need to protect your old data from discovery by others.

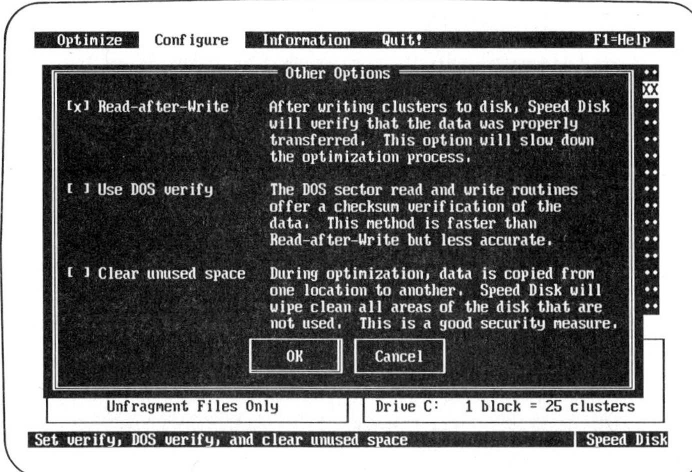

Fig. 5.25
The Other Options screen.

Saving Options to Disk

After you select options from the various Configure menu items, you can save your selections to disk by choosing Save Options to Disk from the Configure menu. Then, when you begin Speed Disk again, these options will still be in effect.

Using the Speed Disk Information Menu

The Speed Disk Information menu enables you to look at a number of pieces of information related to how your disk is optimized. The Information menu is shown in figure 5.26.

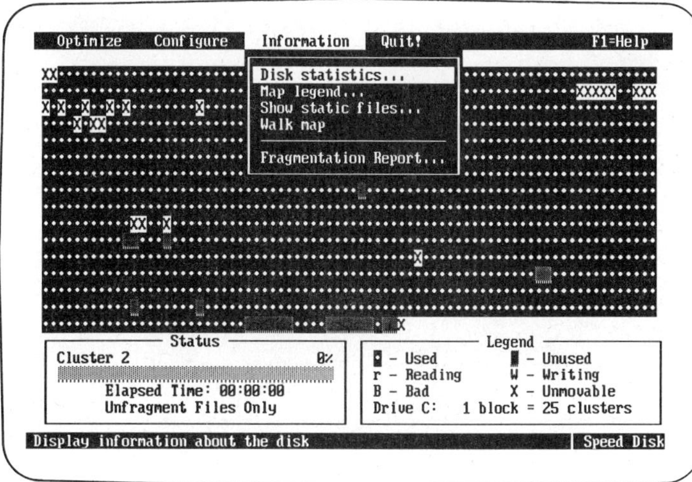

Fig. 5.26
The Information pull-down menu.

The options on the Information menu follow:

- *Disk Statistics:* Gives you information about the disk about to be optimized (see fig. 5.27). The most important information on the Disk Statistics for Drive C: screen is the Percentage of Unfragmented Files field. If this number is 95% or more, you have little fragmentation. If the number is about 90%, you probably should perform an optimization. If it is under 90%, you need a full optimization.
- *Map Legend:* Gives you a key for the symbols used on the disk map that is in view during the optimization (see fig. 5.28).

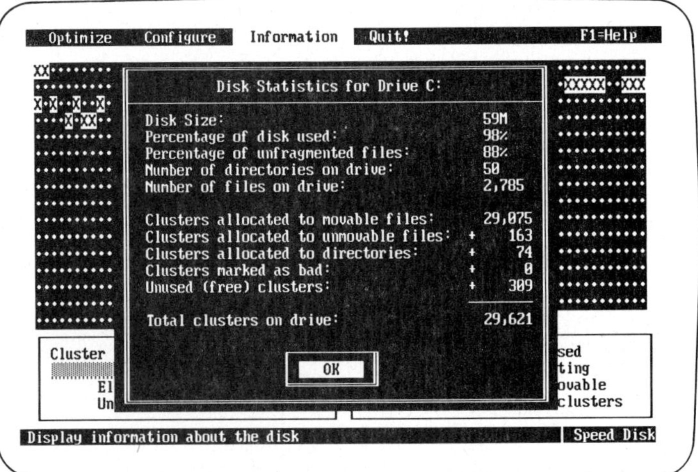

Fig. 5.27
The Speed Disk statistics screen.

Fig. 5.28
The Disk Map Legend screen.

- *Show Static Files:* Gives you a list of files that the program has determined should not be moved (see fig. 5.29).
- *Walk Map:* Displays the disk map and enables you to use the arrow keys to highlight blocks on the map. When you highlight a block, a cluster range is displayed. If you want to know where a bad block is located on disk, for example, you can use the Walk Map option to determine the location of the bad cluster. You may want to examine this cluster by using Disk Editor.
- *Fragmentation Report:* Enables you to examine the amount of fragmentation of individual files (see fig. 5.30). In this figure, the left side of the screen is a directory tree. The PM directory is highlighted, which causes the files for that directory to appear in the list box on the right side of the screen. Notice two files with dots in front of their names. These files are fragmented. The percent of fragmentation is listed under the % column. Files that have 100% listed are completely unfragmented. Any file with 90% or less is considered highly fragmented. The lower this number, the more fragmentation of the file there is.

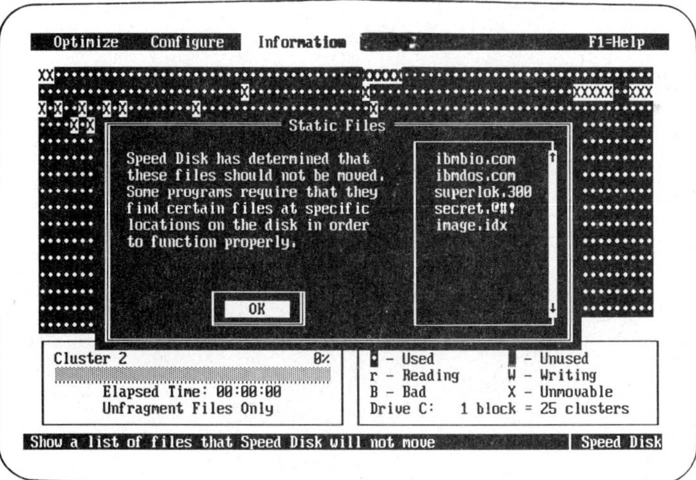

Fig. 5.29
The Speed Disk Static Files list box.

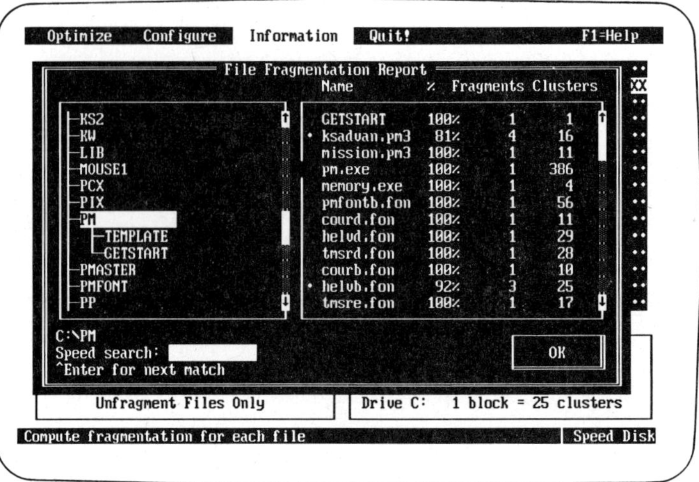

Fig. 5.30
The File Fragmentation Report screen.

Using Speed Disk from the DOS Prompt

You can use the Speed Disk command from the DOS prompt to bypass the menu interface by using the following syntax:

SPEEDISK [*d:*][*switches*]

The available switches for the SD command follow:

Switch	*Effect*
/B	Reboots after the command finishes.
/C	Performs a complete optimization of the disk.
/D	Optimizes the directory only.
/SD[–]	Instructs the command to sort files by date. If the – parameter is included, the sort will be from latest to oldest.
/SE[–]	Instructs the command to sort files by extension. If the – parameter is included, the sort will be in descending alphabetical order.
/SN[–]	Instructs the command to sort by file name. If the – parameter is included, the sort will be in descending alphabetical order.

/SS[–]	Instructs the command to sort by file size. If the – parameter is included, the sort will be from largest to smallest.
/U	Instructs the command to attempt to unfragment as many files as possible without moving parts of the directory structure. Some damaged files may not get unfragmented.
/V	Instructs the command to use verify-after-write date verification.

To perform an optimization of the directories in drive C, for example, you enter the command

```
SPEEDISK C:/D
```

The directory optimization will take place automatically. When optimization is finished, you will be in the Configure menu. Press Esc to return to the DOS prompt. If you include the /B option, your computer reboots after the optimization finishes.

Using Calibrate

You use the Calibrate command to optimize the speed and reliability of reading and writing information to and from your hard disk. In order for Calibrate to know how to optimize your hard disk, it runs a series of tests to determine some of the logical and physical characteristics of your hard disk. Calibrate is specifically for use on your hard disk. It is not intended to work on floppy disks, network disks, RAM disks, assigned disks (DOS ASSIGN command), or substitute disks (DOS SUBST command).

There are two reasons to use the Calibrate command. First, you use it to check your interleave factor (described later) to see if your disk is working efficiently. You need to test the disk only once. Next, if your hard disk is beginning to give intermittent errors when reading and writing files, you need to run Calibrate to evaluate and solve the problem. Norton recommends that you run Calibrate every three months to test your hard disk for problems.

Calibrate can improve the speed at which data is read from your hard disk by adjusting the disk's interleave factor. The interleave factor has to do with the way DOS reads information from your hard disk. Because the hard disk is spinning at a rapid speed, the read/write head cannot always get information off the disk in one long stream. Often, information is read from the disk in 512K spurts of information (a *sector*). As the head is reading information from the disk, for example, it may read one 512K sector, then skip the next sector on the disk while the first sector of information is being sent to the computer, then read the next sector, skip the next, read the next, and so on. The number of sectors skipped between reads is called the *interleave factor*. In this example, the interleave factor is 2 (sometimes called 2:1). Each hard disk has an *optimum interleave factor*—one that makes reading information from the hard disk as fast as possible. Some hard disks, however, may have been formatted at a less than optimum interleave factor. If your hard disk is running at a less than optimum interleave factor, the Calibrate command can adjust your disk to make it work faster. Calibrate adjusts your interleave factor by performing a low-level format. This kind of format does not destroy the data on your disk. It simply adjusts how the information is stored on disk, and tests the reliability of information storage on the disk.

There are some disks on which Calibrate cannot adjust the interleave factor; in other words, it cannot perform a low-level format. In this case, it still can perform some valuable tests, but will not be able to adjust the interleave. When you run the Calibrate program, it will inform you if you have a hard disk that cannot be adjusted. Some of the disk types on which Calibrate cannot adjust the interleave include the following:

- Drives with SCSI or IDE-type controllers
- Drives that are not 100-percent IBM compatible
- Drives with controllers that perform a sector translation
- Drives with on-board disk caching
- Iomega Bernoulli Box drives
- Novell file servers
- Any hard disk with a sector size other than 512K

In addition to the optimization of the speed of your hard disk, Calibrate can perform some tests to improve the reliability of information reading and writing to your hard disk. Calibrate can test each byte of your hard disk for reliability and will move any data that is in danger to a reliable portion of the disk.

Before you run Calibrate the first time, you should back up your hard disk. Although Calibrate is safe and reliable, you may run into problems on drives that are not 100-percent IBM compatible. After you run Calibrate on your computer and verify that your disks are compatible, you no longer need to back up each time you use the program.

Also, before you run Calibrate, you should remove all TSR programs from memory and have only essential device drivers (in your CONFIG.SYS file) in use when you use the Calibrate command. Many times, the easiest way to do this is to boot with your original DOS floppy disk in drive A.

You can run the Calibrate command by choosing it from the Norton menu or by entering the command CALIBRAT at the DOS prompt. If you run Calibrate without any switches, you see an opening screen like the one in figure 5.31. This Calibrate screen gives you a brief description of what Calibrate is about to do. The easiest way to use the program from this point simply is to continue to follow the directions on-screen, which lead you through a standard Calibrate session.

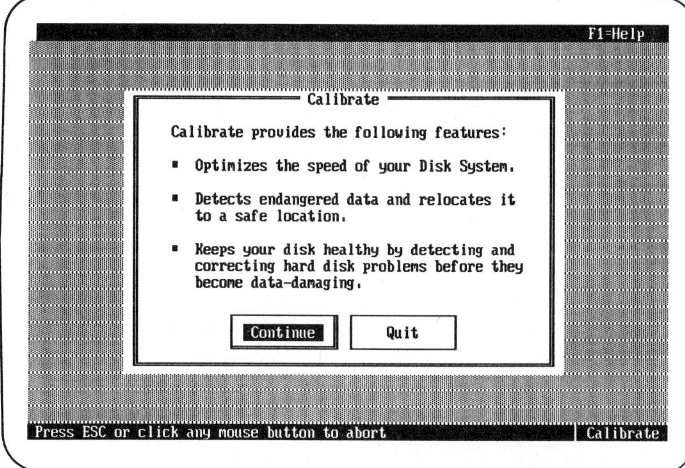

***Fig. 5.31* The Calibrate screen.**

If you have more than one hard disk, Calibrate prompts you to choose which hard disk to analyze. If you have only one hard disk, you are not prompted, but will go directly to the next screen. This screen lists the preliminary tests that will be performed on your hard disk (see fig. 5.32). These preliminary tests will tell Calibrate what it needs to know about the logical and physical characteristics of your disk. Select the Continue option from this screen to go to the next screen.

Interpreting the Calibrate System Integrity Test

When you continue to the System Integrity Testing screen, the System Integrity test begins (see fig. 5.33). As each test is progressing, there will be a blinking dot to the left of the test name. When the test is finished, a check appears beside the name. If the tests determine that your disk is

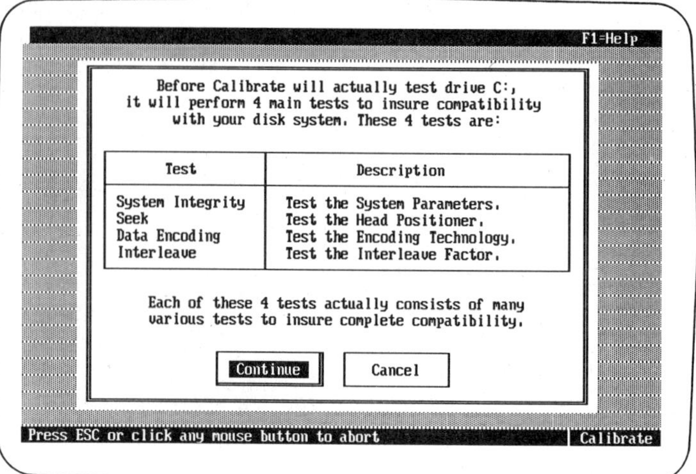

Fig. 5.32
The Calibrate list of tests to be performed.

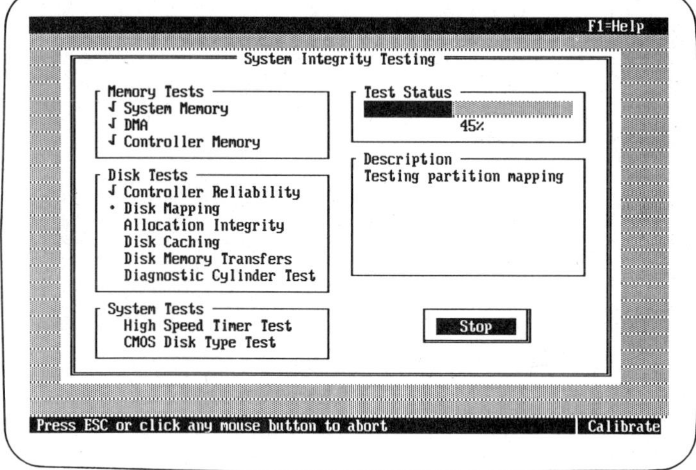

Fig. 5.33
The Calibrate System Integrity Testing screen.

one in which the interleave cannot be adjusted, you see a warning screen like the one in figure 5.34. You still can continue with the other valuable tests, but the interleave options will be skipped.

Interpreting the Calibrate Interleave Test

If calibration is possible, Calibrate will test your disk using a number of possible interleaves. This will take several minutes. When this test finishes, a screen like the one in figure 5.35 appears. This screen is a graphic representation of the results of the interleave test. Your disk will work optimally at the interleave that is lowest on the graph. This interleave number is designated with the caption `Optimal` on the graph. Also, your current interleave will be captioned. If the optimal and current interleaves are different and you want to optimize your disk, use the right- and left-arrow keys to line up the Current and Optimal settings. Then, choose Continue to reset your interleave to the new setting. The actual interleave setting takes place during the pattern testing, described in "Interpreting Calibrate Pattern Testing," later in this chapter. If your disk already is at the optimal interleave, choose Continue to move on to other tests.

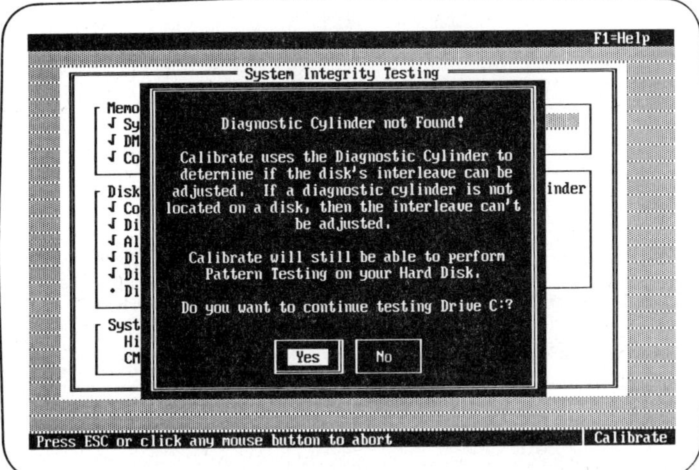

Fig. 5.34
A Calibrate warning message on a disk unable to have interleaving adjusted.

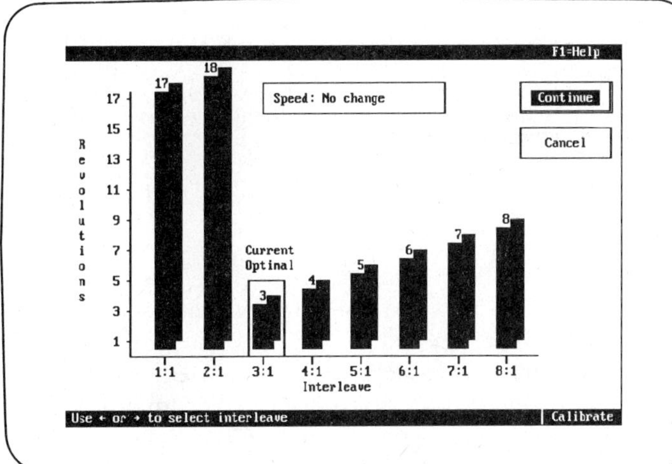

Fig. 5.35
A Calibrate screen displaying the results of the Interleave test.

Interpreting the Calibrate Seek Tests

If you continue with the calibration tests, you see the Seek Test screen (see fig. 5.36). This test examines how fast your read/write head on your hard disk can seek out information on your disk. As the tests are in progress, the movement of the head is animated on-screen, moving back and forth on the picture of the drive in the middle of the screen. There are four tests performed. The Value column gives you the time it takes to perform these four tasks (in milliseconds).

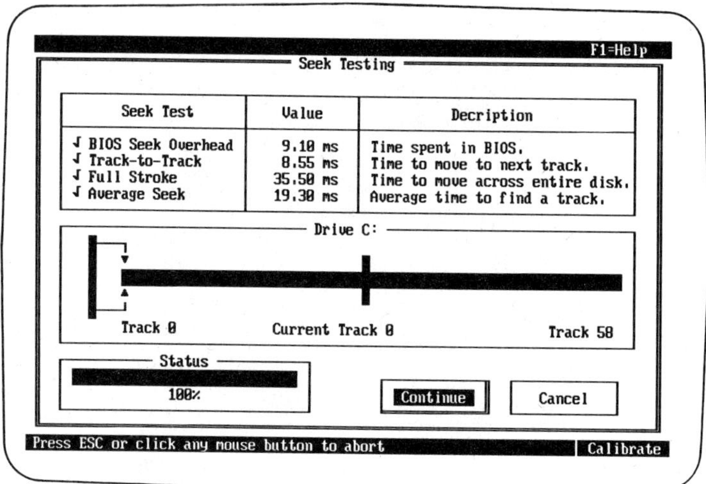

Fig. 5.36
The Calibrate Seek Test screen.

The four tests that the Seek test performs follow:

- *BIOS Seek Overhead:* Tests the time spent getting ready to read information from the disk.
- *Track-to-Track:* Tests how long it takes the head to move to the next track on disk.
- *Full Stroke:* Measures how long it takes to move from one track to another track on the other side of the disk.
- *Average Seek:* Determines how long, on the average, it takes to find and read information from the disk. The Average Seek is the number you most often see quoted in advertisements for hard disks. A fast disk will have an average seek time of less than 20ms. A slow hard disk will have an average seek of from 60ms to 80ms. If you are using disk-intensive application programs on your computer, the average seek time can be a major factor in how efficiently your computer works.

When you begin the Calibrate command from the DOS prompt, you can cause it to skip the Seek test by using the option /NOSEEK in the command line.

Interpreting the Calibrate Data Encoding Test

The Calibrate Data Encoding Testing screen is shown in figure 5.37. This test analyzes the physical characteristics of the hard disk. The information is useful so that the Calibrate program can do further testing, and may be of interest to a technician who is examining a hard disk for problems.

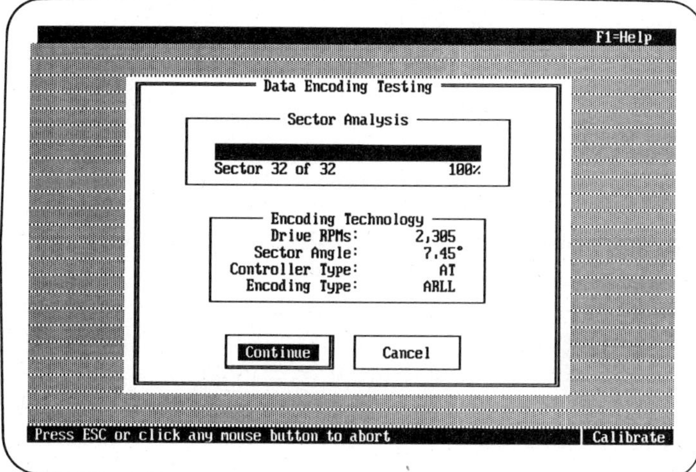

Fig. 5.37* *The Calibrate Data Encoding Testing screen.

Interpreting Calibrate Pattern Testing

You use calibrate pattern testing to test your hard disk for defects. You can choose the thoroughness of this test on the Pattern Testing screen (see fig. 5.38). The options run from No Pattern Testing to Rigorous Pattern Testing. The higher the level of testing, the more time is required. The No Pattern Testing option may take 5 to 10 minutes, and the Rigorous Pattern Testing option may last overnight, depending on the size of your hard disk.

You use pattern testing to test the disk for its read/write capabilities. A pattern of magnetic signals, such as 101010101 is written to the disk, and then read back. Pattern testing uses the alternating 1 and 0 pattern, which is the most difficult pattern to read. If you did not receive a warning that Calibrate could not perform a low-level format, then the pattern testing also performs a low-level format as it tests the disk. This is a non-destructive, safe format (not like a regular format that clears information from the disk).

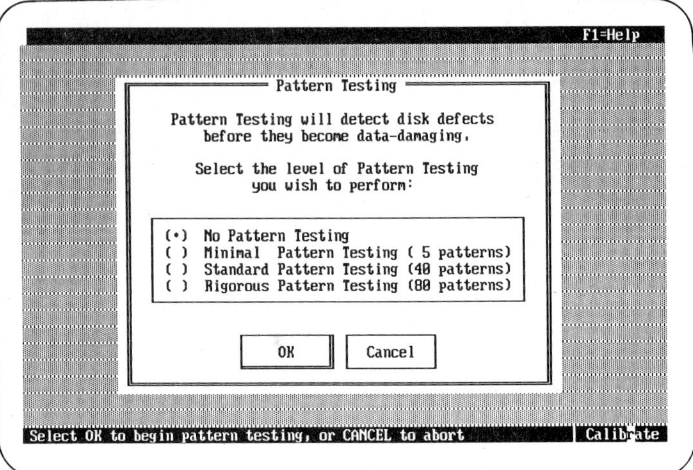

Fig. 5.38 ***The Calibrate Pattern Testing screen.***

Use the No Pattern Testing option if you indicated a new interleave factor in the previous Interleave test. This option is the quickest way to update your interleave factor. Use one of the other pattern-testing options if you have had some problems with your disk, such as losing information or files becoming unreadable. When the pattern test begins, you see a disk map similar to the Speed Disk map that shows the progress of the test. You can interrupt the test safely by pressing Esc. If you stop the pattern-testing/low-level format in the middle of its run, Calibrate will take up where it left off when you begin it again.

Because pattern testing can take some time, Norton has a built-in screen-blanking routine which enables you to blank your screen so that the image will not become imprinted onto your monitor screen. During the pattern testing, press the space bar to blank the screen. While the screen is blank, a floating message will appear occasionally to tell you that the testing is still in progress. Press the space bar again to bring the screen back.

Viewing the Calibrate Report

After all of the Calibrate tests are complete, you see a Report screen like the one in figure 5.39. This report summarizes all of the findings of the tests. Notice that the report is in a list box, so you can use the up- and down-arrow keys to view parts of the report not shown on-screen. It is a good idea to choose the Print option on the Report screen so that you can keep a folder of these reports about your hard disk. These may become important if a technician needs to diagnose problems with your disk in the future. Optionally, you can choose the Save As option to save the report to a file. Choosing Done ends the report screen and returns you to the beginning of the Calibrate program, which displays an option screen for you to choose which disk to test. If you do not want to do further testing, press Esc to return to DOS or to the Norton menu.

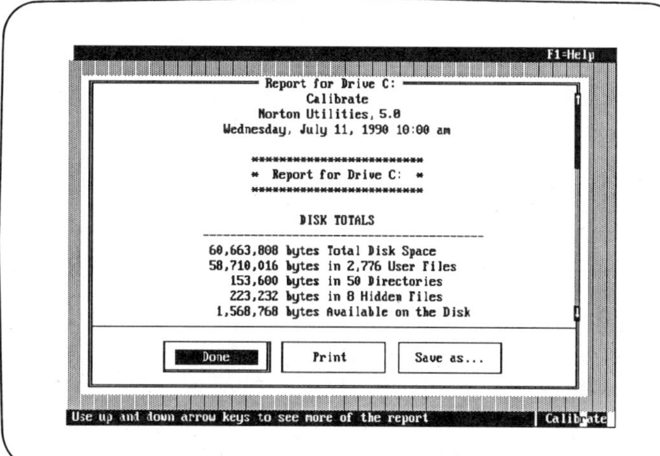

Fig. 5.39
The Calibrate report screen.

Using the Calibrate Command from the DOS Prompt

If you begin the Calibrate command from the DOS prompt, you have several options (switches) that you can choose. The syntax of the Calibrate command is

CALIBRAT [*d*:] [*switches*]

The available switches for the Calibrate command follow:

/BATCH — Does not prompt for any input from the user; returns to DOS when finished. This automates the entire test procedure. If you choose this option, you probably will want to choose one of the /R options as well to create a report of the test findings.

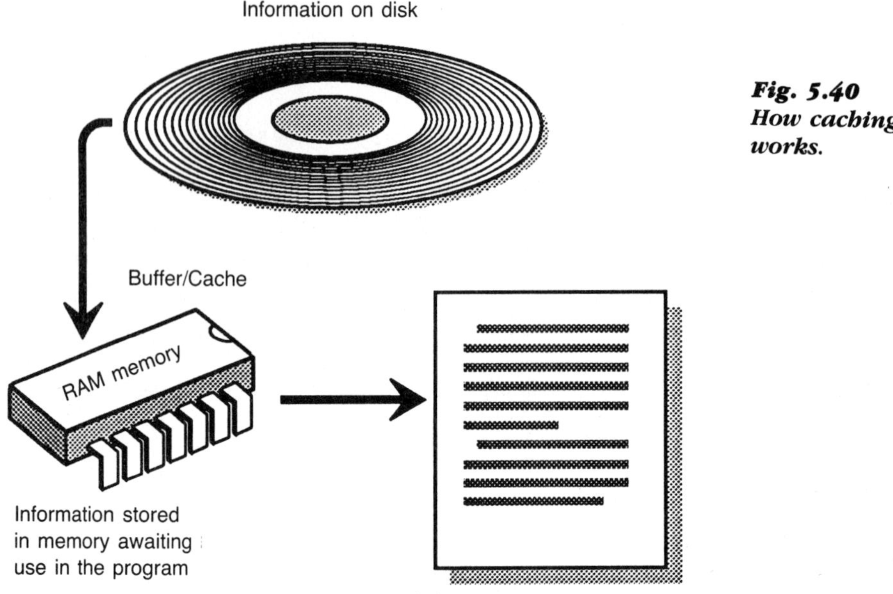

Fig. 5.40
How caching works.

have extra memory that you can use as a disk cache. The more extra memory you can use as a disk cache, the more potential speed you can experience in disk access.

Extra memory is any memory above what your programs normally need. This can be regular DOS memory, which goes up to 640K. If all of your programs in memory (including DOS) use only 320K, then you have some extra memory that you can use as a cache. Other kinds of extra memory are extended and expanded memory. *Extended memory* is memory above the 640K normal DOS limit. *Expanded memory* is add-on memory that can be acessed by certain programs that subscribe to a special way to use memory developed by Lotus, Microsoft, Intel, and AST companies (LIM standard).

Disk cache can provide speed and extend battery life in laptop computers. A disk cache can give your programs an enormous boot in speed. For comparison, reading information from a floppy disk can take around 200ms (milliseconds), while reading information from a hard disk can take 18ms to 80ms. Getting information from RAM takes less than 1ms. A disk cache also can save battery power in a laptop. It does this by making the laptop use the motor on the hard disk less.

The Norton NCACHE program does more than just create an information buffer. By using two features—IntelliWrites and SmartReads—NCACHE tries to guess what data you would read or write from the disk next in order to make the cache contain the information you are most likely to

/NOSEEK	Skips the seek tests. Use this when you do not want Calibrate to test the head-positioning mechanism of the disk. Usually, you need to use Calibrate once without this switch to test the mechanism. Thereafter, use this switch.
/NOFORMAT	Instructs Calibrate to perform pattern testing only and to skip the low-level format.
/PATTERN *n*	Tells Calibrate which testing level (*n*) to use. The parameter *n* can be 0, 5, 40, or 80. The higher the number, the more thorough the test, but the longer Calibrate takes to test the disk.
/R:*file*	Tells Calibrate to generate a report and to write it to the file name specified in the switch. You also must use the /BATCH switch when you use this option.
/RA:*file*	This switch is the same as the /R:*file* switch, but the information is appended to the file rather than becoming a new file.
/X:*drives*	Tells Calibrate to exclude named drives from the test. /X:DE, for example, would exclude disks D and E from testing.

Using Norton Disk Cache

The flow of information from the disk into a computer program is often the source of an information bottleneck. Although you can access information in the computer's RAM almost instantaneously, getting information from a disk can be very, very slow by comparison. If you are using disk-intensive programs, slow disk access can bring your program speed down to a crawl.

A solution to slow disk access is for the computer to read more information from the disk than is needed, and place the extra information into RAM memory—hoping that the next piece of information requested by the program will then be in RAM and therefore be accessed faster. Figure 5.40 shows how the information is read from the disk and stored in a buffer, waiting for the program to request the information. The disk buffer is called a *cache*.

If your computer has 1M of memory, for example, and your software programs can access only 640K of that memory at any one time, then you need. NCACHE does this by analyzing the pattern of past disk access to predict future disk access.

The Norton Disk Cache program is really two programs. One program, NCACHE-F (F stands for Fast), is meant to be used on 80286-, 80386-, or 80486-based computers with expanded or extended memory. The Disk Cache program provides the fastest disk access (cache) possible. The second version of the program, NCACHE-S (S stands for Small), is meant to be used on 8088-based computers, or a computer without much extra memory.

The following descriptions of the NCACHE programs first will cover items common to both versions of the program. Then, a separate section will cover unique features of the F version of the program.

Beginning NCACHE from CONFIG.SYS or AUTOEXEC.BAT

You can use the NCACHE program in one of two recommended ways. You can include the program as a line in your AUTOEXEC.BAT file. Alternatively, you can include the program as a device driver in your CONFIG.SYS file. If you requested that the NCACHE program be installed in the Norton Install program, it was installed as a device driver in your CONFIG.SYS file. The benefit of installing NCACHE in your AUTOEXEC.BAT file is that if you installed it as the last TSR program, you can uninstall it from memory if you need to use the memory to run a large program. The advantage of placing the command in your CONFIG.SYS file is that it will have compatibility with more computers when used in this way.

To place the NCACHE program in your AUTOEXEC.BAT file, you can use the following syntax:

path\NCACHE-F [*parameters*]

Alternatively, you can use NCACHE-S instead of the -F version. The *path* refers to the directory name where the NCACHE-F or NCACHE-S files are stored. To place the program in your CONFIG.SYS file, you can use the following syntax:

DEVICE= *path*\NCACHE-F [*parameters*]

Again, you also could use NCACHE-S, if appropriate. Both of these versions of the command will cause the disk cache to be in effect when you boot your computer. As with the AUTOEXEC.BAT file, you can enter this command from the DOS prompt at any time to begin or end the NCACHE program, using the parameters described later.

A wide variety of optional parameters is explained later in this chapter. You usually can use NCACHE with most default conditions on many computers, however. You should have to refer to the parameters only if you are having problems getting your cache to work correctly. Some ways in which you can use NCACHE follow. The commands listed are what you place in your AUTOEXEC.BAT file, although you can do the same thing by placing DEVICE= in front of the command and placing it in your CONFIG.SYS file.

The following command is used on an IBM PS/2 model 70 computer (80386). Because programs used on this computer never use above the 640K of memory, the NCACHE is set to use 360K of the memory as a cache. The NCACHE program is in the \NORTON directory

```
\NORTON\NCACHE-F EXT=920
```

EXT= tells NCACHE how much extended memory to use. After you enter this command, you see a screen like the one in figure 5.41. Notice in the Extended Memory box at the top middle of the screen that 920K of extended memory is set aside for a cache. In the DOS Memory box to the left of the screen, you can see that the NCACHE-F TSR program in memory is taking 9K of RAM and the Cache manager is taking 61K of memory. This makes 428K RAM available for application programs. If this is too little RAM for your programs, you can use the NCACHE-S version of the program. If you enter the command

```
\NORTON\NCACHE-S EXT=920
```

you see a screen like the one in figure 5.42. On this screen, the NCACHE=S TSR program only takes up 4K and the manager only 2K, leaving 491K of RAM available for your application programs, as shown in figure 5.42. The S version, however, has less features than the F version of the program, as explained later in the chapter.

If you have a computer with no extended memory, such as an 8088 computer with 640 or less memory, you probably would use the S version of the command to specify that some of the DOS memory be used as a cache. Suppose you want to create a small cache of 20K. You would use the command

```
\NORTON\NCACHE-S DOS=20
```

The examples in this section are typical ways of using the NCACHE program. If you use one of these versions of the command, replace the 920 with the amount of extended memory you have available. Alternatively, replace the DOS-20 with the amount of extra DOS memory you are willing to use as a cache. The most common command options you may want to use are the +S and +I options. The +S option enables SmartReads and +I enables Intelliwrites. These options can provide additional speed for some applications such as word processors, spreadsheets, and other programs. These options may not provide additional speed for use with database programs. You may have to experiment with these options to see which combination gives you the best disk access for the type of application programs you run. Another option that you may use is the USEHIDOS=YES option. If you are using an advanced memory manager on your computer such as QEMM or 386-to-the-Max, using the this option will enable NCACHE to use less of your initial 640K DOS memory, and may provide more memory for use in your application programs. If you need further options to make the program run to your needs, see the additional parameters described in the following section.

Fig. 5.41 ***The Norton Cache screen using the F version.***

```
                                  Norton Cache
     DOS Memory              Extended Memory              Expanded Memory
 NCACHE-F:        9 K    Cache:           920 K
 Cache Manag:    61 K
 Available:     428 K    Available:       360 K    Available:            0 K

 Cache Allocated:     0.0K of 920.0K    [00.0%], Now Using:     0.0K  [00.0%]

                                  Cache Options
 DOS=0K     EXT=920K     EXP=0K          BLOCK=512   DELAY=0.0     QUICK=OFF

             Drive Options                           Drive Statistics
            A   C   I   W   S   R   G              Cache Hit Ratio      %Hits
 Drive A:   +   +   -   +   +   D8  128                  0/0           [00.0%]
 Drive B:   +   +   -   +   +   D8  128                  0/0           [00.0%]
 Drive C:   +   +   +   +   +   D8  128                  0/0           [00.0%]

C:\WP50>
```

Fig. 5.42 ***The Norton Cache screen using the S version.***

```
                                  Norton Cache
     DOS Memory              Extended Memory              Expanded Memory
 NCACHE-S:        4 K    Cache:           920 K
 Cache Manag:     2 K
 Available:     491 K    Available:       360 K    Available:            0 K

 Cache Allocated:     0.0K of 920.0K    [00.0%], Now Using:     0.0K  [00.0%]

                                  Cache Options
   DOS=0K                 EXT=920K             EXP=0K              BLOCK=0K

             Drive Options                           Drive Statistics
              A      C      W      G               Cache Hit Ratio      %Hits
 Drive A:     +      +      +      128                   0/0           [00.0%]
 Drive B:     +      +      +      128                   0/0           [00.0%]
 Drive C:     +      +      +      128                   0/0           [00.0%]

C:\WP50>
```

Using NCACHE Parameters and Options

A variety of parameters are available to specify how the NCACHE program creates and uses a disk buffer. The parameters available for both versions of NCACHE follow:

Parameter	*Effect*
BLOCK=*n*	Sets the size of the cache blocks. The *n* is a number in kilobytes. Use large blocks if you are accessing large files and your disk is unfragmented. Use smaller blocks if you access small files or if your disk is fragmented. The S version of the program uses a default value of 8 for the block, and the F version uses a default value of 512.
EXT=*n* or EXT= −*n*	Specifies how much extended memory in kilobytes is to be used by the cache. If a negative value is used, it means to leave that much free memory for use by other programs. The *n* is in kilobytes. EXT=256, for example, means to use 256K of extended memory for the cache.
EXP=*n* or EXP−*n*	Specifies how much expanded memory in kilobytes is to be used by the cache. If a negative value is used, it means to leave that much memory free for other programs to use. EXP=750, for example, means to use 750K of expanded memory for the disk cache. Any expanded memory used must be LIM 4.0 compatible.
DOS=*n* or DOS= −*n*	Specifies how much DOS memory is to be used by the cache. Use this only when you do not have any expanded or extended memory. If a negative value is used, it means to leave that much memory free for other programs to use.
INI=*path*	Tells the command where to look for the file that contains installation options. If your installation options are in your \NORTON directory, for example, you use the parameter INI= \NORTON.

RESET	Resets the cache statistics, which are viewable on the NCACHE status screen.
STATUS	Causes the program to display a number of statistics that enable you to see how effective the cache is working. Figure 5.42, for example, summarizes all of the options you have set. An important part of this screen is the Cache Hit Ratio, which is the ratio of sectors read from the cache to the sectors read from disk. The higher the ratio, the more effective the cache.
UNINSTALL	Removes the command from memory. This command will not work unless the NCACHE program was the last memory-resident (TSR) program loaded into memory.
USEHIDOS = *YES/NO*	Minimizes the use of conventional (low) DOS memory, if high memory is available (if set to Yes). The default for this command is No.
USE HMA = *YES/NO*	Uses the XMS high-memory area to reduce the use of DOS RAM (if set to Yes). This is available only if you have an extended memory manager.

Options for both cache versions follow:

+/−A	Activates or deactivates caching. Use this if you need to deactivate caching in order to run a program in which you do not want caching to be used.
+/−C	Enables or disables caching of additional information. No new information is cached when this is disabled.
F	Flushes the cache (empties it). This causes all writes to disk to be finished.

G=*n*	Specifies a group sector size (the default is 128). Specify a group size smaller than 128 if you are reading small pieces of information from a random file, such as in a database with small records.
+/−W	Enables or disables write-through caching. When write-through caching is disabled, writes are written directly to the disk, bypassing the cache.
+/−I	Enables or disables IntelliWrites. When on, this accelerates disk writes and returns control back to the application before the write is finished.
R=*Dn*	Specifies how may sectors ahead it should read. A specification of R=0 or R=D0 disables read-aheads. R=*n* will cause read aheads always and a specification of R=D*n* will cause read aheads only when the file being read is not a random file. The number of sectors that can be specified is from 0 to 15.
+/−S	Enables or Disables SmartReads. This enables the program to read additional data before it finishes writing all data to disk.

Using NCACHE-F Parameters

The NCACHE-F version of the NCACHE program has a few more parameters than those available to the NCACHE-S version. These descriptions follow:

DELAY=*ss.hh*	Delays writes to the disk in seconds or hundredths of a second (for example, 00.10 is one hundredth of a second). The default is 00.00. Slight writing delays can improve the speed of write-intensive programs.
QUICK=*ON/OFF*	Displays the DOS prompt even when information still is being written to the disk.

Using Batch Files To Simplify NCACHE Options

Because there are so many options in the NCACHE programs, you may consider creating a few batch files to issue versions of the command that you use often. You can place the line

```
NCACHE-F /UNINSTALL
```

in a batch file called UNI.BAT, for example, and make the uninstall procedure easier. Suppose that you want to deactivate NCACHE during the use of a program. You can place the command

```
NCACHE-F -A
```

in a batch file called DEACTIVE.BAT. Then, to reactivate the command, you can have a batch file called ACTIVE.BAT which would contain the command

```
NCACHE-F +A
```

If you use a complicated NCACHE command from the DOS prompt, you can place the command line

```
NCACHE-F USEHIDOS=YES EXT=920 +S +I
```

in a file called CACHE.BAT. Then you only have to enter the command CACHE to begin the NCACHE program. Assigning these batch file names to tasks such as these makes working with long commands with difficult-to-remember options much easier.

Summary

This chapter covered Norton Utilities commands that are useful for getting the most out of your hard disk, including commands that make you knowledgeable about your system (System Information). To keep your disk running at top speed, you need to use the Speed Disk command. You also can use Speed Disk to arrange your files (sort file names) in an order that is convenient and easy for you to use. The Calibrate command enables you to fine-tune your disk access, and the NCACHE programs help you make disk access more efficient. These Norton commands give you much more information about the condition of your disks and the data they hold than the limited DOS disk-analysis commands can provide.

6

Managing the Resources of Your Computer

Previous chapters of this book concentrated on issues of safety and maintenance. This chapter introduces a variety of Norton Utilities commands that make using your computer easier and more fun. The commands covered in this chapter include the Norton Control Center (NCC), Norton Change Directory (NCD), and Batch Enhancer (BE).

These commands enable you to navigate around your computer faster and with less keystrokes than you can with DOS. With these commands, you can modify some of your computer's environmental settings—for example, colors, cursor size, and keyboard rate—and create better batch files.

Changing Your Computer's Settings with the Norton Control Center

The Norton Control Center (NCC) is a utility that enables you to change a number of settings on your computer. You can alter the size of your cursor, your monitor's colors, the number of lines displayed, the date and time, and other settings. The Time Mark (TM) command that you may have used in Version 4.5 of Norton is now in the NCC command for Version 5.0.

You can use the Norton Control Center in command-line or interactive mode. First, this chapter describes interactive mode. Then, you learn about the available options from the command line.

Using the NCC in Interactive Mode

If you enter the command NCC with no quick switches, you enter interactive mode, and the Norton Control Center menu appears (see fig. 6.1).

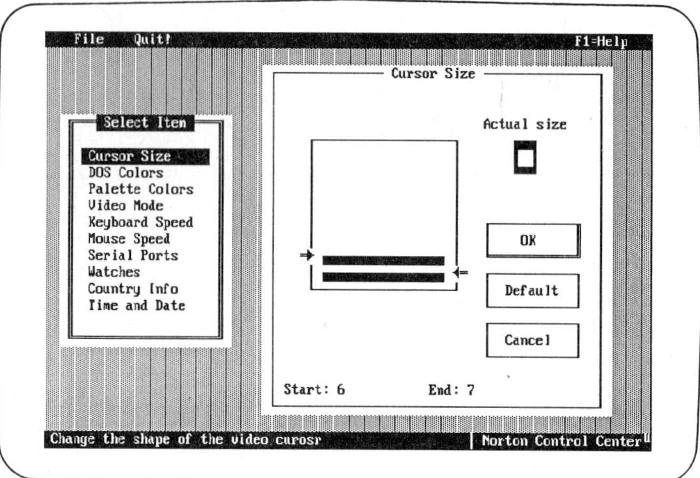

Fig. 6.1
The NCC main menu.

Notice the list of items on the left side of the menu:

- Cursor Size
- DOS Colors
- Palette Colors
- Video Mode
- Keyboard Speed
- Mouse Speed
- Serial Ports
- Watches
- Country Info
- Time and Date

These options represent the settings you can change in the Norton Control Center. The first option, Cursor Size, is highlighted when you enter the NCC command. Using your up- and down-arrow keys, you can highlight one of these menu items. Then, when you press Enter, your highlight moves to the right side of the screen, where you can find information on the item you want to set. You also can use the right- and left-arrow keys or Tab to move to the right or left portion of the screen. Alternatively, point to the area you want with the mouse pointer and click.

After you choose your settings, you can pull down the Files menu at the top of the screen by pressing F10. This menu has two options:

- *Save Settings:* Enables you to save the settings you have chosen to a file. The purpose of saving the settings is so that you can activate the settings at any time from the DOS prompt by entering the NCC command with the /SETALL switch. See the command-line options described later.

- *Load Settings:* Enables you to load previously set NCC options that have been saved in a file.

To end the NCC program, you can choose the Quit option from the menu bar or press Esc.

Setting Cursor Size

The initial screen for setting cursor size is visible on the right side of the screen in figure 6.1. Notice the two lines at the bottom of the rectangle and the squares labeled `Start: 6` and `End: 7`. For this particular video mode, the cursor consists of Lines 6 and 7. (In higher resolution modes, you may have as many as 14 cursor lines.) This combination of Lines 6 and 7 creates a cursor that looks like a small underline—the normal setting for most computers. For some computers in which the cursor may be hard to find—as on some laptops with hard-to-read displays—you may want to create a bigger cursor.

The possible cursor lines range from 1 to 7. If you want the cursor to be bigger, press the up-arrow key to add more lines to the cursor. Figure 6.2 shows a selection that makes the cursor appear as a square rather than an underline. (Normally, the cursor, as you have sized it, appears in the square in the upper right corner of the screen, but this is not shown in figures 6.1 and 6.2.)

After you size your cursor, press Enter to select OK and return to the NCC menu, where you can change another setting or press Esc to end the NCC command.

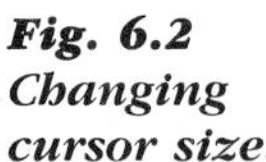

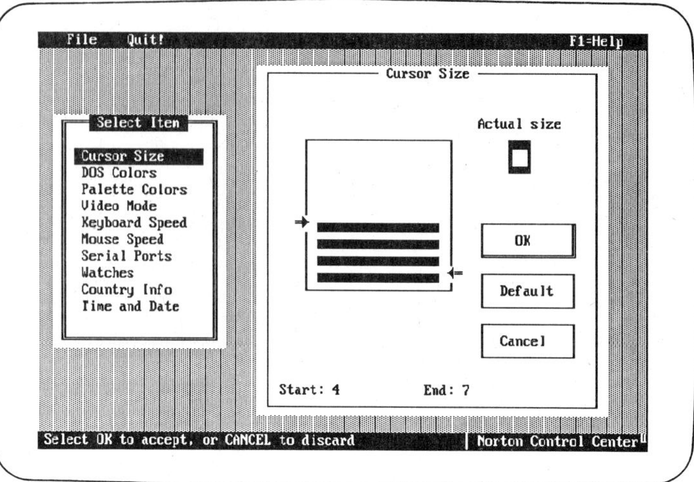

Fig. 6.2
Changing cursor size.

Setting Monitor Colors

With the DOS Colors option, you can choose color settings for your computer. These settings depend on the kind of monitor you have. Some computers support only a few colors, and others support hundreds. If you are tired of the black and white you normally see when using DOS, you can use DOS Colors to choose colors that better fit your mood or decor.

After you choose DOS Colors, a screen similar to figure 6.3 appears. You have three settings: Text Color, Background, and Border Color. You can move between these settings by using the arrow keys. The Text Color box contains examples of how text will appear with a variety of colors. The list contains white on black, for example, yellow on black, white on blue, red on blue, and dozens of other color combinations. To choose a color combination, scroll through this list. Arrows on the right and left point to the color currently chosen. The text at the right bottom of the DOS Colors box that begins `this is an example` shows what text on-screen will look like with the currently chosen option. The Background box contains two options: Blinking and Bright.

After you choose the color options you want, choose OK at the bottom of the box to return to the Select Item menu. If you want to revert to the default colors, choose Default. If you want to revert to the previously set colors and return to the Select Item menu, choose Cancel.

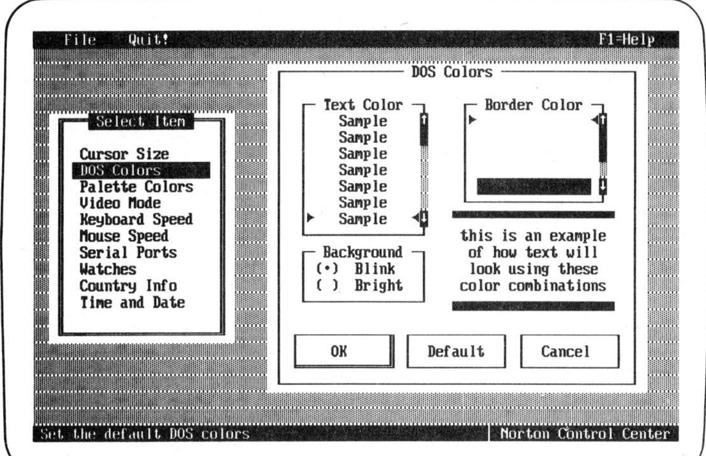

Fig. 6.3
Changing the DOS color settings.

Setting Palette Colors

Notice that the NCC menu has another color option—Palette Colors. This option is available for EGA and VGA monitors only. In the DOS colors option, you can use only 16 colors at a time even if your monitor can display more colors. You use the Palette option to choose which 16 colors you want to use. If your monitor supports more than 16 colors, you can use the Palette Colors option to select alternative colors to be used as the 16 DOS colors. You can change the normal DOS blue to a lighter shade of blue, for example. On some computers, you have as many as 256 possible colors that you can use as your 16 DOS colors.

After you choose the Palette Colors option, a screen similar to figure 6.4 appears. This is a list of 16 colors plus black. Although you cannot see the actual colors in this black and white figure, you can see the names of the colors to the left of the black box. To choose an alternate color for one of these original DOS colors, point to the original DOS color you want to change and choose the Change option from the four options at the bottom of the Palette Colors screen. To choose Change, press Tab or the right-arrow key to move your cursor to the Change box and press Enter, or point to Change with your mouse pointer and click. This brings up another color menu that lists many alternate colors. You can scroll through this list to find a new color, and press Enter to choose it as the replacement for the original DOS color you chose to change. Then you will be back to the screen in figure 6.4. If you chose a blue-green to replace DOS's original blue, therefore, DOS will display a blue-green color where it would usually display blue on-screen.

If you want the colors to all revert back to the normal DOS colors, choose Default from the Palette Colors screen. After you select the colors you want, choose OK. If you want to cancel this option and revert to the colors as they were when you began NCC, choose Cancel.

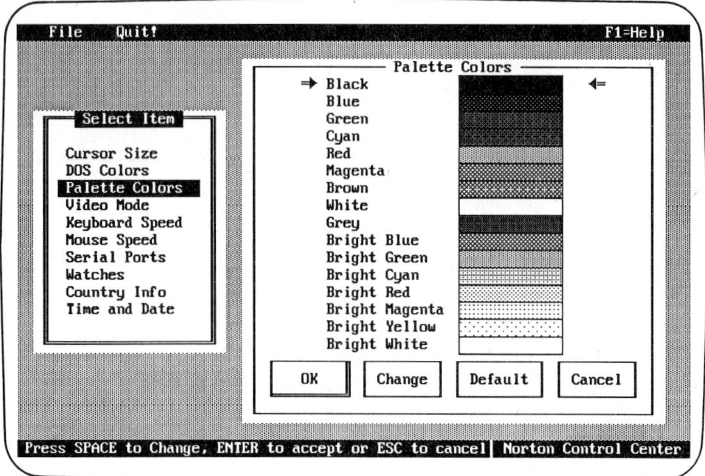

Fig. 6.4
The Palette Colors menu screen.

Setting the Video Mode

Although the normal DOS monitor displays 25 lines per screen, some monitors, EGA and VGA in particular, can display more. Using the Video Mode option from the NCC menu, you can choose a new video display for your computer (see fig. 6.5). Note that the available options on the Video Mode menu include 25-line color, 40-line color, and 50-line color. A filled radio button appears beside the current video setting. You also can choose black and white or color mode from this screen. Use the up- or down-arrow key to point to the option you want and press the space bar to lock it in. Then, press Enter to exit this option, or point to OK with your mouse and click. Select Cancel to cause the video mode to revert to its previous state.

Setting Keyboard Speeds

The IBM PC keyboard has several settings that you can change with the NCC command to suit your tastes. If you are a speed typist, for example, you may want to make the keyboard more responsive. If you select the Keyboard Speed option from the NCC main menu, you see a screen simi-

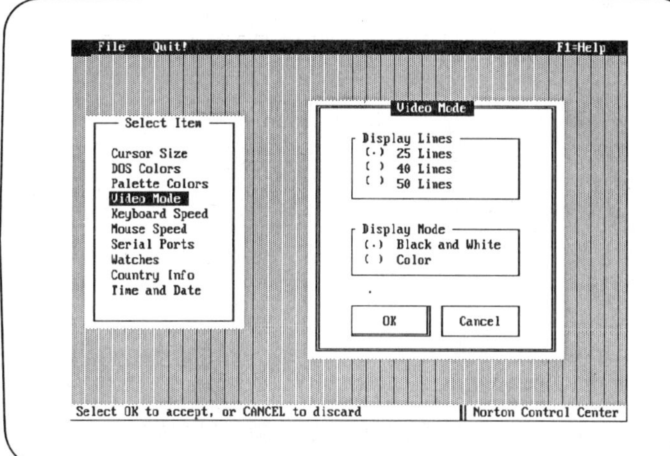

Fig. 6.5
Choosing a video mode.

lar to figure 6.6. (The Keyboard Speed option is not available on some early versions of the PC.) If your computer will not support a change in keyboard speeds, Norton displays a message that this option will not work on your computer.

The Keyboard Speed screen has two areas to set keyboard options. You use the top area to set the keyboard rate, and you use the bottom area to set the delay before auto repeat. *Keyboard rate* refers to how quickly a letter repeats when you hold down that letter's key, and *delay before auto repeat* refers to the amount of pause after you press a key and before it begins repeating. To set each of these parameters, you use the arrow keys to move the bar to the corresponding graphic control pictured on-screen. Move between the two settings by using the up- and down-arrow keys. Set the rates with the right- and left-arrow keys. Alternatively, point to a slide graph with your mouse pointer and, pressing the button, drag the setting to the desired spot. To choose quickly the Fast settings for the keyboard speed and repeat, you can select the Fast button at the bottom of the Keyboard Speed screen.

The normal delay rate before repeating is .500 second. You can change this to a minimum of .250 second or a maximum or 1.00 second. The normal repeat speed is 10.9 characters per second (cps). You can change this to a minimum of 2 cps or to a maximum of 30 cps.

You can experiment with these settings and type information on the Keyboard Test Pad to see how your new settings affect the keyboard rate. Press and hold down the A key, for example, and notice two things: how

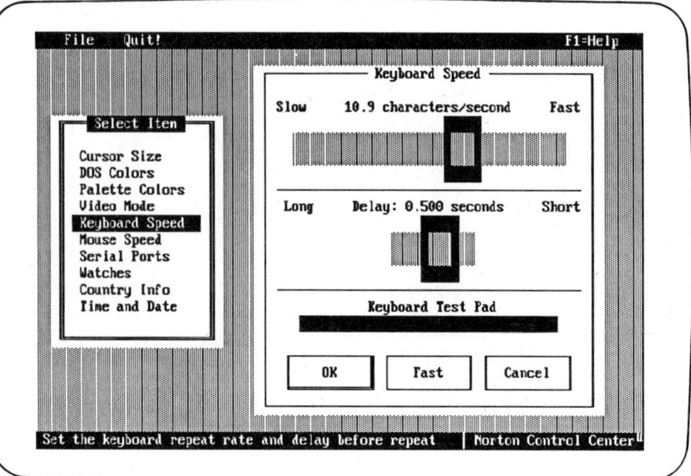

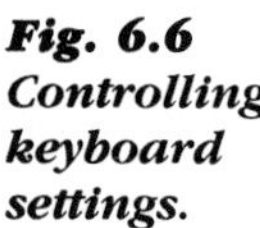
Fig. 6.6 Controlling keyboard settings.

much delay occurs before the letter starts repeating, and how fast the letter repeats. When you are satisfied with your settings, choose OK to return to the Select Item menu. You can choose Cancel to revert to the previous speed settings.

Setting Your Mouse Speed

If you are using a mouse, you may want to adjust the sensitivity of the mouse. That is, how the movement of the mouse corresponds to the movement of the mouse pointer on-screen. A slow sensitivity means that you must move the mouse more to see a movement on-screen. Fast sensitivity means that a small movement of the mouse on your mouse pad will be big on-screen. If you select the Mouse Speed option from the Select Item box, you see a screen like the one in figure 6.7. The default sensitivity setting is 50, and you may set it from 0 to 100. Set the sensitivity by using the right- and left-arrow keys. Alternatively, point to the setting with your mouse pointer, press and hold the button, and drag the setting to the desired spot.

Choosing Settings for Your Serial Ports

With NCC, you can choose the settings for your serial ports. You need to do so if you have a printer or other device working through your serial port that requires such settings. A printer (or modem, plotter, and so on) attached to a serial port, for example, may require a setting of 2400 baud,

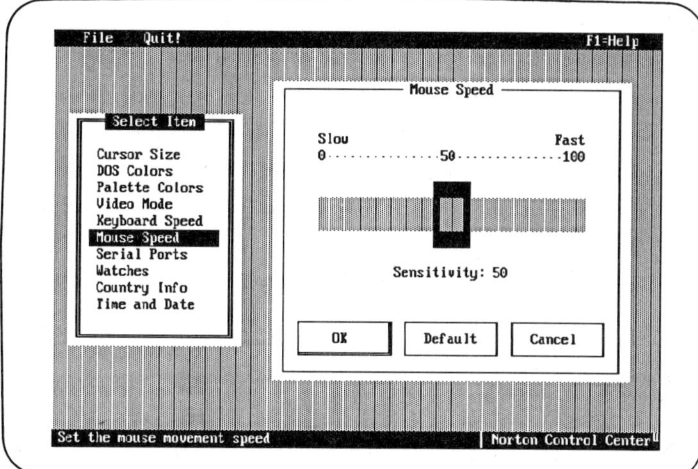

Fig. 6.7
Setting mouse speed.

no parity, 8 data bits, and 1 stop bit. Usually, if you need to choose serial settings for communications to a peripheral device (such as a printer) or to another computer, these settings are specified in your peripheral device's documentation or by the computer to which you will be connecting.

If you choose Serial Ports from the NCC main menu, the Serial Ports screen appears (see fig. 6.8). On this screen, you can set the baud setting, parity, data bits, and stop bits for up to four COM (serial) ports.

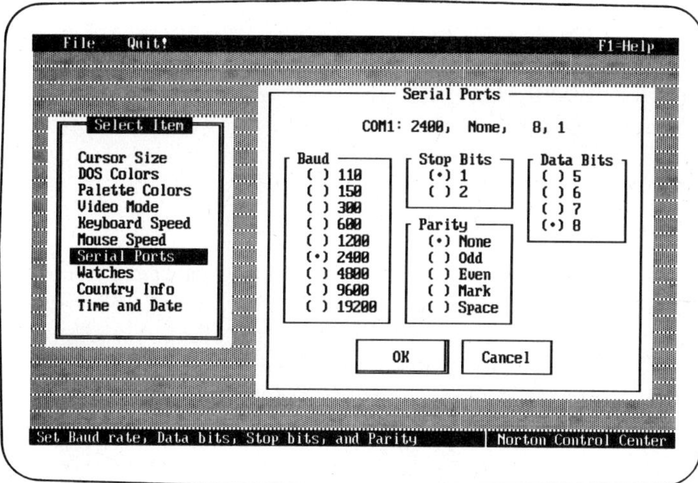

Fig. 6.8
Selecting settings for serial ports.

These settings on the Serial Ports screen define how data communications take place through the serial ports:

- *Baud*: Defines the speed of the communications. Common baud settings are 110, 150, 300, 600, 1200, 2400, 4800, 9600, and 19200. The higher the baud setting, the faster the communication.
- *Parity*: Defines the type of error-checking protocol to be used: None, Odd, Even, Mark, and Space. The most common setting is None.
- *Data Bits*: Defines how many bits of information are included in each communication pulse. This number is 5, 6, 7, or 8.
- *Stop Bits*: Defines how many stop-bit signals are sent with each pulse of information. Stop bits are usually set at 1 or 2.

Use the arrow keys to point to the settings you want and press the space bar to lock in a setting in each option box. Alternatively, point to the desired setting with your mouse and click to select it. Choose OK to lock in all selections, or choose Cancel to revert back to the previous settings.

Setting and Observing Stopwatches

Norton Utilities provides four stopwatches to enable you to time certain events. You can use the Watches option on the NCC menu, to observe and reset these clocks. When you use the NCC command with the /START or /STOP options, the elapsed times appear on-screen. The results of a /START or /STOP may scroll off screen, however, and if so, you can view the time by using the NCC Watches option. You also can use the Watches option to reset the clocks before timing something (see fig. 6.9). You can choose which watch to use by selecting one of the four radio buttons. Then, you can reset the watch or start it by choosing Start or Reset at the bottom of the screen. Choose OK to return to the Select Item menu.

Setting Country Info

Because PC computers are used in a number of countries, there needs to be a way to specify how certain items are formatted so that they match the generally used standard of a country. In the United States, for example, dates are usually written in the MM-DD-YY format, but in Europe, dates are written in the DD-MM-YY format. Other formats that change from country to country are time, currency, lists, and numbers. The Country Info item enables you to set these items for your computer. If you are

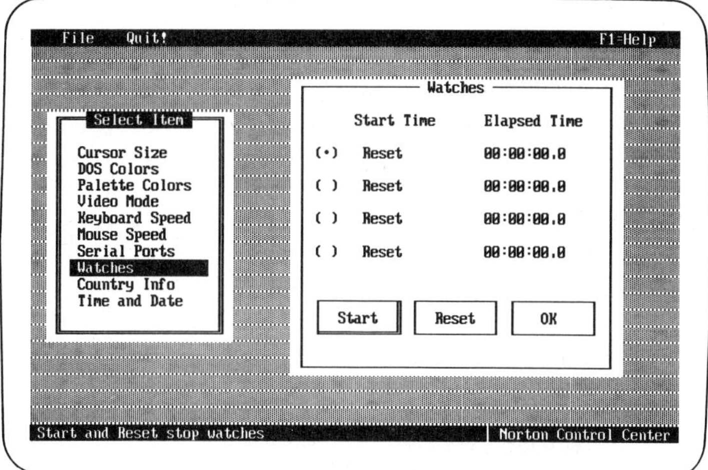

Fig. 6.9 The Norton Control Center Watches settings.

preparing a report to be sent to Europe, for example, you temporarily may change the Date format so that the report is understandable by Europeans.

For the Country Info option to work, you must have the COUNTRY.SYS driver in your CONFIG.SYS file. If the COUNTRY.SYS driver is not there, a screen appears, giving you your current settings, but you will not be able to make any changes. If you can make changes, you will see a screen like figure 6.10.

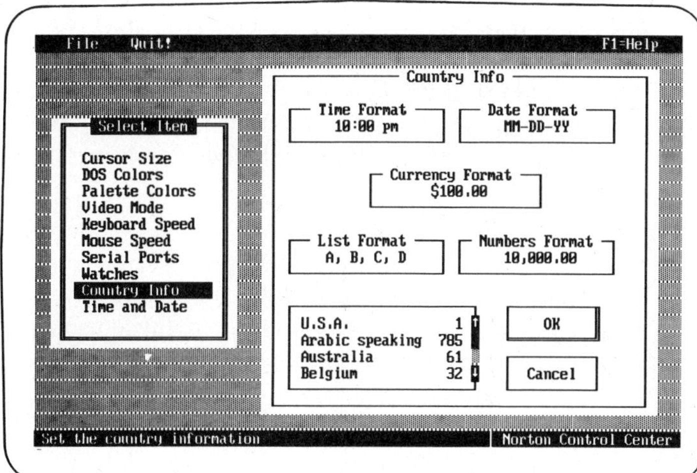

Fig. 6.10 The Norton Control Center Country Info settings.

If you want to be able to change your country settings, place a line like the following in your CONFIG.SYS file:

```
COUNTRY=001,850 C:\DOS\COUNTRY.SYS
```

The 001 specifies US and 850 is a selection for a character set. The other common character set used in the US is 437. See your DOS manual or *Using PC DOS* (Que, Chris DeVoney) for more information on country settings. Also, you need to enter the following command from the DOS prompt (or in AUTOEXEC.BAT):

```
NLSFUNC \DOS\COUNTRY.SYS
```

assuming that you have stored the COUNTRY.SYS driver in a directory named \DOS. After you include the proper COUNTRY.SYS driver in your CONFIG.SYS file, reboot, and enter the NLSFUNC command, you can change your country settings in NCC.

On the Country Info screen, you see a list box at the bottom left listing a number of countries, including U.S.A., Arabic Speaking, Australia, and so on. If you choose a country from this list, the country info information changes to match that country's normal usage. After selecting a country, choose OK to lock in the formats. Choose Cancel to revert back to the original setting.

Setting Time and Date

If your clock battery fails, your date and time settings for your machine will not be correct. On some computers, particularly the AT, you have to use the diagnostics disk to reset the date and time so that the computer remembers the settings. The NCC Time and Date option enables you to set these parameters without booting up with the diagnostics disk (see fig. 6.11). You can use the Time and Date option to set the date and time for a number of DOS computers, but some computers may not respond to your setting. You just have to experiment to see whether this NCC option works for your computer.

To set the date or time, use the arrow keys to point to the number that you want to change in the Date or Time box. Then use the plus (+) or minus (−) key to change the number up or down. (Alternatively, you simply can enter the numbers.) Choose OK to lock in the change, or choose Cancel to return the date and time to their previous settings.

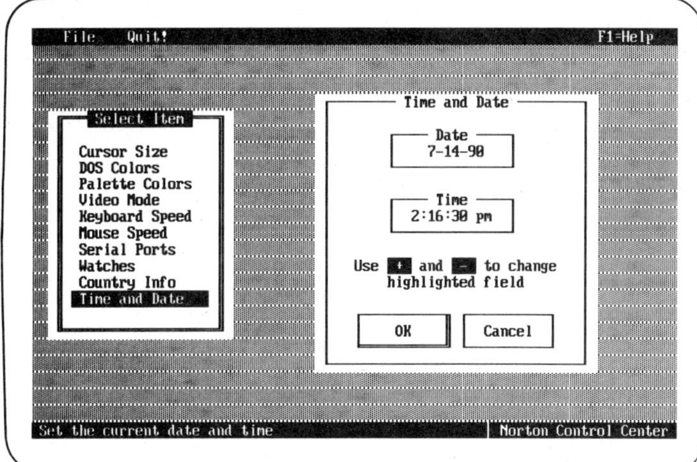

Fig. 6.11 *The Norton Control time and date settings.*

Saving NCC Settings to Disk

After you make your selections from the NCC menu, you can save your new settings to a file. If you press F10 from the NCC menu, the File pull-down menu appears. Choose the Save Settings option. When prompted for the name of a file, type a file name and press Enter. The settings you changed in NCC are saved to that file.

After you save the information to a file, you can use command-line switches to reset NCC to the settings you have saved. Suppose that you chose certain colors, as well as several other settings, that you want to use all the time. You saved this information to a file named SETTINGS.NCC. You can place the NCC command in your AUTOEXEC.BAT file with the /SETALL switch, using the following command:

```
NCC \NORTON\SETTINGS.NCC /SETALL
```

This command reactivates all of the settings (color choices, cursor size, and so on) that you saved in NCC.

In this case, the SETTINGS.NCC file was in the \NORTON directory, so the path name was necessary. Otherwise, the file would be activated from the root (\) directory. If you do not want to include the command in your AUTOEXEC.BAT file, you can enter the same NCC command from the DOS prompt. Additional command-line options are described in the next section.

Using NCC in Command-Line Mode

A number of settings that you can choose interactively in Norton Command Center also can be set from the DOS prompt by using NCC command-line options. The syntax for the NCC command in command-line mode is

NCC [*filespec*][*switches*]

or

NCC [*quick switches*]

The *filespec* in the first version of the command refers to a file that contains system information specifications. Before you use this version of the command, you must create this file by using NCC in interactive mode to choose the settings you want and then save the information to a file. (See the preceding section, "Saving NCC Settings to Disk.")

The available switches for the first version of the NCC command follow:

Switch	*Effect*
/SETALL	Tells NCC to read the information in the file named by *filespec* and to set all the parameters.
/CURSOR	Tells NCC to read the information in the file named by *filespec* but to set only the cursor size.
/KEYRATE	Tells NCC to read the information in the file named by *filespec* but to set only the keyboard rates.
/PALETTE	Tells NCC to read the information in the file named by *filespec* but to set only the palette colors.
/COM*n*	Tells NCC to read the information in the file named by *filespec* but to set only the information for serial port (COM port) specified by *n* (*n* = 1, 2, and so on).
/DOSCOLOR	Tells NCC to read the information in the file named by *filespec* but to set only the previously chosen DOS colors for foreground, background, and border.
/DISPLAY	Tells NCC to read the information in the file named by *filespec* but to set only the display.

If you have not created a settings file by running the NCC command in interactive mode, you can use the second version of the NCC command. With this version, you can set a few options by using certain Quick switches, which include the following:

Switch	*Effect*
/BW80	Places the monitor in black-and-white mode with 25 lines and 80 columns.
/CO80	Places the monitor in color mode with 25 lines and 80 columns.
/25	Places the monitor in 25-line mode (same as /CO80).
/35	Places the monitor in 35-line mode. This option is supported by EGA monitors only.
/40	Places the monitor in 40-line mode. This option is supported by VGA monitors only.
/43	Places the monitor in 43-line mode. This option is supported by EGA monitors only.
/50	Places the monitor in 50-line mode. This option is supported by VGA monitors only.
/FASTKEY	Sets the keyboard rate at its fastest possible value.

To set your VGA computer so that 50 lines are displayed on-screen and so that the keyboard rate is the fastest value, for example, use this command:

```
NCC /50/FASTKEY
```

You also can set system stop watches by using the following switches in NCC:

Switch	*Effect*
/START:*n*	Tells NCC to begin the stopwatch number *n*, where *n* can be from 1 to 4.
/STOP:*n*	Tells NCC to stop the stopwatch number *n*, where *n* can be from 1 to 4.
/N	Tells NCC not to display the current time and date.
/L	Tells NCC to display the time and date on the left side of the monitor.
/LOG	Tells NCC to format the output of the command so that it can be printed in report form.
/C:*comment*	Tells NCC to display the text string *comment* when the command is executed. This is useful for documenting what timer is being reported. If the comment contains any blanks, the entire comment must be surrounded with quotes.

Changing, Making, and Removing Directories Using Norton Change Directory

You use the NCC command to manage the hardware settings on your computer; you use the Norton Change Directory (NCD) command to manage your software—the files on disk. With NCD, you can manage efficiently your directories on disk, and you can navigate easily between the directories. NCD really is two commands in one. When used in a command-line mode, the command is a substitute for the DOS CD, MD, and RD commands, which you use to change, make, and remove directories. When used in interactive mode, NCD is a directory-management tool. NCD is one of the most useful commands from Norton Utilities.

Using NCD in Interactive Mode

If you enter the NCD command with no parameters, you are placed in interactive mode, and a graphic representation of your directory structure appears on-screen (see fig. 6.12). The disk in this figure has four levels of directories. You can see that directory ONE-A has a subdirectory called TWO-A that has a subdirectory called THREE-A that has a subdirectory called FOUR-A. ONE-B has a subdirectory named TWO-B, and directory ONE-C has no subdirectories.

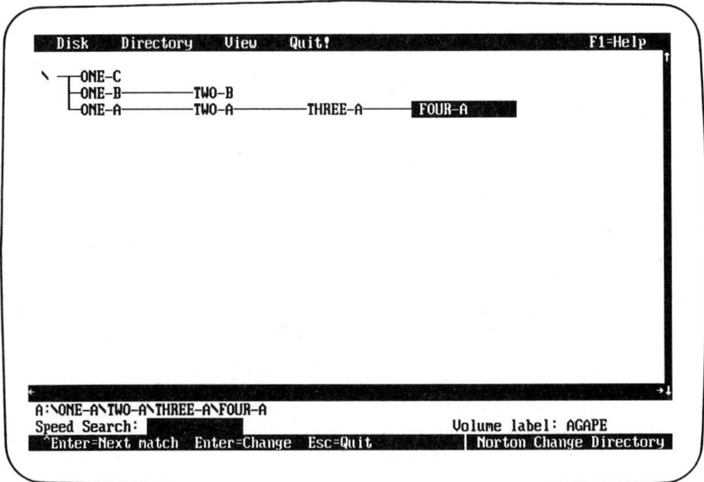

Fig. 6.12 Using Norton Change Directory in interactive mode.

To move to any directory on disk, use the arrow keys to highlight the directory you want and then press Enter. You exit from the NCD command, and end up in the directory you chose at the DOS prompt.

You can do much more than just change directories on this screen. Notice the menu bar at the top of the screen with the menu options Disk, Directory, View, and Quit. Press F10 to open the menu bar, or point to one of the options with your mouse pointer and click.

The Disk menu contains the following options:

- *Change Disk...F3:* Enables you to select from a list the disk for which you want to display the directory tree.
- *Rescan Disk...F2:* Tells NCD to update its file TREEINFO.NCD that contains the names of all of the directories. If you have added or removed a directory without using the NCD command, you need to select this option to make sure that the directory tree on-screen is accurate.
- *Volume Label...Alt-V:* Enables you to change the volume label on the disk or to add a volume label if there is not one present. This function replaces the old VL command in Norton 4.5.

Notice that each of these items has a command key associated with it. You can access the Change Disk option by pressing F3, for example, even if the Disk menu is not pulled down.

The Directory menu contains the following options:

- *Print Tree...Alt-P:* Enables you to print a copy of the directory tree to the printer. If your directory tree is too big to fit on-screen, this is a good way to get a copy where you can see the whole tree at once.
- *Rename...F6:* Renames a directory. Highlight the directory you want to rename, press F6, or choose the Rename option. Then type the new name and press Enter. Remember that you cannot rename a directory in DOS, so this feature is particularly useful. In fact, if you have had to recover from the DOS RECOVER command or if you have unformatted a disk without the use of the IMAGE.DAT file, all directories named in the root directory are changed into obscure machine-generated names. The only way to retrieve the original names is to rename the directories with the NCD Rename feature.
- *Make...F7:* Enables you to make a new directory. Highlight the directory to which you want to add a subdirectory and press F7 or choose the Make option. A new directory then appears on the graph. Enter a name for the new directory and press Enter.

- *Delete...F8:* Removes a directory. Highlight the directory (it must not contain any files or subdirectories) and press F8 (Delete).

The View menu contains the following items:

- 25 lines
- 40 lines
- 50 lines

A check mark appears at the front of the selection that is being used currently (usually 25 lines). When directories become large, they may not fit entirely on the Norton Change Directory screen. The View menu enables you to choose to display more lines on-screen, if your monitor type supports it. With an EGA screen, you can display 40 lines. With a VGA screen, you can display 50 lines on-screen.

You can quit NCD by choosing Quit or pressing Esc.

Using NCD in Command-Line Mode

In command-line mode, you enter the NCD command at the DOS prompt and include options to define what you want to do. The syntax for the Norton Change Directory (NCD) command is

NCD [*dirname*] [*switches*]

or

NCD MD [*dirname*][*switches*]

or

NCD RD [*dirname*][*switches*]

The *dirname* is the name of the directory you want to change to, make, or remove. The *switches* associated with the NCD command include /R and /N. The /R switch updates the file TREEINFO.NCD, which contains information about your directory tree structure. The /N switch instructs the NCD command *not* to write the file TREEINFO.NCD. If you are using NCD on a write-protected disk, you need to use the /N switch.

To change directories by using the NCD command, you enter NCD plus the name of the directory to which you want to change. Suppose that you want to change to a directory on disk named \ONE-A\TWO-A\THREE-A\FOUR-A. Using the DOS CD command, you would have to enter the entire path name to go to that directory:

CD \ONE-A\TWO-A\THREE-A\FOUR-A

Using the NCD command, you enter only the name of the destination directory, as in

```
NCD FOUR-A
```

In fact, you need to enter only enough characters in the name to make it unique, so you could enter the command

```
NCD FOUR
```

or maybe even

```
NCD F
```

If you had more than one directory beginning with the letter F, the NCD command would switch to the first directory beginning with that letter. If you enter the command again (press F3 and Enter), NCD switches to the next directory beginning with the letter F. As you are naming your directories, you may want to choose unique names to make the NCD command that much faster to use. The more complicated your directory structure, the easier changing directories becomes with the NCD command.

You also can use the NCD command rather than the DOS MD and RD commands to make and remove directories. To make a directory, such as \FIRST\SECOND, enter the command

```
NCD MD \FIRST\SECOND
```

To delete that directory, enter

```
NCD RD \FIRST\SECOND
```

You may be tempted to pass up the NCD command for MD and RD, but a good reason exists for using NCD instead. The first time you run the NCD command, Norton analyzes your entire directory structure and stores it in a file (TREEINFO.NCD) for quick access. If you use the DOS versions of RD and MD, the Norton file is not updated. If you use the NCD versions of MD and RD, the Norton file is updated, and changing directories continues to be quick and easy.

If you accidentally use the RD or MD command, you can update the Norton file TREEINFO.NCD by using the /R switch with the NCD command.

Creating Batch Files Using Batch Enhancer

The Norton Batch Enhancer (BE) is a powerful set of commands in its own right. Batch Enhancer gives you more flexibility in creating batch files.

Batch files normally consist of a number of DOS commands listed one after another. When a batch file is executed, DOS acts on these DOS commands. The DOS language, however, has a few holes when it comes to creating useful batch files. You may want to prompt for input in a batch file and branch according to the user's response, for example. Also, being able to set colors, draw windows or boxes, and print text anywhere on-screen from a batch file would be helpful. Norton's Batch Enhancer fulfills these needs.

The syntax for the Batch Enhancer command is

BE *subcommand*

or

BE *filespec*

The available *subcommands* for BE are ASK, BEEP, BOX, PRINTCHAR, ROWCOL, WINDOW, and SA.

You can use the BE command at the DOS prompt, but it generally is used in a batch file. For example, the following command produces a standard system beep:

BE BEEP

In a batch file, you may want to include this command at the end to signal when a process is finished.

Each BE subcommand has its own parameters, which are described in the following sections.

Using the Ask Subcommand

The Ask subcommand enables you to capture a user's response and to act on it. You can use the Ask command to create menus. If you use the Ask command in your AUTOEXEC.BAT file, you can control the way your computer is booted—for example, sometimes you may want to load memory-resident programs like Sidekick at boot time, and sometimes you may not.

The syntax of the Ask subcommand is

BE ASK *prompt*[,*keys*][DEFAULT=*key*]
[TIMEOUT=*n*][ADJUST=*n*][*color*]

The *prompt* is a text string that you want to display on-screen. (You need to enclose it in double quotation marks.) The cursor is placed after the prompt to anticipate a single-character user response.

A simple example of the BE ASK command follows. Suppose you want your AUTOEXEC.BAT file to give you the option of booting with no memory-resident programs. You would want it to ask the question:

```
Skip memory resident programs (Y/N)
```

If you press Y, you want it to skip loading memory-resident programs. If you press N, you want it to go ahead and load those programs. You would use the ASK command

BE ASK "Skip memory resident programs (Y/N)", YN

Notice that the expected responses are listed as the keys Y and N (YN). The next few lines tell what to do when one of the choices is made. This is done with the DOS IF ERRORLEVEL commands. For example,

IF ERRORLEVEL 2 GOTO DOMEMORY
IF ERRORLEVEL 1 GOTO SKIP

If you press N, an ERRORLEVEL code 2 is generated and these commands send the flow of the batch file to a label named DOMEMORY. If you press Y, an ERRORLEVEL code 1 is generated and the flow if the batch file is sent to a label named SKIP. If you press any key, the computer beeps and the Ask command continues to wait for a Y or an N. A listing of how the complete batch file may look using the ASK command follows:

```
ECHO OFF
CLS
BE ASK "Skip memory resident programs (Y/N)",YN
IF ERRORLEVEL 2 GOTO DOMEMORY
IF ERRORLEVEL 1 GOTO SKIP
:DOMEMORY
REM place commands for memory resident programs here
:SKIP
REM place the rest of the AUTOEXEC.BAT commands here
```

The REM lines are remarks about where to place the commands that load memory-resident programs and where to place other AUTOEXEC.BAT commands.

Using the Ask subcommand's DEFAULT=*key* parameter, you can specify what Enter means. DEFAULT=Y, for example, would mean that the user pressing Enter is the same as choosing Yes.

Using the TIMEOUT=*n* parameter, you can specify how long the Ask command waits for an answer before taking the DEFAULT answer. *n* is the number of seconds to wait.

If menus get big, you may want to adjust the answer. You may have a two-layer menu, for example, with the first layer having 10 options. When BE returns an errorlevel in the second layer, you may want to adjust the errorlevel by 10 so that it matches your IF...GOTO statements.

The ADJUST= option is used when you have multilayered menus. That is, one menu calls another menu. When this happens, your second menu would return to an ERRORLEVEL number of 1, 2, 3, and so on—but this number could get confused with the ERRORLEVEL number set by the first menu. ADJUST= enables you to make the ERRORLEVEL numbers higher so that they will not conflict with some used already. If your first menu has four options, for example, it could end up with an ERRORLEVEL value of 1 to 4. Then, on a subsequent menu, you would include an ADJUST=4 command to make your next menu begin with ERRORLEVEL values of 5, 6, and so on. You then would use the resulting ERRORLEVEL number to branch to the proper location in the batch file.

You also can set colors in the ASK statement. The color options are described in "Using the Screen Attributes (SA) Subcommand," later in this chapter. For example, including WHITE ON BLUE in the BE ASK command line causes the prompt to appear as white letters on a blue background. The color selection will be in effect only for the Ask prompt.

Using the Beep Subcommand

The Beep subcommand produces a tone or series of tones. This command can come in handy if you are creating a batch file that performs a lengthy operation. You can use Beep to tell you audibly that the batch file is finished or is at a certain stage of the process.

The syntax for this subcommand is

BE BEEP [*switches*]

or

BE BEEP [*filespec*][/E]

If you include a *filespec*, the file specified should contain a list of tones to play. When used with a file specification, the /E switch instructs the BE BEEP command to echo the text in the file to the screen.

If you do not include a *filespec*, you specify the tones to play by using *switches*. The switches available for the BE BEEP command are listed in table 6.1.

Table 6.1
Switches for the BE BEEP Command

Switch	*Description*
/D*n*	Specifies the duration of a tone in measurements of 1/18th of a second. Thus, D3 specifies that the tone be sounded for 3/18th of a second.
/F*n*	Specifies the frequency of a tone, where *n* is cycles per second (Hertz). The switch /F440, for example, plays a tone at 440 cycles per second. The larger the value of *n*, the higher pitched the tone.
/R*n*	Specifies that the tone be repeated *n* times.
/W*n*	Specifies a wait in durations of 1/18th of a second. The switch /W3, for example, causes a wait of 3/18th of a second. You usually use this as a wait between beeps.

The following command plays a tone at 440 cycles per second for one second (18/18), waits half a second (9/18), and then plays the tone again:

```
BE BEEP /F440 /D18 /R2 /W9
```

Using the Box Subcommand

The Box subcommand enables you to draw rectangular boxes on-screen. Boxes are helpful for emphasizing on-screen messages and for creating menus.

The syntax for the Box subcommand is

BE BOX *top,left,bottom,right*[SINGLE|DOUBLE][*color*]

The *top* and *left* parameters specify the row number and column number, respectively, of the upper left corner of the box. Likewise, the *bottom* and *right* parameters specify the row number and column number of the lower right corner of the box.

The SINGLE or DOUBLE parameter specifies whether the edges of the box should have a single or double line. The *color* specifies color choices, (see "Using the Screen Attributes (SA) Subcommand," later in this chapter).

An example of using the Box subcommand is

```
BE BOX 2,10,10,70 SINGLE
```

This command draws a single-line box beginning at the 2nd row, 10th column and extending to the 10th row and 70th column of the screen.

Using the Delay Subcommand

The Delay subcommand enables you to cause a batch file to suspend operation for a period of time. Suppose your batch file is displaying information on-screen. You may want to build in a delay so that the information can be read before some other information is printed on-screen. The syntax for the Delay subcommand is

BE DELAY [*time*]

where time is measured in 1/18 of a second. Thus, the command

BE DELAY 18

causes a one-second delay.

Using the Print Character Subcommand

The Print Character subcommand enables you to print a character a specified number of times. The Print Character command can come in handy if you are drawing images on-screen—perhaps highlighting a message, making a menu look fancy, and so on.

The syntax of the Print Character subcommand is

BE PRINTCHAR *character,repeats* [*color*]

The *character* can be any ASCII character. You can specify a number of *repeats* up to 80. The *color* parameter is described in the section on the Screen Attributes (SA) subcommand.

Tip: In the BE PRINTCHAR command, you can use characters from the extended IBM character list—ASCII characters from 128 to 255—if your program can access them. (Some editors, such as WordStar, may not be able to access the IBM extended characters.) To use the Greek letter beta (β) in the BE PRINTCHAR command, for example, hold down the Alt key, type the ASCII code 225 on the numeric keypad, and release the Alt key. (The ASCII codes for the extended character set are listed in the back of most DOS or BASIC manuals.) The letter β should appear on-screen. To print the character 20 times, you would enter the command

BE PRINTCHAR β,20

Using the Row Column Subcommand

The Row Column subcommand is used to place the cursor somewhere on-screen before you write a message to the screen. Using the Row Column command, you can place information anywhere on-screen and be creative in designing menus or messages.

The syntax for the Row Column subcommand is

BE ROWCOL *row,col*[,*text*][*color*]

The *row* parameter represents the number of the on-screen row where you want the cursor to appear—normally 1 to 25. The *col* is the number of the column on-screen, normally 1 to 80. The *text* is a message you want to display at the location specified. Enclose your message in double quotation marks. The *color* parameter is described in the next section.

Suppose that you are designing a menu screen and you want the text "ABC Company, Inc." to appear on the top line of the screen. You can use this command:

BE ROWCOL 1,33,"ABC Company, Inc."

The 1 specifies the top line of the screen and the 33 specifies that the message will begin in the 33rd column. This will center the message on-screen.

Using the Screen Attributes Subcommand

The Screen Attributes subcommand enables you to specify colors and other features of the screen. Using screen attributes, you can design your screen by highlighting text in different colors, boldness, and blinking. This feature can be useful in bringing attention to messages on-screen or making your menus look more colorful.

The syntax for the Screen Attributes subcommand is

BE SA *main-setting* [*switches*]

or

BE SA [*intensity*][*foreground*][ON *background*][*switches*]

The options for *main-setting* are Normal, Reverse, or Underline. Choices for *intensity* are Bright, Bold, or Blinking. Bright and Bold are identical. Choices for *foreground* or *background* colors are White, Black, Red, Magenta, Blue, Green, Cyan, or Yellow. The available *switches* follow:

Switch	*Effect*
/N	Instructs the Sceen Attributes subcommand not to set border color.
/CLS	Clears the screen after setting the screen attributes. This enables you to see the effects of the Screen Attributes command immediately on-screen.

The Screen Attributes subcommand is helpful not only as a command in Batch Enhancer but also directly from DOS. To set your monitor to a blue background with white letters, for example, use the command

```
BE SA WHITE ON BLUE
```

This setting sets the color for the entire screen. It is in effect until you change it with another command.

Using the Window Subcommand

The Window subcommand is similar to the Box subcommand. Like the Box subcommand, Window draws rectangular boxes. It also gives you the option to draw the rectangle with a shadow and to zoom the box onto the screen. You can use the Window command to create menus or to highlight messages on-screen.

The syntax for the Window subcommand is

BE WINDOW *top,left,bottom,right* [*color*] [SHADOW] [ZOOM]

The *top* and *left* parameters specify the row number and column number, respectively, of the upper left corner of the box. The *bottom* and *right* parameters specify the row number and column number of the lower right corner of the box.

The SHADOW parameter adds a shadow to the right and bottom edges of the window, which gives the window the effect of standing out on-screen. ZOOM makes the window appear to grow from a small rectangle to a rectangle that fits into the size indicated by the top, left, bottom, and right parameters. The *color* options are described in the preceding section.

For example, the command

```
BE WINDOW 2,10,10,70
```

creates a rectangle on-screen.

Creating Batch Files with DOS and Batch Enhancer Commands

By combining DOS batch commands and Norton Batch Enhancer commands, you can create batch files that are neat programs. Figure 6.13 shows a batch file that uses DOS batch commands and several Batch Enhancer commands to create a menu system for your computer. This file is named MENU.BAT.

```
echo off
:begin
cd\norton
be sa white on blue
cls
be window 2,10,12,65 white on red shadow zoom
be rowcol 3,30 "My Special Menu"
be rowcol 5,16 "Exit to DOS..........................D"
be rowcol 6,16 "Begin Norton Integrator..........N"
be rowcol 7,16 "Begin WORDPERFECT.........W"
be rowcol 8,16 "Begin EXCEL...................... E"
be rowcol 10,16
be ask "Choose an option letter: ",dnwe default=D
if errorlevel 4 goto excel
if errorlevel 3 goto word
if errorlevel 2 goto norton
if errorlevel 1 goto thatsall

:excel
cls
cd\excel
win386 excel
goto begin

:word
cls
cd\wp50
wp
goto begin

:norton
cls
cd\norton
ni
goto begin

:thatsall
be sa white on blue
cls
```

Fig. 6.13
The batch file MENU.BAT.

When you issue the MENU command from the DOS prompt, a screen like the one in figure 6.14 appears. As you can see in Lines 6 through 12 of the batch file in figure 6.13, the menu was made by first drawing a box with the WINDOW subcommand and then using the ROWCOL subcommand to give the menu a heading and to locate the items for the menu. The ASK command captures the user's response, which is evaluated by the IF ERRORLEVEL commands. Each menu choice points to a label in the batch file, which begins a program or exits to DOS. If you choose a program by pressing N, W, or E, the program associated with that selection begins. After the program returns to DOS, the batch file continues to operate and displays the menu again.

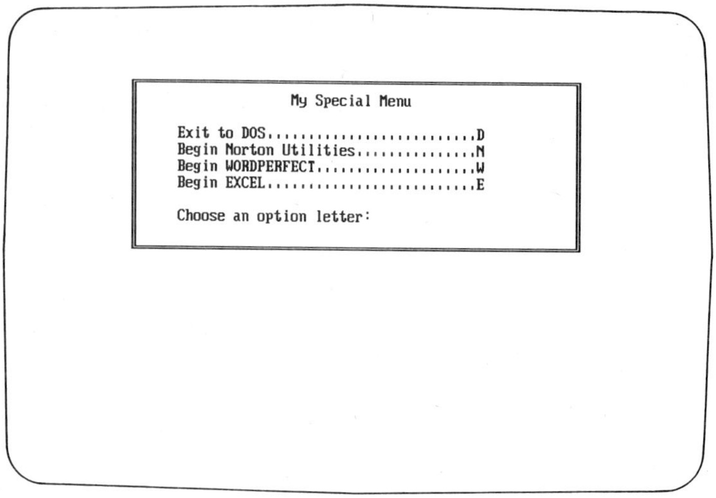

```
                  My Special Menu

Exit to DOS..........................D
Begin Norton Utilities...............N
Begin WORDPERFECT....................W
Begin EXCEL..........................E

Choose an option letter:
```

Fig. 6.14 The screen displayed by the batch file MENU.BAT.

Tip: Notice in figure 6.13 that the MENU.BAT program was created to run from the \NORTON directory. It runs fastest from this directory because the BE command is located in this directory and thus is loaded fastest. If you use a menu program like this one, be sure that you place it in the directory that contains the NORTON BE.EXE Batch Enhancer program. If you use the BE command in another directory, DOS will search the directories defined in your DOS path for the BE.EXE program. If the \NORTON directory is early in the path, the execution of the BE command will be faster than if the \NORTON directory is later in the path.

Summary

Norton Utilities contains a number of programs that can jazz up the workings of your computer. You can set colors, graphically manage your directories, find files and text anywhere on disk, place comments on files, time events, and much more. All users have their own ideas about what makes their computers work intuitively for them. With the programs described in this chapter, you have a number of tools to make your computer behave exactly as you want it to.

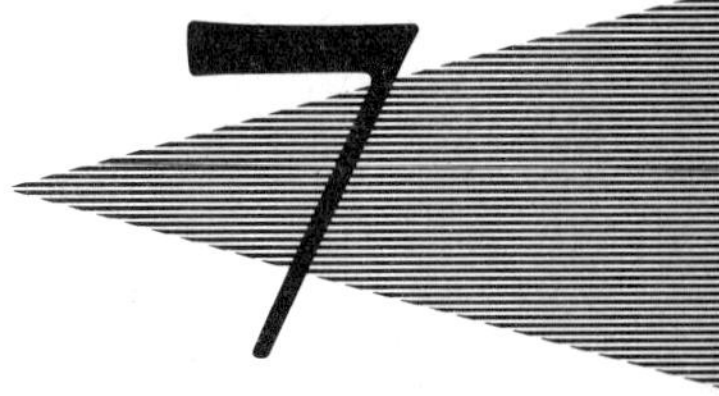

Using Norton Utilities Commands

This chapter lists alphabetically the commands in Norton Utilities Version 5.0; use this chapter as a handy reference when you want to learn about a command quickly. Commands from the previous version of Norton Advanced Utilities (4.5) also are listed, with references to the new Version 5.0 command that replaces the old command. Each brief command description refers you to the chapter in this book that contains a more complete description of the command.

Several options are used in many of the Norton Utilities 5.0 commands. In this book, the following conventions apply to those options:

- In the command syntax, items enclosed in [brackets] are optional.
- For words written in italic, substitute the appropriate word. For example, to use the DISKREET [*switches*] syntax, you may type DISKREET /ON or DISKREET /CLOSE.
- The [*d:*] option is a designation for the disk drive name, such as drive A, B, C, or D.
- The [*filespec*] option is a designation for a file specification. Unless noted, this specification can include a path name. For example, the file specification for a file named MYFILE.TXT in the \WP50 directory is \WP50\MYFILE.TXT. Usually, you can use the asterisk (*) and question mark (?) DOS global file characters (wild cards) in file specifications. For example, *.TXT specifies all files with the TXT extension.

- The [*color*] option refers to a selection of colors. A color designation could be White on Blue, for example. Using colors is described in Chapter 6.

Several global switches are available when you use a Norton command from the DOS prompt. You should place these switches on the command line after the command:

Switch	*Effect*
/G0	Tells Norton command that you have a EGA or VGA monitor. Produces a graphic mouse pointer if you are using a mouse and causes display boxes to use graphic symbols instead of character-based symbols (for example, uses round circles, or *radio buttons*, instead of check boxes).
/G1	Tells Norton command that you have an EGA or VGA monitor. Disables use of the graphic mouse pointer. Causes display boxes to use graphic symbols, as with /G0.
/BW	Tells Norton command that you are using a monochrome display so that it displays black-and-white instead of color screens.
/LCD	Tells Norton command that you are using an LCD (laptop computer) display so that the command will use colors that have been specifically chosen by Norton to appear best on this kind of display.
/NOZOOM	Tells Norton command not to use the zoom-style dialog box.

To use one of these switches, for example, you would type

```
DISKTOOL /G0
```

Batch Enhancer (BE)

Chapter 6

The Batch Enhancer (BE) command consists of a series of subcommands intended to supplement the DOS batch commands. The syntax for the Batch Enhancer command is

BE *subcommand*

or

BE *filespec*

If a list of subcommands is stored in a file, you use the second version of the BE command. You also can enter BE commands from the DOS prompt, as in the first version of the BE command. See Chapter 6, "Managing the Resources of Your Computer," for more information about BE and all its subcommands.

ASK

The BE subcommand ASK waits for a response from the user and stores the response in the DOS errorlevel variable. You usually need to use the DOS IF ERRORLEVEL GOTO LABEL command after ASK. The syntax is

BE ASK *prompt*[,*keys*][DEFAULT=*key*][TIMEOUT=*n*]
[ADJUST=*n*][*color*]

The following command displays the prompt `Enter Menu Choice:` and waits for your input:

BE ASK "Enter Menu Choice: ",ABCD,DEFAULT=D,TIMEOUT=60

When you press A, B, C, and so on, the BE ASK command sets the ERRORLEVEL code; the first key becomes ERRORLEVEL 1, the second key is ERRORLEVEL 2, and so on. If you do not press a key during the TIMEOUT period of 60 seconds, the DEFAULT option (D) is used.

BEEP

The BE subcommand BEEP creates a tone and uses this syntax:

BE BEEP [*switches*]

or

BE BEEP [*filespec*][/E]

The *switches* available for the BEEP subcommand include the following:

Switch	*Effect*
/D*n*	Specifies the duration of a tone in measurements of 1/18th of a second. Thus, /D3 specifies that the tone be sounded for 3/18th of a second.

/F*n*	Specifies the frequency of a tone, where *n* is cycles per second (Hertz). The switch /F440, for example, plays a tone at 440 cycles per second.
/R*n*	Specifies that the tone repeat *n* times.
/W*n*	Specifies a wait in durations of 1/18th of a second. The switch /W3, for example, causes a wait of 3/18th of a second.
/E	Instructs the BE BEEP command to echo the text in the file to the screen (when used with a filespec).

The following command creates a sound at a frequency of 440 Hertz, pauses for 10/18th of a second, and sounds the tone again:

```
BE BEEP /F440 /R2 /W10
```

BOX

The BE subcommand BOX draws a box on-screen. The syntax for the BOX subcommand is

BE BOX *top,left,bottom,right*[SINGLE|DOUBLE][*color*]

Descriptions of the BOX parameters follow:

Parameter	*Effect*
top	Specifies the row number of the upper left corner of the box
left	Specifies the column number of the upper left corner of the box
bottom	Specifies the row number of the lower right corner of the box
right	Specifies the column number of the lower right corner of the box
SINGLE	Produces a box with single lines (default)
DOUBLE	Produces a box with double lines

Remember: Items in uppercase are key words in the command—they appear in the command as written. The parameters in italics represent some number or option to be placed into the command. For example, *top*=3, *left*=2, and so on.

The following command draws a box on-screen with the upper left corner positioned two lines from the top of the screen and 10 columns from the left:

```
BE BOX 2,10,20,70 DOUBLE
```

The lower right corner of the box is 20 lines from the top of the screen and 70 columns from the left. The rectangle drawn uses double lines.

DELAY

The BE subcommand DELAY causes the batch file to delay for a specified length of time. The syntax of the DELAY subcommand is

BE DELAY [*time*]

where time is measured in 1/18 of a second, or in *ticks*. The command

```
BE DELAY 18
```

would delay for one second.

PRINTCHAR

The BE subcommand PRINTCHAR prints a character a specified number of times. The syntax of the PRINTCHAR subcommand is

BE PRINTCHAR *character,repeats* [*color*]

The *character* can be any ASCII character, and you can specify *repeats* up to 80.

The following command prints the asterisk (*) character 20 times on-screen, all in one line:

```
BE PRINTCHAR *,20
```

ROWCOL

The BE subcommand ROWCOL places the cursor at a designated location on-screen and optionally displays text at that location. The syntax for the ROWCOL subcommand is

BE ROWCOL *row,col*[,*text*][*color*]

The *row* parameter represents the number of the on-screen row where you want the cursor (and any specified text) to appear (usually 1 to 25), and *col* is the number of the on-screen column (usually 1 to 80). If you include a *text* parameter in the command, that text is written to the screen at the designated location. The *color* parameter specifies the color of the text on-screen—see "Screen Attributes (SA)."

The following command places the cursor 10 lines from the top of the screen and five columns from the left, and prints at that location the text specified within the quotes:

BE ROWCOL 10,5,"Make a selection using the cursor keys."

Screen Attributes (SA)

The BE subcommand SA sets color attributes for the screen. The syntax for the Screen Attributes (SA) subcommand is

BE SA *main-setting* [*switches*]

or

BE SA [*intensity*][*foreground*][ON *background*][*switches*]

The options for *main-setting* are Normal, Reverse, or Underline. Choices for *intensity* are Bright, Bold, or Blinking. Bright and Bold are identical. Choices for *foreground* and *background* colors are White, Black, Red, Magenta, Blue, Green, Cyan, and Yellow. The available switches follow:

Switch	*Effect*
/N	Instructs the SA subcommand not to set border color
/CLS	Clears the screen after setting the screen attributes

The following command causes on-screen characters to appear in bold white on a blue background. When this command is given, it also clears the screen.

BE SA BOLD WHITE ON BLUE/CLS

WINDOW

The BE subcommand WINDOW draws a window on-screen, with optional shadow and zoom features. The syntax for the WINDOW subcommand is

BE WINDOW *top,left,bottom,right* [*color*][SHADOW][ZOOM]

Descriptions of the WINDOW parameters follow:

Parameter	*Effect*
top	Specifies the row number of the upper left corner of the window
left	Specifies the column number of the upper left corner of the window
bottom	Specifies the row number of the lower right corner of the window
right	Specifies the column number of the lower right corner of the window
SHADOW	Adds a shadow to the right and bottom edges of the window
ZOOM	Zooms the window onto the screen—the window starts as a small rectangle and grows to full size

The following command draws a box on-screen with the upper left corner positioned two lines from the top of the screen and 10 columns from the left:

BE WINDOW 2,10,20,70 SHADOW ZOOM

The lower right corner of the box is 20 lines from the top of the screen and 70 columns from the left. The window zooms onto the screen and has a shadow.

Calibrate

Chapter 5

You use the Calibrate command to optimize the speed and reliability of reading and writing information to your hard disk. Calibrate is capable of performing a non-destructive, low-level format, which enables you to check your disk for reliability without destroying the information on disk.

You should make sure any memory-resident programs (TSRs) are *not* loaded and that only essential device drivers (in your CONFIG.SYS file) are in use when you use this command. The syntax of the Calibrate command is

CALIBRAT [*d:*] [*switches*]

The available switches for the Calibrate command follow:

Switch	*Effect*
/BATCH	Does not prompt for any input from the user. Returns to DOS when finished.
/NOSEEK	Skips the seek tests. Use this when you do not want Calibrate to test the head-positioning mechanism of the disk. Usually, you need to use Calibrate once without /NOSEEK to test the mechanism.
/NOFORMAT	Instructs Calibrate to perform pattern testing only and to skip the low-level format.
/PATTERN *n*	Tells Calibrate which testing level (*n*) to use. The parameter *n* can be 0, 5, 40, or 80. The higher the number, the more thorough the test; however, the higher the number, the longer Calibrate takes to test the disk.
/R:*file*	Tells Calibrate to generate a report and to write it to the file name specified in the switch. You must use the /BATCH switch also when you use /R:*file*.
/RA:*file*	Performs the same function as the /R:*file* switch, but the information is appended to the file rather than creating a new file.
/X:*drives*	Tells Calibrate to exclude named drives from the test. /X:DE would exclude disks D and E from testing, for example. If your computer has allocated non-existent drives, you must use this switch to exclude those drives from the tests.

Directory Sort (DS)

The Directory Sort (DS) command for Norton Utilities 4.5 has been incorporated into the Speed Disk (SPEEDISK) command for Version 5.0.

Disk Editor

Chapter 4

The Disk Editor is similar to the old Norton Utilities main program. The Disk Editor enables you to view and edit the entire contents of a diskette or hard disk. The Disk Editor is useful when you are not able to recover information by using Norton Disk Doctor II. You must have a good understanding of how disks work, however, to be able to use this program effectively. The syntax for the Disk Editor is

DISKEDIT [*d:*] [*path*] [*filename*] [*switches*]

The available switches for the DISKEDIT command follow:

Switch	*Effect*
/M	Tells DISKEDIT to operate in Maintenance mode. This enables the program to bypass DOS and look directly at the contents of a disk.
/X:[*d*][*d*]	Tells DISKEDIT to exclude certain drives from absolute sector processing. /X:DE would exclude disks D and E from testing, for example. If your computer has allocated non-existent drives, you must use this switch to exclude those drives from being available.

The Disk Editor is an interactive program that you operate from a menu.

Disk Information (DI)

The Disk Information command in Norton Utilities 4.5 has been integrated into the System Information command in Version 5.0.

Disk Monitor

Chapter 3

The Disk Monitor command helps you protect your information on disk from accidental or unauthorized destruction. Disk Monitor contains three main features: Disk Protect, Disk Light, and Disk Park. The Disk Protect feature prevents the unauthorized use of your files on disk without your approval. The Disk Light feature places a disk-access light on your monitor so that you can see when your disk is being used. The Disk Park feature moves the read/write head on you hard disk to a safe location for moving your computer. You should run Disk Monitor interactively the first time to choose the type of protection you want (files, system areas, entire disk, and floppy format). The Disk Monitor command creates the file DM.INI; then you can use this command from the DOS prompt. The syntax for using the Disk Monitor command from the DOS prompt is

```
DISKMON [switches]
```

The available switches for the DISKMON command follow:

Switch	*Effect*
/STATUS	Tells DISKMON to display a summary of the Disk Monitor status on-screen.
/PROTECT– or or /PROTECT+	Tells DISKMON to turn the protect feature on (+) or off (–). When this feature is turned on, protection is set to your selections that were stored in DM.INI when you selected those items from previously running the command interactively.
/LIGHT+ or or /LIGHT–	Tells DISKMON to turn the Disk Light feature on (+) or off (–).
/PARK	Tells DISKMON to park all drives.
/UNINSTALL	Uninstalls the DISKMON program from memory, if that program was the last TSR loaded into memory.

Disk Test (DT)

The Disk Test (DT) command for Norton Utilities 4.5 has been incorporated into the Norton Disk Doctor II command for Version 5.0.

Disk Tools

Chapter 4

Disk tools are a set of six utilities that contain data-protection and recovery features. These tools enable you to do the following:

- Make a disk bootable
- Recover from DOS's RECOVER command
- Revive a defective diskette
- Mark a cluster
- Create a rescue disk
- Restore with a rescue disk

The Disk Tools program operates interactively. To begin the program from the DOS prompt, enter the command

DISKTOOL

Diskreet

Chapter 3

Diskreet is a program that enables you to protect files so that they cannot be accessed by anyone without permission (the user must know a password). Files stored by Diskreet are encrypted so that they are unreadable, even by the DISKEDIT program. In order for the DISKREET program to work, the following line must be in your CONFIG.SYS file:

DEVICE=*path*\DISKREET.SYS

where *path* is the name of the directory where your Norton files are stored. When you boot your computer, this line tells DOS to make the DISKREET driver available for use. The syntax for using Discreet from the DOS prompt is

DISKREET [*switches*]

The available switches for the DISKREET command follow:

Switch	*Effect*
/ENCRYPT:*filespec*	Encrypts the specified files.
/DECRYPT:*filename*	Decrypts the specified files.
/PASSWORD:*your password*	Tells the Diskreet command what password to use for encryption or decryption.
/SHOW[:*d*]	Instructs the Diskreet command to show the hidden drives (NDISKS) being used to store files.
/HIDE[:*d*]	Instructs the Diskreet command to hide the specified drive (NDISK).
/CLOSE	Instructs the Diskreet command to close all NDISKS.
/ON	Instructs the Diskreet command to enable the Diskreet driver.
/OFF	Instructs the Diskreet command to disable use of the Diskreet driver.

File Attributes (FA)

The File Attributes (FA) command in Norton Utilities 4.5 has been incorporated into the File Find command in Version 5.0.

File Date (FD)

The File Date (FD) command in Norton Utilities 4.5 has been incorporated into the File Find command in Version 5.0.

File Find

Chapter 6

The File Find command helps you find files by name in any directory on disk, search for text in files, set file attributes, and set dates and times on file names. The File Find command uses the following syntax:

FILEFIND [*d:*][*filespec*] [*search-text*] [*switches*]

The filespec option may include global file characters such as a question mark (?) or an asterisk (*). Some special filespec forms follow:

.	Search entire current drive
.*.*	Search only current directory
:.*	Search all drives

The switches available for the FILEFIND command follow:

Switch	*Effect*
/S	Includes all subdirectories in search.
/C	Includes current directory in search.
/CS	Makes search case-sensitive.
/A[+/−]	Sets archive bit. The plus (+) sets the archive and the minus (−) unsets the archive bit. If neither + nor − is included, the command lists files with the archive bit set.
/R[+/−]	Sets the read-only bit. The plus (+) sets read-only and the minus sign (−) unsets the read-only bit. If neither + nor − is included, the command lists files with the read-only bit set.
/HID[+/−]	Sets the hidden bit. The plus (+) sets the hidden file and the minus sign (−) unsets the hidden bit. If neither + nor − is included, the command lists files with the hidden file bit set.

/SYS[+ / −]	Sets the system file bit. The plus (+) sets the system bit and the minus (−) unsets the system bit. If neither + nor − is included, the command lists files with the archive bit set.
/CLEAR	Clears all file attributes.
/D*date*	Tells the File Find command what date to place on the files that match the file specification. The *date* should be in the format MM-DD-YY. (The date format may be different if your computer uses a non-US-country code.)
/T*time*	Tells the File Find command what time to place on the files that match the file specification. The *time* should be in the format HH:MM:SS (military time). (The time format may be different if your computer uses a non-US-country code.)
/NOW	Sets the time and date to the current system time and date.
/TARGET:*d*	Tells File Find to determine whether the files specified in the filespec will fit on the target drive D.
/O:*file*	Instructs File Find to save output lists from the command to the file named.
/BATCH	Tells File Find to exit the program automatically and return to the DOS prompt.

The following command sets the date and time on all files on the diskette in drive A to 1-1-91 and noon:

```
FILEFIND A:*.* /D010191 /T12:00:00
```

The following command produces a list of the files stored on drive C that match the *.DRV file specification:

```
FILEFIND C:*.DRV
```

This list reports the file name, size, date, time, and file attributes.

File Fix

Chapter 4

You use the File Fix command to diagnose and repair damaged dBASE, Lotus 1-2-3, or Symphony files. File Fix examines the contents of damaged files and attempts to reconstruct the files. Many files can be repaired automatically, but some will require intervention by the user to make judgment decisions on how to fix the file. File Fix runs in interactive mode. To begin the program at the DOS prompt, enter the command

FILEFIX [*filename*]

where *filename* is the name of the file you want to fix.

File Info (FI)

The File Info (FI) command for Norton Utilities 4.5 is not included in Version 5.0.

File Save

Chapter 3

The File Save command moves files that you have deleted to a less used part of the hard disk so that those files will remain recoverable for a longer period of time. After the part of the disk that contains a deleted file is used, any deleted files occupying that space become unrecoverable. The File Save command usually is included in the AUTOEXEC.BAT file so that it is in effect whenever you delete files. The File Save command is a memory-resident (TSR) program. The syntax of the File Save command is

FILESAVE [*switches*]

The available switches for the FILESAVE command follow:

Switch	*Effect*
/STATUS	Displays the status of the File Save command.
/ON	Enables the File Save command to move deleted files to a safe area.

/OFF	Disables the File Save command, so deleted files are not affected. The File Save command remains in memory, but does not function unless you have turned the /ON switch back on.
/UNINSTALL	Removes the File Save command from memory if File Save was the last memory-resident (TSR) command loaded.

File Size (FS)

The File Size (FS) command for Norton Utilities Version 4.5 has been integrated into the FINDFILE command in Version 5.0.

Format Recover (FR)

The Format Recover (FR) command in Norton Utilities 4.5 has been integrated into the Unformat command in Version 5.0.

Image

Chapter 3

The Image program captures important information about the files on your hard disk and saves that information to a file named IMAGE.DAT. If your disk is formatted, the information in the IMAGE.DAT file can help the UNFORMAT program restore your files. To keep the IMAGE.DAT file current, you usually will place the Image command in your AUTOEXEC.BAT file so that the file will be updated each time you boot your computer. The syntax for the Image program is

```
IMAGE [switch]
```

The only switch for this command is /NOBACK. This switch instructs the command not to create the backup file IMAGE.BAK.

Line Print (LP)

The Line Print (LP) command in Norton Utilities Version 4.5 is not included in Version 5.0. You can use the DOS command PRINT to print the contents of a file to the printer.

List Directories (LD)

The List Directories (LD) command in Norton Utilities 4.5 has been integrated into the Norton Change Directory command in Version 5.0.

Norton Change Directory (NCD)

Chapter 6

The Norton Change Directory (NCD) command enables you to manage your directories on disk, to quickly change from directory to directory, and to print a directory tree. NCD gives you more control over directory names than you have with the normal DOS commands. The NCD command is suited particularly for use interactively, but you also can use it from the DOS prompt. In command-line mode, the syntax for the Norton Change Directory (NCD) command is

NCD MD *dirname* [*switches*]

or

NCD RD *dirname* [*switches*]

or

NCD *dirname* [*switches*]

These commands replace the DOS commands MD, RD, and CD. You use the NCD MD command to make a directory; you use the NCD RD command to remove a directory, and you use the NCD command to change directories.

The switches associated with the NCD command follow:

Switch	*Effect*
/R	Updates the file TREEINFO.NCD, which contains information about your directory tree structure.
/N	Instructs the NCD command *not* to write the file TREEINFO.NCD. If you are using NCD on a write-protected disk, you need to use this switch.

To use the NCD command interactively, enter the command with no directory name. The directory screen and a menu appear, from which you can change, make, remove, or rename directories.

To create a directory named \WP50\REPORTS interactively, for example, use the command

NCD MD \WP50\REPORTS

To use the NCD command to change directories, you type *NCD* plus the name of the directory to which you want to change. To change to the directory \ONE-A\TWO-A\THREE-A\FOUR-A, for example, use the command

NCD FOUR-A

Norton Control Center (NCC)

Chapter 6

The Norton Control Center (NCC) command enables you to control hardware settings, including display colors, keyboard rates, and clock settings. You can use the Norton Control Center command in command-line or in interactive mode. The syntax for the NCC command in command-line mode is

NCC [*filespec*][*switches*]

or

NCC [*quick switches*]

The *filespec* in the first version of the command refers to a file that contains system-information specifications. Before you use this version of the command, you must create this file by using NCC in interactive mode to choose the settings you want and then saving the information to a file.

The available switches for the first version of the NCC command follow:

Switch	*Effect*
/SETALL	Instructs the NCC command to read the information in the file named by *filespec* and to set all the parameters.
/CURSOR	Instructs the NCC command to read the information in the file named by *filespec* but to set only the cursor size.
/KEYRATE	Instructs the NCC command to read the information in the file named by *filespec* but to set only the keyboard rates.
/PALETTE	Instructs the NCC command to read the information in the file named by *filespec* but to set only the palette colors.
/COM*n*	Instructs the NCC command to read the information in the file named by *filespec* but to set only the information for serial port (COM port) specified by *n* (*n* = 1, 2, and so on).
/DOSCOLOR	Instructs the NCC command to read the information in the file named by *filespec* but to set only the previously chosen DOS colors for foreground, background, and border.
/DISPLAY	Instructs the NCC command to read the information in the file named by *filespec* but to set only the display.

If you have not created a settings file by running the NCC command in interactive mode, you can use the second version of the NCC command. With this version, you can set a few options by using certain quick switches, which include the following:

Switch	*Effect*
/BW80	Places the monitor in black-and-white mode with 25 lines and 80 columns.

/CO80	Places the monitor in color mode with 25 lines and 80 columns.
/25	Places the monitor in 25-line mode (same as /CO80).
/35	Places the monitor in 35-line mode. This option is supported only by EGA monitors.
/40	Places the monitor in 40-line mode. This option is supported only by VGA monitors.
/43	Places the monitor in 43-line mode. This option is supported only by EGA monitors.
/50	Places the monitor in 50-line mode. This option is supported only by VGA monitors.
/FASTKEY	Sets the keyboard rate at its fastest possible value.

To set your VGA computer so that 50 lines are displayed on-screen and so that the keyboard rate is the fastest value, use this command:

```
NCC /50/FASTKEY
```

You also may use the Control Center to set system stop watches by using the following switches:

/START:*n*	Tells NCC to begin the stopwatch number *n* where *n* can be from 1 to 4.
/STOP:*n*	Tells NCC to stop the stopwatch number *n* where *n* can be from 1 to 4.
/N	Tells NCC not to display the current time and date.
/L	Tells NCC to display the time and date on the left side of the monitor.
/LOG	Tells NCC to format the output of the command so that it can be printed in report form.
/C:*comment*	Tells NCC to display the text string comment after you execute the command. This is useful for documenting which timer is being reported. If the comment contains any blanks, you must surround the entire comment with quotes.

To access Norton Control Center interactively, enter the NCC command without using any file specification. The Control Center menu appears, enabling you to choose interactively the options that you can set by using switches in the command-line mode.

Norton Disk Cache

The Norton Disk Cache program enables you to specify how much RAM memory in your computer should be used as a buffer when the computer is reading information from disk. The larger the cache, the faster your disk access will tend to be. In order for Disk Cache to work, there should be a command in your CONFIG.SYS file as follows:

DEVICE=*path*\NCACHE-F.EXE [*parameters*]

or

DEVICE=*path*\NCACHE-S.EXE [*parameters*]

The *path* refers to the directory name where the NCACHE-F or NCACHE-S files are stored. The F version of the cache program is designed to give you more speed in your disk access. The S version of the cache program also gives you more speed, but it does not use as much memory. (You normally would use this version on an 8088-based computer.)

Parameters for both versions of NCACHE follow:

Parameter	*Effect*
BLOCK=*n*	Sets the size of the cache blocks.
EXT [=*n*] EXT [=−*n*]	Specifies how much extended memory the cache will use. If a negative value is used, it leaves that much memory free for use by other programs.
EXP [=*n*] EXP [=−*n*]	Specifies how much expanded memory the cache will use. If a negative value is used, it leaves that much memory free for use by other programs.

Parameter	*Effect*
DOS [=*n*] DOS [=−*n*]	Specifies how much DOS memory the cache will use. Use this only when you do not have any expanded or extended memory. If a negative value is used, it leaves that much memory free for use by other programs.
INI=*path*	Tells the command where to look for the file that contains installation options.
RESET	Resets the cache statistics.
STATUS	Displays a number of statistics that enable you to see how effective the cache is working.
UNINSTALL	Removes the command from memory. This command will not work unless the NCACHE program was the last memory-resident (TSR) program loaded into memory.
USEHIDOS [= *YES/NO*]	Minimizes the use of conventional (low) DOS memory if high memory is available (if set to Yes). The default for this command is No.
USE HMA [=*YES/NO*]	Uses the XMS high-memory area to reduce the use of DOS RAM (if set to Yes). This is available only if you have an extended-memory manager.

Parameters available only for NCACHE-F follow:

Parameter	*Effect*
DELAY=*ss.hh*	Delays writes to the disk in seconds or hundredths of a second. For example, 00.10 would be one hundredth of a second. The default is 00.00.

Parameter	*Effect*
	Slight writing delays can improve the speed of write-intensive programs.
QUICK[=*ON*/*OFF*]	Displays the DOS prompt on-screen even when information still is being written to the disk.

Options for both cache versions follow:

Parameter	*Effect*
+/−A	Activates or deactivates caching.
+/−C	Enables or disables caching of additional information. New information is cached when this is disabled.
F	Flushes the cache (empties it). This causes all writes to disk to be finished.
G=*n*	Specifies a group sector size. (The default is 128.)
+/−W	Enables or disables write through caching.
+/−I	Enables or disables IntelliWrites. When this is on, disk writes accelerate and control is returned to the application before the write is finished.
R=*Dn*	Specifies how may sectors should be read ahead. A specification R=n always causes read aheads. A specification of R=n causes read-aheads only when the file being read is not a random file.
+/−S	Enables or disables SmartReads. This enables the program to read additional data before it finishes writing all data to disk.

Norton Disk Doctor II

Chapter 4

The Norton Disk Doctor (NDD) command finds and corrects, if possible, physical or logical problems on a disk. The syntax of the Norton Disk Doctor command is

NDD [*d:*] [*d:*][*switches*]

The *d:* designations are disk drive names; you can specify more than one. The switches available for the NDD command follow:

Switch	*Effect*
/QUICK	Omits the test for bad cylinders, but tests the partition table, boot record, root directory, and lost clusters.
/COMPLETE	Tests for bad cylinders on the disk plus partition table, boot record, root directory, and lost clusters.
/R:*file*	Instructs NDD to output a report about the results of its testing to the file named. Use with /Quick or /Complete.
/RA:*file*	Same as /R, but appends the report to the file instead of making a new file. Use with /Quick or /Complete.
/X:*d*	Excludes drive *d* from examination.

Use Norton Disk Doctor whenever you experience problems in accessing a file or when you get a DOS error message concerning the operation of a disk. NDD is your first line of defense to prevent these problems from getting worse and to solve the problems before any data is lost.

If you enter the NDD command with no switches, you operate in interactive mode. The Disk Doctor menu appears, from which you can choose to diagnose the disk or choose Common Solutions (make a disk bootable, revive a defective disk, or recover from DOS's Recover command).

Norton Integrator (NI)

The Norton Integrator (NI) command in Norton Utilities Version 4.5 has been integrated into the NORTON command in Version 5.0.

The Norton Main Menu

Chapter 1

The NORTON command begins the Norton Utilities main menu. From this menu, you can run any of the other Norton Utilities utility programs. Also, this menu contains brief Help files that describe the purpose and syntax of each utility. To begin the Norton program from the DOS prompt, enter the command

NORTON

Norton Utilities Main Program (NU)

The Norton Utilities main program (the NU command) in Norton Advanced Utilities Version 4.5 has been integrated into the DISKEDIT command in Version 5.0.

Quick Unerase (QU)

The Quick Unerase (QU) command in Norton Utilities Version 4.5 has been integrated into the UNERASE command in Version 5.0.

Safe Format

Chapter 3

The Safe Format command prevents you from accidentally formatting a disk that contains important information and provides some safety checks for those times when you do format a disk. The syntax of the Safe Format command is

SFORMAT [*d:*][*switches*]

You may have renamed the SFORMAT command FORMAT to replace the DOS command. If so, the format for the SFORMAT (FORMAT) command is

FORMAT [*d:*][*switches*]

(SFORMAT.EXE is renamed FORMAT.EXE.) Many of the available switches for the SFORMAT command are similar to the DOS FORMAT switches. You can use the following DOS-like switches with the SFORMAT command:

Switch	*Effect*
/B	Leaves space for system files
/S	Places system files on disk
/V:*label*	Places a volume label on disk
/1	Formats as single sided
/4	Formats as 360K (in 1.2M drive)
/8	Formats with 8 tracks per sector
/N:*n*	Specifies number of tracks per byte (*n* = 8, 9, 15, or 18)
/T:*n*	Specifies number of tracks (*n* = 40 or 80)
/F:*size*	Specifies size of diskette (*size* = 360 or 720)

The following switches are unique to Norton's Safe Format command:

Switch	*Effect*
/A	Uses automatic mode (in batch files)
/*size*	Specifies size of diskette (*size* = 360 or 720)
/Q	Uses Quick Format mode
/D	Uses DOS FORMAT mode
/C	Uses Complete Format mode (for diskettes only)

To format a disk with system files and place the volume label MYDISK on the disk, for example, use this command:

```
SFORMAT B:/S/V:MYDISK
```

You can use the Safe Format command in interactive mode by entering SFORMAT (or FORMAT) with no switches. From the Safe Format menu, you can choose the drive to format, the size of the disk to format, whether to copy system files to the disk, which (if any) volume label to put on the disk, and which format mode to use (Safe format, Quick format, DOS format, or Complete format).

Speed Disk

Chapter 5

The Speed Disk command reorganizes your disk so that fragmented files can be unfragmented. Files also may be packed and rearranged to help your disk run at top speed. The syntax of the Speed Disk command is

SPEEDISK [*d:*] [*switches*]

The available switches for the Speed Disk command follow:

Switch	*Effect*
/B	Reboots after the command finishes.
/C	Performs a complete optimization of the disk.
/D	Optimizes the directory only.
/SD[−]	Instructs the command to sort file by date. If the − parameter is included, the sort will be from most recent date to oldest date.
/SE[−]	Instructs the command to sort files by extension. If the − parameter is included, the sort will be in descending alphabetical order.
/SN[−]	Instructs the command to sort by file name. If the − parameter is included, the sort will be in descending alphabetical order.
/SS[−]	Instructs the command to sort by file size. If the − parameter is included, the sort will be from largest to smallest.
/U	Instructs the command to attempt to unfragment as many files as possible without moving parts of the directory structure. Some damaged files may not be capable of unfragmenting.
/V	Instructs the command to use verify after write-date verification.

You also can run Speed Disk in interactive mode. In interactive mode, you can choose the options mentioned as switch options. Also, you can choose which files not to move and which files to place first on the disk (nearest track 0).

System Information

Chapter 5

The System Information command provides information about your computer (computer type, equipment in use, ROM-BIOS information, and so on) and performs tests that enable you to compare your computer's performance to the performance of other computers. The syntax of the System Information command is

SYSINFO [*d:*][*switches*]

The available switches for the System Information command follow:

Switch	*Effect*
/AUTO:*n*	Tells the command to operate in automatic mode. The *n* parameter specifies a delay of N seconds between screens.
/DEMO	Tells the command to operate in demo mode.
/TSR	Tells the command to show all TSR (terminate-and-stay resident) programs in memory.
/N	Tells the command to skip the live memory probe. On some computers, the live memory probe forces you to reboot after the SYSINFO test. Use the /N switch to get around this problem.

Text Search (TS)

The Text Search (TS) command in Norton Utilities Version 4.5 has been integrated into the FILEFIND command in Version 5.0.

Time Mark (TM)

The Time Mark (TM) command in Norton Utilities Version 4.5 has been integrated into the Norton Command Center in Version 5.0.

Unerase

Chapter 4

The Unerase command enables you to recover erased (deleted) files. You can unerase only files that have not been overwritten by other files. See the FILESAVE command. The syntax of the UNERASE command is

UNERASE [*filespec*]

You may use the global file characters ? and * to specify which files you want to erase. For example, the command

UNERASE *.BAK

looks for all erased files with the BAK extension. UNERASE may prompt you to provide the first character of the name of the file to be unerased. Follow the prompts on-screen after entering the command.

Unformat

Chapter 3

You use the UNFORMAT command to bring back information on a formatted disk. This command works best if you used the IMAGE command to store a copy of the system areas of your disk, or if you formatted the disk by using Safe Format. (see IMAGE and Safe Format). The syntax of this command is

UNFORMAT [*d:*]

where *d:* is the name of the disk to unformat. If your hard disk has been formatted, do not copy anything onto the hard disk before attempting to use UNFORMAT. In this case, you should run the Norton program from a floppy disk. After entering the UNFORMAT command, follow the instructions on-screen.

Unremove Directory (UD)

The Unremove Directory (UD) command in Norton Utilities Version 4.5 has been integrated into the UNERASE command in Version 5.0.

Volume Label (VL)

The Volume Label command in Norton 4.5 has been incorporated into the NCD command in Version 5.0.

Wipe Disk

The WIPEDISK command in Norton Utilities Version 4.5 has been integrated into the WIPEINFO command in Version 5.0.

Wipe File

The WIPEFILE command in Norton Utilities Version 4.5 has been integrated into the WIPEINFO command in Version 5.0.

Wipe Info

The WIPEINFO command overwrites information on disk in such a way that the information cannot be recovered. This includes wiping files or the entire disk. The syntax of the WIPEINFO command is

WIPEINFO *d:*[*disk or file switches*] [*common switches*]

The disk switch available for the WIPEINFO command follows:

Switch	*Effect*
/E	Causes the command to overwrite information only that currently is unused or that is in *erased* files—files marked for erase by the DOS ERASE command but otherwise recoverable.

The file switches available for the WIPEFINO command follow:

Switch	*Effect*
/N	Uses No-wipe mode, which causes the WIPEFILE command to behave like the ERASE command. The file is marked as erased but is not overwritten.
/K	Also wipes any slack space allocated to a file.
/S	Wipes out files that match the *filespec* in subdirectories also.

The common switches available for the WIPEINFO command follow:

/G*n*	Uses a government-standard overwriting procedure. The default for *n* (number of overwrites) is 3. Although the default is 0, the /G switch overrides this default,. When you include the /G switch, the value written to disk is ASCII value 246.
/R*n*	Overwrites the disk *n* times. The default is 1.
/V*n*	Selects the value that is to be used to overwrite information on the disk. The value can be from 0 to 255.

To wipe disk D using the governmental standard, for example, enter the command

```
WIPEINFO D:/G
```

Part III

A Closer Look at Norton Commander

Includes

Using Norton Commander as an Enhancement to DOS

Norton Commander Advanced Topics

8

Using Norton Commander as an Enhancement to DOS

Norton Commander, Version 3.00, is a program that enables you to perform a variety of tasks on your computer in a menu-like environment rather than from the standard DOS command line. Instead of having to remember the syntax of the DOS COPY command, for example, you are led through the Commander copy process with a series of menus and prompts.

Commander is not just a substitute for some DOS commands; it also provides you with a number of features that are not found in DOS. You can use Commander, for example, to view the contents of a variety of database, spreadsheet, and word processing files without having to use the respective application programs. Also, Commander enables you to execute several of the Norton Utilities commands, such as those used to display a sorted directory, set file attributes, find files, set an EGA monitor to display more than 25 lines, and more.

One of the main features of Norton Commander is convenience. It is a bit like an automatic transmission in a car. You can get by with a manual transmission, but an automatic transmission often makes driving the car easier and more pleasurable. In the same way, many of the things that you can do in Commander you can do also in DOS or in Norton Utilities. Commander automates those commands through its menu structure, however, making the "driving" of the computer easier for you. Commander is particularly helpful for beginning users who have not memorized DOS and Norton commands.

This chapter introduces you to the basics of using Norton Commander. The chapter is arranged according to how you would normally use Norton Commander and not necessarily by the order of the options in the on-screen menus. You first learn how to display and access the various Commander menus. Most of the action takes place on the Commander's left and right panels, so the potential contents of the panels and options for controlling the display of these panels are discussed.

After the preliminary description of how Commander works, the chapter turns to how to manage and manipulate your directories and files; how to look at files from spreadsheets, databases, and word processors; how to use the Commander editor to edit ASCII files; and how to customize Commander to your particular tastes.

Getting To Know the Norton Commander Screen

If you have not installed Norton Commander, refer to the instructions in Appendix C. Then start Commander by typing *nc* at the DOS prompt and pressing Enter. If you want the Commander program to begin each time you boot your computer, place the NC command as the last line in your AUTOEXEC.BAT file. Refer to Appendix A for information on the AUTOEXEC.BAT file.

When you start Norton Commander, you see a screen similar to the one in figure 8.1. Under normal installation, Commander is set up to display

```
                                   C:\NC
        Name           Size        Date      Time
..                  ►UP--DIR◄    1-28-90    7:48p
123view   exe         52464     10-23-89    3:00p
chkmail   bat           342     10-23-89    3:00p
dbview    exe         61026     10-23-89    3:00p
inread    me           1312     10-23-89    3:00p
mci       exe        103396     10-23-89    3:00p
mci       hlp         27050     10-23-89    3:00p
mcidrivr  exe         71272     10-23-89    3:00p
nc        exe          3100     10-23-89    3:00p
nc        hlp         45727     10-23-89    3:00p
nc        ini           476      2-10-90    3:10p
ncmain    exe        139274     10-23-89    3:00p
paraview  exe         62596     10-23-89    3:00p
pcxview   exe         46094     10-23-89    3:00p
rbview    exe         67966     10-23-89    3:00p
read      me            974     10-23-89    3:00p

..                  ►UP--DIR◄    1-28-90    7:48p
C:\NC>
1Help  2Menu  3View  4Edit  5Copy  6RenMov  7Mkdir  8Delete  9PullDn  10Quit
```

Fig. 8.1
The opening Norton Commander screen.

initially only a directory panel on the right half of the screen and a function key bar at the bottom of the screen. However, the screen actually has four places where you can choose options (or directory or file names): the menu bar, the function key bar, the left panel, and the right panel.

Although only the function key bar and the right panel are visible on the initial screen, you easily can display the menu bar at the top of the screen and the left panel. The commands for turning on and off the screen components are listed in table 8.1.

Table 8.1
Commands for Displaying the Commander Screen Components

Screen Component	*Command To Toggle Display*
Menu bar	F9
Left panel	Ctrl-F1
Right panel	Ctrl-F2
Function key bar	Ctrl-B

Note: In Version 2.00, F9 turns on the menu bar, but does not turn it off again, as in Version 3.00. In Version 2.00, press Esc to turn off the menu.

As discussed in Chapter 2, "An Overview of Norton Commander 3.00" several methods of accessing options are available. You can use the point-and-shoot method with the keyboard or the mouse. After the menu appears, you also can press a hot key to choose an option. The hot key usually is the first letter of the option name, or it is the only capitalized letter in the option name. Another method of accessing options is by using control commands. To give a control command, you hold down the Ctrl key and then press another key. If a control command requires the key combination of Ctrl and the letter C, for example, the command is shown in this book as Ctrl-C. If there is a control command equivalent to a menu option, it appears to the right of the option name on the menu.

Using the Menu Bar and its Pull-Down Menus

After you press F9 (PullDn), a menu bar appears at the top of the screen (see fig. 8.2). (You also can use the mouse to display the menu bar. Just point to the top line of the screen and hold down the left button.) This menu bar enables you to access five Commander menus: Left, Files, Commands, Options, and Right. When the menu bar is on, you can use the right- and left-arrow keys (or the mouse) to point to a menu option. If you press Enter or click the left mouse button when an option is highlighted, a pull-down menu appears.

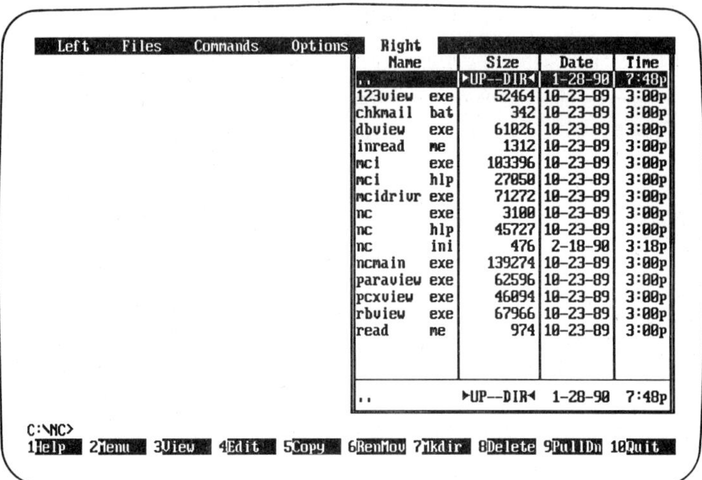

Fig. 8.2
Displaying the Norton Commander menu bar.

The first four pull-down menus are shown in figures 8.3 through 8.6. (The Left and Right menus are similar, so the Right menu is not shown in a figure.) The Left menu controls what you see in the left panel, and the Right menu controls what you see in the right panel. The Files menu enables you to choose Commander options that deal with files. The Commands menu gives you access to a number of disk-management commands similar to some of the Norton Utilities commands. The Options menu enables you to choose various options about how Commander information is displayed on your computer. These menus are described in more detail in subsequent sections of this chapter.

Using the Function Key Bar

The function key bar appears at the bottom of the screen when the Norton Commander is in operation. If you are using a mouse, you can select one of the function key options by pointing to it with the mouse and clicking the left button. If you are using the keyboard, press the function

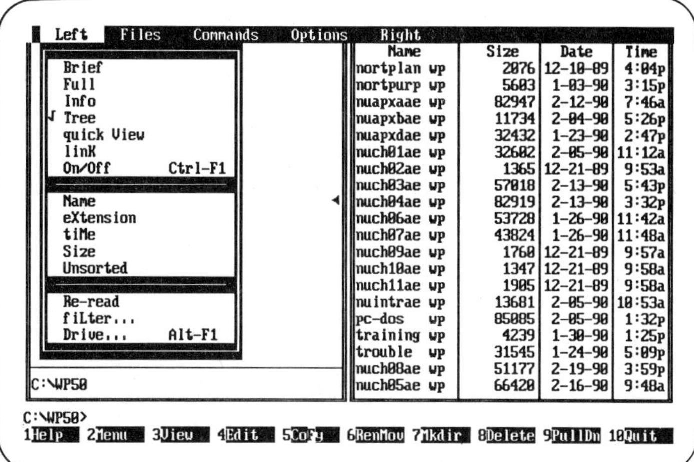

Fig. 8.3 The Norton Commander Left menu.

```
 Left   Files   Commands   Options   Right
                                  Name            Name            Name
  Help                  F1       kfeature        wp        mrs   nortplan wp
  User menu             F2       nortrep         survey    pm3   nortpurp wp
  View                  F3       nu1230    arc   hplaseii  prs   nuapxaae wp
  Edit                  F4       wp50-89   arc   standard  prs   nuapxbae wp
  Copy                  F5       int       bas   wp{wp}    set   nuapxdae wp
  Rename or move        F6       rwconfig  dct   wp{wp}en  sup   nuch01ae wp
  Make directory        F7       rwrules   dct   wp{wp}en  ths   nuch02ae wp
  Delete                F8       rwwords   dct   adsurvey  txt   nuch03ae wp
                                 test      doc   pc-dos1   txt   nuch04ae wp
  file Attributes                wpsmall   drs   pc-dos2   txt   nuch06ae wp
  Send files                     right     exe   wp-move   txt   nuch07ae wp
                                 spell     exe   wp-out    txt   nuch09ae wp
  select Group        Gray +     wp        exe   b-loops   wp    nuch10ae wp
  uNselect group      Gray -     wpright   exe   compare   wp    nuch11ae wp
                                 wp        fil   dos-out   wp    nuintrae wp
  Quit                  F10      wphelp    fil   geriat    wp    pc-dos   wp
                                 wphelp2   fil   howdisk   wp    training wp
                                 que       frm   nort-que  wp    trouble  wp
                                 wp{wp}en  lex   nortdue   wp    nuch08ae wp
                                 keys      mrs   nortout   wp    nuch05ae wp
C:\WP50>
1Help  2Menu  3View  4Edit  5Copy  6RenMov  7Mkdir  8Delete  9PullDn  10Quit
```

Fig. 8.4 The Norton Commander Files menu.

key that corresponds to the menu number. To choose the Help option (1), for example, press F1. The meanings of each of the function keys are described in the following sections.

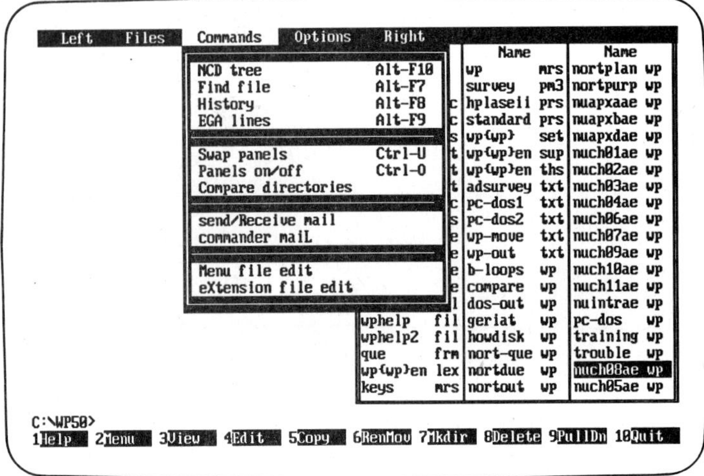

Fig. 8.5
The Norton Commander Commands menu.

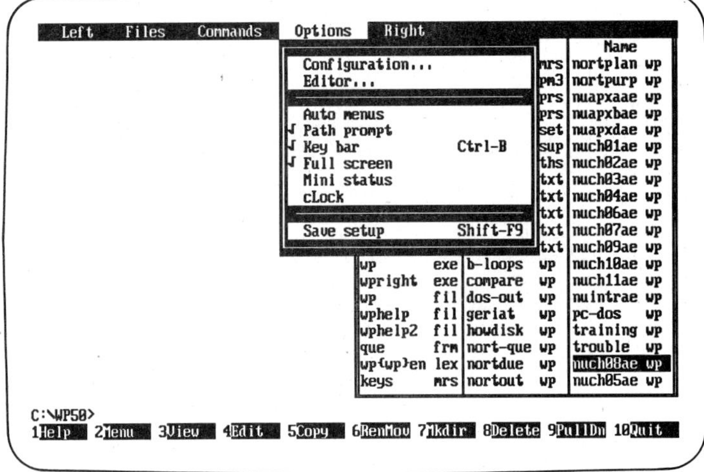

Fig. 8.6
The Norton Commander Options menu.

One of the first function keys you should learn about is F10, which is the Quit key. If you want to end Norton Commander, just press F10. A small dialog box appears in the center of the screen, asking you to verify that you want to quit. To end Commander, press Y, highlight Yes and press Enter, or point to Yes with the mouse and click the left button.

Using the Right and Left Panels

The contents of the right and left panels are controlled by the options on the Right and Left pull-down menus. Depending on your preferences, these panels can contain

- A brief directory of files (names only)
- A full directory of files (including dates, times, and sizes)
- A graphic representation of the directory tree
- Information about the directory and disk
- The displayed contents of a file

When you activate the left and right panels in Commander by pressing Ctrl-F1 or Ctrl-F2, you see a display like the one in figure 8.7. Usually, the left panel is set up to display the directory tree structure of the disk and the right panel is set up to display the files belonging to the directory that is selected in the left panel.

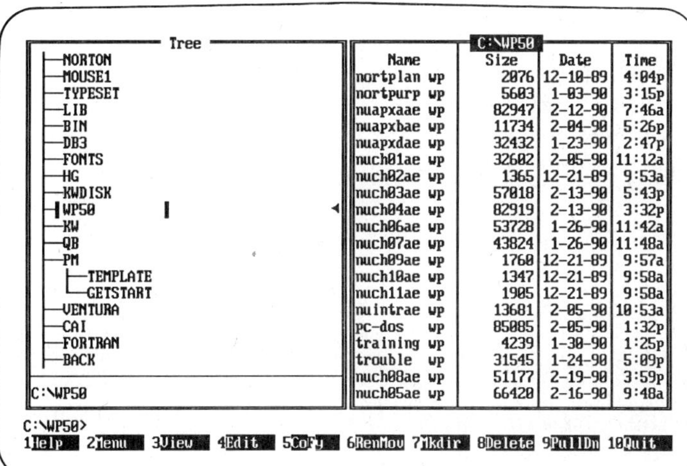

Fig. 8.7 ***The Norton Commander screen with both panels activated.***

You can access information in only one panel at a time. When both panels are displayed, you move from one active panel to the other by pressing the Tab key (or by pointing with the mouse to a panel and clicking the button to activate). When a panel is activated, you can use the arrow keys to highlight files or directories that you want to access or use in some way.

If you want to swap the current left and right panels on-screen, choose the Swap Panels option from the Commands menu (or press Ctrl-U). The reasons for swapping panels are purely aesthetic, because you can perform the same operations regardless of which panel holds the information. Using the Swap Panel option is much quicker, however, than swapping manually by choosing other options for each panel.

Using the DOS Prompt and the History Option

Notice that the DOS prompt also appears on the Norton Commander screen, directly above the function key bar. As mentioned previously, you can use Commander menus to access commands or you can enter DOS commands from the DOS prompt.

Commander also offers another convenient feature for entering DOS commands. If you have entered a DOS command recently and want to repeat that command, you can use Commander's History option to review and choose any of the last 15 commands entered at the DOS prompt.

You can access the History option by choosing it from the Commands menu or by pressing Alt-F8. A panel then appears on-screen, listing up to 15 commands. You can use the up- and down-arrow keys or the mouse to point to one of the commands and press Enter (or click the right mouse button) to execute the command.

Controlling the Left and Right Panel Displays

With DOS's DIR command, you can look at the contents of only one directory at a time. Also, when you want to use one of the directory's files in a command such as COPY or RENAME, you must spell out the full file name—and you had better not make any typing mistakes! Using Norton Commander's left and right panels, you can display twice as much on-screen as you can with DOS. Also, you can point to and select the files or directories you want to use without having to worry about typing them or spelling them correctly. These features are only a few reasons why using Commander's right and left panels is easier than using DOS commands.

As mentioned previously, you press Ctrl-F1 to toggle the left panel on and off and Ctrl-F2 to toggle the right panel on and off. Commander provides several other keyboard commands for controlling the panel display and manipulating the files and directories listed in the panels. These shortcuts are listed in table 8.2.

Table 8.2
Using the Keyboard To Control Panel Display

Key	*Effect*
↑	Scrolls panel information up
↓	Scrolls panel information down
Enter	Changes to a directory if you highlight that directory name and press Enter (works like an NCD command). Begins the program if you highlight a program file name (a BAT, EXE, or COM file, for example). Has no effect if you press Enter with any other file name highlighted.
Ctrl-PgUp	Changes to the parent directory
Ctrl-\	Changes to the root directory
Gray +	Selects a group of files
Gray −	Unselects a group of files
Alt-*file name*	Speeds search for a file name
Ins	Selects/unselects file at cursor
Ctrl-Enter	Copies file or directory name to command line
Ctrl-P	Turns inactive panel on or off
Ctrl-O	Turns both panels on or off
Ctrl-U	Switches panels

You can change to another directory by typing the command

NCD *dirname*

at the DOS prompt. If you prefer to use point-and-shoot techniques, you can change directories in several other ways. This is similar to performing an NCD\ command. You then can highlight any directory name and press Enter to change to that directory (or point with the mouse and double-click). Remember the shortcut keys Ctrl-PgUp to change to the parent directory, and Ctrl-\ to change to the root directory.

At times, you may want to select from a directory panel a number of files at the same time (for example, to copy a group of files with the F5 key). You can select a particular group of files by using the gray + and gray − keys, which are usually located at the right of the keyboard. If you press the gray + key, you are prompted to enter all files to include in a selection. You can enter *.TXT, for example, to include all files with a TXT extension. The selected files then appear highlighted in the panel. To exclude files from the list, press the gray − key. You can press gray − and then type *b.**, for example, to exclude all files that begin with the letter B. After selecting files, you can use the function key commands to copy, rename, move, or delete these files.

The Alt-*file name* command enables you to find quickly a file in a directory. Suppose you are looking for a file named SAMPLING.TXT—however, there are 200 files in the directory. Of course, you can scroll until you find it. An easier way, however, is to press Alt-S. A small dialog box appears at the bottom right of the screen. The highlight in the directory panel points to the first file in the list that begins with the letter "s." After you press the second letter (A), the highlight moves to the first file name in the directory that matches "sa." Usually, by pressing a few letters, you soon locate the file you have in mind. You then can use that file in a command such as copying the file, renaming it, and so on.

The Ctrl-Enter command enables you to copy quickly the name of a highlighted file to the DOS command area. Suppose you want to enter the following command at the DOS command prompt:

```
WP50 FY8990RT.WP5
```

Instead of typing the whole command (and possibly misspelling the file name), you can highlight the file name in the directory panel. Then enter the WP50 and press Ctrl-Enter. The name FY8990RT.WP5 then appears on the DOS command line, and you have entered the command you wanted.

As mentioned previously, to control exactly what information appears in the panels—and how it appears—you use the options on the Left and Right pull-down menus. The following sections describe these menu options.

Displaying Files in Brief and in Full

The Brief and Full options on the Left and Right menus determine how files are displayed on a panel. The Brief option lists only the file names; the Full option lists the file names with the size, date, and time for each file. Using the Brief option enables you to display more file names at one time. An example of a right panel display after you select the Brief option is shown in figure 8.8. If you have many files in a directory and are interested only in the names, you can use the Brief option to avoid having to scroll to find the files you want to access.

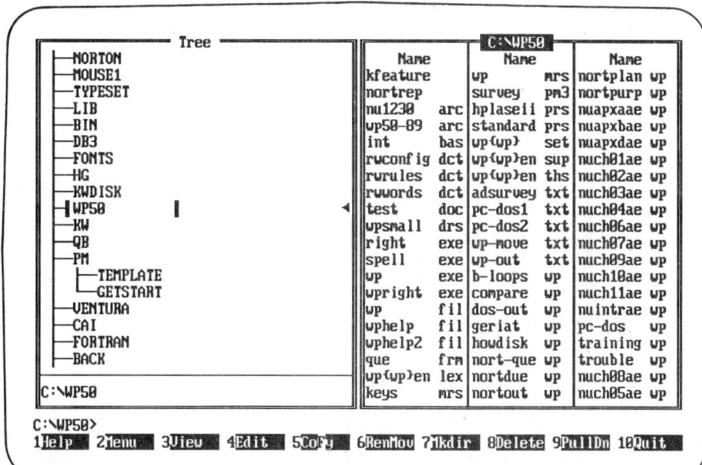

Fig. 8.8 Displaying the right panel in brief mode.

Displaying Summary Information

When you select the Info option from the Left or Right menu, the corresponding left or right panel displays summary information about the current drive, similar to information you would get with the DOS CHKDSK command (see fig. 8.9). The top part of the Info panel tells you the amount of memory available, the disk size and disk space available, the number of files in use, and how much space is taken up by the files.

Note that the bottom part of the Info panel in figure 8.9 includes the message `No 'dirinfo' file in this directory`. The DIRINFO file is a file that contains a brief description of the directory. You may place information in this file that gives information about the contents of the directory. In the \WP50 directory, for example, you can place the message "This directory contains WordPerfect Version 5.0." If you want to create such a DIRINFO file, press F4 (Edit). A small edit window appears at the bottom of the Info window. Enter your summary information, and then press F10 to save the DIRINFO file. Then whenever you display the Info panel for that directory, your description appears at the bottom of the panel.

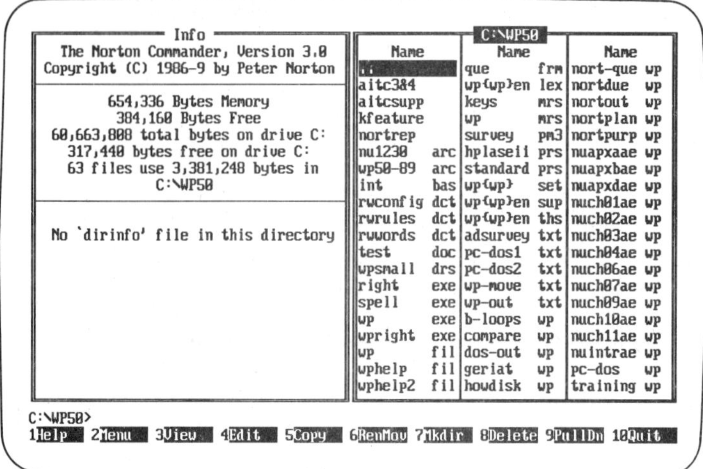

Fig. 8.9 Displaying the Info panel.

After you display the Info panel, you can return the panel to its previous state by pressing Ctrl-L, or you can choose another panel option from the Left or Right menu.

The Info option is useful for several reasons. The Bytes Free figure tells you how much RAM is available to be used by an application program. Usually programs have a minimum requirement for them to run. You can display the Info panel to check whether you have enough memory to run a particular application program. Commander uses about 13K of memory. When you begin an application, you actually have 13K more memory available to you than what is reported in the Info window. This is because Commander frees itself from memory when an application program begins and then restarts itself when the program finishes. Also, Info tells you how many bytes are free on a disk. This information can be important if you need to copy files to the disk. Displaying the Info panel can save you the trouble of trying to copy files that the disk cannot handle. Also, if you don't know the size of one of your diskettes, you can get that information from the total bytes message.

Displaying a Directory Tree

Choosing the Tree option from the Left or Right menu displays a graphic tree of the disk directory structure, as is shown in the left panel of figure 8.8. After you activate a panel containing a directory tree, you can use the up- and down-arrow keys to select a directory as the current directory.

(To select a directory in the Tree panel with a mouse, point to the directory name and click the left button.) If the other panel is set up to display file names, that panel displays the file names associated with the selected directory.

Sorting Files

File names displayed in the panels may be listed in a number of sorted orders, according to options on the Left and Right menus. You can list files in order by name, extension, time of creation, and size, or you can choose to have the files listed in unsorted order, which is how they would normally appear in a DOS DIR list. To select a sort option, highlight the Name, Extension, Time, Size, or Unsorted option and press Enter. Alternatively, press the uppercase letter to select an option. If you are using a mouse, highlight the option and release the left button. After you choose a sort option, a check mark appears to the left of the option in the menu.

Sort orders are helpful if you are trying to locate files by some criteria, such as when they were created or what extension was used. By displaying the files in the appropriate sorted order, you may be able to locate files more quickly.

Filtering Files

The Filter option enables you to select which files are displayed in a panel. When you choose Filter from the Left or Right menu, a dialog box appears in which you can choose the type of files to display. Figure 8.10 shows a Filter dialog box. Your choices include all files, executable files, or a custom list of files. If you choose the custom option, you must then enter a file specification—using the question mark (?) or asterisk (*) wildcard characters—to describe the files to include. If you want to list only files with the PIX extension, for example, choose a custom list and enter a *.PIX file specification.

Changing Drives

The Drive option on the Left and Right menus enables you to specify which drive should be used for the panel. When you choose this option, a dialog box displays a list of the possible drive names. Choose a drive and press Enter, and the panel reflects the change.

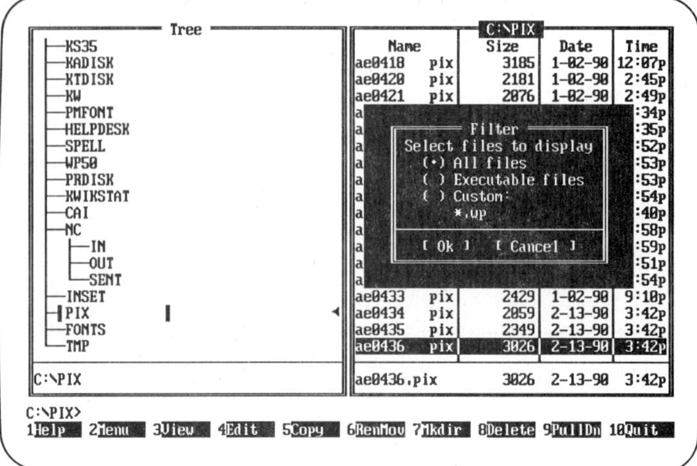

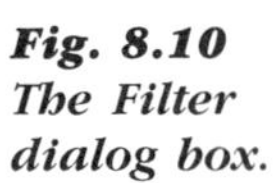
Fig. 8.10
The Filter dialog box.

Rereading and Updating File Information

The Re-read option on the Left and Right menus makes Commander reread file information from disk and update information in a panel. The program often performs this operation automatically when a change is made. If you change a disk in a drive or modify a file with a memory-resident program, however, you should choose the Re-read option to make sure that Commander has up-to-date knowledge about the files on disk. Choosing Re-read when the directory tree is activated ensures that Commander has current information about all directories on disk.

Viewing Files

The Left and Right menus' Quick View option displays the contents of a file that is highlighted in the other panel. You can view the contents of files from programs such as Lotus 1-2-3, WordStar, WordPerfect, dBase III, and others—even if you don't have those application programs. You also can view graphic files that match the Z-Soft PCX standard. The Quick View option is similar to the F3 (View) key (see "Viewing Files with F3," later in this chapter). The Quick View option, however, initially displays only half a screen rather than the full-screen F3 view. Figure 8.11 shows a screen that contains a quick view panel of a Mosaic Twin spreadsheet file.

Notice in the function key bar that the F3 key, which previously had been labeled View, is now Zoom. When a quick view panel is displayed, you can press F3 (Zoom) to expand the view from a half-screen panel to the full screen.

```
         Mosaic Twin View                           C:\TWIN
A1: 'Commander Company Cash Flow Anal      Name          Size     Date     Time
      A          B          C          addendum txt    12900  2-12-87  2:22a
1  Commander Company Cash Flow Analy   hercules txt     4627  2-12-87  2:22a
2              Jan        Feb          install  txt     1020  2-12-87  2:22a
3  REVENUES  ------     ------         readme   txt      934  2-12-87  2:22a
4  Sales      1277.5    1463.16        visavis  txt     4746  2-12-87  2:22a
5  Royalites     577        577        mba      wk1     4273  5-23-89  8:22a
6  Other          23         44        tsumc    wks     2932  1-26-90 12:48p
7  Interest     5.83       3.94        aaa      wkt     1800 12-23-89  2:26a
8  TOTAL     1883.33     2088.1        aeck89   wkt    42801  2-06-90  9:25p
9            ------     ------         aeck90   wkt    21820  2-15-90  7:30p
10                                     balance  wkt     2550  2-15-90  7:25p
11 EXPENSES  ------     ------         books    wkt     4092 12-21-89 11:17a
12 Commissio    2332        600        bryant   wkt     4200 12-23-89  9:50a
13 Phone      125.84                   caiman   wkt     2352 11-26-89 10:17p
14 Printing       70       50.7        cashflow wkt     9064  1-11-90  7:53p
15 COGS        59.89     322.19        command  wkt     8625  2-18-90  3:43p
16 State Fees                          dec89    wkt    13954  1-20-90  4:17p
17 Postage     79.81     193.17        expen88  wkt     2776  2-05-89  7:26p

command.wkt          8,625             command.wkt      8625  2-18-90  3:43p

C:\TWIN>
1Help  2Menu  3Zoom  4Edit  5Copy  6RenMov  7Mkdir  8Delete  9PullDn  10Quit
```

Fig. 8.11 ***Using the Quick View option.***

Linking Information

The Link option on the Left and Right menus enables you to move information quickly between two computers. The Link option may be handy particularly if you use a laptop computer. To update your desktop computer with information on your laptop (or vice versa), you can use the Link option to copy files back and forth between computers. This option is an advanced feature and is covered in Chapter 9.

Turning the Panels On and Off

The On/Off option on the Left and Right menus toggles the corresponding panel off and on. This option has the same effect as pressing Ctrl-F1 or Ctrl-F2. At times, you may want to see what is "behind" a panel—for example, after you perform a DOS command and information scrolls onto that part of the screen. Norton Commander offers a few other shortcuts for turning panels on and off. Pressing Ctrl-P turns on and off the inactive panel, and Ctrl-O turns on and off both panels.

Managing Your Directories with Norton Commander

Norton Commander enables you to access and manage your directories on disk. Using Commander, you can make new directories by pressing a function key, access a version of the Norton Change Directory (NCD) command similar to the command in Norton Utilities, and compare directories. Table 8.3 summarizes the options used to perform these tasks.

Table 8.3
Commands for Managing Directories

Task	*Function Key*	*Menu Command*
Make directory	F7	NCD Tree option on Commands menu
Access NCD program	Alt-F10	NCD Tree option on Commands menu
Compare directories		Compare Directories option on Commands menu

Creating Directories with Mkdir (F7)

The F7 (Mkdir) key enables you to make a new directory on disk. After you press F7, you are prompted to enter the name of the new directory. Enter the full path name. To make a directory named KWIKSTAT as a subdirectory of the root directory, for example, type the name *kwikstat*. To make a directory named LETTERS as a subdirectory of the WP directory, type *wp**letters*. When you use the F7 (Mkdir) command, the Norton Commander and Norton Utilities information file TREEINFO.NCD is updated so that the NCD command works properly without having to rescan. You also can make a directory with Norton Commander's NCD command.

Navigating Directories with the NCD Tree Option

The NCD Tree option is similar to the Norton Utilities Norton Change Directory (NCD) command. Chapter 6, "Managing the Resources of Your Computer," contains a more detailed description of that command. The NCD Tree option enables you to navigate among the directories on disk. This capability becomes more useful as your directory structure grows more complex.

You can choose the NCD Tree option from the Commands menu or by pressing Alt-F10. When you do so, you see a display similar to the one in figure 8.12. After this directory tree is displayed, you can change to a directory simply by moving the highlight to that directory's name. You do not need to press Enter after you highlight a directory name. Commander changes automatically to that directory. If you want to press Enter after you highlight a directory before Commander changes directories, turn off the Auto Change Directory option. See "Setting Commander Configuration," later in this chapter, for more information. If you are using a mouse, point to a directory and click the left button to change directories. Table 8.4 lists the specific movement keys available from the Tree screen.

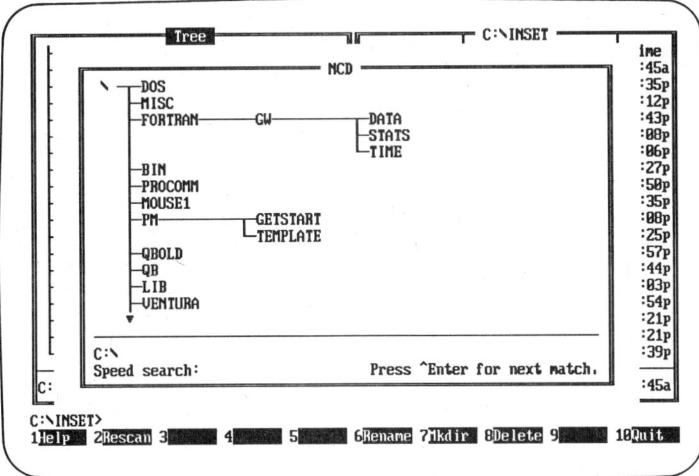

Fig. 8.12
After choosing Norton Commander's NCD Tree option.

Table 8.4
Using Cursor-Movement Keys in Commander NCD

Key	*Effect*
↑, ↓, ←, →	Moves in direction of arrow
PgUp, PgDn	Moves up and down tree on page (19 directories at a time)
Home	Moves to beginning of tree
End	Moves to end of tree
Gray +	Moves forward one directory entry in the list
Gray −	Moves backward one directory entry in the list

Other keyboard shortcuts are available when you are working on the NCD Tree screen. To select a directory, type its name. You may not have to type the entire directory name for it to be selected. When you begin typing, NCD begins a *speed search*, matching the letters you type to the directory names. You need to type only enough letters to make the name unique. To choose the \FORTRAN\GW\STATS directory from the tree displayed in figure 8.12, for example, you need to press only an S at the Speed Search prompt, because no other directories or subdirectories begin with that letter. After you press S, the directory name \FORTRAN\GW\STATS is highlighted on-screen. Then press Enter to choose the directory. (If more than one directory name began with an S, when you pressed S, the first directory in the directory list would be highlighted. To search for the next match, you could press Enter.) Table 8.5 summarizes Shortcut Commander NCD keyboard commands. Note also that several function keys are listed in the table. These keys are located at the bottom of the NCD Tree display and are described in more detail in the following sections.

Choosing the Rescan Option (F2)

The F2 (Rescan) key causes NCD to rescan a disk to update the directory structure and the TREEINFO.NCD file, which contains the tree structure information. If you make or remove a directory with the DOS MD or RD command rather than the NCD command, for example, the TREEINFO.NCD file becomes out of date. When you rescan to make sure that this file contains current information, the NCD Tree command works faster. The Rescan option has the same function as the Re-read option on the Left and Right menus.

Table 8.5
Using Keyboard Shortcuts in Commander NCD

Key	*Effect*
Any letter	Begins speed search to select a directory
Ctrl-Enter	Searches for next match
Enter	Changes directory
F2	Rescans and rebuilds TREEINFO.NCD file
F6	Renames a directory
F7	Makes a new directory
F8	Deletes a directory
Esc or F10	Quits NCD

Choosing the Rename Option (F6)

The F6 (Rename) key enables you to rename a directory. DOS has no equivalent feature. To rename a directory, follow these steps:

1. On the Tree screen, highlight the directory to rename.
2. Press F6 (Rename).
3. Type a new name.
4. Press Enter.

Choosing the Mkdir Option (F7)

The F7 (Mkdir) key on the NCD Tree screen enables you to make a new directory. First point to the directory that will be the parent directory of the new directory; then press F7 and type the new directory name. If you want to create a subdirectory of MISC named TMP, for example, point to MISC on the tree, press F7, and type *tmp*. The result is a directory named \MISC\TMP. To create a subdirectory of the root directory, highlight the \ directory before pressing F7. When you create a directory by using F7, the TREEINFO.NCD file is updated automatically.

F7 works only with the NCD tree; in other places, a dialog box appears in which you can enter the name of a new directory to make.

Choosing the Delete Option (F8)

The F8 (Delete) key enables you to remove a directory. The directory must contain no files or subdirectories. To delete a directory, simply highlight the directory name and press F8. When you delete a directory with this method, the TREEINFO.NCD file is updated automatically.

Using the Compare Directories Option

The Compare Directories option enables you to compare the contents of two directories. Before you use this command, you must display one directory in the right panel and another in the left panel. Then open the Commands menu and choose the Compare Directories option. Files having the same name but more recent dates than a file in the other directory are highlighted. This feature can be helpful if you want to compare similar directories. Suppose that you want to make sure a directory on a floppy has all the latest files that are on the hard disk directory—you can use the Compare Directories option. You also can use the Compare Directories option to make both directories identical by copying unmatching files to the other directory.

Figure 8.13 shows the comparison of two directories named \CAI2DISK on drives A and C. In the left panel, the file AEAPPHLP appears on-screen in a different color, signifying that it does not appear in both directories.

A:\CAI2DISK					C:\CAI2DISK				
Name		Size	Date	Time	Name		Size	Date	Time
..		►UP--DIR◄	4-30-90	1:35a	..		►UP--DIR◄	1-19-90	8:51a
a	img	512	12-01-89	1:01a	a	img	512	12-01-89	1:01a
aeapp	hlp	1427	12-01-89	1:01a	apple	img	896	12-01-89	1:01a
apple	img	896	12-01-89	1:01a	b	img	640	12-01-89	1:01a
b	img	640	12-01-89	1:01a	ball	img	256	12-01-89	1:01a
ball	img	256	12-01-89	1:01a	beetle	img	512	12-01-89	1:01a
beetle	img	512	12-01-89	1:01a	brun40	exe	76816	10-08-87	5:57p
brun40	exe	76816	10-08-87	5:57p	c	img	512	12-01-89	1:01a
c	img	512	12-01-89	1:01a	cai-util	exe	57178	1-19-90	2:30p
cai-util	exe	92525	4-30-90	10:01p	cai	exe	74831	2-14-90	11:04a
cai	exe	112229	4-30-90	9:49p	caidoc	enc	67196	1-19-90	7:55a
caidoc	enc	67196	1-19-90	7:55a	cat	img	768	12-01-89	1:01a
cat	img	768	12-01-89	1:01a	cat1	img	646	12-01-89	1:01a
cat1	img	646	12-01-89	1:01a	cat2	img	653	12-01-89	1:01a
cat2	img	653	12-01-89	1:01a	cat3	img	635	12-01-89	1:01a
cat3	img	635	12-01-89	1:01a	cat4	img	646	12-01-89	1:01a
cat4	img	646	12-01-89	1:01a	create	bat	16	1-19-90	9:56a
create	bat	16	1-19-90	9:56a	create	cai	17329	1-19-90	9:56a
create	cai	17329	1-19-90	9:56a	crehelp		1408	12-01-89	1:01a
crehelp		1408	12-01-89	1:01a	d	img	640	12-01-89	1:01a

A:\CAI2DISK>

1Help 2Menu 3View 4Edit 5Copy 6RenMov 7Mkdir 8Delete 9PullDn 10Quit

Fig. 8.13 Comparing directories.

Managing Your Files with Norton Commander

Along with providing easy management of your directories, Norton Commander enables you to manage your files on disk with options that exceed what you can do with DOS alone. Using Commander, you can copy, rename, move, and delete files. You also can set file attributes and find files on disk. Table 8.6 summarizes the options used to perform these tasks.

Table 8.6
Commands for Managing Files

Task	*Function Key*	*Option*
Copy files	F5	Copy option on Files menu
Rename files	F6	Rename or Move option on Files menu
Move files	F6	Rename or Move option on Files menu
Delete files	F8	Delete option on Files menu
Set Attributes		Set file attributes options such as Read-only, Archive, Hidden, and System on the Files menu.
File Find	Alt-F7	Find File option on Commands menu

The use of these options is described in the following sections.

Copying Files

You can access the Copy option by pressing F5 (Copy) or by choosing Copy from the Files menu. With the Copy option, you can copy one or more files to another disk or location. This copy procedure is similar to the DOS COPY command. When you use the Commander Copy command, however, you are prompted for the information on which files to copy and where to copy them. You therefore do not have to remember the correct DOS COPY command syntax.

To copy a file, follow these steps:

1. Display in a panel the files that you want to copy. Change to the appropriate directory by using the NCD Tree option or by pointing and shooting on the directory name on the other panel that displays the directory tree.

2. Select the file or files to copy. If you want to copy a single file, highlight that file on the Commander panel. To copy multiple files, select those files by using the gray + and gray − keys.

3. Press F5 or choose Copy from the Files menu. Commander prompts you to specify where to copy the files (see fig. 8.14).

Tip: When you are working on a disk with many files, you may want to limit the files that appear on a panel. You can do this by setting the filter to display files that match some file specification. If you are working only with *.EXE files, for example, then set the filter to display only those files.

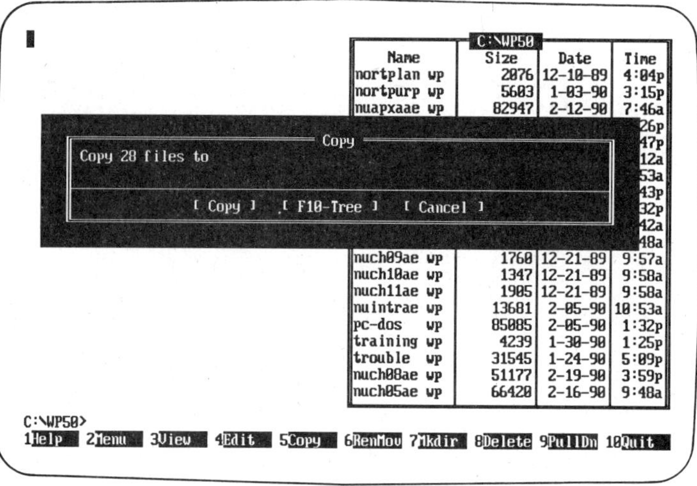

Fig. 8.14
A message asking you to specify a copy destination.

4. Specify the destination. Enter the name of a disk drive such as A:, a path name such as \WP, or a combination such as C:\WP. When specifying the destination, you can press the F10 key to display a tree of the available directories. From this tree, you can then highlight the directory to which you want the files copied. After you type or select the destination, press Enter and the copy commences.

Another way to copy files (regardless of the panels displayed) is to press Shift-F5 when your cursor is at the DOS prompt. Commander asks you to enter the specification for the file or files to copy and the destination (see fig. 8.15). You also can press F10 to display a directory tree. From this tree, you can highlight a directory name and then press Enter to select it as the destination. (You also can select with a mouse.)

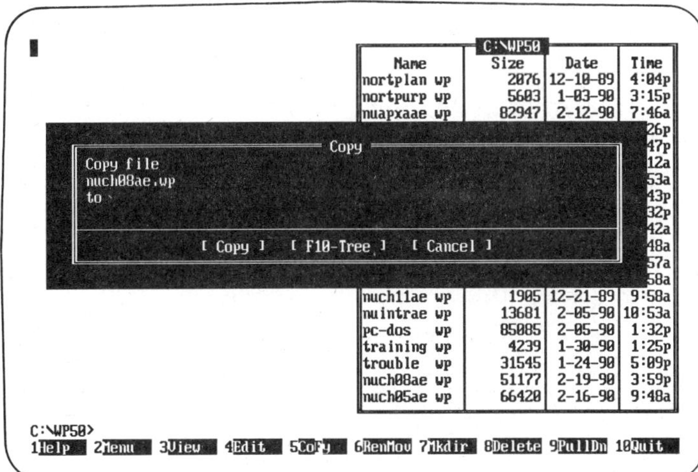

Fig. 8.15 *Using the manual copy process.*

Renaming or Moving Files

The Rename or Move option, which you access from the Files menu or by pressing F6 (Rename), enables you to rename one or more files within the same directory or to move one or more files from one location on disk to another location on that disk or another disk. The Rename process works much like the Copy option but simply changes the name of a file within a directory rather than copying the file. You use the Move option to specify a destination other than the current directory. A Move operation copies the file or files to the new destination and erases the original file or files. DOS offers no equivalent Move command.

To rename or move a file, follow these steps:

1. Select the file or files to rename or move. If you want to move or rename a single file, highlight that file on the Commander panel. If you want to rename or move multiple files, select those files by using the gray + and gray − keys.

2. Press F6 or select the Rename or Move option from the Files menu.

3. To rename the selected file or files, specify the destination as a file name or a file specification containing the wild cards * or ?. If you selected all files with the WP extension (*.WP), for example, you may type *.*bak* as the destination. This operation renames all files having the WP extension to files with a BAK extension.

To move the selected file or files, enter a destination disk or directory different from the current one. You can press F10 to display a tree of the available directories on disk and select the destination by highlighting the directory name. If you enter a destination that is a different directory (or different drive), the selected files are moved to the new location and maintain their original names. If you choose a destination and also include a file specification, the files are moved *and* renamed. If you selected all files with the WP extension in the \WP directory on drive C, for example, and you specify a new destination as A:\WP*.BAK, the files are moved from the original C:\WP directory to the A:\WP directory and are renamed from WP files to BAK files.

If the file being copied or moved exists already in the target directory, commander asks

```
Do you wish to write over the old file?
```

You may choose from the Overwrite, All, or Skip options. Overwrite enables you to copy or move a file. The All option enables you to use Copy and Move for all other files to be copied or moved. Skip means that you want to skip this particular copy or move.

To perform a rename or move operation manually, press Shift-F6. Commander prompts you to enter the files to rename or move and the destination. You can press F10 to select a destination directory from the directory tree.

Deleting Files

The Delete option, which you access from the Files menu or by pressing F8, enables you to delete one or more files. Follow these steps:

1. Select the file or files to delete. To delete a single file, highlight that file on the Commander panel. To delete multiple files, select those files by using the gray + and gray − keys.

2. Press F8 (Delete) or select Delete from the Files menu. A dialog box asks

   `Do you wish to delete (filename)`

   and gives you Delete and Cancel options. Choose the Delete option to delete the files or Cancel to cancel the procedure.

Figure 8.16 shows the FILE3.BAK file highlighted on the right panel. If you press F8, the Delete dialog box appears. Choose Delete to delete the highlighted file.

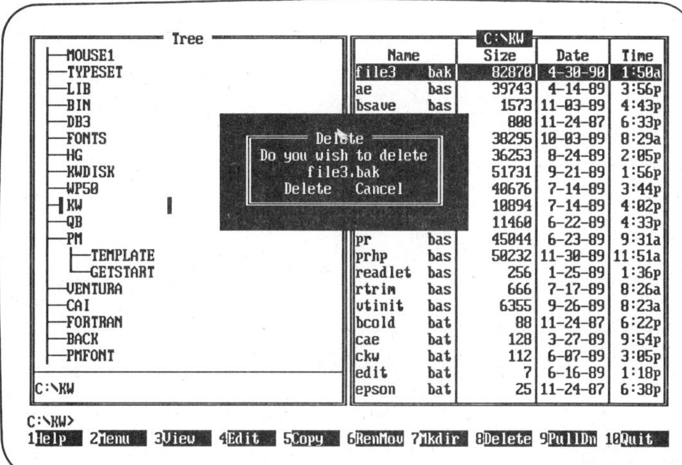

***Fig. 8.16** The FILE3.BAK file highlighted on the right panel.*

To delete files manually, press Shift-F8. Commander prompts you to enter the file specification of the files to delete. To delete all files with the BAK extension, for example, type **.bak*.

Setting File Attributes

File attributes enable you to set the Read-only, Archive, Hidden, and System settings for files. These attributes are the same as those described for the Norton Utilities File Find command. For a more detailed description of these terms, see Chapter 3, "Protecting Your Files with Norton Utilities." You can set file attributes in Norton Commander by choosing the File Attributes option from the Files menu. Follow these steps to set file attributes:

1. Select the file or files for which you want to set attributes. If you want to set a single file, highlight that file on the Commander panel. To set attributes for multiple files, select those files by using the gray + and gray − keys.
2. Open the Files menu and select the File Attributes option to display the dialog box shown in figure 8.17.

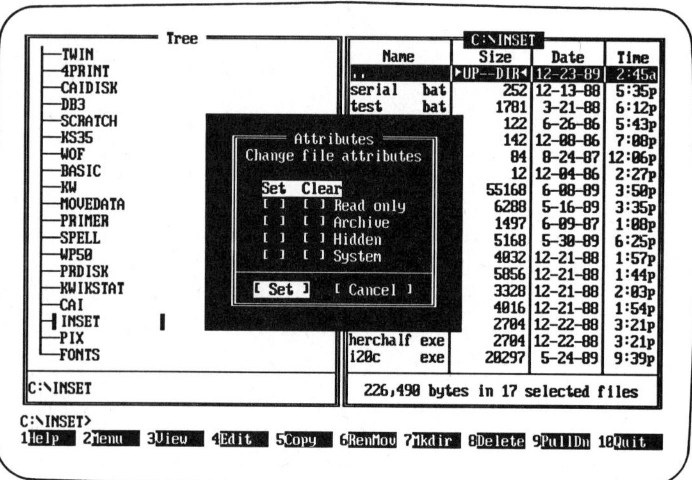

Fig. 8.17
The dialog box for setting file attributes.

3. Place the cursor in one of the option boxes and press the space bar to place an X in the box to select the option. Placing an X in the Set column sets the attribute on, and placing an X in the Clear column sets the attribute off. If you are using a mouse, point to the appropriate option box and click the left button to select.
4. Highlight the Set option at the bottom of the dialog box and press Enter to activate the settings, or choose Cancel to cancel the procedure.

Finding Files

The Commander's Find File option is similar to the Find File command in Norton Utilities. With Find File, you can locate files on disk by searching for matching file specifications. You can choose the Find File command by selecting it from the Commands menu or by pressing Alt-F7.

When you choose the Find File option, you are given a `File(s) to find:` prompt. To search for a single file, such as REPORT.90, enter the full file name at the prompt. To search for a group of files, such as all files with the CAI extension, enter a file specification that includes wild cards, such as *.CAI.

After you enter the file name or specification, press Enter to initiate the search. If a file matching the file specification is found, the directory, the file name, size, and date and time the file was created appear on-screen. If many files matching the specification are found, they are listed on-screen, grouped in their respective directories. Figure 8.18 shows a screen that gives the results of a Find File operation for all files matching the specification *.CAI.

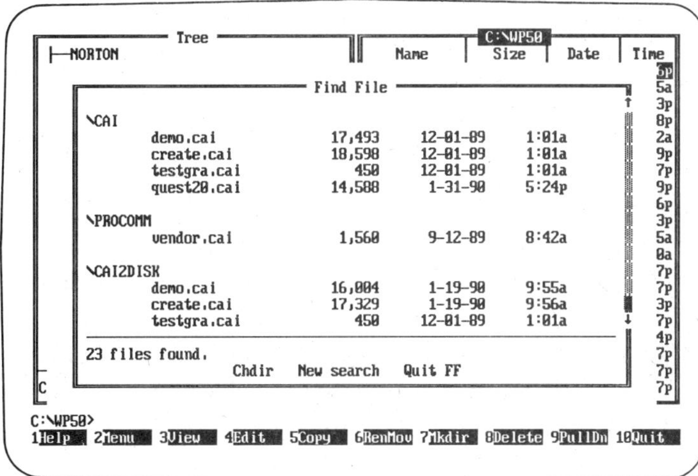

Fig. 8.18 ***The results of a Find File operation.***

To move to the directory containing the file you are interested in, use the up- and down-arrow keys to highlight the file and then press Enter.

Viewing Files with F3

The F3 (View) function key command is one of the handiest features of Norton Commander. This command enables you to examine the contents of a file without having to use an application program. To look at a dBASE III database, for example, you normally have to start the dBASE III program, enter a command to get the file you want, and then enter another command to look at the contents of a file. With Commander, however, you simply highlight the file name on-screen and press F3. If you want to enter manually the name of a file to view, press Shift-F3. Commander then prompts you for the name of the file you want to view.

You can use the View option on a number of data-storage file types used by major software programs. See the following list for compatible programs; this information is not exhaustive, however, because a number of other programs create files that use the file formats of the popular programs listed. For example, the programs PC-FILE:db from Buttonware and KWIKSTAT from TexaSoft create and use dBASE III type files. Thus, you also can view PC-FILE:db and KWIKSTAT files with Norton Commander's View option.

Spreadsheet Programs

Lotus 1-2-3 (releases 1.x and 2.x)
Lotus Symphony
Microsoft Excel
Microsoft Multiplan 4.0
Borland Quattro
Microsoft MS Works
Mosaic Twin
Words & Figures
VP-Planner Plus

Database Programs

dBASE II, III, III PLUS, and IV
FoxBASE
Nantucket Clipper
Paradox
R:BASE
Microsoft MS Works
dbXL
Reflex

Word Processing Programs

WordPerfect 4.2 and 5.0
Microsoft MS Word 4.0 and 5.0
Microsoft Windows Write
Microsoft Works
XyWrite
WordStar Pro, WordStar 2000
MultiMate
All word processors and editors that create ASCII text files

Graphics Programs

All programs that create Z-Soft standard PCX-type (Paintbrush) files. This feature may be restricted according to your monitor's ability to display colors and your computer's memory.

The following sections describe how to use the View option to view databases, spreadsheets, and word processing files.

Viewing Database Files

Norton Commander recognizes common database files for the programs in the previous lists. To view the contents of a dBASE III file, for example, highlight the file name in a panel and press F3. Figure 8.19 shows the screen that is displayed when you select a database file named MAGAZINE.DBF. The information displayed is the first record of the database. Using the up- and down-arrow keys, you can page through the database records and examine them one at a time. You cannot change any of the information in the database, however, when using the Commander View option.

At the top of the view screen, you can see information about which view method is being used to display the contents of a file. For example, figure 8.19 indicates dBASE View.

The number of the record being viewed and the total number of records in the database appear at the top right of the screen. In figure 8.19, the message 1/324 means that the database contains 324 records and you are currently viewing record 1.

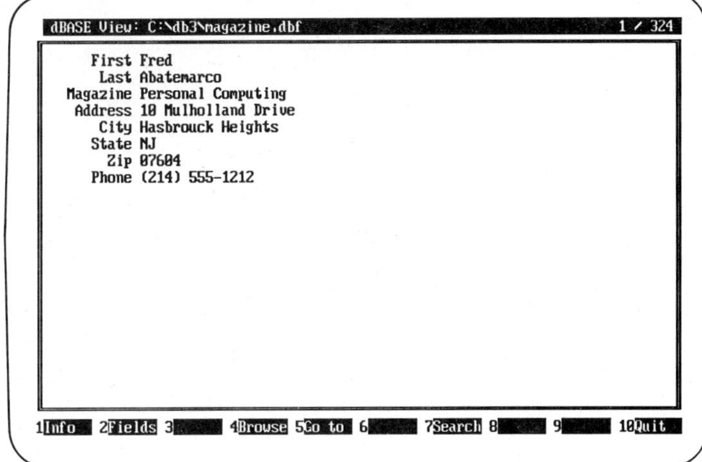

Fig. 8.19 Using the View option to view a dBASE III database file.

Notice also the function key options at the bottom of the dBASE View screen. The F1 (Info) option gives you information about the database structure. The F2 (Fields) option lists the field names and characteristics. The F4 (Browse) option mimics the dBASE III Browse command and places one record per line on-screen. The F5 (Go to) option enables you to specify a record number to display. The F7 (Search) option enables you to search for text within the database, and the F10 (Quit) option exits the view and returns you to Commander. Table 8.7 lists these these function keys and other command and movement keys that you can use when viewing database files.

When you first view a database, a single record is displayed on-screen. If you press F4, the display changes to look much like a browse in dBASE, with one record displayed per line. Figure 8.20 shows this for the MAGAZINE database. Using this method, you can see multiple records at a time. However, notice that only the first three fields of the record are displayed. To view the information off the screen to the right, press the right-arrow key until information in the other fields appears. To return to viewing a single record at a time, press F4 again.

Suppose that you want to find information in a particular record—you want to find the phone number of Sam Jones, for example. If you press F7, a Search dialog box appears where you can enter a search key. Figure 8.21 shows how you enter the information to search for the name "Jones." After entering the search key and pressing Enter, the first record containing Jones (in any field) appears on-screen. If this is not the Jones you are looking for, you can press Shift-F7 to continue the search.

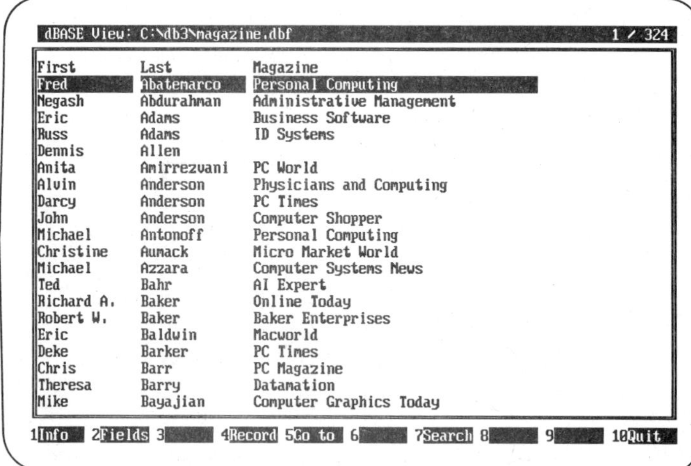

dBASE View: C:\db3\magazine.dbf
1 / 324
First Last Magazine
Fred Abatemarco Personal Computing
Negash Abdurahman Administrative Management
Eric Adams Business Software
Russ Adams ID Systems
Dennis Allen
Anita Amirrezvani PC World
Alvin Anderson Physicians and Computing
Darcy Anderson PC Times
John Anderson Computer Shopper
Michael Antonoff Personal Computing
Christine Aumack Micro Market World
Michael Azzara Computer Systems News
Ted Bahr AI Expert
Richard A. Baker Online Today
Robert W. Baker Baker Enterprises
Eric Baldwin Macworld
Deke Barker PC Times
Chris Barr PC Magazine
Theresa Barry Datamation
Mike Bayajian Computer Graphics Today
1Info 2Fields 3 4Record 5Go to 6 7Search 8 9 10Quit

Fig. 8.20 ***Viewing a record from the MAGAZINE database.***

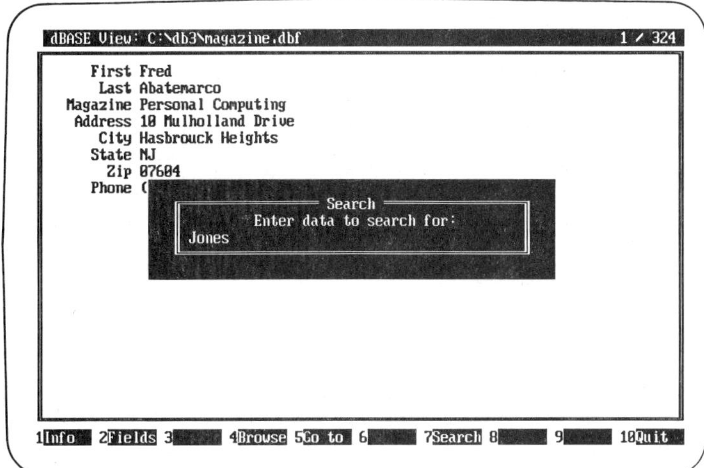

***Fig. 8.21* Searching a record for the name "Jones."**

If you know the record number of the record you want to view, you can press F5. You are prompted to enter the record number, and then that record is displayed.

At times, you may need to know the structure of a database. You may be working on a program to merge information from the database, for example, and need to know field names and widths. When you are viewing a database, you can press F2 to display the structure of the database, as shown in figure 8.22. This gives you information about the field names, types, widths, and decimals used (if any).

To exit the view screen, press Esc or F10 and you return to Commander.

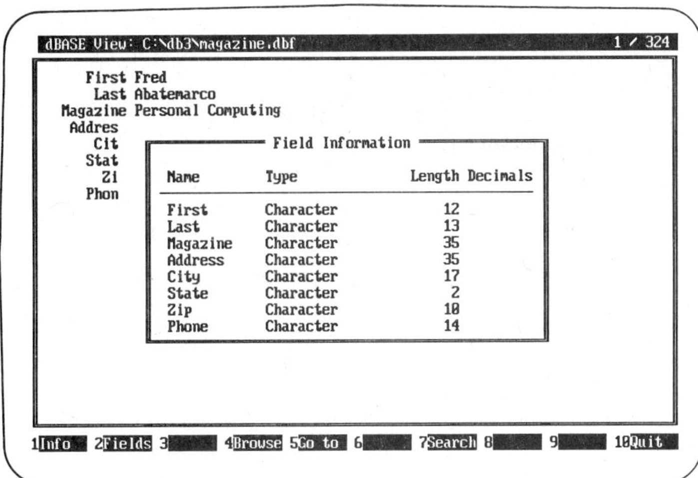

***Fig. 8.22* Displaying the structure of a database.**

Table 8.7
Keyboard Commands for the Database View

Key	*Effect*
↑ or Ctrl-E	Goes back one field
↓ or Ctrl-X	Goes forward one field
PgUp or Ctrl-R	Moves up one page or to previous record
PgDn or Ctrl-C	Moves down one page or to next record
Gray −	Goes to previous record
Gray +	Goes to next record
Ctrl-Home or Ctrl-PgUp	Goes to first record
Ctrl-End or Ctrl-PgDn	Goes to last record
F1	Displays file information
F2	Displays field information
F4	Browses
F5	Goes to record
F7	Searches
Shift-F7	Continues a search
Ctrl-Pause	Stops a search
Esc or F10	Quits View and returns to Commander menus

Viewing Spreadsheet Files

Norton Commander recognizes common spreadsheet files for the programs listed in the "Viewing Files with F3" section. To view the contents of a Mosaic Twin file, for example, highlight that file name in a panel and press F3. Figure 8.23 shows the screen displayed after you select the file named COMMAND.WKT. From the WKT extension, Commander knows that the selected file was created by Mosaic Twin, which is a spreadsheet program similar to Lotus 1-2-3.

```
Mosaic Twin View: C:\twin\command.wkt
A1: 'Commander Company Cash Flow Analysis for 1990
        A          B        C        D        E        F        G        H
1  Commander Company Cash Flow Analysis for 1990
2               Jan      Feb      Mar      Apr      May     June     July
3  REVENUES   ------   ------   ------   ------   ------   ------   ------
4  Sales      1277.5  1463.16   1828.4    821.4   2143.4   2751.2  2827.06
5  Royalites     577      577     1154     1154     1154      577      577
6  Other          23       44       21       11        2       34       22
7  Interest     5.83     3.94     1.04     1.32     1.11     1.23     1.22
8  TOTAL     1883.33   2888.1  3004.44  1987.72  3300.51  3363.43  3427.28
9             ------   ------   ------   ------   ------   ------   ------
10
11 EXPENSES   ------   ------   ------   ------   ------   ------   ------
12 Commissio    2332      600     1154  3057.13   1546.5  1338.07   711.27
13 Phone      125.84            146.13    162.4   196.55    94.01   314.14
14 Printing       70     50.7    11.47            385.57    84.33   182.88
15 COGS        59.89   322.19    57.09    51.23   608.12   640.29   508.87
16 State Fees                      160                                 25
17 Postage     79.81   193.17   130.82   115.21   117.74   356.84   451.22
18 Dues                    50       68            240.61
19 Cont Ed    240.67                                  24
20 Writing              94.65
1Help 2 3 4 5Goto 6 7Search 8 9 10Quit
```

Fig. 8.23 Using the View option to view a Mosaic Twin spreadsheet file.

At the top of the view screen, you can see information about which view method is being used to display the contents of a file. In figure 8.23, the first line indicates Mosaic Twin View. The second line of the screen shows the name and contents of the cell being viewed.

In this view screen, the F1 (Help) key displays information about cursor-key movements and the function-key commands. The F5 (Go to) option enables you to choose the area of the spreadsheet to display. The F7 (Search) option enables you to search for text within the spreadsheet, and the F10 (Quit) option exits the view and returns you to Commander. Table 8.8 shows these function keys and other command and movement keys that you can use when viewing spreadsheet files.

If you want to search the database for particular information, you can use the F7 (Search) key. If you want to find the label containing the word "Taxes," for example, you can press F7 and then enter the search word in the Search dialog box, as shown in figure 8.24. After you press Enter, the first cell containing a match is highlighted in the spreadsheet. If that is not the label you are looking for, press Shift-F7 to continue the search. If you already know the cell name of the cell you want to view, press the F5 (Go to) key, and then enter a cell address (for example, A5 or N50). Press Esc or F10 to end View and return to Commander.

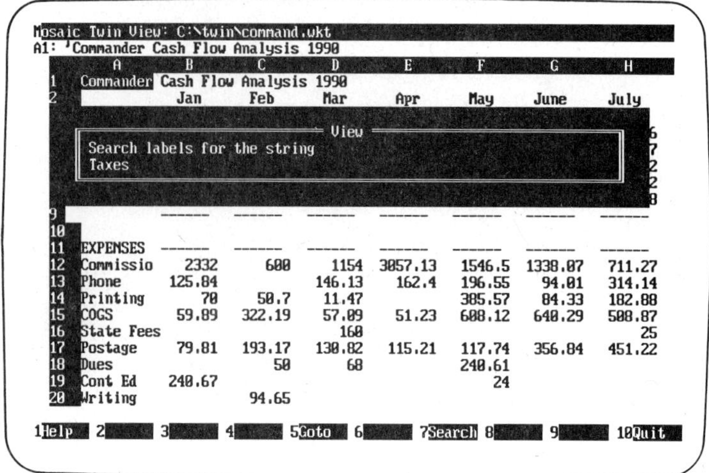

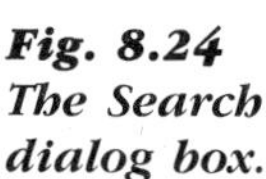

Fig. 8.24
The Search dialog box.

Table 8.8
Keyboard Commands for the Spreadsheet View

Key	*Effect*
Home	Goes to top left cell
End	Goes to last active cell
← or Ctrl-S	Moves one cell left
→ or Ctrl-D	Moves one cell right
↑ or Ctrl-E	Moves one cell up
↓ or Ctrl-X	Moves one cell down
PgUp or Ctrl-R	Moves one page up
PgDn or Ctrl-D	Moves one page down
Tab or Ctrl-→	Scrolls one page right
Shift-Tab or Ctrl-←	Scrolls one page left
F5	Goes to record
F7	Searches
Shift-F7	Continues search
Esc or F10	Quits View and returns to Commander menus

Viewing Word Processor Files

Norton Commander recognizes common word processing files for the programs listed in the "Viewing Files with F3" section. To view the contents of a WordPerfect file, for example, highlight that file name in a panel and press F3. A view of a WordPerfect file is shown in figure 8.25.

```
WordPerfect View: C:\wp50\ch08ae.wp5     Col 0      72,390 Bytes      1%

Norton Commander, Version 3.00, is a program that enables you to
perform a variety of tasks on your computer in a menu-like
environment rather than from the standard DOS command line. Instead
of having to remember the syntax of the DOS COPY command, for
example, you are led through the Commander copy process with a
series of menus and prompts.

Commander is not just a substitute for some DOS commands; it also
provides you with a number of features that are not found in DOS.
You can use Commander, for example, to view the contents of a
variety of database, spreadsheet, and word processing files without
having to use the respective application programs. Also, Commander
enables you to execute several of the Norton Utilities commands,
such as displaying a sorted directory, setting file attributes,
finding files, setting an EGA monitor to display more than 25
lines, and more.

One of the main features of Norton Commander is convenience. It is
a bit like an automatic transmission in a car. You can get by with
a manual transmission, but an automatic transmission often makes
driving the car easier and more pleasurable. In the same way, many
of the things that you can do in Commander you can do also in DOS
1Help  2Unwrap 3      4Hex   5      6      7Search 8Viewer 9      10Quit
```

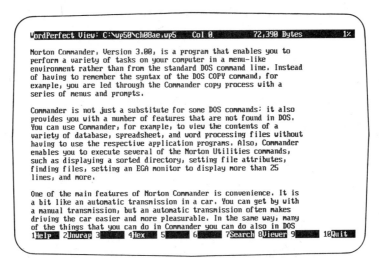

Fig. 8.25
Using the View option to view a WordPerfect file.

At the top of the view panel, you can see information about which view method is being used to display the contents of a file. The top line in figure 8.25 indicates WordPerfect view. (If the view type is inappropriate for this file you can use the F8 key to choose another view type. You may be trying to view a WordPerfect file using the WordStar view type, for example.) The top line of the view screen also displays the file name, the current column location of the cursor, the size of the file in bytes, and a percent that represents the amount of the file that has been paged off the top of the screen.

In this screen, the function key F2 (Unwrap) enables you to toggle word wrap on and off. When text is wrapped, text that would exceed the right margin is wrapped around to the next line. When text is unwrapped, it may exceed the right margin. You can use the cursor-movement keys to display information past the right margin. The F4 (Hex) key enables you to examine a file in Hex (hexadecimal) code. This feature may be useful if you are looking for some special character codes in a file. Sometimes files contain characters that are not normally printable on-screen, for example.

These "ghost" characters can cause problems when you try to edit or print the file. If you display the file in Hex format, you can locate these unusual characters and then edit them out of your file using your editor. The F7 (Search) key enables you to search for text within a file. The F8 (View) key enables you to change the view type to another type available for word processors (see the "Viewing Files with F3" section). The F10 (Quit) function key quits the View option and returns you to Commander. Table 8.9 shows these function keys and other command and movement keys that you can use when viewing word processor files.

When you select a file to view, Norton is able to decipher the kind of database files and spreadsheet files from the extension. For example, DBF files are dBASE databases and WKS files are Lotus 1-2-3 spreadsheets. However, word processors usually enable you to name your files using any extension. Many times, Norton is able to figure out what kind of file you are attempting to display, and it will use the word processor view type it thinks most appropriate. If Norton is wrong, however, you will have to select manually the view type by pressing F8 and then selecting the view you think is appropriate. Figure 8.26 shows the Select Viewer dialog box.

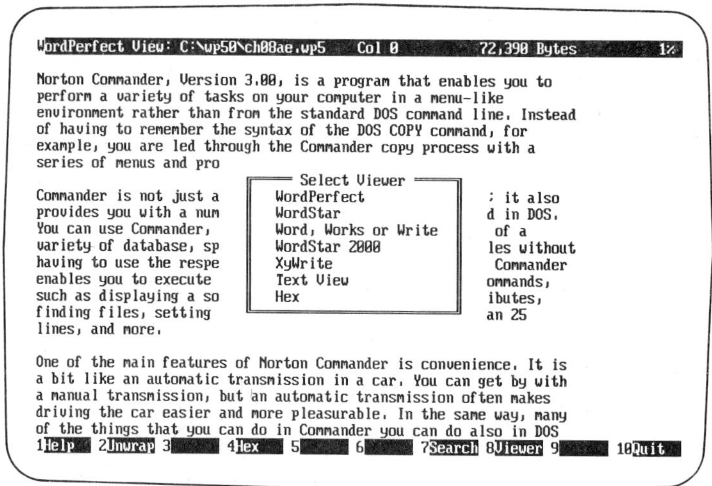

Fig. 8.26* *The Select Viewer dialog box.

Because many word processing documents are long, it may take time to scroll through a document to look for a specific piece of information. If you know some key word that will be near the paragraph you are looking for, you can use the F7 (Search) key to help locate the information. Suppose that you are looking for a paragraph about a virus, for example. To find this paragraph, press F7. A dialog box appears (similar to the ones previously discussed for database and spreadsheet views). Enter the key word "virus" and press Enter. The lines around the first occurrence of "virus" appear on-screen. If this is not the paragraph you are looking for, press Shift-F7 to continue the search until you find the information you are looking for. To end a search that is taking a very long time, press Ctrl-Break or Esc.

Press Esc or F10 to quit the view and return to Commander.

Table 8.9
Keyboard Commands for the Word Processing View

Key	*Effect*
↑ or Ctrl-E	Scrolls up
↓ or Ctrl-X	Scrolls down
← or Ctrl-S	Scrolls left
→ or Ctrl-D	Scrolls right
Ctrl-← or Ctrl-A	Scrolls left 40 columns
Ctrl-→ or Ctrl-F	Scrolls right 40 columns
PgUp or Ctrl-R	Moves one page up
PgDn or Ctrl-C	Moves one page down
Home, Ctrl-Home, or Ctrl-PgUp	Goes to beginning of file
End, Ctrl-End, or Ctrl-PgDn	Goes to end of file
F2	Toggles word wrap on/off
F3	Returns to quick-view panel (available only if the view screen was originally a quick-view panel)
F7	Searches for text
Shift-F7	Continues search
Ctrl-Break or Esc	Stops a search
F8	Selects view type
Esc or F10	Quits

Editing ASCII Text Files

In addition to enabling you to view files, the Edit option (or the F4 key) from Commander's Files menu enables you to edit ASCII text files. You can use this feature to edit files up to 25K (about 25,000 characters) in length. The command is ideal if you need to create or modify batch files (such as AUTOEXEC.BAT) or other ASCII text files.

Using the Commander Editor

The Commander editor is a full-screen editor similar to a word processor editor. To use it to edit an existing file, highlight the file name in a Commander panel and then press F4 or choose Edit from the Files menu. If you want to enter manually the name of the file to edit, press Shift-F4. Commander then prompts you to enter the file name. Figure 8.27 shows the editor being used to edit the file CONFIG.SYS.

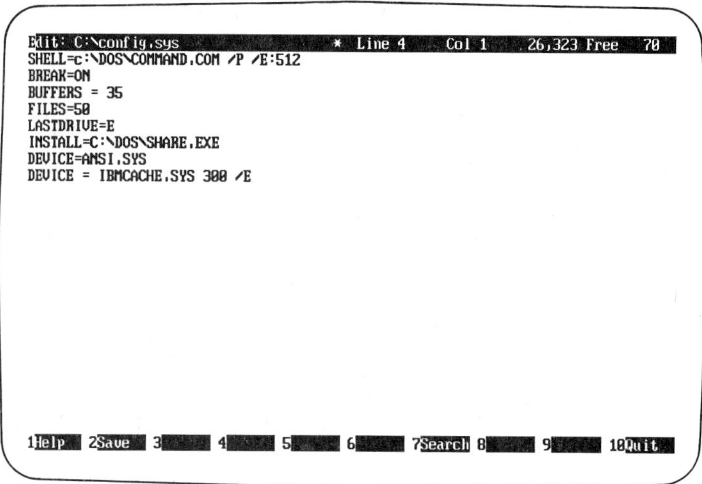

Fig. 8.27* *Editing the CONFIG.SYS file.

Most of the commands in the editor, particularly the cursor-movement commands, are the same as they would be in any full-screen editor. Several editor commands deserve some added explanation, however. The Ctrl-Q command, for example, is used to enter special characters into a file. Suppose that you want to enter the ASCII Escape character in a file as a part of a printer code or for some other reason. Normally, if you press Esc, you quit the editor and return to Commander. However, if you press

Ctrl-Q first, and then press Esc, the Esc character is placed in the file as if you had typed it in like any other character. (It appears as an arrow on-screen.)

Press F2 to save the file you edited. This saves the file under the original file name that you chose from the Commander panel. If you want to use a new name, press Shift-F2 and you are prompted to enter a new name. If the file is long and you want to search for a particular word or phrase, you can press F7. You then are prompted to enter the search word. If the first word found is not the one you are looking for, press Shift-F7 to repeat the search. To end the editor, press Esc or F10. Remember to save the file before quitting if you want your edits to be saved to disk.

Table 8.10 lists the cursor-movement and editing keys that you can use in the Commander editor.

Table 8.10
Using Cursor-Movement and Editing Keys in the Commander Editor

Key	*Effect*
↑ or Ctrl-E	Scrolls up
↓ or Ctrl-X	Scrolls down
← or Ctrl-S	Scrolls left
→ or Ctrl-D	Scrolls right
Ctrl-← or Ctrl-A	Moves one word left
Ctrl-→ or Ctrl-F	Moves one word right
Home	Goes to beginning of line
End	Goes to end of line
PgUp or Ctrl-R	Moves one page up
PgDn or Ctrl-C	Moves one page down
Ctrl-Home or Ctrl-PgUp	Goes to beginning of file
Ctrl-End or Ctrl-PgDn	Goes to end of file
Backspace	Deletes character to left
Del or Ctrl-G	Deletes character at cursor
Ctrl-Backspace or Ctrl-W	Deletes one word left

Table 8.10 *continued*

Key	*Effect*
Ctrl-T	Deletes one word right
Ctrl-Y	Deletes line
Ctrl-K	Deletes to end of line
Ctrl-Q	Quotes next character
F1	Accesses help
F2	Saves file
Shift-F2	Asks for "save as" name
F7	Searches for text
Shift-F7	Continues search
Esc or F10	Quits editor and returns to Commander
Shift-F10	Saves and quits editor

Using a Substitute Editor

Normally, when you choose an edit option, Commander uses a built-in editor. You can, however, specify that Commander use an editor of your choice. You may want to use your editor as a substitute editor if you are familiar with it and prefer using it instead of the Commander editor. From the Options menu, choose the Editor option. You then are prompted to choose the built-in editor or an external editor. To choose the Built-in option or the External option, use the arrow keys to highlight your choice on the Edit menu and press the space bar.

If you choose the External option, Commander prompts you to enter the command used to begin the editor. Enter this command followed by an exclamation mark (!) if you want to use only a file name when editing, or type *!.!* after the command if you want to use a file name plus an extension. If you are using the WP editor in the \WPROC directory, for example, you should enter the following command to indicate that you want the full file name used when editing:

```
\WPROC\WP !.!
```

The path name (\WPROC) is necessary if that is how you must start the editor when you enter the command from the DOS prompt. If you do not use a ! or !.!, Commander uses !.! as a default.

Customizing the Norton Commander Screen Display

Norton Commander has several options with which you can customize how the program looks on your screen. For example, you can change the number of lines displayed (if you have an EGA or VGA monitor), thus enabling Commander to display more information per screen. Also, you can control Commander's screen-blanking feature, whether hidden files and directories appear in displayed directories, and other options.

Controlling the Number of Lines On-Screen

The EGA Lines option enables you to set your EGA or VGA monitor to display more than the normal 25 lines per screen. You can access this option by choosing EGA Lines from the Commands menu or by pressing Alt-F9. The command works as a toggle switch. If you have an EGA monitor, choosing the command toggles between the normal 25-line mode and a 43-line mode. If you are using a VGA monitor, you toggle between 25- and 50-line modes. Displaying more information on-screen may simplify your access to files and directories. The only problem with these 43- and 50-line modes is that the characters are smaller than normal and may be more difficult to read—you may need to wear your bifocals!

Tip: If your CONFIG.SYS file in the root directory contains the command line DEVICE=ANSI.SYS, the number of lines that can be displayed on-screen is limited to 25. Thus, even if you enter the 43-line EGA mode or 50-line VGA mode, your monitor still displays only 25 lines. You can remove this command from the CONFIG.SYS file to enable your monitor to display a larger number of lines per screen. Or, if you are using DOS 4.0 or higher, include the switch /L in the command, which displays 43- and 50-line screens. Before you decide to remove the ANSI.SYS command, be aware that some programs need it in order to work properly. You will have to check your particular applications to see if they require ANSI.SYS in order to operate.

Choosing Other Screen Options

The Options menu gives you several screen options from which to choose. Like the EGA Lines option, these options operate as toggle switches, turning the features off and on. When an option is on, a check mark appears beside the option name in the Options menu. The following options are available from the Options menu:

- *Auto Menus*: See Chapter 9. This is an advanced feature.
- *Path Prompt*: Controls whether the DOS prompt includes a path name. If you are in the \WP directory with the Path Prompt turned off, for example, the DOS prompt (on drive C) is

  C>

  With Path Prompt on, the prompt is

  C:\WP>

  Most users prefer the second version of the prompt (which includes the path) because it tells you which directory is being used currently.
- *Key Bar*: Determines whether the Function Key menu appears at the bottom of the screen.
- *Full Screen*: Determines whether the right and left panels extend from the top to the bottom of the screen or are only half that size.
- *Mini Status*: Controls the status line at the bottom of each panel. When the Mini Status option is turned on, the status line shows the name, size, date, and time for the highlighted file or directory. If you have made a selection of files, the status line gives a count of the number of files selected. If the Mini Status option is off, the status line does not appear.
- *Clock*: Determines whether a clock appears at the upper right corner of the Commander screen. Choosing to have the clock displayed is only a convenience and serves no other purpose.

When you exit Norton Commander, changes in screen options, such as which panels are displayed and how, revert back to whatever was in effect when you first started Commander. To save any changes so that they will be in effect the next time you use Commander, you must choose to save the setup by selecting the Configuration option from the Options menu and then choosing Auto Save Setup.

Setting Commander Configuration

After you select the Configuration option from the Options menu, you see a dialog box like the one in figure 8.28. Notice that this box has five areas of settings: Screen Colors, Screen Blank Delay, File Panel Options, Tree Panel Options, and Other Options.

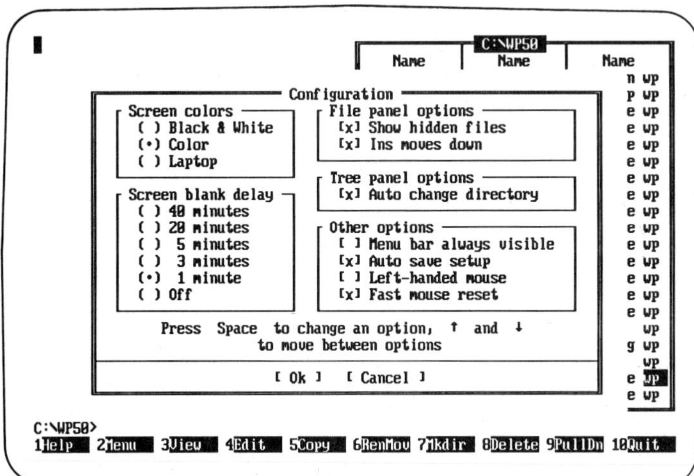

Fig. 8.28
The Configuration dialog box.

Setting Screen Colors

In the Screen Colors area, you can tell Commander that you want information displayed on a color monitor, a black-and-white monitor, or a laptop monitor. Select or deselect the type of monitor by using the arrow keys to move the highlight and pressing the space bar. If you are using a mouse, you can point to the appropriate option and click the left button.

Setting Blank Screen Delay Options

The Screen Blank Delay options enable you to choose how long Commander waits until automatically blanking out your screen. Blanking out the screen saves your monitor from possible *burn in* of an image. (On some screens, if you leave an image on-screen for a long time, a trace of the image remains on-screen like a ghost.) The default time used in Commander before blanking the screen is five minutes.

When Commander blanks out the screen, you see a random pattern of white dots on a black background, resembling stars in the sky. The dots come and go so that you can tell that the computer is working. When the screen is blanked out, you can press any key or move the mouse to bring back the working screen. Commander blanks out the screen only when you are at the DOS prompt—not when you are in a program, such as a word processor. You can choose to turn off the blanking feature or to set the wait from 1 minute to 40 minutes by using the arrow keys to highlight the appropriate option in the Screen Blank Delay area and then pressing the space bar to lock the option into place. If you are using a mouse, point to the option and click the left button.

Setting File Panel Options

The File Panel Options area of the Configuration dialog box enables you to indicate whether you want hidden files to appear in directories. You also can choose the meaning of the Ins key when marking files. If you mark the Ins Moves Down option, you can select files from a panel by repeatedly pressing the Ins key. Each time you press Ins, the cursor moves down to the next file. If you do not mark Ins Moves Down, the highlight does not move down to the next file after you press Ins. You instead have to select options with arrow keys and the space bar or with the mouse.

Controlling Automatic Display of Directory Files

The Tree Panel Options area gives you one option: Auto Change Directory. If you turn on this option, you tell Commander that when you highlight a directory in a tree, you want the other panel to display the files contained in the highlighted directory. Select the Auto Change Directory option with arrow keys and the space bar or with the mouse.

Setting Other Configuration Options

Other options available in the Configuration dialog box include choosing to have the menu bar always visible at the top of the screen (by default it is not visible); automatically saving any changes you make to the configuration during a session (it is on by default); specifying whether you are using a left-handed mouse, which reverses the functions of the left and right buttons (the right mouse is the default); and turning on the fast mouse reset. If the fast mouse reset is on, Commander can return more quickly from a command if you are using a COMPAQ or PS/2 model computer with a mouse port. Select options in the Other Options area with arrow keys and the space bar or with the mouse.

Summary

This introductory look at Norton Commander showed you how to access the Commander menus and described the meaning of most menu options. You learned how to use Commander as a substitute for DOS commands such as Copy, Rename, and Delete. Commander also has a Move function to move files, which cannot be performed in DOS. The Commander NCD command is an important part of managing your directories on your hard disk. With NCD, you can choose directories from a graphic tree, make new directories, change directories, and remove directories. With NCD, you can rename a directory—something that DOS cannot perform. Using the View file options, you can use Commander to view quickly the contents of a number of word processing, spreadsheet, and database files. You also can use Commander to set screen colors, save your monitor screen by using screen blanking, and more. For information on advanced Norton Commander options, move on to Chapter 9.

Norton Commander Advanced Topics

The Norton Commander features covered in Chapter 8 are straightforward commands that you can use without any advanced computer knowledge. Although the topics in this chapter require more knowledge about how a computer works, they also introduce you to some of the more exciting features of Norton Commander. In this chapter, you learn to use menus to customize your computer so that it works the way you think it should work. You learn to shortcut your access to programs so that you can point to files on-screen and have the application program come up immediately. You also discover how to use Commander Mail to send messages by electronic mail (E-Mail) and Commander Link to transfer information quickly from one computer to another.

Creating and Using Menus in Commander

Each person has his or her own particular selection of programs. You may use WordPerfect, Microsoft Excel, and dBASE III, for example. Another person may use PC-FILE, Procomm, Kwikstat, and 10 other programs. To begin any one of these programs on your computer, you may need to enter several commands. You first may change the directory, then run a preliminary setup program, and then run the actual program, for example. If you use the computer infrequently or have many different directories and programs, you may forget the command sequences for all your programs. You may wish that you had a menu of programs so that you could just choose a program and automatically issue all necessary commands to begin the program. That is exactly what you can do with a Norton Commander user menu.

A *user menu* is a list of items that appears on-screen (like a dialog box) from which you can choose options. A series of commands (usually DOS commands) is associated with each of the options on the user menu. After you choose a menu option, Commander issues these commands in sequence as if they were entered from the DOS prompt, much like a batch file does. Usually, these commands begin a program.

Two kinds of user menus are available: main and local. You use the same commands to create both menus. The primary physical difference between the menus is the directory in which they are stored. The main menu is stored in the \NC directory. Local menus are stored in other directories. The main functional difference between a main menu and a local menu is that *local menus* usually contain selections that deal with programs in a local directory, whereas a *main menu* usually contains selections that pertain to programs in a number of different directories.

You activate a user menu by pressing F2 while the Commander program is running and the DOS prompt is on-screen. If a local menu is located in the current directory, that menu appears. If no local menu exists, Commander accesses the main menu from the \NC directory. If no menu is available in either place, you get an error message after you press F2.

Thus, the first (and perhaps the only) menu you usually need to create is the one in the \NC directory—the main menu. If it is the only user menu, you can access it whenever you press F2—from any directory. This setup is the simplest and least complicated. If you want different menus in other subdirectories, however, you need to create local menus. (You can have local menus without having a main menu.) You may want to have a local menu in a subdirectory that contains a number of programs you want to access. In your accounting directory, for example, you may want to have a menu of options available to run programs that do posting, end-of-month runs, trial balances, and so on, but you do not want all these options cluttering up the main menu. You therefore may choose the broad topic Accounting from the main menu, which brings up the local menu that has the detailed accounting choices. Alternatively, because some systems are used by more than one person, you may want to have different menus loading different batch files to start various programs. You could have one batch file that causes WordPerfect to load with a particular data file directory, for example, and another batch file that causes Ventura to call from a particular customer a chapter information file.

Creating User Menus

You create a user menu in Norton Commander by selecting the Menu File Edit option from the Commands menu. You then enter lines of information in a file to tell Commander which selections you want to display in the menu and what should happen when a user chooses any of those menu items. You can place four basic kinds of lines in the menu file:

- *Comment lines* begin with a single quotation mark ('). These lines do not influence how the menu looks or functions. Comment lines are optional and are provided only so that you can document what the menu file does. Comments are helpful to other users who may have to change the file in the future, or may be helpful to you if you have to return to the file a year later.

- *Menu items* begin with a single character, called a hot key, followed by a colon (:). To create a menu item called Begin WordPerfect that is chosen when a user presses W, for example, enter this command in the menu file:

  W: Begin WordPerfect

  The W (the hot key) must be in the far left column of the file (flush left). If you enter a noncomment line flush left (any line without a letter and a colon or an apostrophe that is flush left), it becomes a menu item without a hot key. When the menu comes up, the user has to choose the item by highlighting it with the arrow keys and pressing Enter, or by pointing and shooting with a mouse.

- *DOS commands* or other commands are listed on the lines following a menu item. These commands must *not* be flush left. You must indent these commands by placing a tab or one or more blank spaces in front of the text.

- *Blank line separators* should be inserted after each menu item. To create a blank line, press Enter.

To create a typical user menu, follow these steps:

1. Start Norton Commander from the DOS prompt if the program is not running already.

2. Open the Commands pull-down menu from the menu bar.

3. Select the Menu File Edit option from the Commands menu.

   A dialog box similar to the one in figure 9.1 appears.

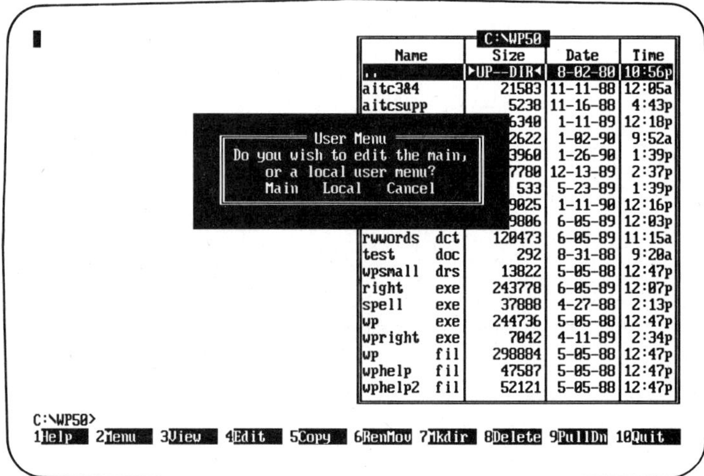

Fig. 9.1
Creating a user menu.

4. You are given the option to create a main menu, a local menu, or to cancel the command. In this example, choose Main. The Commander User Menu Edit screen appears (which is really a version of the Commander editor discussed in the preceding chapter), with the file named NC.MNU in the \NC directory on-screen and ready for you to edit (see fig. 9.2). (If you choose to edit a local menu in another directory, the edit screen displays the NC.MNU file for you to edit in the specified directory.) Notice the help box at the bottom of the editor screen in figure 9.2. This screen summarizes the file format for creating a user menu.

Fig. 9.2
The Norton Commander User Menu Edit screen.

5. In the menu file, enter lines that define your user menu. For example, the lines associated with beginning the WordPerfect program are

   W: Begin WordPerfect
   NCD \WP50
   WP

   Note that the menu item line, W: Begin WordPerfect, is flush left in the file, and the other lines are indented. Figure 9.3 shows an example of information entered in the editor to create a menu with three menu selections. Each menu selection begins with a single letter followed by a colon and a brief description of the menu option. Following each menu option are some DOS commands that invoke the appropriate program. The Procomm program, for example, begins with two commands. First, the NCD \PROCOMM command changes to the \PROCOMM directory. Then, the PROCOMM command begins the Procomm program.

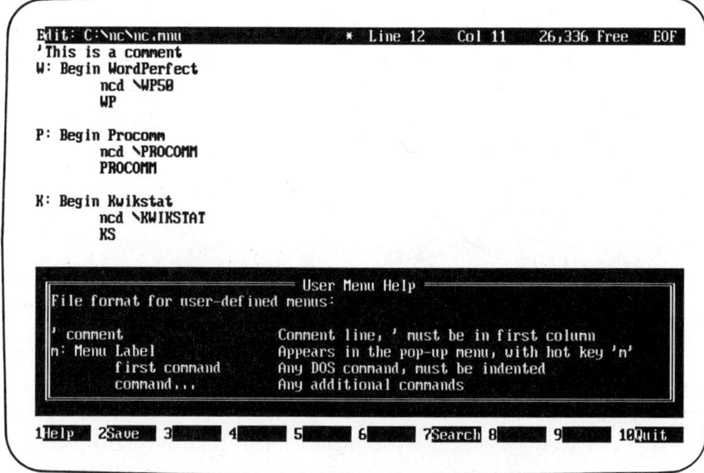

***Fig. 9.3* Sample menu entries on the User Menu Edit screen.**

6. Save the menu file by pressing F2 (Save).
7. Quit the menu editor by pressing F10 (Quit).

Invoking User Menus

After you create a menu, you can open it by pressing the F2 (Menu) key from the Norton Commander screen. Remember that if a local menu exists in the current directory, Commander opens that menu. If no local menu exists, Commander opens the main menu located in the \NC directory. Figure 9.4 shows how the sample menu created in figure 9.3 would look on-screen.

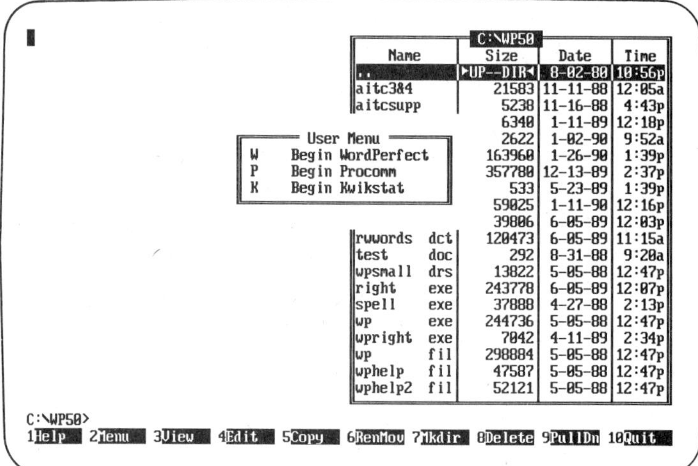

Fig. 9.4
The sample menu in use.

To choose an option on this menu, you can use one of three methods: pressing the option's hot key, highlighting the option and pressing Enter, or double-clicking the option with a mouse. To end the user menu without choosing an option, press Esc.

Automating Menus

If you are taking advantage of Commander's menu capabilities, you may want to set up the program to display your user menu whenever you start Commander. You may create a series of menus, for example, to help a novice use a variety of application programs. With this design, a user never has to issue a DOS command.

You can automate the user menu system by choosing (turning on) the Auto Menus option on the Options menu. When Auto Menus is turned on (a check mark appears beside it on the menu), the local or main menu (whichever is appropriate to the current directory) opens whenever you begin Commander. Keep in mind, however, that after you or another user ends the menu by pressing Esc or by choosing some other menu item, the user menu disappears. You must press F2 to redisplay the menu.

You can design local menus so that they always come back to the main menu, however. For example, the commands that you may use in the main menu to begin WordPerfect could be

```
W: Begin Word Perfect
   NCD \WP50
   WP
   NCD \NC
```

The first line tells the program that the W hot key is associated with the menu item Begin WordPerfect. The second line begins the commands that are used if a user chooses the W option from the menu. This line changes to the \WP50 directory, which contains the WordPerfect program. The third line begins the WordPerfect program. The fourth line changes back to the \NC directory so that the main menu again appears. Thus, after you exit from WordPerfect, the command NCD \NC is issued automatically, which brings you back to the \NC directory and the main menu.

Defining File Extensions in Commander

Another element of Norton Commander that takes some of the work out of accessing application programs is the file-extension feature, which you can use to define meanings for file extensions. After Commander knows the definition of a file extension, you can select any file with that extension from a panel, and Commander begins the appropriate application program necessary to use the file. Recall that a file specification is of the form *filename.ext*, where *ext* is the file extension. If you have defined WP as an extension for WordPerfect, for example, and you then select the file REPORT.WP from a panel, Commander automatically begins WordPerfect with the file REPORT.WP on-screen and ready to edit.

To tell Commander the meanings of various extensions, you must enter information into the file NC.EXT in the \NC directory. To create or edit this file, follow these steps:

1. Open the Commands pull-down menu from the menu bar.
2. Select the Extension option from the Commands menu.

   You see a screen similar to the one in figure 9.5. The help box at the bottom of this screen summarizes the format of an extension command. You now are in the Commander editor.

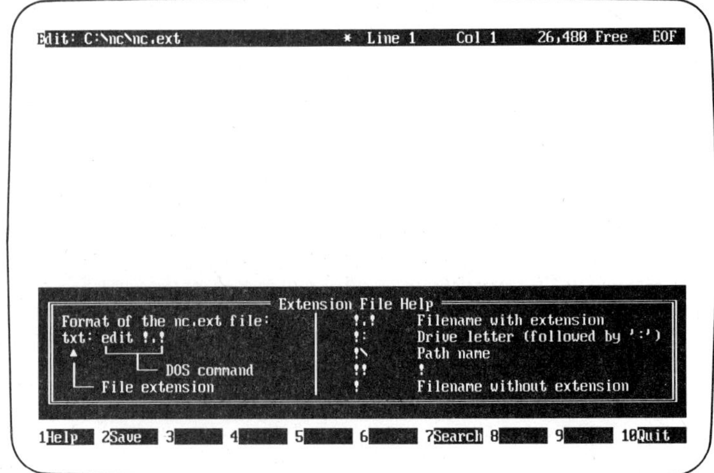

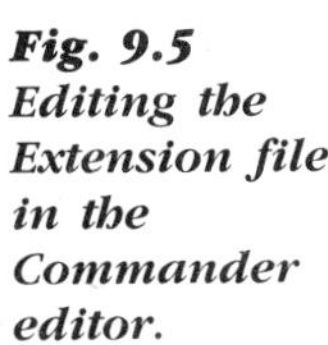
***Fig. 9.5* Editing the Extension file in the Commander editor.**

3. For each extension that you want to define, type a line of information, using the following format:

   ext: command !.!

   where *ext:* is the extension that you are defining. For example, this parameter could be DOC: for Microsoft Word files using the DOC extension, FOR: for FORTRAN programs using the FOR extension, and so on. The second part of the line contains the *command* required to begin the program associated with the defined file extension. You can include a path to the command if necessary. The !.! means that the command is to be followed by a file name with an extension, causing WordPerfect to load automatically the selected file into the program to begin editing. To tell Commander to use the command WP from the directory \WP50 to edit a file with a WP extension, for example, you use the following specification:

   WP: C:\WP50\WP !.!

   or

   WP: C:\WP50\WP !.WP

   The !.! syntax is a part of Norton Commander's extension definition. It is similar to DOS's *.* wild-card specification. The use of the !.! specification is a way to define what parameter should be placed on the command line when the program you have specified begins. In the preceding example, you can use !.WP or !.! because both keep the extension WP in the file specification. The meanings of !.! and related specifications are detailed in table 9.1.

Table 9.1
Specifying Parameters in the Extension Definition

Specification	*Meaning*
!.!	File name with extension
!	File name without extension
!:	Drive letter followed by a colon
!\	Path name

You must choose the specification in the command line according to what the application program expects in order for the selected file to be accessed. Thus, the specification ! indicates that the file name without an extension is to be placed in the command line. The specification !:!.! means that the drive name and a colon would appear before the file name and extension. If you do not place a !.! specification in the extension definition line, Commander begins the application program but does not automatically access the selected file.

As another example, suppose that you defined the specification

CAI: \CAI\CAI !:!\!

Then, if you choose the file DEMO.CAI, the command generated would contain the current drive (!:), the current pathname (!\), and the file name without the extension (!). Therefore, if you were in the C:\TMP directory when you chose this file, the DOS command used to start the program would be \CAI\CAI C:\TMP\DEMO.

Figure 9.6 shows an extension file containing a variety of definitions. The first definition is for WordPerfect. The second is to edit files with FOR (FORTRAN) extensions with an editor named Edit, and the third is to begin the CAI program (PC-CAI, a computer-aided instructional program).

After you enter your extension definitions, save them by pressing F2 (Save). End the editor by pressing F10 (Quit). To abandon the edit without saving, press Esc or F10 without first pressing F2. You then can highlight a file name on a Commander panel and press Enter or double-click to begin using that file in the proper program. To return to this extension file (\NC\NC.EXT) to change, add, or remove any of your definitions, choose the Extension option again from the Commands menu.

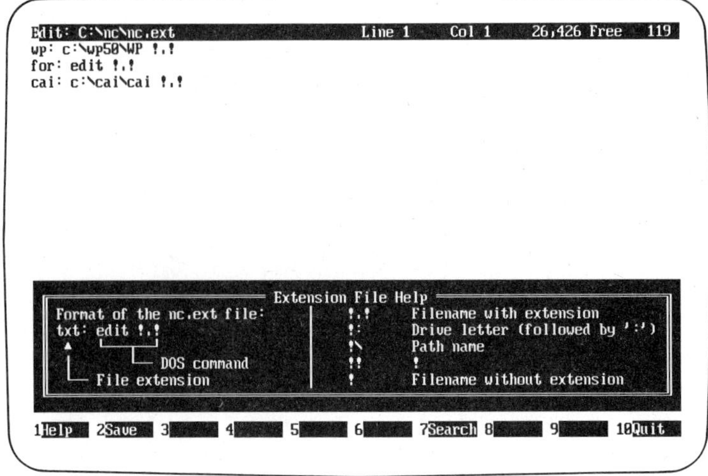

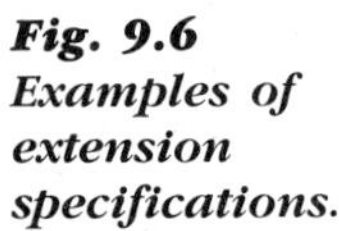
Fig. 9.6 ***Examples of extension specifications.***

Using Commander (MCI) Mail

The Commander menu and extension features enable you to access information easily on your computer. Commander Mail enables you to send and receive information to and from other computers through the MCI electronic network. Specifically, the options you have with MCI Mail include the following:

- *You can send and receive electronic mail (E-mail).* Electronic mail is information in a computer file. You write a message on your computer and send the message to someone who has an MCI account. You also can send ASCII text files as electronic mail. The message is routed electronically to the specified electronic address (the recipient's computer), and the recipient can then read the message.

- *You can send a letter through Commander Mail to the MCI network and have that letter printed on paper and mailed to a designated address.* To do so, you write the letter on your computer and send it and the address to the MCI network. MCI prints the letter and puts it in the mail.

- *You can send information to a FAX machine through MCI Mail.* You create a letter on your computer and send the letter to the MCI network with a FAX number. MCI then sends the letter to the appropriate FAX machine.

- *You can send messages to other electronic mail services, such as CompuServe and Telemail X.400.* This feature is useful if you want to send electronic mail to someone who is not an MCI subscriber but is a subscriber on CompuServe or Telemail.

MCI Mail is a convenient way to communicate quickly. It is particularly well suited for members of an organization or colleagues who live in diverse places. Messages can be sent at the convenience of the sender and received at the convenience of the recipient. Also, messages arrive much faster than they do by express mail and have the clarity of a letter as opposed to the possible misinterpretations that characterize voice messages. Using MCI Mail, salespeople can send orders to the home office at the end of each day, and journalists can communicate with their offices and send messages and stories quickly—the possibilities for improved communications are endless.

Using Commander's MCI interface rather than MCI's interface (which you can use if you dial MCI) means that you do not have to use a communications program (such as ProComm, Crosstalk, and so on), you can do all of the work of preparing and reading communications off-line (which saves phone connect time), and you can use the Commander's simple pull-down user interface.

Reviewing the Requirements for Using MCI Mail

As mentioned in Chapter 2, you need an MCI account and some computer hardware to use MCI Mail. To get an MCI account, call (800) 444-6245. MCI will assign you a user name and a password, which you typically will receive by mail within several days.

You also need to have a modem hookup on your computer. Generally, personal computers have two kinds of modem hookups: internal and external. An internal modem fits inside your computer in one of the expansion slots. An external modem is connected to a communication port on your computer with a serial cable.

With an internal modem, all you see from the outside are phone jacks on the back of the computer. One of those jacks is labeled "To Line." To hook your modem into the phone system, you must run a phone line from the To Line jack in the back of the computer to the phone wall jack. Usually another jack in the back of the computer is called "To Phone." You can use this jack to hook up a normal telephone. Figure 9.7 illustrates this hookup.

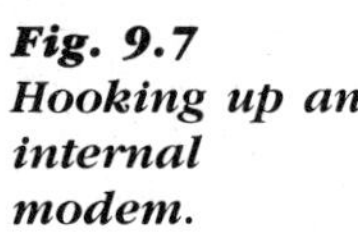

Fig. 9.7
Hooking up an internal modem.

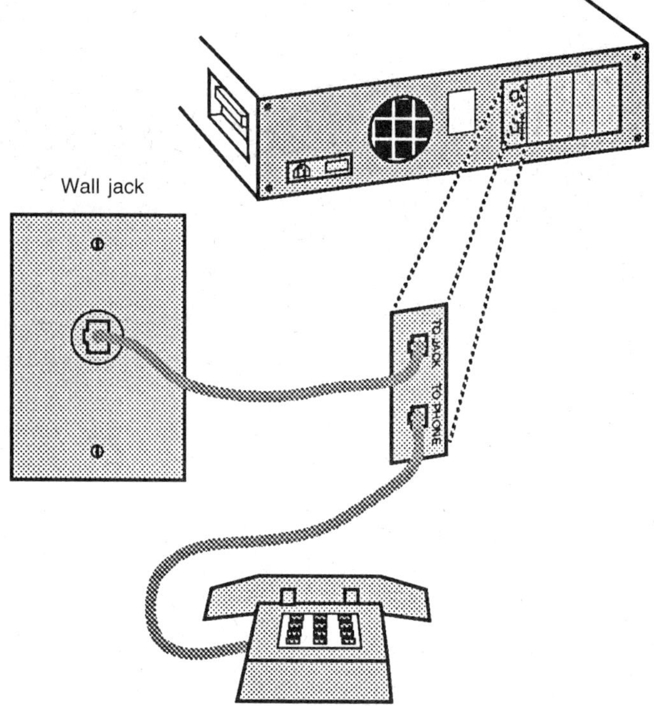

An external modem is hooked into your computer through a serial port, usually the COM1 or COM2 port. Your COM port is usually a 25-pin (RS-232) connector, as illustrated in figure 9.8. IBM AT type machines use a 9-pin connector. A cable is attached to the COM port on the back of the computer and also attached to the modem. A phone line then is hooked into the modem (in the To Line jack) from the phone wall plug. Optionally, you can have a regular phone hooked into the modem's To Phone jack. This hookup is illustrated in figure 9.9.

MCI supports modems using speeds of 300, 1200, and 2400 baud. The baud rate is the speed at which your computer modem transmits and receives information. Although a baud rate of 300 is slow, 1200 and 2400 baud are acceptable. Speeds of up to 9600 baud will soon be commonplace.

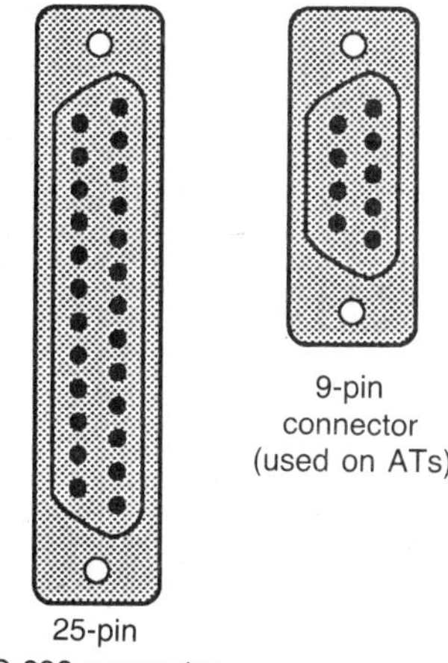

Fig. 9.8
25-pin and 9-pin serial connectors.

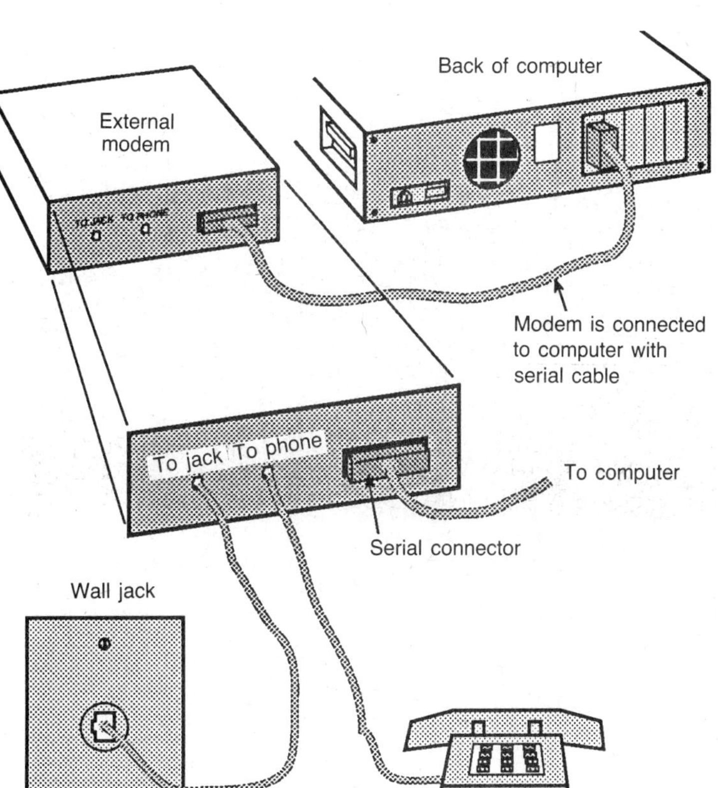

Fig. 9.9
Hooking up an external modem.

Tip: If you do not currently have a modem, here are some tips on what to look for. The faster the speed of the modem, the more quickly you can send and receive messages over the phone lines. The quicker the communication, the shorter the phone call and (usually) the less the cost to access services like MCI. (You are charged for the time connected.) Probably the most commonly used modems today are 2400 baud. If you are on a tight budget, however, you can buy a 1200 baud modem for less than $100. Using a slow, 300-baud modem is not a good idea.

Also, you need to get a Hayes-compatible modem. Modems are operated through a command language (similar to how a PC DOS computer is operated through DOS commands). Hayes-compatible modems use the AT command set, which is what Norton Commander is set up to use when talking to a modem.

The advantage of using an internal modem is that it does not need your communication port, which you may want to use for something else. Using an internal modem makes changing from computer to computer difficult, however, because you have to take your computer apart to remove the modem. An external modem has an important advantage in that you easily can switch it and use it on more than one computer by simply unplugging the cable from one computer and plugging it into another. The disadvantage of the external modem is that it takes up more room on your desk. Other than these convenience considerations, the internal and external modems operate the same way.

As soon as your computer is set up with a modem and you have an MCI account, you can start sending messages.

Setting up Commander Mail To Communicate with MCI Mail

To set up Commander Mail for use, open the Commands menu from the menu bar and choose the Commander Mail option. The first time you choose Commander Mail, you see a screen like the one in figure 9.10. This screen tells you that you must go through a setup procedure before you can use Commander Mail. You need to have your MCI account information handy. If you do not want to set up Commander Mail at this time (if you do not have your account number yet), press Esc to end this option. Press Enter to proceed with the setup.

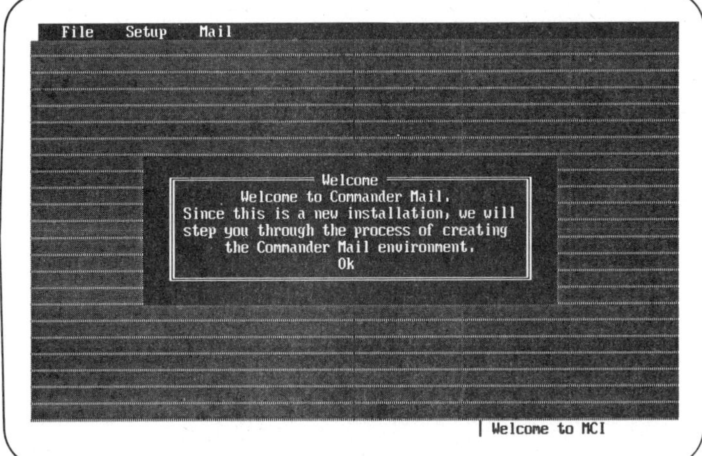

Fig. 9.10
The initial Commander Mail setup message.

Adding, Deleting, and Modifying Accounts

If you proceed with Commander Mail setup, the first item you see is the Account 1 dialog box (see fig. 9.11). In this box, you enter information about your MCI account. First you must enter your MCI account name, which is often the first letter of your first name followed by your full last name. No blanks are included in the MCI account name. After entering your name, enter your password and MCI ID. These pieces of information are all contained in the Welcome to MCI Mail kit that you receive in the mail after you subscribe.

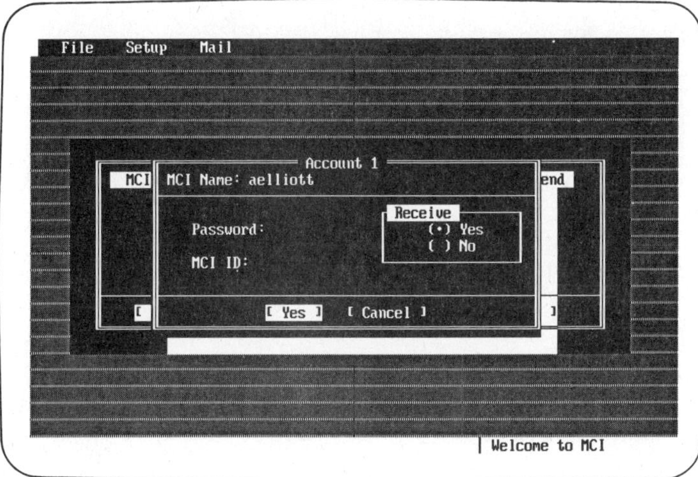

Fig. 9.11
Setting up an MCI account.

After you finish entering your account information, you are prompted to indicate whether you want to receive mail. Check Yes (press Y) to be able to send *and* receive MCI electronic mail, or No (press N) if you do not want to receive mail and plan to use MCI Mail only to send information. Choose Yes at the bottom of the screen to confirm the information for this account. The MCI Account List box appears. If more than one person with MCI accounts will be using Commander Mail on this machine, you can add additional accounts by choosing the Add option. If you need to change or remove one of the accounts after you enter it, highlight the account and choose the Modify option to make changes or the Delete option to remove the account. When you finish making additions, modifications, or deletions, choose OK to save the list.

After you finish entering your account information, the MCI Account List dialog box appears again (see fig. 9.12). This time it contains information about your account. Highlight your MCI name and choose the Use option to tell Commander Mail to charge your account for messages being sent. Commander will use this account for all future uses of MCI mail unless you choose another account. If you enter only one account, that account is highlighted and will be the one you use.

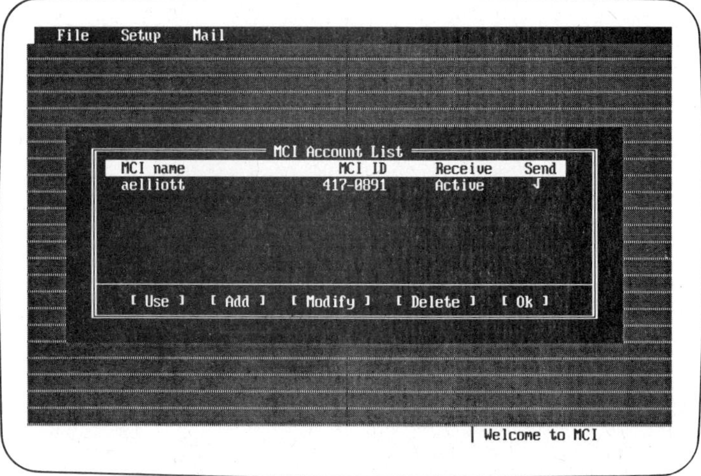

Fig. 9.12 ***The completed MCI Account List dialog box.***

Specifying Directories for Message Storage

During the setup procedure, the next dialog box that appears indicates the directories where MCI messages will be stored (see fig. 9.13). The default directories are \NC\OUT, \NC\IN, and \NC\SENT. The OUT directory stores outgoing mail, the IN directory stores incoming mail, and the SENT directory stores copies of messages you have sent already. You can type new names for these directories or accept the defaults. To enter new names, use the arrow keys to highlight the directory to change, type a new directory name, and press Enter. When the directory names are as you want them, choose the Yes option in the dialog box. To choose Yes, you can press Y, press Tab to move the highlight to Yes and then press Enter, or point to Yes with your mouse and click.

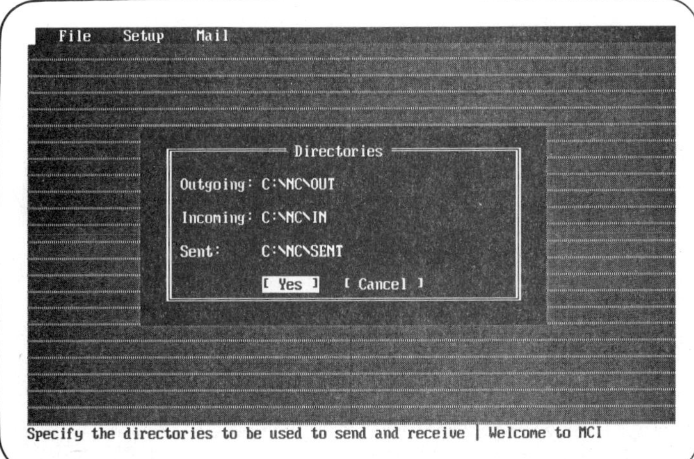

Fig. 9.13
The dialog box in which you can accept or modify the outgoing, incoming, and sent directories.

Specifying Your Modem Setup

You must next tell Commander Mail about your modem setup. Figure 9.14 shows the Modem dialog box. The Port setting indicates which serial port is being used for your modem. If you have only one serial port on your machine, you are using COM1. If you have two serial ports, you need to check your system's documentation to determine which port you are using. Usually, the COM1 port is any built-in port on your computer and the COM2 port is a port added with an expansion card.

The Dialing option indicates whether your telephone exchange uses tone or pulse dialing. Some older exchanges use only pulse dialing. If you can use phones with only rotary dials, your exchange supports only pulse dialing. If you are able to use a phone with a touch-tone numeric pad, your exchange supports tone dialing. If you do not know whether your telephone exchange supports tone dialing, call your telephone operator.

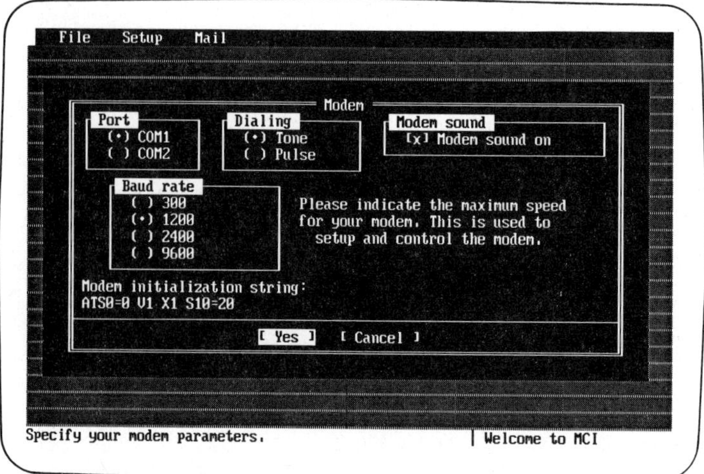

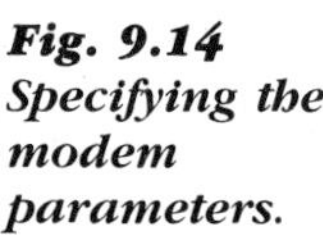
Fig. 9.14 Specifying the modem parameters.

The Modem Sound option indicates whether you want to hear the dialing process as it is taking place. (If your modem does not have a speaker, you will not hear the dialing even if you check this option.) The advantage of hearing the dialing process is that you can tell if the call is going through properly. If you have a speaker modem but you do not hear the dialing taking place, it may mean that you have selected the wrong COM port. You can hear easily if something interferes with connection (such as a busy signal). If you cannot hear the dialing process, you must wait for a message from the computer before you know whether the connection has been made properly. Usually, this takes less than 30 seconds.

The Baud Rate option indicates the speed that you are using. For the fastest communication, choose the highest baud rate your modem can support—up to 2400 baud. The baud rates supported by your modem should be listed in your modem documentation. Commander has a 9600 baud option; however, as of the print time of this book, MCI does not support this speed.

Note the Modem Initialization String field at the bottom of the Modem dialog box. The *modem initialization string* is a code set by Commander Mail for using your modem. The code in figure 9.14 is for a Hayes-compatible modem, which is the most common type of modem. If you are using a Hayes-compatible modem, you do not have to know which initialization string to use. Commander Mail supplies the necessary code automatically. Unless you are a sophisticated user who likes to try different ways of doing things, you should never have to change this code. If you are using a non-Hayes-compatible modem, you need to check your documentation for the proper initialization string.

After you choose all the proper options on the Modem dialog box, choose Yes to save these parameters.

Specifying the Phone Number

The next setup dialog box asks for the phone number to be used to communicate with MCI Mail (see fig. 9.15). Your Welcome to MCI Mail information kit contains the phone numbers you can use:

(800) 234-6245 for 300- and 1200-baud modems
(800) 456-6245 for up to 2400-baud modems

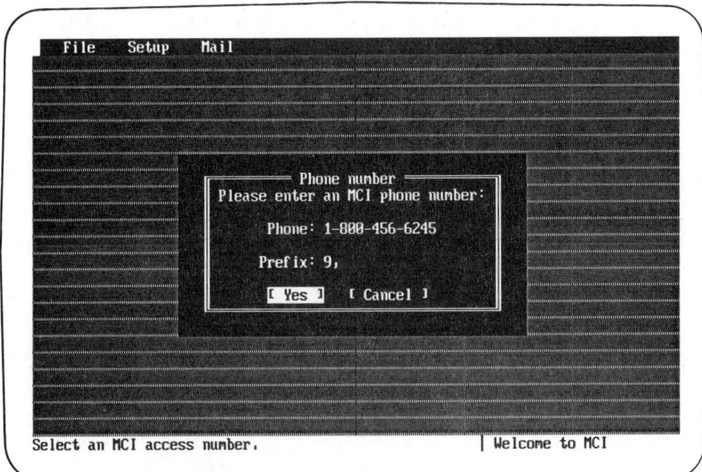

Fig. 9.15 Specifying the MCI phone number.

Thus, if you are using a 300- or 1200-baud modem, use the first number. If you are using a 2400-baud modem, use the second number. Type the appropriate number in the Phone Number dialog box. The Prefix entry is any number or series of numbers that you must type to get an outside line. In many businesses, this prefix is 9. When you have entered the phone number and any necessary prefix, choose Yes to save this information.

At this point, the Commander Mail setup program begins creating the directories you specified in the Directories dialog box. A new directory dialog box appears in sequence for each of the three new directories—IN, OUT, and SEND (or another three directories if you changed the names).

Figure 9.16 shows the new directory dialog box that asks whether you want Commander to create the \NC\IN directory. Choose the Mkdir option to make these directories on your hard disk. (To choose Mkdir, press M, use the arrow keys to highlight Mkdir and then press Enter, or point to Mkdir with a mouse and click once.) If you cancel the creation of a directory, MCI Mail returns you to the DOS prompt. If you try to run MCI Mail, you are prompted again to make the directories needed. You will not be able to run MCI Mail until these directories exist.

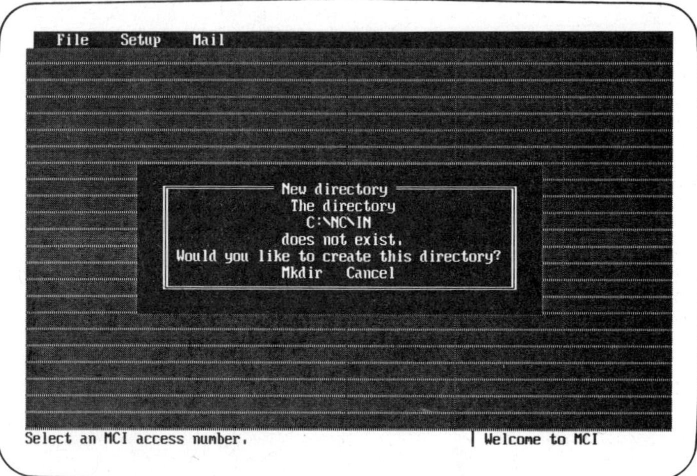

Fig. 9.16 Making the IN directory during setup.

At this point, you have reached the end of the setup procedure. A dialog box appears with the following message:

```
Commander Mail has now created the parameter file, MCI.INI,
required to run the communications driver, MCIDRIVR.EXE.
```

This message tells you that the choices you have selected in the setup procedure are stored in the file MCI.INI and that the program now is ready to begin communications.

Beginning a Mail Session

After you set up the MCI Mail parameters, as described in the preceding section, a screen like the one in figure 9.17 automatically appears after you choose the Commander Mail option from the Commands menu. This screen, the In Box screen, holds any messages that have been received and are waiting to be read. The first time you use Commander Mail, no messages appear on this screen.

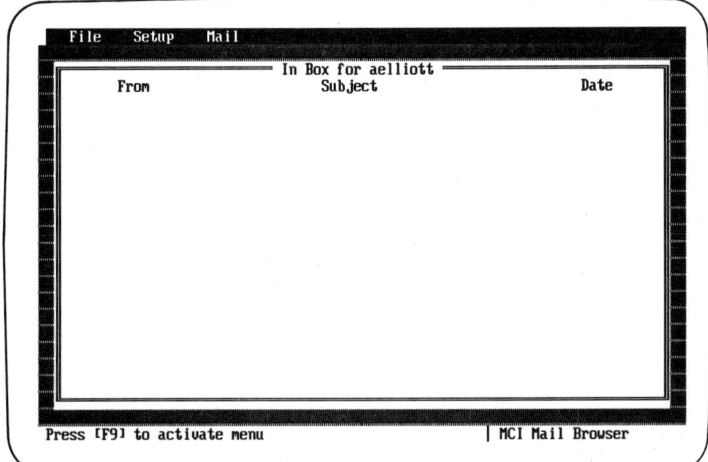

Fig. 9.17 ***The In Box screen.***

Notice the Commander Mail menu bar at the top of the screen. Three pull-down menus are available: File, Setup, and Mail. To move your cursor to this menu bar, press F9 or point to the menu bar with the mouse. Use the arrow keys to point to a menu and then press Enter to display the menu (or point with a mouse and click).

Using the File Menu To Get Help

The first menu is the File menu (see fig. 9.18). It contains three options: Help, About MCI, and Quit. You can activate the first option (Help) also by pressing the F1 key. The Help option provides brief information about how to use various parts of Commander Mail. The About MCI option lists phone numbers for MCI phone support and the MCI support mailbox. The Quit option ends your Commander Mail session.

Using the Setup Menu To Establish Communications Settings

The second menu is the Setup menu (see fig. 9.19). It contains six options: Address Book, MCI Accounts, Schedule, Phone, Modem, and Directories. The following sections discuss each of these options.

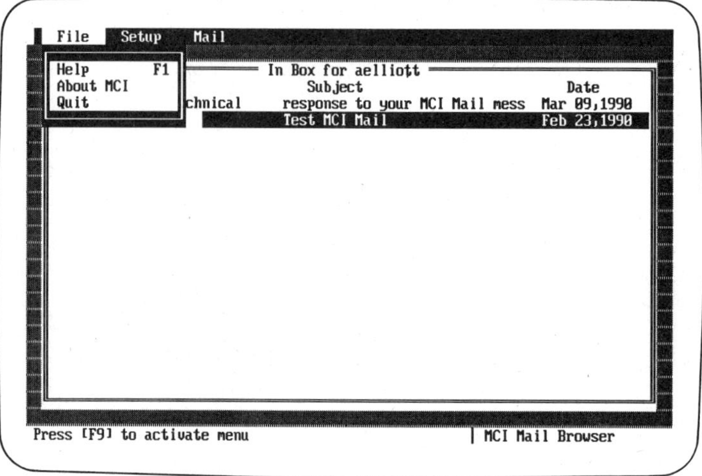

***Fig. 9.18* Commander Mail's File menu.**

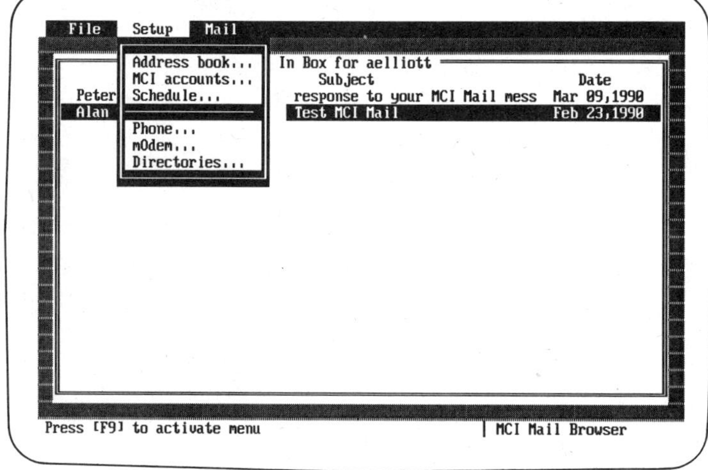

***Fig. 9.19* Commander Mail's Setup menu.**

Adding Addresses to the MCI Address Book

The Address Book option enables you to create a list of addresses of people to whom you plan to send messages. After you choose this option, you see the MCI Address Book dialog box. Figure 9.20 shows an address book that contains only one address. At the bottom of the box are four options:

- *Add:* Adds a name to the address book.
- *Modify:* Changes the currently highlighted address.

- *Delete:* Deletes the currently highlighted address.
- *OK:* Exits the Address Book dialog box and returns you to the Setup menu.

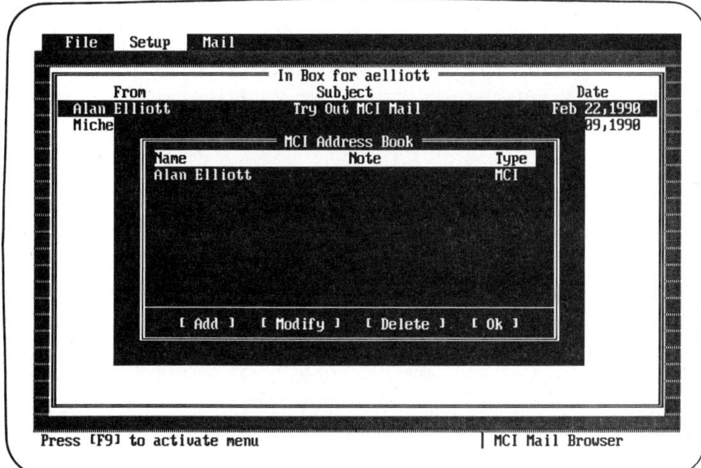

Fig. 9.20 ***The MCI Address Book dialog box.***

After you choose to add an address to the address book, you see another dialog box, like the one in figure 9.21. In this box, you must choose how to send the message to this address. You have five options:

- MCI Instant
- Paper Mail
- FAX
- Telex
- External Mail System

If you will be sending messages to the same person, but using different methods (MCI or a FAX, for example), you must enter an address for each way that you want to send the messages.

If you choose MCI Instant, you see a screen similar to the one in figure 9.22. On this screen you enter the information about the MCI account to which the message will be sent. You must know the MCI user name or the MCI account number for this address. If you know one but are unsure about the other, just enter the one you know. The information you put in the name, note, location, and organization fields appears on the electronic message you send. The lighter, highlighted area next to each part of the address indicates how many characters you can enter for that address component. After you enter information in the Name field, press Enter to move to the next field. You also may use the arrow keys to move from field to field.

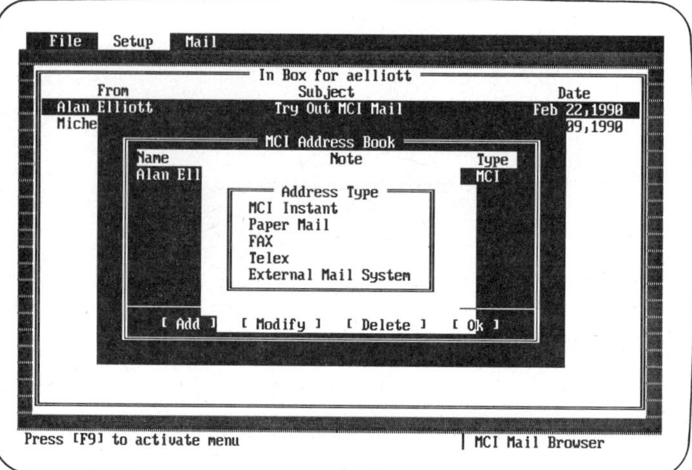

Fig. 9.21
The dialog box for indicating address type for an Address Book entry.

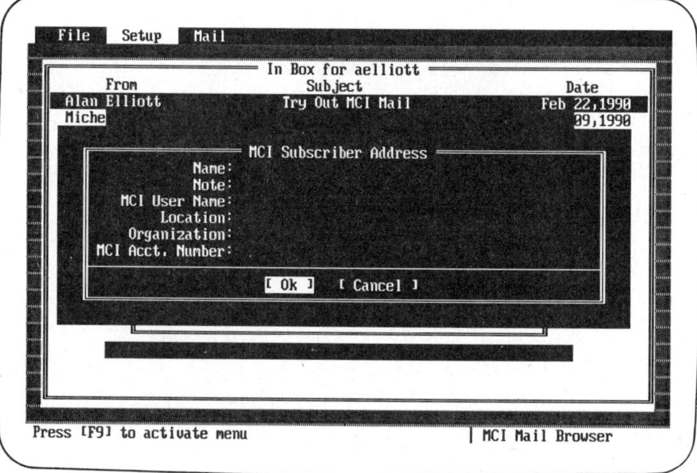

Fig. 9.22
Entering an MCI subscriber address.

If your recipient is not an MCI account holder, you can choose Paper Mail in the Address Type dialog box. You may want to use MCI Paper Mail rather than send the letter yourself for several reasons. You may like the important-looking, telegram-like style of MCI letters. You may find this method easier than writing and printing the letter yourself. Also, if you are away from your office, you may want to write and send letters directly from your computer—from a hotel room, a conference, or anywhere that you can plug your computer into a phone plug. After you choose the Paper Mail option, Commander prompts you to enter information for the following fields:

Name:
Note:
Country:
Title/Company:
Addr. Line 1:
Addr. Line 2: City:
State:
Zip Code:

Type information for each field and press Enter to move to the next field. Use the arrow keys to move from field to field if you need to make any corrections. The information you enter is used to address the letter that MCI then sends by regular mail. For a paper address, you *must* include a name and address. The Note, Addr Line 2, and Title/Company fields are optional. Move the highlight to the Ok option and press Enter (or select Ok with the mouse) to end the entry process.

If you want to send your message to a FAX machine, you can choose the FAX option in the Address Type dialog box. For this option, you are asked to enter information for the following fields:

Name:
Note:
Phone #:
Retry:

You *must* include a name and phone number, but the Note and Retry fields are optional. In the Retry field, you can enter the number of hours that MCI should keep trying to send the message if it cannot get through. The default is 4 hours. You can enter a number between .5 and 12 hours. If you cannot reach the FAX number (it may be busy, for example), MCI continues to try to send the FAX for the length of time specified in the Retry field. After you send the FAX successfully or have exhausted all entries, you receive an electronic mail message from MCI telling you whether it was successful in sending the FAX.

If you want to send a message to a Telex address, choose Telex from the Address Type dialog box. Then supply information for the following fields:

Name:
Note:

Country:
Telex Number:
Answerback:

The Name and Telex Number fields are required. If you leave the Country field blank, Commander Mail uses USA as the default. Do not use the Answerback field unless you know your recipient's answerback code. (*Answerback* is a verification code used by some Telex subscribers as a safety feature.)

Note: You also can receive Telex messages through MCI Mail. Your telex number is 650 plus your MCI ID number. If your MCI ID is 123-4567, for example, then your Telex number is 6501234567. Messages sent by Telex appear in your MCI Commander Mail In Box as electronic messages.

To send a message to a person on an electronic mail service other than MCI, you must choose External Mail System as the Address Type. You then are asked to supply information for the following fields:

Name:
Note:
Mailsystem:
MBX Info 1:
MBX Info 2:
MBX Info 3:

The Name, Mailsystem, and MBX Info 1 fields are required. The Mailsystem field contains the name of the electronic mail service, such as CompuServe. (No other mail systems are currently supported.) The MBX Info 1 field contains the ID number for that service, such as 12345,789. The MBX Info 2 and 3 fields are reserved for future use. MCI periodically adds new services that it can reach. Your correspondence from MCI will explain any future uses for these fields.

After you add addresses to your address book, they appear in the MCI Address Book dialog box when you create a message. You then can highlight an address and select it to be used as the recipient of the message.

Editing and Deleting Addresses

Eventually, you probably will need to modify or delete some addresses. To modify an address, open the Setup menu and choose the Address Book option. Highlight the address to be modified (using the arrow keys or a mouse), and then choose the Modify option. The address appears, and you can use the arrow keys to move from field to field, making necessary corrections to the address. Highlight the OK option and press Enter (or click OK with a mouse) to save the modification.

To delete an address, choose the Address Book option from the Setup menu. Highlight the address to be deleted (using the arrow keys or a mouse), and choose the Delete option. Then highlight the OK option and press Enter (or click OK with a mouse) to save the change.

Specifying MCI Accounts

The MCI Accounts option on the Setup menu enables you to choose which account should be used to send messages. You can add new accounts, modify current accounts, or delete accounts. This procedure is the same as when you added your first account during the setup procedure.

A person's name or other information may change, for example. To modify an account after you complete the initial setup, choose the MCI Accounts option from the Setup menu. The account list appears on-screen. You then can highlight the account to change and choose the Modify option. Commander Mail displays the information on-screen so that you can edit it. Press Esc when you finish modifying the account. Choose OK to save the modified account list.

Deleting an existing account is similar to modifying one. To delete an account, choose the MCI Accounts option from the Setup menu. When the account list appears, highlight the account to delete and choose the Delete option. Then choose OK.

Setting MCI Mail To Run Automatically

The Schedule option on the Setup menu enables you to specify when and if Commander Mail automatically calls MCI. You can set up Commander Mail to send and receive messages unattended during the night when rates are lower, for example. Any received messages are on your computer when you come to work the next day. You may have a number of salespeople sending in orders daily. You can set up Commander Mail to call MCI automatically several times during the day to collect messages being sent in—and to send your salespeople confirmations that their orders were received.

After you choose the Schedule option, a Schedule dialog box like the one in figure 9.23 appears. You have two choices—to use MCI Mail on demand or on a schedule. Using MCI on demand means that you manually choose when to contact MCI Mail. If you choose the Use Schedule Below option, MCI Mail initiates calls at the times specified. To specify times to initiate an MCI call, type up to eight different times in the dialog box at the designated locations. Then choose Yes to close and return to the Setup menu.

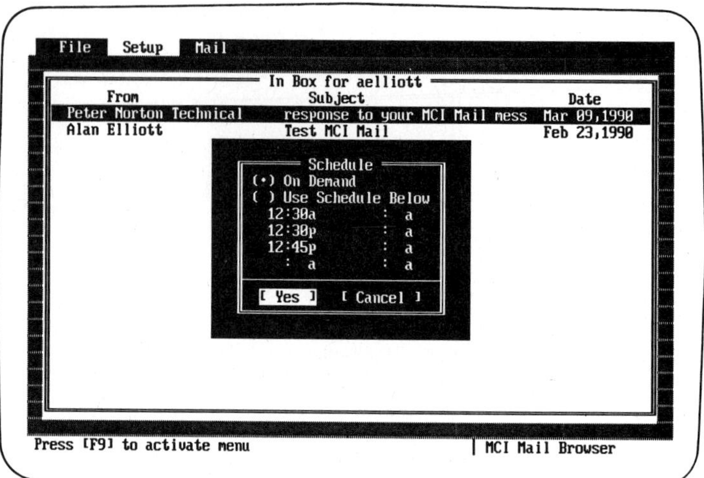

Fig. 9.23 ***Completing the Schedule dialog box for automatic communications.***

For Commander Mail to operate in automatic mode, you must begin the MCIDRIVR program from the DOS prompt. After you set up the times in the Schedule dialog box for Commander to call MCI Mail, load the MCIDRIVR program by entering the following command at the DOS prompt:

```
MCIDRIVR
```

After you enter this command, the Commander MCI Mail program becomes a background program and you are returned to the DOS prompt where you can run other programs. Even if you are using another program at the time, Commander Mail initiates a call at the scheduled times and sends all messages you currently have in your Out Box and receives any messages that are waiting for you.

When you enter the MCIDRIVR command at the DOS prompt, you have several switches to choose from that control features of this program. Table 9.2 lists the switches available for the MCIDRIVR command.

Table 9.2
Switches for the MCIDRIVR Command

Switch	*Effect*
/N	Initiates a session *now*. The program immediately dials the MCI phone number and sends and receives messages. The command MCIDRIVR/N, for example, begins an MCI session immediately, even if it was not in the schedule.
/E	Enables the driver. You use this switch if the MCIDRIVR program is in memory but is disabled.
/D	Disables the driver. This switch leaves the MCIDRIVR in memory but disables it (turns it off temporarily).
/A	Aborts the current communications session.
/X	Exits (terminates) the current session and removes the driver from memory.
/S	Sets the status. Sets the DOS ERRORLEVEL to 0 if the driver is waiting for a scheduled event, or sets ERRORLEVEL to 1 if the driver is currently in a communications session. You can use this switch in a batch program. For more information, see the discussion of the Norton Utilities Batch Enhancer program in Chapter 6.

Changing the MCI Phone Number

The Phone option on the Setup menu enables you to change the MCI phone number and prefix used in calling MCI Mail. MCI will contact you if the number you use to access MCI services changes. The dialog box displayed by the Phone option is the same dialog box that you used in the initial setup procedure to specify the MCI phone number.

Changing Modem Settings

The Modem option on the Setup menu enables you to change the settings for your modem, which you may need to do if you install a different modem. Your new modem may run at a different speed than your original modem, for example. The modem settings include communications port, tone or pulse dialing, modem sound, baud rate, and initialization string. The dialog box displayed by the Modem option is the same dialog box that you used in the initial setup procedure to specify modem settings.

Changing Message Directories

The Directories option on the Setup menu enables you to change the names of the directories that you use to store outgoing messages, incoming messages, and sent messages. Remember that these directories are usually set as \NC\OUT, \NC\IN, and \NC\SENT in the setup procedure. You may want to change directories, for example, from drive C to another disk if drive C is getting full and cannot store all the messages being received.

Using the Mail Menu To Manage Messages

You use the Mail menu from the Commander Mail menu bar to manage your incoming and outgoing messages. The Mail menu is shown in figure 9.24. The four basic tasks that you perform with the Mail menu options are creating, sending, receiving, and reading messages.

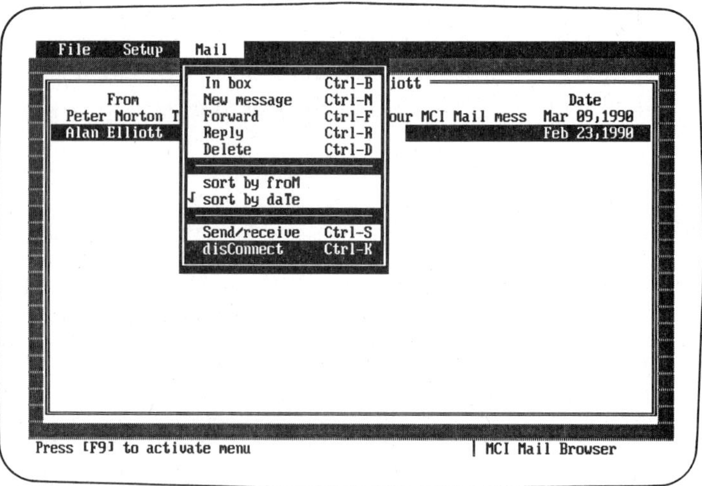

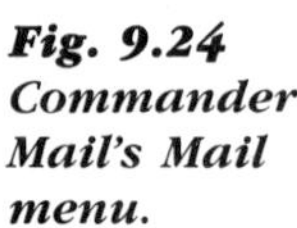

Fig. 9.24 Commander Mail's Mail menu.

To mail an electronic message you follow these three basic steps:

1. Choose the New Message option and select the destination of your message from your MCI Address Book.
2. Write the message using the Commander editor and save it to disk.
3. Send the message by choosing the Send/Receive option.

This sequence is one you will probably follow most often when using the Mail menu. The following sections discuss how to use these and other options on the Mail menu to manage your incoming and outgoing mail messages.

Creating Messages

After you choose the New Message option from the Mail menu, you see a screen similar to the one in figure 9.25. At the top of the screen, you enter information that tells MCI where to send the message. These fields are To, CC (carbon copy), Subject, Attach, and Handling. The To field is the only required field. To enter information in the To field, make sure that the field is highlighted and then press Enter to display the Edit Send List dialog box (see fig. 9.26).

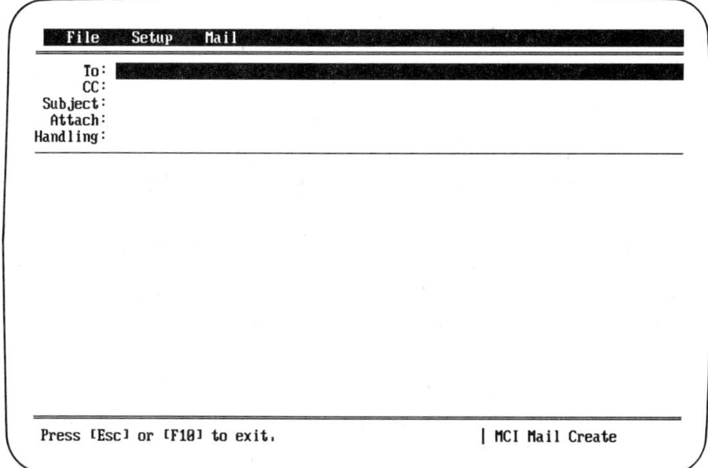

Fig. 9.25* *Creating a message.

The Edit Send List dialog box creates a list of names to whom your message should be sent. Choose the List option to display the current list of names in your address book. Your address book appears on-screen as figure 9.27 shows. You can choose an address from this list to indicate where to send your message. To choose an address, use the up- and down-arrow keys to highlight the address. Then choose Select by pressing S, using the right- and left-arrow keys to highlight Select and pressing Enter, or pointing to Select with the mouse and clicking. You are returned to the Edit Send List dialog box, and the name you highlighted appears in the box. Choose List and repeat this process for as many addresses as you want to select. Notice the Add option in the Address Book dialog box. If

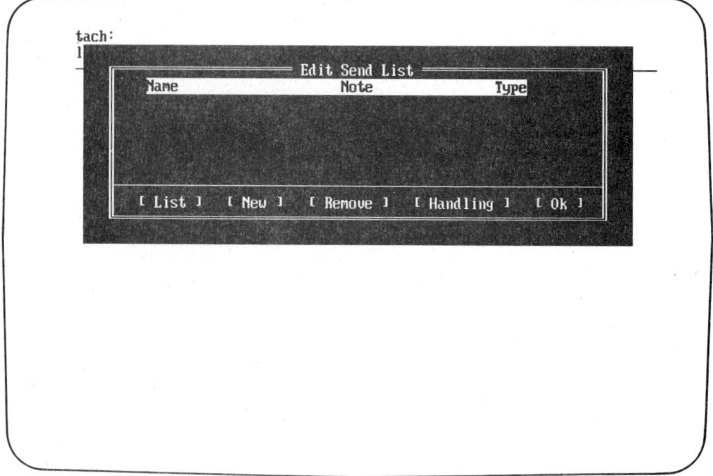

***Fig. 9.26* The Edit Send List dialog box for specifying message recipients.**

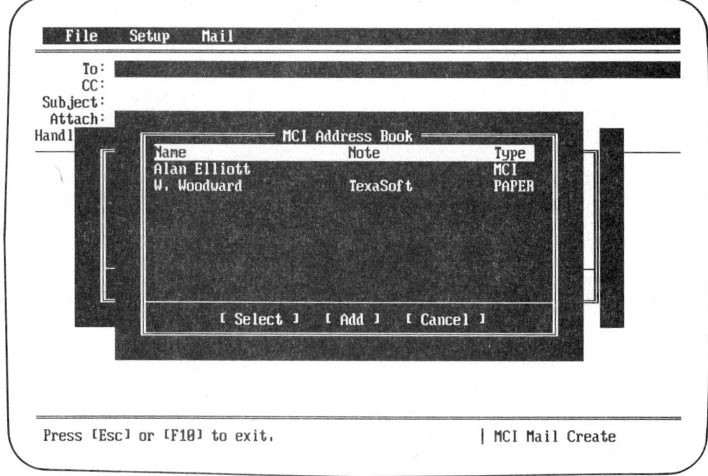

***Fig. 9.27* The Address Book.**

you choose the Add option you can add a new address to your Address Book. The Cancel option cancels the Address Book and returns you to the Edit Send List dialog box without adding any names.

If you choose the New option in the Edit Send List dialog box, you can enter all of the information needed to send a message. You are asked whether you want to add this name to your address book. The Remove option enables you to delete a name from the list. The Handling option enables you to choose several ways of handling your message. After you choose the Handling option, a dialog box appears where you can enter one of four options, as described in table 9.3. After you list all of the names in the Edit Send List dialog box where you want to send this message, choose OK.

Table 9.3
Using the Handling Options

Option	*Effect*
Receipt	Indicates that you want to receive a receipt verifying that the recipient has received the message.
4hour	Specifies priority delivery of the message.
Charge	Specifies a charging code. This code can be anything you want, because it is for your internal use only. The code, however, cannot contain any blank spaces. (You choose Charge and then type a code.)
Alert	Causes the recipient to be notified by telephone that an MCI message has been sent. You must supply the recipient's phone number.

You can select names for the CC field of the New Message screen in the same way you select names for the To field. You can type any information in the Subject field. The Attach field is used to specify the name of a file to include with the message. This file must be an ASCII text file. If you want to include the file named SALES.TXT from the C:\REPORT directory, for example, type the following line in the Attach field:

```
C:\REPORT\SALES.TXT
```

You use the Handling option to specify the same handling for all recipients in the send list. When you choose a Handling option for this message, it is in effect for all addresses in the list. You cannot specify the Alert option on one address, for example, and not on another in the same message.

When you have entered in the New Message screen all the information about where to send the message, type the actual message in the bottom half of the screen. In this screen, you are using the Commander editor, which uses all the keystroke commands mentioned in Chapter 8. After you type the message, press F10. You are given the option to save the message or to end without saving. The message is saved to your \NC\OUT directory and waits there to be sent.

Sending and Receiving Messages

After you create a message, you need to connect to the MCI network to send and receive messages. Choosing the Send/Receive option from the Mail menu instructs Commander Mail to begin a communications session. A communications session performs the following tasks:

1. Calls the MCI Mail service.
2. Sends any messages you currently have in the Out Box.
3. Receives messages from MCI and puts them in your In Box.

If you use the Schedule feature to have Commander Mail automatically send and receive mail, it performs this entire Send/Receive procedure without any human intervention. When you manually choose the Send/Receive option, you see the Send/Receive MCI Mail screen, from which you can monitor the progress of the communication to MCI Mail and the sending and receiving of messages. The box in the upper left corner lists six activities that will be taking place:

- Initializing
- Dial Service
- Get into MCI
- Send Mail
- Receive Mail
- Terminate Session

While each of these activities is taking place, a dot blinks to the left of the item. As the session completes each one of the activities, a check mark appears next to the item. The *initializing* process is when your computer establishes contact with your modem. The *dial service* activity is when the MCI phone number is being called. If your modem has a speaker and you have chosen to hear the sound, you should hear the dialing. Note that the lower left box also displays information about what is happening. This includes messages about your modem setup—the baud rate or the MCI name of the phone number being dialed, for example. While you are connected to MCI, the message `Connected to MCI` appears. When the session is over, the message `Hanging Up` appears, and then a message stating the length of the session appears. Boxes on the right side of the screen give you information about the progress of the session. The Total Session box is a bar graph that shows you how much of the session has gone by. The Current Activity graph shows the progress of some activity such as sending or receiving messages. The MCI and Commander Activity areas display messages such as `Wait`, `Receive`, and `Send`, which give the status of the modem activity.

After connecting to MCI, Commander Mail sends your account name and password to MCI. If these names are correct, you are logged into MCI. After you log in, any messages in your Out Box (the \NC\OUT directory) are sent, and any messages from MCI that are waiting to be received are placed in your In Box (the \NC\IN directory). Then the session is terminated.

The Sent and Received messages in the lower left corner of the screen tell you how many messages were sent and how many were received. The time spent logged into MCI is displayed in the Current Timer area of the screen. When the session is over, you can go to your In Box to examine any messages.

Reading Messages

You use the In Box option on the Mail menu to examine incoming messages. Figure 9.28 shows a sample In Box screen containing messages to be read. To look at a message in this list, highlight it and press Enter. If you are using a mouse, point to the message and double-click the left button. The message then appears on-screen. If it is too long to fit, you can use the PgUp and PgDn keys to see more of the message (see fig. 9.29). Press Esc to exit the message and return to the In Box.

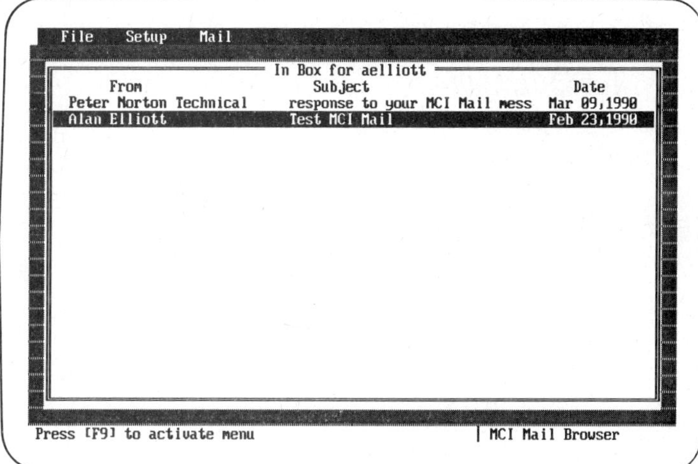

Fig. 9.28
A sample In Box screen containing two messages.

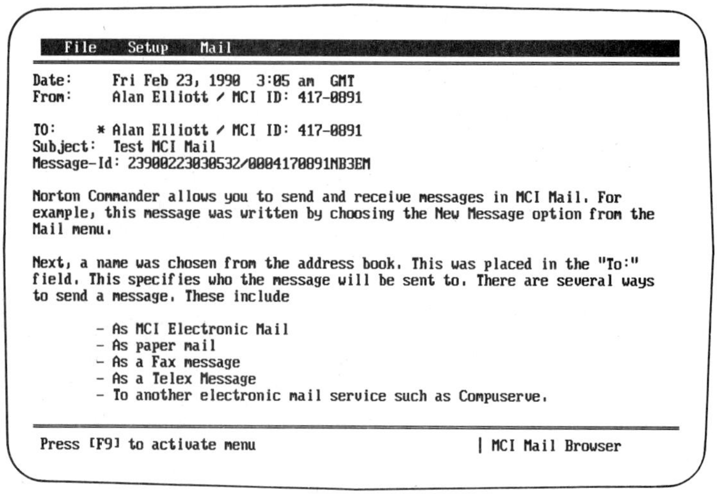

```
 File   Setup   Mail

Date:      Fri Feb 23, 1990  3:05 am  GMT
From:      Alan Elliott / MCI ID: 417-0891

TO:      * Alan Elliott / MCI ID: 417-0891
Subject:  Test MCI Mail
Message-Id: 23900223030532/0004170891NB3EM

Norton Commander allows you to send and receive messages in MCI Mail. For
example, this message was written by choosing the New Message option from the
Mail menu.

Next, a name was chosen from the address book. This was placed in the "To:"
field. This specifies who the message will be sent to. There are several ways
to send a message. These include

        - As MCI Electronic Mail
        - As paper mail
        - As a Fax message
        - As a Telex Message
        - To another electronic mail service such as Compuserve.

 Press [F9] to activate menu                          | MCI Mail Browser
```

Fig. 9.29* *Viewing a message.

Using Other MCI Mail Options

In addition to creating, sending, receiving, and reading messages, other tasks are necessary to manage your electronic mail. These tasks include forwarding, replying to, deleting, sorting, and printing messages, as well as disconnecting. Options for these functions—with the exception of printing—also are found on the Mail menu.

Forwarding Messages

If you choose the Forward option from the Mail menu, you can select a message in your In Box and forward it to a person in your address list. This option enables you to send to a third party a message you have received from someone else.

Replying to Messages

The Reply option on the Mail menu enables you to choose a message from your In Box and reply to that message. When you choose to reply, the To field in the message editor is automatically completed with the name of the person who sent you the message. Type a message, and it is stored in the Out Box to be sent the next time you use the Send/Receive option.

Deleting Messages

Choosing the Delete option from the Mail menu enables you to delete a message that is currently in your In Box. You should periodically delete these messages to free up space on your hard disk. Another way to delete messages from the In box is to move those files to another directory. You can use the Commander Move command (F6), for example, to move all files in the directory \NC\IN (which is your In box) to another directory.

Sorting Messages

Commander Mail sorts the messages in your In Box by the name of the sender or by the date. Choose Sort by From or Sort by Date from the Mail menu to designate the sorting method you prefer. A check mark appears next to the option that is currently in effect. If you typically only have a handful of messages in your In Box, either sort will do, because you easily can see all the message names on one screen.

Printing Mail Messages

One option that is not directly provided by Commander Mail is a feature to print a message. Because the messages are ASCII text files, however, you can print messages from your IN, OUT, or SENT directory by using DOS PRINT. To print the message in the In Box named ELLIOTT.U00, for example, you can use the following command at the DOS prompt:

```
PRINT \NC\IN\ELLIOTT.U00
```

Disconnecting Communications

During an MCI Send/Receive session, you may want to cancel the communications before they are completed. You can do so by opening the Mail menu and choosing the Disconnect option. You can press Esc or Ctrl-K to end the session. For example, you may begin a session, realize that the messages being sent are wrong, and then want to cancel the session quickly.

Using Commander Link

Commander Link enables you to link two local computers and to copy or move files from one computer to the next. It also enables you to rename or delete files on either computer. Link may come in handy if you are upgrading from one computer to another and want to copy your old files to a new computer. The feature also can be helpful if you use a desktop computer and a laptop. In many cases, laptops use 3 1/2-inch diskettes and desktop computers use 5 1/4-inch diskettes. Commander Link enables you to access files from the laptop without copying the file to some middle computer that has 3 1/2- and 5 1/4-inch drives.

Commander Link has two requirements:

1. Your two computers must be attached by a serial null modem cable connected to the COM1 or COM2 port on each computer.

2. Norton Commander must be running on both computers.

You can buy null modem cables from most computer supply stores. A null modem is not like the modem that you use to connect your computer to the phone system because it does not actually modulate or demodulate the communication signal. It simply feeds the signal from one computer to the next. Basically, a null modem is a serial cable with some of the wires crossed. These cables cost about the same as a normal serial cable. After you attach the null modem cable and start Norton Commander on both computers, you are ready to use Commander Link. Figure 9.30 shows how the null modem cable is connected to two computers.

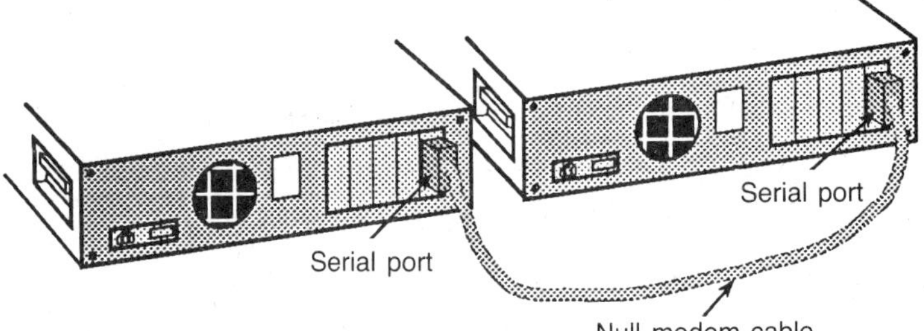

Fig. 9.30
The null modem cable connected to two computers.

To begin Commander Link, choose the Link option from the Left or Right pull-down menu. A dialog box like the one in figure 9.31 appears. Note that the Mode options include Master and Slave. One computer must be designated as the master, and the other as the slave. All commands are then given from the master machine. Using your arrow keys, highlight the Master or Slave option for each computer and press the space bar. A dot between the parentheses indicates the selected option.

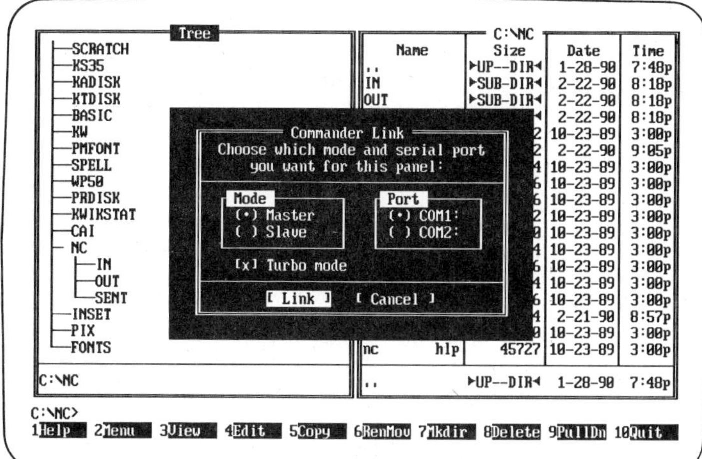

Fig. 9.31 The Commander Link dialog box.

The Port options are COM1 and COM2. For each computer, choose the Port option that corresponds to the serial port where you have attached the cable. The Turbo Mode option maximizes the speed of the communications between master and slave computers. If you have trouble communicating, turn off this option on both computers and try again.

To begin the link procedure, choose the Link option at the bottom of the Commander Link dialog box by using the arrow keys or by pressing L. You then can access files in the slave machine or the master machine by using the Copy, Rename/Move, and Delete options on the master machine. You cannot use DOS commands to access files across the link.

After you set up the link on the master and slave machines, you see panels similar to the ones in figure 9.32. In this example, the left panel reports the directory of the slave machine. Notice that the directory indicator at the top of the panel reads `Link:C:\KWIKSTAT`. This message indicates that the slave (linked) machine is set to the C:\KWIKSTAT directory. The master machine's directory is on the right panel and is set at C:\NC. Using the menu bar (for the left panel, in this example), you can change the directory listing of the slave machine to a full or brief listing. Because of the way the Link program operates, none of the other settings work for the slave machine. The keyboard on the slave machine does not respond when the machine is set to slave mode.

You also can change directories on either machine. If the slave machine is currently set to a subdirectory, for example, such as C:\KWIKSTAT in figure 9.32, choose the .. name on the directory list to switch to the root directory of the slave machine. From there, you can point to and choose

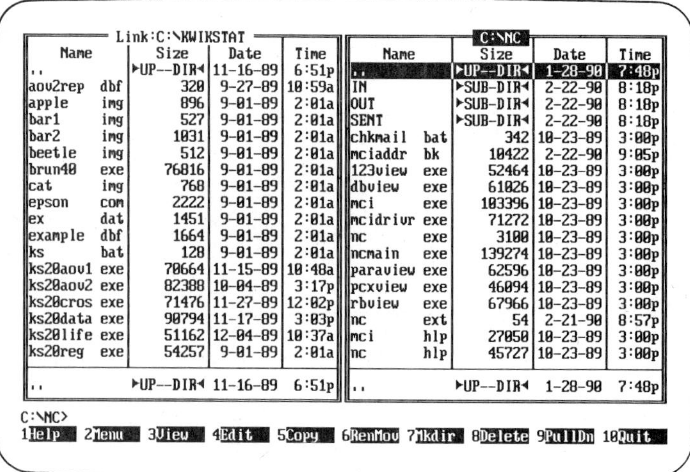

Fig. 9.32 Panels showing master and slave directories.

another directory on the slave machine. You can choose a directory on the master machine in the same way.

You can copy files to or from the master and the slave and you can delete or rename files on the master or the slave machine. Where the files are copied, moved from, deleted, or renamed is determined by which panel you are operating in. If you are operating from the link panel, which represents the linked (slave) machine, then deleting a file deletes a file on the slave machine. If you delete a file on the nonlink panel, you are deleting a file on the master machine. Basically, think of the link panel as being just another directory, although it happens to be on another machine.

In Commander Link, you use the Norton Commander Copy, Rename/ Move, and Delete commands in essentially the same way you always do—just as if you were using two directories on the same hard disk. (See Chapter 8 for more information.)

The following steps describe how to copy files from the slave machine to the master machine:

1. Select the file or files to copy.

   If you want to copy a single file, highlight that file on the Commander panel. You may have to change directories on the link (slave) panel to locate the file.

   If you want to copy multiple files, move your cursor to the slave directory panel and press the gray + key. You then are prompted to specify files to include. Enter a file name or a file specification, which can include the asterisk (*) or question mark (?) wild-card characters, and press Enter. The selected files appear highlighted. (Also, you can press the gray – key to select files to exclude.)

2. Press F5 (Copy). Commander prompts you to specify where to copy the files to the master machine.

3. Select the destination.

   A default destination often appears on-screen. To accept that destination, press Enter. Otherwise, enter the name of a disk drive such as A:, a path name such as \WP, or a combination such as C:\WP. When specifying the destination, you can press F10 to display a tree of the available directories on the master machine. From this tree, you can highlight the directory to which you want to copy the files.

4. Press Enter, and the copy commences.

5. End the link by choosing the Link option from the master machine's Right or Left menu. This step disables the link and returns the master and slave machines to normal operation.

   To give you an idea of how quickly operations can occur in linked machines, a test copy of a 90,794-byte file took only 18.27 seconds. In other words, the file was copied at about 5,000 bytes per second.

Summary

This chapter covered advanced Norton Commander features. These capabilities generally take a little more time to learn and use, but they provide some of the more exciting aspects of the program. The menu options enable you to customize Commander menus to fit your particular needs. The communications options—Mail and Link—enable you to communicate around the world or to the computer on the next desktop. In all, Norton Commander provides a number of powerful features with which you can make better use of your computer resources.

Part IV

Backing Up with Norton Utilities

Includes

Protecting Your Information with Norton Backup

10

Protecting Your Information with Norton Backup

The Norton Backup program enables you to copy information quickly from your hard disk to a number of floppy disks. You use this procedure to make a backup copy of the information on your hard disk so that you can recover the information that was lost because of mechanical failure, an accident, or sabotage. Although Norton Utilities also provides ways of recovering erased files and formatted hard disks, it cannot recover data from a mechanically damaged disk. The Norton Backup program is a separate program that you can purchase; it is not a part of Norton Utilities or Commander.

If you have not installed Norton Backup, refer to the installation instructions in Appendix C.

If your computer is jolted or dropped (which happened to many computers in the recent San Francisco earthquake), the read/write head in your hard disk may scratch the surface of the magnetic platter. When this happens, you may be unable to read information from the disk. Also, with the proliferation of computer viruses these days, the information on your hard disk could be erased or compromised by a malicious software program. More commonly, you accidentally may erase files on your disk, overwrite files with erroneous information, or format your disk. Keeping backups of your hard disk is an easy way to protect your information from these kinds of dangers.

The Norton Backup program is a perfect complement to the protection given to your information by Norton Utilities. If you already have learned how to use Utilities or Commander, you will adapt easily to Norton Backup's menu interface. As with Norton Utilities and Norton Commander, you may use a mouse or the arrows on the cursor keypad to choose options with the easy-to-use point-and-shoot menu access.

Norton Backup also is easy to use from a conceptual viewpoint. With very little experience, you can learn how to use the program to perform basic backups of your system. With a little more experience, you can use Backup's advanced features. Norton Backup also has some advantages over the DOS BACKUP and RESTORE commands.

To run the DOS BACKUP command, you must enter the command from the DOS prompt and carefully include a list of switches and parameters describing your backup. With Norton Backup, however, you make your choices through menu selections. You also have more control in selecting which files to back up and in automating the backup process than you do with DOS's BACKUP command.

This chapter describes how to use Norton Backup to back up your hard disk and to restore information to your hard disk when you need it. Before you learn the specifics of using Norton Backup, you should develop a backup strategy. This process is covered in the next section. The "Performing a Basic Backup and Restoring Information to Your Hard Disk" section, later in this chapter, covers how to use Norton Backup to perform a simple and quick backup of your system by using the Norton Backup menus. The "Using Advanced Features of Norton Backup" section covers options on how to customize the backup procedure and how to implement a consistent organization-wide backup process. The "Automating Norton Backup" section describes methods of programming the backup procedures so that you can back up with a minimum number of keystrokes.

Creating and Implementing a Backup Strategy

To use any backup program effectively, you need a backup strategy. Many people are not sure how often they should back up. This is a difficult question to answer in a book, because the frequency of backups will vary with each person. The amount of backups depends mainly on the value of your information. If you use your computer for playing games and using programs that do not store information (such as communications programs, entertainment programs, and so on), you do not need to back up very often—the information on your computer does not change often, so there is little value in having more than one backup copy. If you are a stockbroker and keep valuable financial information on daily sales and commissions, however, you will probably want to back up every day. A good rule of thumb is that you should back up if the effort of doing so is less than the pain of redoing the original work.

A backup strategy is presented in this chapter that will meet the needs of most business situations in which people must back up some information weekly. If you need to back up more than this, make the backup time frames shorter. If this plan asks you to back up too much for your situation, make the time frames longer.

One of the important parts of a backup strategy to keep in mind is that you are protecting your data from a variety of disasters—not just a hard disk crash. Accordingly, your strategy should include a provision for off-site storage of your information. Therefore, many situations call for a backup procedure that creates more than one version of the backup. For example, use the following strategy:

1. Perform a backup of your computer and keep the copy of that backup at home or in another building. You can use this backup in the event of a disaster that destroys your computer and office. Perform this backup once a month.

2. Perform another backup and keep this copy in your office. You will use this backup if your computer disk is damaged or if you lose files on disk, but your computer still is okay. Perform this backup once a week or more.

3. If needed, you can make daily backups of only those files that have been changed or created since the last backup.

Again, the frequency of your backup should be geared toward how much information you are willing to lose—a day, a week, or a month.

Another part of the backup strategy deals with selecting which files to back up. You usually do not need to back up all files on your hard disk. If you lose your hard disk files and still have your master copy of your WordPerfect program disks, for example, you can reinstall that program from the original disks—you do not need a backup copy. Usually, backups should concentrate on files that contain information you use or files that would be hard to reinstall or recreate. Norton Backup enables you to select which kinds of files *not* to back up. Therefore, you can save a lot of time by not backing up EXE and COM files that you can reinstall easily from original program disks.

Also, for your daily or weekly backups, you do not have to back up all files each time. Norton Backup enables you to perform an incremental backup, which backs up only files that changed since the last backup. Therefore, if you are performing daily backups, you may want to perform your full backup on Friday, and incremental backups on Monday through Thursday.

A backup program will do you little good unless you use it on a regular basis—do not wait until disaster strikes before deciding to implement a backup strategy. Norton Backup makes the backup chore easy and efficient.

Performing a Basic Backup and Restoring Information to Your Hard Disk

To begin the Norton Backup program to back up or restore files, you enter the command

NBACKUP

from the DOS prompt.

Figure 10.1 shows the Norton Backup main menu. There are four options on this menu: Backup, Restore, Configure, and Quit. Select one of these options by using the arrow keys to highlight an option and then pressing Enter. If you are using a mouse, you can point to the desired option and click the left mouse button.

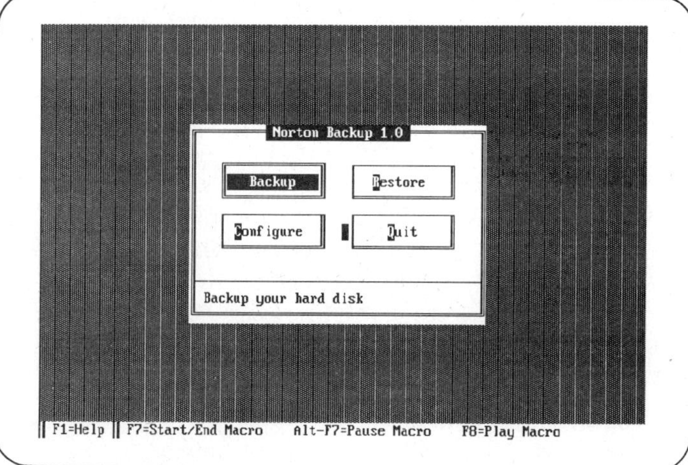

Fig. 10.1 ***The Norton Backup main menu.***

You use the Configure option to reset your configuration that was set originally when you installed Norton Backup. The Quit option ends the Norton Backup program and returns you to the DOS prompt. The Backup and Restore options are discussed in "Using Advanced Restore Features" and "Automating Norton Backup," later in this chapter.

In this chapter, you learn how to perform a backup and restore by using Norton Backup's basic options. After you are comfortable with the basics of using Norton Backup, you may want to use some advanced options which enable you to automate the backup process.

Backing Up Your Entire Hard Disk

After you choose the Backup option from the Norton Backup main menu, you see a menu similar to the one in figure 10.2. Notice that one letter in each option name is highlighted. To select one of the options to use, you can press the highlighted hot key (for example, the T key to select Backup To), use the arrow keys to highlight your choice and press Enter, or point to the option with the mouse and click the left mouse button once.

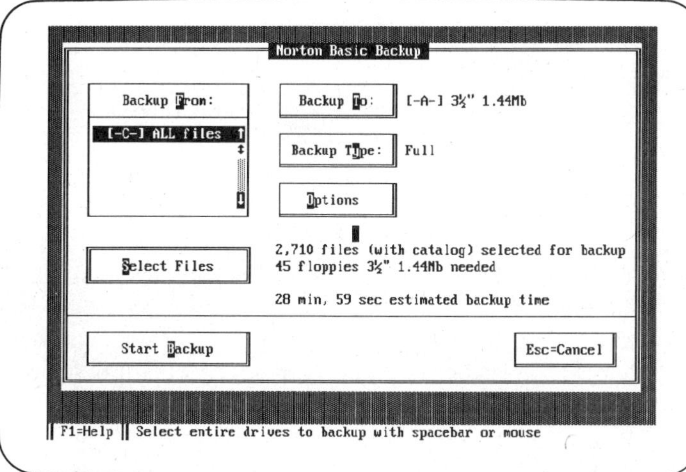

Fig. 10.2
The Norton Basic Backup menu.

To perform a backup of your hard disk to floppy disks, you must be sure that the Backup From and Backup To settings are correct. The Backup From setting should be the name of your hard disk. Usually, this is drive C.

If you have more than one hard disk, you will need to use the arrow keys (or a mouse) to select the hard disk to back up from. Similarly, you need to make sure that the Backup To selection is set to the floppy disk on which you want to store the information. Usually, this is set to drive A. If you have other floppy disk drives and want to back up to one of them, select the Backup To option. A list of the available disks appears from which you can choose the disk to back up to (see fig. 10.3).

The default backup type is Full. This backs up all selected files on the Backup From drive to the Backup To drive. The next section discusses how to change the default backup and how to select which files to back up.

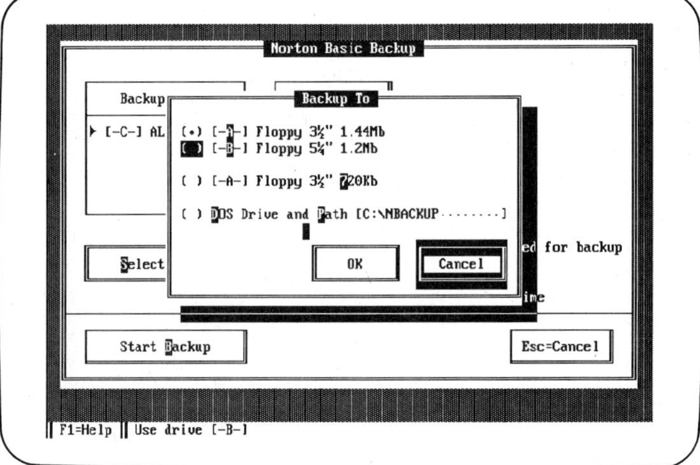

Fig. 10.3
The Backup To dialog box in Norton Backup.

To the right of the Select Files option on the Norton Basic Backup screen is a description of the number of files scheduled to be backed up and an estimate of the number of disks needed to perform that backup. You do not need to format these disks, because the Norton Backup procedure performs a format as the backup is in progress. Norton Backup also provides an estimate of the time required to perform the backup.

Tip: It is very important to match your diskette size with the disk drive you are using for backup. Do not try to use a 5 1/4-inch, 360K diskette, for example, in a drive meant for a 5 1/4-inch, 1.2M diskette. Similarly, do not use a 3 1/2-inch, 720K diskette in a 3 1/2-inch, 1.44M drive.

At the bottom of the Norton Basic Backup screen are the choices Start Backup and Esc=Cancel. If you decide to cancel this backup, press Esc. To begin the backup, select the Start Backup option.

When you begin the backup procedure, you see a screen similar to the one shown in figure 10.4. The top left of the screen contains a diagram of the directories on your hard disk and the top right of the screen displays the files in the highlighted directory. As the backup progresses, you will see the progress being made as the highlight moves down the directory tree.

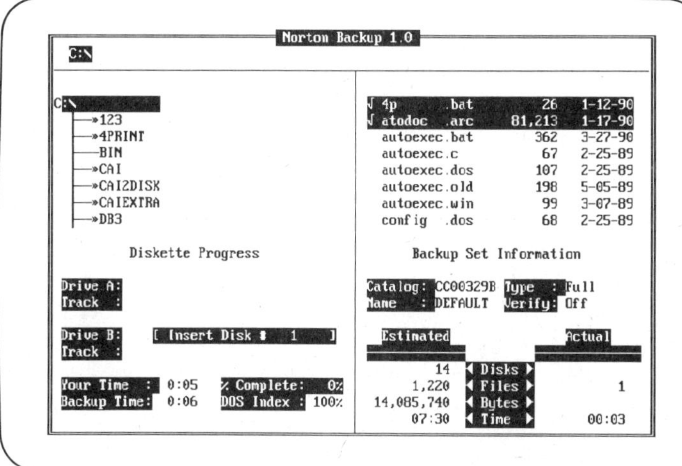

Fig. 10.4 ***The Norton Backup screen shows the progress of the backup process.***

At the bottom right of the screen is a set of statistics and information about the backup. As the backup progresses, information about the number of disks used and the estimated and actual time for the backup is displayed.

During most of the backup, you will be watching the information at the bottom left of the screen. Notice in figure 10.4 that the prompt `Insert Disk #1` is highlighted (it will probably be blinking on your screen). After you insert a disk, the backup begins and a small bar shows the progress of the backup to that disk. When the first disk is full, the message `Insert Disk #2` appears. The disk light on your disk drive will not go out; this is to keep the motor running to prevent the time lost when the motor has to stop and restart. Take out Disk #1 and insert Disk #2 into the drive. You must plan to stay at your computer during the backup process so that you can change disks as soon as you are prompted.

Each time a disk is full, you get a message to insert the next disk. This continues until the backup is finished.

Note: Be sure to label properly each diskette with its backup number. You will need to know the number of each backup disk when you restore files from the diskettes back to the hard disk.

Backing Up Selected Files

Norton Backup enables you to select which files to back up. In the Basic Backup screen in figure 10.2, notice the Select Files option. Choose this option to tell Norton Backup which files you want to back up. After you choose Selected Files, you see the Select Backup Files screen (see fig. 10.5). This screen is divided into two parts. The left part shows the directory structure on your hard disk. Directories with names preceded by a chevron (») contain files that you have selected to back up. If an arrow (→) precedes a directory name, this indicates that all files in that directory are selected to be backed up.

The highlighted directory has its file names displayed on the right side of the Select Backup screen (in fig. 10.5, this is the FORTRAN directory). File names that are preceded by a check mark (✔) are selected for backup. File names that are preceded by a dot (.) or a blank are excluded from the backup. You may select entire directories (including all files) to back up, or you may select individual files to back up.

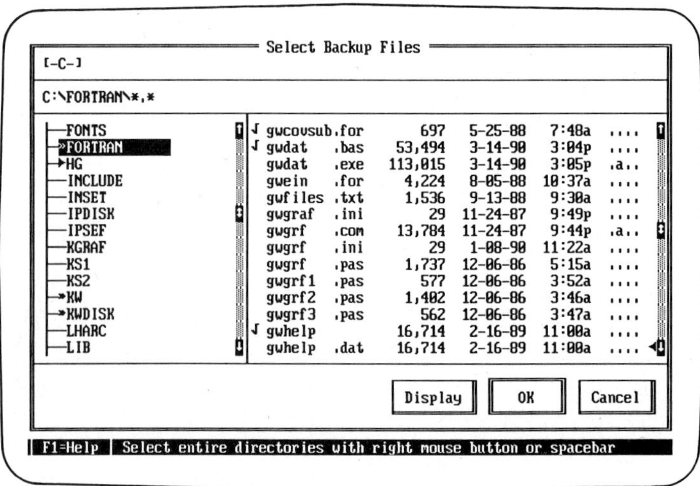

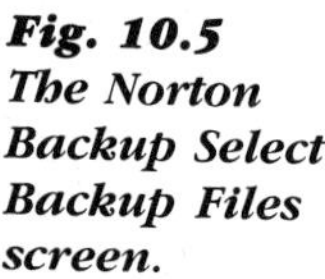

Fig. 10.5
The Norton Backup Select Backup Files screen.

Selecting and Deselecting Entire Directories To Back Up

To select all of the files in a directory to be backed up, highlight a directory name on the left side of the screen. If your cursor is not on the left side of the screen, press the left-arrow key or point to the directory with a mouse and click the left button. After you select a directory, you can press the space bar to select or deselect the files in that directory. After you select the files for backup, the file names are preceded by a check mark. When you deselect the files, the file names are preceded by a dot or a blank.

Selecting and Deselecting Groups of Files

It is common to want to select or deselect files containing the same extension. You may want to deselect all files with the EXE extension, for example. You can do this by performing the following steps:

1. Choose the Display option from the Select Backup Files screen. To select this option, press Tab until the Display option is highlighted and then press Enter, point to Display with your mouse and click the left button once, or press D. A dialog box appears similar to the one in figure 10.6. In this box, you indicate which files to display on the right side of the Select Backup Files screen. Choose to display the files *.EXE, for example.

   Now, when you point to a directory name on the left side of the screen, only .EXE files will appear on the right side.

2. Press the space bar to deselect or select all EXE files in that directory.

   You can be in any directory when you specify certain files to select. After you specify that only EXE files should be displayed, they will be the only files displayed, regardless of which directory you move to. To change this display specification, you must return to the Display option and change your selection criteria.

You can go through this process several times to eliminate other kinds of files that you do not want to back up, such as COM, OBJ, and LIB files—files that you can restore from master program disks.

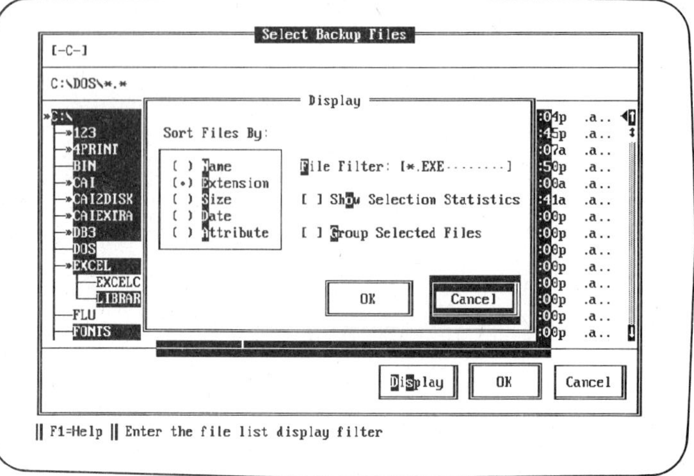

Fig. 10.6 *The Display dialog box from the Select Backup Files screen.*

Selecting and Deselecting Individual Files

There may be individual files that you want to select or deselect after you have selected or deselected entire directories or types of files (EXE). To select or deselect a file, highlight the directory containing the files on the left side of the Select Backup Files screen. Use the right arrow key to move your cursor to the right side of the screen. Point to the file to be selected or deselected and press the space bar. When the file is checked, it will be backed up (selected); otherwise, the file will not be backed up (deselected).

Performing a Backup with the Selected Files

After you go through the process of selecting files for backup, the backup process is the same as for a full backup, as described in "Backing Up Your Entire Hard Disk," earlier in this chapter. From the Norton Basic Backup menu, choose the Start Backup option and follow the prompts on-screen.

Performing Incremental Backups and Copies

If you perform backups on a regular basis, there usually is no need to perform a full backup each time. You can save on the amount of time you spend doing backups by performing incremental backups.

Suppose that you perform a backup every day. On Friday, you could perform a full backup (and take it home during the weekend). Then, on Monday through Thursday you could perform an incremental backup—backing up only the files that have changed that day.

Performing incremental backups means that you will be backing up updated copies of files that you backed up on Monday. This means that you will have a growing stack of diskettes containing the backup of your hard disk. This is why you want to start over every Friday with a full backup to consolidate all of the file changes made during the week—this cuts down on duplicated files and on the number of diskettes used. Also, when you decide to restore a file, it becomes more of a problem finding the right file if you have multiple copies of it backed up.

Your computer (or, more specifically, DOS) keeps track of which files have been backed up. The archive attribute is set when a file is backed up. This archive attribute (or *flag*) is an on/off switch that is stored by DOS with the file name. The archive attribute tells DOS whether a file has been backed up. When the archive attribute on a file name is set, therefore, DOS knows that the file has been backed up. When you alter a file or create a new file, DOS unsets the archive attribute. When you perform an incremental backup, DOS looks for the files that do not have the archive attribute set, and it backs up those files only. Then, DOS sets the archive attribute for these new files as they are backed up. When you perform your next incremental backup, only new or changed files since the last incremental backup are backed up. (See the discussion on the FA command in Chapter 3 for more information on archive flags.)

To perform an incremental backup, choose the Backup Type option from the Norton Basic Backup screen. You see a dialog box like the one in figure 10.7. From this Backup Type box, choose the Incremental option by pressing I to select Incremental, or by pointing with your mouse to the ( ) before Incremental and clicking.

After you select the incremental type backup, the backup process is the same as for a full backup (see "Backing Up Your Entire Hard Disk," earlier in this chapter). From the Norton Basic Backup menu, choose the Start Backup option and follow the prompts on-screen.

Using Other Backup Types

There are several other selections in the Backup Type dialog box. The Full option and Incremental options are discussed earlier in the chapter.

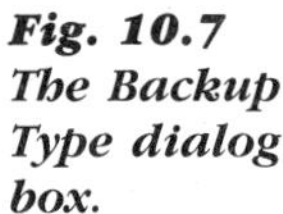

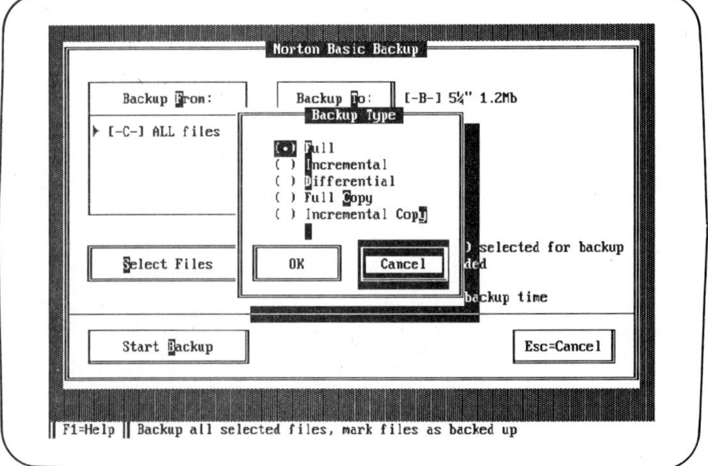

Fig. 10.7 The Backup Type dialog box.

The Differential option is similar to the Incremental option—it backs up files that you changed or created since the last backup—but it does not set the archive attribute on a file like the Incremental option. When you perform a differential backup, therefore, your computer keeps no record of the backup. There may be occasions when you want to back up changed files, but you do not want to set the archive attribute. You may use Backup to copy files from one computer to another, for example. In this case, you do not want the copy to count as a backup.

The Full Copy option is similar to the Full option, but it does not set the archive attribute like a regular full backup does. You may want to perform a full backup without disturbing your normal backup procedure, which relies on the archive attributes being set for incremental backups. You may want to use Backup to copy the contents of the entire hard disk to a new computer, for example. However, because this backup does not fit into your normal daily, weekly, or monthly backup scheme, you do not want this backup to set the archive attributes and disturb your normal backup set of disks.

The Incremental Copy option enables you to perform a backup of selected files that you changed or created since the last backup without setting the archive attribute. This option provides you with a complete set of backup disks for these files—not just "add-on" disks for the full backup. (A normal incremental backup creates disks that depend on a previous full copy to be restored. You can use Incremental Copy to restore files without relying on a previous full backup.) The Incremental Copy option makes it easier to restore these files to another disk. You can use this procedure to transfer files to another computer without messing up your normal incremental backup procedure.

Using Backup Options

There is one selection remaining on the Norton Basic Backup screen to be discussed. This is the Options selection, which enables you to select backup options. The options screen is shown in figure 10.8.

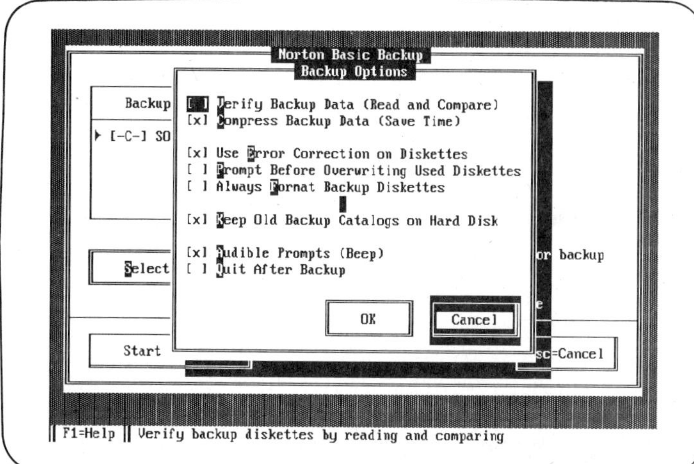

Fig. 10.8
The Backup Options dialog box.

On the Backup Options menu, an item is selected if an X appears to its left. Use the arrow keys to point to a selection, and use the space bar to place an X or remove an X from the selection (or point to an option with the mouse and click the left button). You can select the following options from the Backup Options menu:

- *Verify Backup Data:* Causes Norton Backup to double-check the information as it is written to disk. This slows down the backup process, but gives you more assurance that the backup is correct. Usually, you should not have to use this option. However, if your disk drives are old or have had read and write problems in the past, you may want to choose this option as an added measure of protection.

- *Compress Backup Data:* Compresses the data written to disk so that more information can be written to each disk. This means that you will be able to use fewer disks. When the Compress selection is off, backup will be faster, but it will take more diskettes. You usually will want to choose this option.

- *Use Error Correction on Diskettes:* Provides additional checking of the information as it is written and read to and from the backup disks. If your data is very critical, you may want to use this extra measure of safety. Also, you may use the Verify Backup option to verify that the information written to disk matches the original files exactly. Use this option as a special safety feature of Norton Backup.

- *Prompt Before Overwriting Used Diskettes:* Causes Norton Backup to prompt you before writing information to a previously used diskette. This could save you from accidentally writing over important information. It also may slow down the backup process.

- *Always Format Backup Diskettes:* Causes Norton Backup always to format disks as the backup is taking place. You may want to use this if the disks you are using for backup were formatted on an older version of DOS.

- *Keep Old Backup Catalogs on Hard Disk:* Causes Norton Backup to keep old backup catalogs (containing backup information) each time you perform a backup. Otherwise, when you perform a full backup, the old catalogs are deleted. You may want to select not to keep old catalogs in order to conserve disk space.

- *Audible Prompts:* Determines whether a beep will be sounded when Norton Backup prompts you to change disks and for other warnings.

- *Quit After Backup:* Determines whether Norton Backup will return to the Backup menu or to DOS after it performs the backup.

Restoring Backed-Up Files

You may never have to use your backup disks to restore files. However, when disaster strikes, those backup disks suddenly become very valuable. You may restore one file from your backup diskettes to your hard disk, a selected number of files, or all files.

The restore process is managed from the Norton Basic Restore screen, as shown in figure 10.9. To display this screen, choose the Restore option from the Norton Backup main menu. Before choosing the Start Restore option from the Norton Basic Restore screen, you need to check several options—Restore From, Catalog, Options, and Select Files.

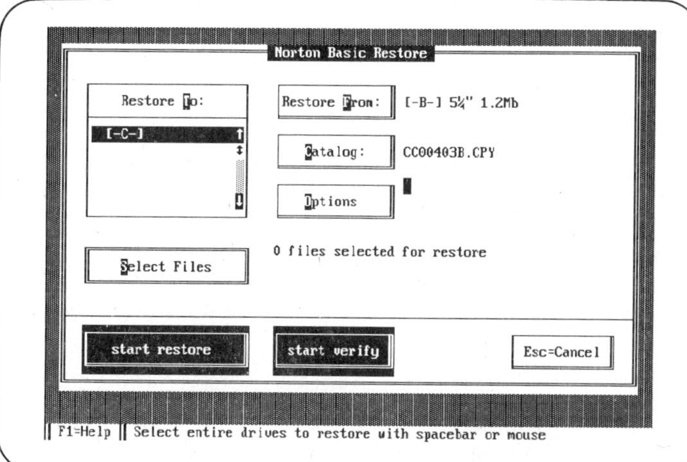

Fig. 10.9
The Norton Basic Restore menu.

Choosing Restore From

You chose the Restore To setting during the configuration process when you installed Norton Backup. The Restore From selection also will reflect what you chose during installation. If you need to use another disk drive to restore the disks, you can select the Restore From option and change the setting.

Choosing the Restore Catalog

Each time you perform a restore, Norton Backup keeps a copy of the catalog of files restored. After you select the Catalog option from the Norton Basic Restore menu, you see the Select Catalog screen (see fig. 10.10). Notice the list of catalog files in the middle of the screen. A catalog of each backup is kept on your hard disk and on the last diskette of the backup floppies. Because you may have multiple backups (one-day old, a week old, and so on), you must choose from this list of catalogs which will be used to perform the restore.

From the Select Catalog menu you can view or print the contents of a catalog by highlighting its name in the center of the screen and choosing View/Print. You use the Retrieve option to retrieve a catalog from the last floppy of a backup. If you are restoring to a machine or hard disk that did not create that backup, for example, you must retrieve the catalog. You use the Rebuild command to rebuild a catalog if the last disk of a backup has been damaged. After you indicate which catalog to use, choose the Load option, which loads that catalog and returns you to the Restore menu.

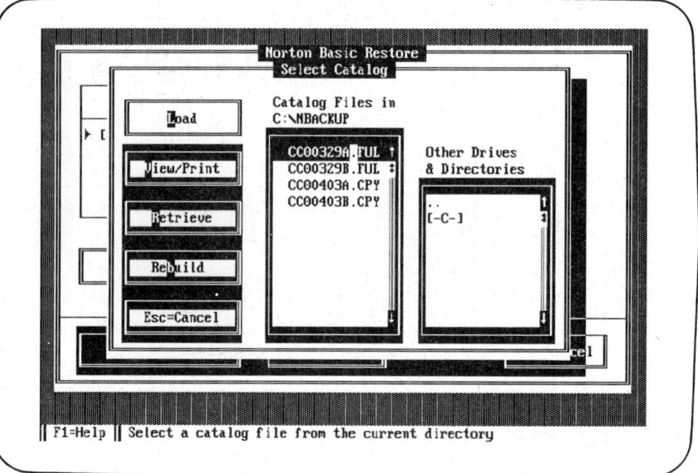

Fig. 10.10 ***The Select Catalog menu.***

Selecting Restore Options

When you choose the Options menu from the Norton Basic Restore menu, you see a screen similar to the one in figure 10.11. Skip the Options menu if you do not want to set any of these options by pressing Esc or by pointing to Cancel with your mouse and clicking.

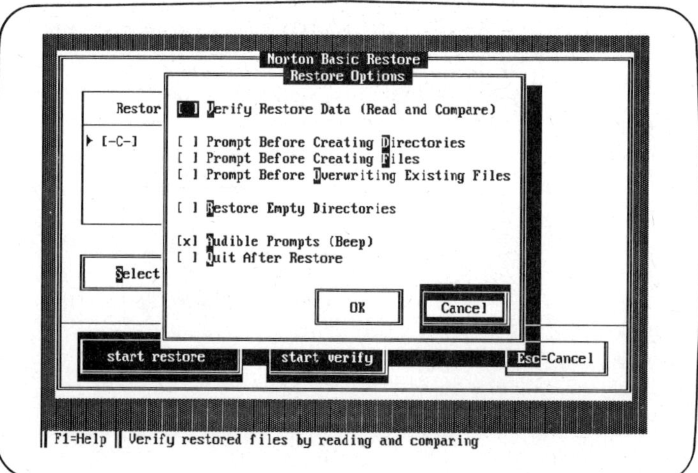

Fig. 10.11 ***The Restore Options dialog box.***

The Verify Restore Data option on the Restore Options menu causes Norton Backup to double-check the contents of the file after it is copied to the hard disk. This will slow down the restore, but may be advisable if you have had any difficulties in performing a successful restore.

The Prompt options cause Norton Backup to prompt you before overwriting existing directories or files or before creating new files on disk. Choosing these options drastically increases the amount of interaction you will have during the restore process—but may be necessary if there is a possibility that the restore will overwrite valuable information on your hard disk. If you are restoring files that may overwrite important existing files, you should use this option as a precautionary measure.

Restore usually will not restore empty directories unless you choose the Restore Empty Directories option. You may turn off audible prompts by deselecting the Audible Prompts option. After you select all of the options you want by placing an X to the left of the option name, choose OK to close this dialog box and return to the Basic Backup menu. If you choose Cancel instead of OK, all options return to their previous states and you return to the Basic Backup menu.

Selecting Files To Restore

After you choose the Select Files option from the Norton Basic Restore menu, you see the Select Restore Files screen (see fig. 10.12). This screen is similar to the Select Backup Files screen. You choose files to restore in the same way you choose files to back up. When you choose a file to restore, a check mark appears beside the file name (like the one next to the file BIG.DBF in figure 10.12). You may choose one file, several files, an entire directory, or all directories to restore.

If you choose files to restore that already may be on disk, you may want to choose one or more of the prompt selections in the Options menu (see the "Selecting Restore Options" section).

The Show Versions option on the Select Restore Files screen enables you to see information about several versions of a file. You may have incrementally backed up the file called SALES.DBF every day, for example. In this case, there would be several versions of this file on the backup diskettes. To choose the proper version to restore, highlight the file name on-screen and select the Show Versions option, which displays the versions with the date and time they were created. From this list, select the proper version to restore.

After you make your selections for which files to restore, choose the OK option and you will return to the Norton Basic Restore menu.

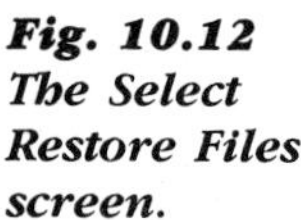

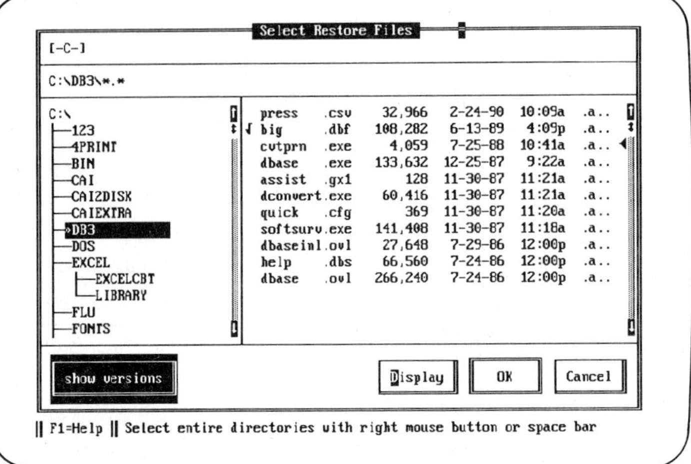

Fig. 10.12
The Select Restore Files screen.

Starting the Restore

After you select which files to restore, select the Start Restore option from the Norton Basic Restore menu. A screen similar to the one in figure 10.13 appears. An Alert screen prompts you to insert a diskette into the disk drive. Place the proper diskette into the drive and choose Continue. Follow the prompts on-screen to complete the restore process.

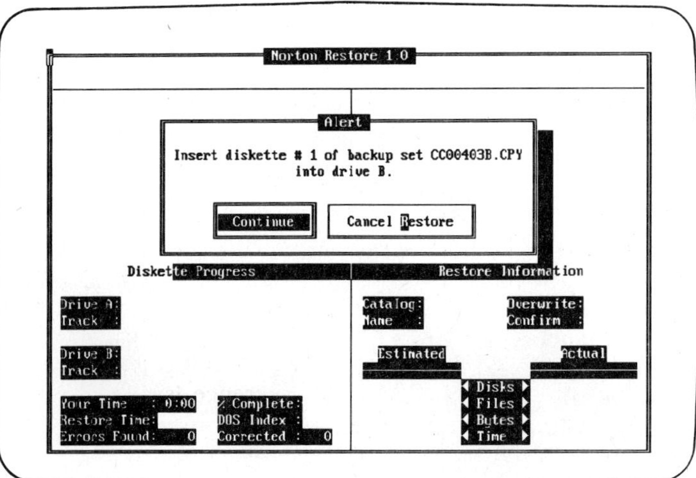

Fig. 10.13
The Alert dialog box tells you which backup disk to insert.

Tip: What can you do if your hard disk and your Norton Backup program is destroyed? If you are restoring your files to a new or reformatted hard disk, follow these steps:

1. Install the Norton Backup program to the new or reformatted hard disk.

2. Insert the last diskette of your most recent backup (or the backup you want to use to restore your files) into your disk drive.

3. Begin the backup by typing *nbackup* and choose Restore from the Norton Backup main menu.

   The Norton Basic Restore screen appears. Make sure that the Restore From option refers to the disk where your backup diskette is located.

4. Choose the Catalog option from the Norton Basic Restore screen, and then choose the Retrieve option from the Select Catalog menu. This accesses catalog information that Norton uses to restore files. Choose the latest catalog file and press Esc to exit this option.

5. Select all files to be restored.

6. Insert Disk 1 of the backup disks into the disk drive, choose Start Restore from the Norton Basic Restore screen, and follow the prompts on-screen.

Verifying that a Restore is Possible

Even with all of the checks and double-checks, it is possible for a set of backup disks to become unusable. This could be from environmental factors such as magnetism, heat, or cold. Disks also can become unusable because of the deterioration of the magnetic surface on the diskette.

You can check a set of backup disks by performing a verify immediately after creating the disks or any time in the future. You begin a verify just like you begin a restore. The only difference is that instead of choosing the Start Restore option on the Norton Basic Restore menu, you choose Start Verify. A Verify is similar to a Restore, but it will not actually restore the files to the disk; it examines the files to see if they can be restored.

You should perform a verify on the first backup you create on your computer to ensure that everything is okay. If you are going to use a set of diskettes to move information from one computer to another—you may want to take the diskettes to your new home on the coast, for example—you should verify that the backup disks are okay before taking them to your new location. Otherwise, you may be disappointed.

Some companies run a periodic check of a disaster-recovery plan. For example, what happens if your office burns down? Can you recover your data? You can simulate the recovery of your computer information by performing a verify on your backup disks. Performing such a simulation on a quarterly basis is a good test of the integrity of your backup plan as well as a test of the disks. After you perform the simulation, you need to ask yourself if you are satisfied with the amount of information that you would be able to recover after a disaster.

Using Advanced Features of Norton Backup

Performing a backup and restore using advanced features is similar to performing a basic backup and restore. The main difference is that Norton enables you to set up prescribed backup procedures and additional backup and restore options by using the advanced features. Follow these steps:

1. Choose the Configuration selection from the Norton Backup main menu.

   The Norton Backup Configuration menu appears, enabling you to set the program level, mouse characteristics, type of video display, and other settings related to your computer.

2. Select the Program Level option from the Configuration menu and set it to Advanced. Use the arrow keys to highlight the Program Level option on the Norton Backup Configuration screen and press Enter. Alternatively, point to the Program Level option with a mouse and click (see fig. 10.14). The Program options are Basic, Advanced, and Preset. Select Advanced and then select OK to return to the Configuration menu.

3. Save the new configuration by choosing the Save Configuration option from the Norton Backup Configuration menu. Exit the Configuration menu by choosing OK.

The following information describes how to perform a backup using the advanced backup options. Because many of these options are the same as in a basic backup, only the advanced options are emphasized.

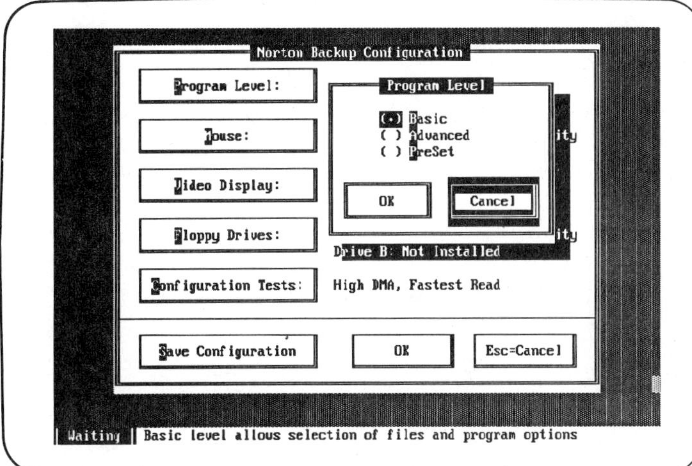

Fig. 10.14
The Norton Backup Configuration dialog box.

Using the Advanced Backup Menu

After you choose the advanced program level for the Norton Backup configuration, choose the Backup option from the main menu. The Norton Advanced Backup menu appears (see fig. 10.15). Notice that this menu is similar to the Basic Backup menu except for the addition of the Setup File

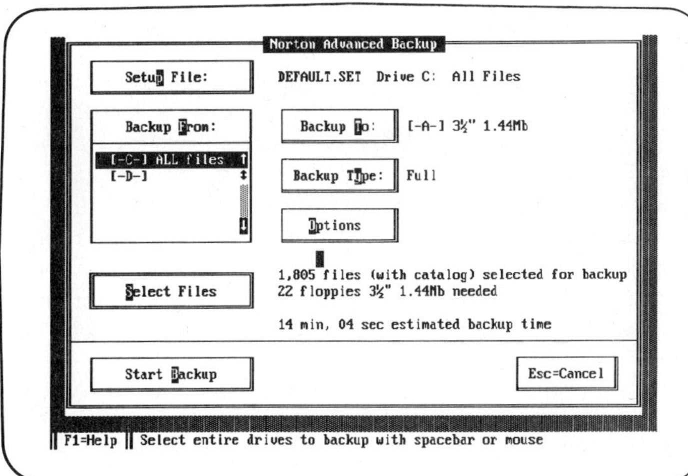

Fig. 10.15
The Norton Advanced Backup menu.

option at the top left of the screen. Creating and using setup files is discussed in "Creating and Using Setup Files," later in this chapter.

Using Advanced Select Files Options

After you choose Select Files from the Advanced Backup screen, the Select Backup Files screen appears (see fig. 10.16). Notice the addition of the selections—Include, Exclude, and Special—at the bottom left of the screen. These options are not available in the Basic Backup program level. The Include and Exclude options enable you to include or exclude groups of files to be backed up.

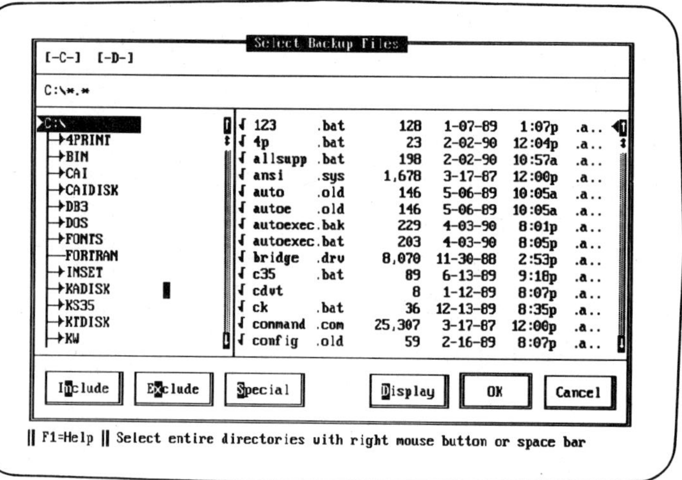

Fig. 10.16
The Advanced Select Backup menu.

If you choose the Include option, the Include Files dialog box appears (see fig. 10.17). To include files, enter the appropriate path for the directory at the path prompt and a global file specification at the file prompt. Type **.exe* to match all files with an EXE extension, for example. If you mark the Include All Subdirectories option with an X, all matching files in subdirectories also are included. Each time you indicate an Include Files specification and choose OK, that specification is added to a list, and the Include Files screen reverts to the state shown in figure 10.17. You now can enter another specification to include on the list. You can list a number of file specifications to include—such as *.EXE, *.COM, *.TXT, and so on.

To view the list of included and excluded files, choose the Edit Include/Exclude List option from the Include Files dialog box. The Edit Include/Exclude List screen appears (see fig. 10.18). By using the up- and down-arrow keys to highlight one of the items on the list, you then can choose to edit the item, delete it from the list, or copy it by choosing one of the options at the bottom of the dialog screen. Choose OK when your list of included and excluded files is correct.

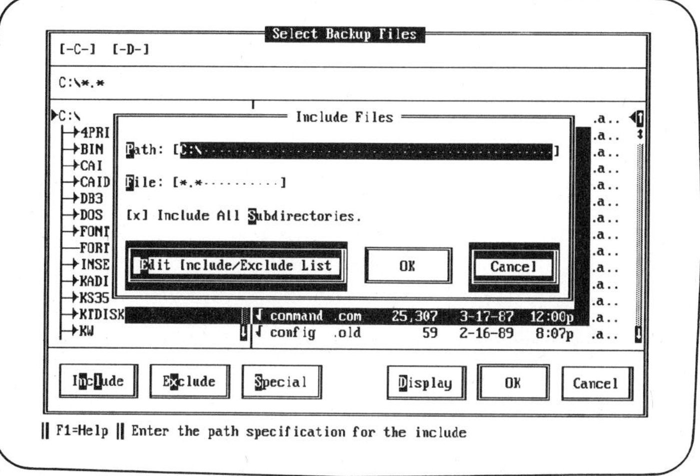

Fig. 10.17
The Include Files dialog box.

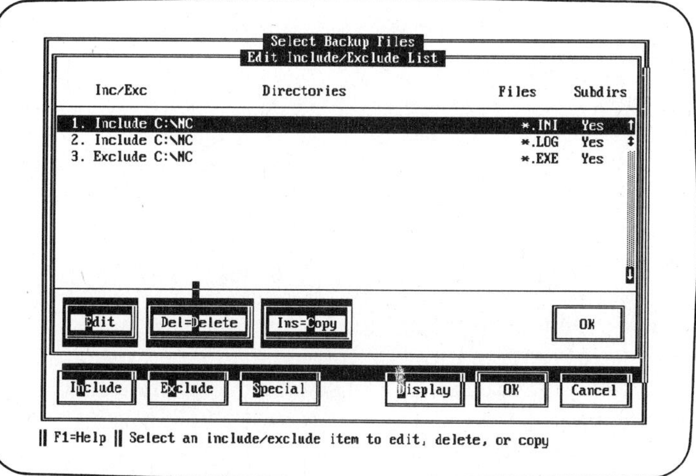

Fig. 10.18.
The Edit Include/Exclude List screen.

Another option on the Select Backup Files screen is the Special option (fig. 10.19 shows the Special Selection dialog box). This option enables you to select a date range of files to back up. After you choose the Date Range option from the Special Selection menu, you are prompted to enter a beginning and ending date. The date range 1-1-90 to 12-31-90, for example, backs up only files created in 1990. You also can select options to exclude the following:

- Read-only files
- System files
- Hidden files

Using arrow keys and the space bar or a mouse, place an X in the selection box in front of the file types to exclude from backup. If you choose the Copy Protected Files option on the Special Selections menu, you are prompted to enter a list of copy-protected files to exclude from backup.

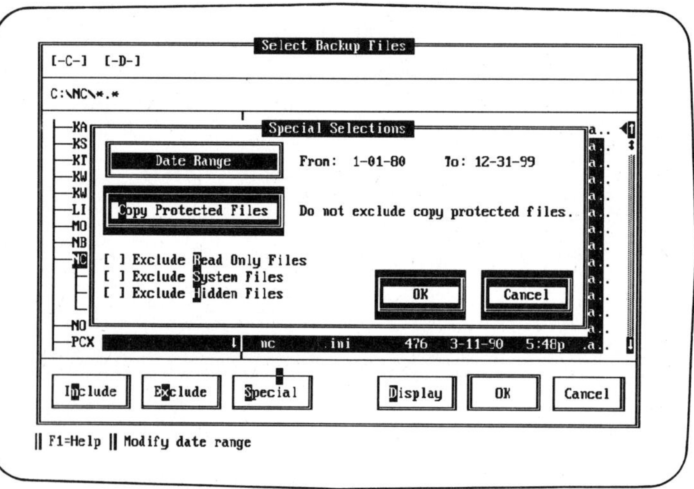

Fig. 10.19. ***The Special Selections dialog box.***

Selecting Advanced Backup Options

After you choose Options from the Norton Advanced Backup screen, you are presented with a different set of options than when using the basic backup procedure. The Backup Options screen for advanced backup is shown in figure 10.20.

The Data Verification option causes the backup procedure to verify the data more thoroughly as it is written to the backup disks. Norton Backup compares the backup file to the original file to verify that the backup copy is exactly the same as the original. This slows down the backup procedure, but may be worth it to protect very important data.

You can choose from three options with the Data Compression option:

- *Save Time:* Does little compression, but is quicker and uses more diskettes.
- *Save Disks (low):* Does more compression and takes fewer disks, but is slower than the Save Time option.
- *Save Disks (high):* Performs maximum compression and takes fewest disks, but is slow.

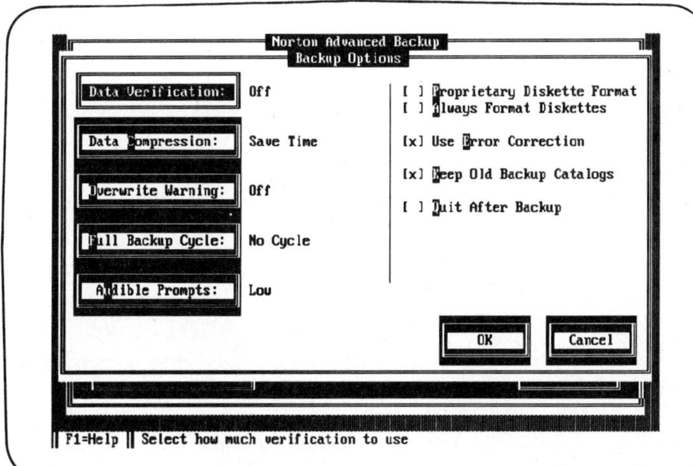

***Fig. 10.20** The Advanced Backup options.*

If you set the Overwrite Warning option to On, you are prompted each time before the program overwrites backup diskettes that already contain data.

The Full Backup Cycle option enables you to specify the number of days between full backups. If you set this cycle to 7, for example, when you attempt to do a partial backup on the 7th day, you will get a message telling you that you should be doing a full backup. You may set the Audible Prompts option to Off, Low, or High.

Other selections on the Backup Options screen are listed on the right half of the screen. If you select Proprietary Diskette Format, Norton uses a special technique of formatting the disk which is faster than the normal DOS format. If you select Always Format Diskettes, the backup procedure formats each backup disk as information is written to the disk, even if the disk already has been formatted. This is a safety check to make sure that the disk does not contain any bad sectors, but it may slow down the backup process.

When you choose User Error Correction, Norton writes additional information to each disk that can be used by Norton to recover damaged disks, but it takes up more space on the disk. If you select Keep Old Backup Catalogs, Norton does not delete accumulated catalogs from previous backups. If you are overwriting old backup disks for a new backup, you probably do not want to keep the old catalogs.

The Quit After Backup option causes Norton Backup to return to the DOS prompt after it finishes a backup. You generally use this when you are running Backup from a batch process (see "Automating Norton Backup," later in this chapter).

Creating and Using Setup Files

You use setup files to capture all of the backup settings and selections you have made for a backup so that you will not have to repeat that process again. You can give each setup selection a name so that you can choose the backup setup from the Setup File option on the Norton Advanced Backup menu. You may have a Weekend setup that backs up the entire disk, for example, which is what you want to do on Fridays. Another setup may be called Weekday, which is an incremental backup that you want to perform on Monday through Thursday.

To create a setup file, fill in all of the fields for the options described in the Advanced Backup menu—Backup To, Backup From, Backup Type, Options, and Select Files. Then, choose the Setup File option. A screen similar to the one in figure 10.21 appears. On this screen, name the setup

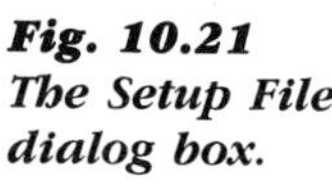

Fig. 10.21
The Setup File dialog box.

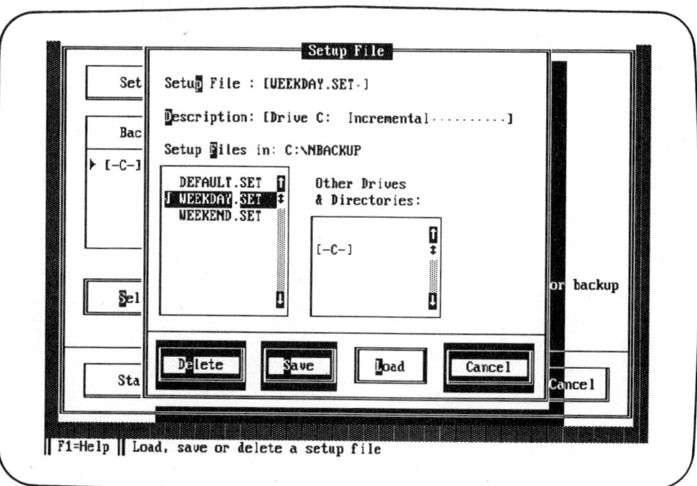

file and enter a description containing up to 24 characters (press Tab or Shift-Tab to get to these fields, or point and click with a mouse). After you enter a new name and description for the setup, choose the Save option.

After you have several setup files defined, you can choose the Setup File option from the Advanced Backup menu and choose the kind of backup to perform. The current selection will be displayed on the Advanced Backup menu next to the Setup File option.

Tip: If you are in charge of backups in an organization, you can make standard setup files and distribute them to the entire organization—to each person using Norton Backup. This would enable nonsophisticated users to perform backups without having to understand all of the procedures for setting options and selecting files. Simply copy the SET and SLT files, which are created when you save a setup to each computer using Norton Backup. This makes that setup available on each person's computer. You also can include some backup automation to make the backup even more easy to perform. These techniques are discussed later.

Using Advanced Restore Features

The Advanced Restore procedure is similar to the Basic Restore process (see "Restoring Backed-Up Files," earlier in the chapter), with the addition of a few options. These options include the Setup File option and different Restore options.

Using a setup file option in an advanced restore enables you to capture and then reuse all of the settings you want to use in a restore operation. You create and select setup files by using the same process described in "Using Advanced Select Files Options." The Advanced Restore screen has a different set of restore options than does the Basic Restore screen. The Advanced Restore Options menu is shown in figure 10.22. Some of these options are the same as on the Basic Restore screen. Those that are different will be described here.

After you select the Data Verification option, a dialog box appears from which you can choose one of several methods of verification:

- *Off:* Provides no verification, but offers the fastest speed when restoring files.
- *Sample Only:* Verifies every eighth track of data.

- *Read Only:* Reads the data after it has been written.
- *Read and Compare:* Reads the data and compares it to the data on the backup diskette. Requires the most amount of time, but provides the highest amount of safety.

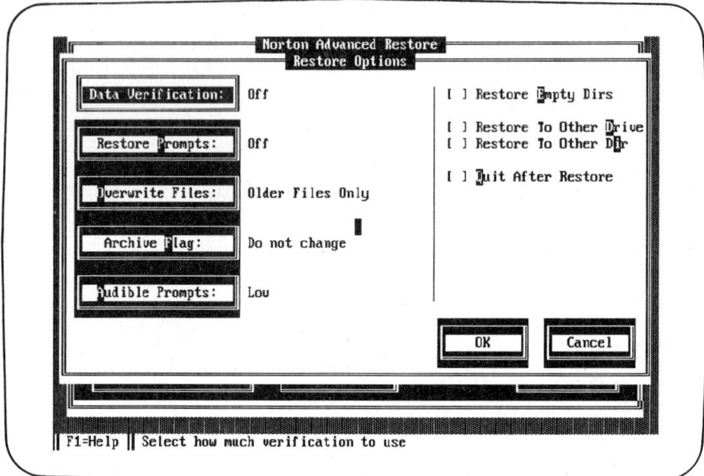

Fig. 10.22
The Advanced Restore options.

The Restore Prompts option, when on, causes the program to prompt you before it restores a new directory or creates a new file on the target drive. Using prompts can slow down the restore process considerably, but they provide a greater amount of safety.

You can choose from three settings for the Overwrite Files option:

- *Never Overwrite Files:* Prevents the accidental overwriting of files already in existence on disk. Choose this if you do not want restored files to replace same-named files already on disk.
- *Always Overwrite:* Causes the restore to copy all files specified by the Restore selection, even if it overwrites a same-named file already on disk.
- *Overwrite Older Files:* Causes the restore to overwrite only files with a date that is older than the one from the backup files. The default setting is to overwrite older files only.

These options do not affect files being restored that do not have same-named files already on disk.

You can set the Archive Flag option to Do Not Change, Mark as Backed Up, or Marked as *not* backed up. The archive flag is normally set to Do Not Change. This means that if a file to be restored sees the same file already on disk, it will not change its archive flag as a result of the restore. The Mark as Backed Up option turns off all archive flags on restored files, and the Mark as Not Backed up option turns on the archive flag for all files restored. Usually, the default condition is the best, but there may be special circumstances—such as restoring to a new machine—when you want to have more control over the setting of the archive flag. Of course, you also can use the Norton Utilities FA command to set the archive flag.

You can set Audible Prompts to Off, Low, or High.

There are several other selections on the right side of the Restore Options screen. The Restore Empty Dirs option, if selected, enables the restore process to recreate empty directories that may have been backed up.

The Restore To Other Drive and Restore To Other Dir options enable you to redirect where the restored files will go. If you select one of these options, a dialog box appears, where you can define the destination of the restore.

All other options and procedures on the Advanced Restore screen are the same as on the Basic Restore screen. To continue with the restore process, set all options according to your needs and choose the Begin Restore option from the Advanced Restore main menu.

Automating Norton Backup

If you always perform the same type of backup, using the same options, you can automate the backup procedure so that you can begin a backup with just a few keystrokes. You can automate the backup process by using macros or the DOS prompt command level options.

Using Macros To Capture and Replay Commands

You can think of a macro as a tape recorder—it records your keystrokes and plays them back again. You can use a macro to capture a series of keystrokes that choose certain backup or restore procedures. Then, when you want to repeat the same process later, you can replay the macro.

Before creating a macro, plan carefully which keystrokes you will need. Also, after you create a macro, test it before using it on a regular basis. You cannot use the mouse when recording a macro. The macro you will make will be associated with the setup file currently in use. Therefore, make sure that you first choose the correct setup file.

To begin the recording process, press F7. The message `Recording` should appear at the lower left corner. As you progress through your keystrokes, you will be *simulating* a backup or restore—not actually performing one. Therefore, instead of pressing Enter and the space bar to select certain options, use the following simulation keys:

Press	*To Simulate*
Ctrl-Enter	Enter
Ins	On
Del	Off

When you select files to be included or excluded in a backup, use Ins to select and Del to deselect—not the space bar. Whenever you would press Enter, use Ctrl-Enter instead.

To stop recording, press F7 again. To play back your recording, press F8. Always check out your macro before distributing it to other users. Because this macro is associated with a setup file, it will be available for use whenever you use that setup file. You even can begin a macro from the DOS prompt, as described in the next section.

You can use a macro to automate the backup procedure for a user that is uncomfortable in dealing with these kinds of tasks. Record a backup session so that users can repeat the same backup with a batch file command, as described in the next section.

Using Batch Files To Automate Backup

Another method of automating the backup and restore process is by including commands on the DOS command line. To begin the NBACKUP program and automatically use the WEEKEND setup file, for example, enter the following command at the DOS prompt:

```
NBACKUP WEEKEND
```

If there is a macro associated with the WEEKEND setup file, you can cause the macro to begin automatically by using the DOS command:

```
NBACKUP @WEEKEND
```

You can enter these commands at the DOS prompt or as a line in a batch file. If you created a macro for the weekend backup process, therefore, you can create a batch file named WEEKEND.BAT, which contains commands such as these:

```
echo off
echo This is a batch file for Weekend backups
cd\nbackup
nbackup @weekend
cd\
echo -----------The backup is finished----------
```

Then, you or another user only will have to enter the command

```
WEEKEND
```

at the DOS prompt to begin the backup process.

Summary

You can use Norton Backup at two levels of sophistication: basic and advanced. The basic backup procedures enable you to perform backups without having to be concerned about choosing many options. On the other hand, you also can use Norton Backup in advanced mode, which enables you to select from a wide variety of backup options. If you are setting up a controlled backup process for yourself or an organization, Norton Backup has features that enable you to automate the backup process so that you can perform sophisticated backups and restores with a minimum amount of user intervention.

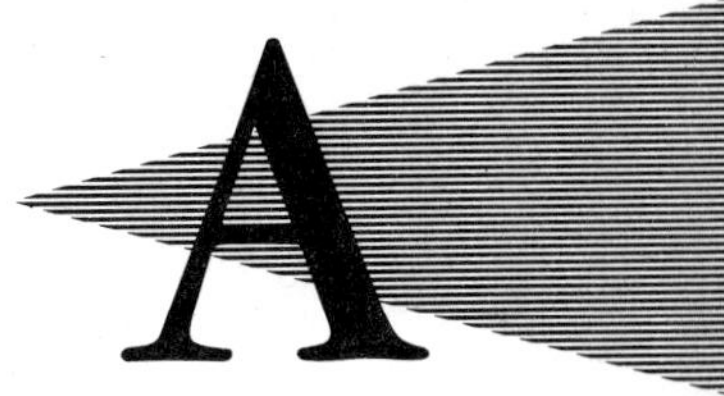

Introduction to DOS

DOS, which stands for disk operating system, is a software program that manages the resources of the computer. On the IBM personal computer, this operating program is called PC DOS. IBM-compatible computers use a nearly equivalent DOS called MS-DOS, which stands for Microsoft DOS. Microsoft is the company that designed DOS for the IBM family of personal computers.

In everyday events—banking, filing, and checking your coat—items are stored and retrieved. Information is just one more thing that needs to be stored somewhere so that it can be retrieved later. Because the computer deals mainly with information, having a "manager" that puts information somewhere and then later retrieves it makes sense. On the computer, DOS is the manager, and you are the one that makes requests about what to do with the information stored on the computer.

For DOS to understand what you want it to do, you have to speak its language. This appendix introduces the basic concepts and commands—the language—of DOS. If you are a computer beginner, read this entire appendix before using the book, because the book frequently references DOS commands and concepts. If you are familiar with some parts of DOS, you may not need to read the entire appendix. Instead, you can study only the topics that you want to learn more about and those that will be helpful to you while using this book (and your computer). The topics covered in this appendix include the following:

- Learning how DOS works
- Reviewing commonly used DOS commands
- Managing a hard disk by using DOS commands
- Using batch and system files

- Using the DOS EDLIN editor
- Using DOS to back up information on your hard disk

Understanding How DOS Works

Before learning *what* specific tasks DOS can do, you must first understand *how* DOS works. Before you can do that, however, you must understand the concept of computer files. You can relate computer files to paper files that are used in the workplace. You undoubtedly are familiar with manila folders in a file cabinet. Each folder contains information about some person, item, contract, and so on. Computer files operate under the same idea. Like a physical file, a computer file contains information. This information may be your resume, your monthly budget, an economics report, or a software program. Rather than physical pieces of paper, you have electronically stored information on the disk.

Somehow, the computer needs to keep track of all the files on disk. Also, a facility is needed for making copies of files, erasing files, and performing other managerial functions concerning the resources of the computer. DOS manages these resources under the direction of you, the computer operator.

This appendix begins with a summary of the changes DOS has undergone since its inception. You then learn how DOS gets your computer going, how to name and use DOS files, and how to issue DOS commands.

Reviewing the Evolution of DOS

When the IBM PC was first introduced in October 1981, it operated under the PC DOS operating system, Version 1.0. Since that time, PC DOS has undergone several changes, and newer versions have been released. Because you are likely to find several versions in use in any business or university, knowing some of the differences among the various versions is helpful. Some earlier versions of PC DOS are not fully compatible with the newer versions.

The primary reason for continually changing DOS is so that it can support new storage devices introduced on new versions of the PC. Usually, these changes have to do with advancements in disk storage. When the PC was first introduced, it supported only single-sided diskettes—disks that stored information on only one side. When double-sided disks were introduced, a new version of DOS was required, and DOS Version 1.1 was released. Along with supporting new disk devices, new versions of DOS also have improved and changed some other features, such as support for new kinds of monitors and other peripherals.

The various changes in PC DOS are outlined in table A.1. Changes in DOS are typically considered *upwardly compatible*. That is, new versions of DOS usually are able to read information from disks created with old versions of DOS—but not always. A major change was made in DOS 2.0, for example, in the way information is stored on disk. The result is that a diskette formatted with DOS 2.0 cannot be read on a machine that uses DOS 1.1 or DOS 1.0. Also, because hard disks were first supported with Version 2.0 of DOS, the Norton Utilities programs covered in this book are based on the assumption that you are operating with DOS Version 2.0 or higher.

Table A.1
The Versions of PC DOS

Version	*Primary Feature(s)*
1.0	Supports single-sided diskettes (160K)
1.1	Supports double-sided diskettes (320K)
2.0	Supports hard disks and a subdirectory file structure (double-sided disks, now 360K)
2.1	Supports the half-height diskettes on the IBM PCjr
3.0	Supports the 1.2M floppy and other new functions of the IBM PC AT
3.1	Supports networking
3.2	Supports 720K 3 1/2-inch floppy diskettes, laptop computers, and networking
3.3	Supports 1.44M 3 1/2-inch floppy diskettes and the PS/2 series of computers
4.0	Features pull-down menus and supports drive use past the previous 32M limit

Booting the Computer

The computer hardware by itself does not "know" how to do many tasks. What it *can* do is match patterns of 0s and 1s and use those patterns to follow commands that programmers have stored in the computer's memory. Because the computer knows so little, a way is needed to "teach" it quickly what to do. That teaching process occurs when the computer is booted.

Within the PC, a small amount of information always is present in the ROM (read-only memory). This memory contains the BIOS (basic input-output system) and some other diagnostic and language programs. This memory does *not* contain DOS. How then, can the computer operate? When you turn on the computer, it has only the most primitive instructions. The computer knows enough, however, to look for DOS on a disk in the disk drive. The computer "pulls itself" to life by reading its instructions from the DOS program on disk. In computer jargon, loading DOS into memory is called *booting* the machine, which comes from the old saying "pulling yourself up by your own bootstraps." This booting process occurs whenever you turn on the computer. After you load DOS into memory from your diskette or hard disk, the computer can perform many management functions. Most of these functions are ways of accessing and manipulating information on disk.

At times, you may need to reboot the computer. A program bug, for example, may cause the computer to freeze, so that it will not respond to program commands anymore. Your only chance for recovery may be to reboot. One obvious way to reboot is to turn off the machine and then turn it back on. This process is called a *cold boot*. Electronic equipment, however, is particularly sensitive to being turned on and off. The computer's electronics stabilize when the power is turned on. Many times, if an electronic component is going to fail, it does so after you first turn it on—when it gets the initial burst of power.

Because of this danger of failure, the system gives you a built-in way to restart the computer without turning off the power. This method of rebooting is called a *warm boot*. To perform a warm boot, hold down the Ctrl and Alt keys and press Del. Hold down all three keys for a second, let up on all keys, and the computer reboots. Some computers have restart buttons that also perform warm boots.

After you boot your computer properly, you are ready to store and use information.

Naming and Using DOS Files

As mentioned previously, files stored on a computer are like manila folders stored in a file cabinet. Some identifying name usually is written on each folder's tab. If the folder contains the budget for May 1991, for example, the tab may say "BUDGET MAY 91." If the folder contains a copy of the annual report, the tab may say "ANNUAL REPORT." The name on the tab gives a short description of the contents of the file. Also, you usually do not place folders in file drawers at random. All the Budget files may be in one drawer and all the Report files may be in another drawer. In fact, you may reserve an entire file cabinet for reports, while another cabinet may contain only financial information. You should name and organize files on the computer in the same way.

Specifying File Names

Just like the name tab on a paper folder, each computer file has a name (called a *file name*). A file name should briefly describe the contents of the file. Your resume may be named RESUME, for example, and the May 1991 budget may be named BUDMAY91. When you create related files, select names that are similar. If you are writing a three-part paper, for example, you may want to create three separate files named PART1, PART2, and PART3. If you are collecting monthly data, you may want to name the files containing the information MAY91, JUNE91, and JULY91.

Although you usually create files from applications rather than from DOS, the file names you use must obey DOS guidelines.

A DOS file name can contain up to eight characters, including all letters (upper- and lowercase) and numbers, but it cannot contain spaces or the following punctuation marks:

. ' \ / [ ] : | < > + = ; * ? and ,

Some programs enable you to use a space in a file name, but not on the DOS level, so you should avoid using spaces.

Using File Extensions

In the case of computer files, the name includes a second part, called the *extension*, which you can use to specify the type of file—whether it is a word processing or a database file, or a letter or a budget. You can include up to three characters in the extension, which you separate from the file name by a period (.). You can name the resume file you create with the WordPerfect word processor RESUME.WP, for example, or you can name the letter you write concerning a certain project PROJECT.LET. This extended form of the name is called the file specification, or *filespec* for short. You also may include a drive name in your file specification such as C: or A:—for example, C:MYFILE.DOC.

DOS and other software programs commonly follow certain conventions in the use of file extensions, because extensions often tell the computer what kind of information is in the computer file. Files on disk that contain DOS commands usually end with the extension COM. BASIC language programs end with the extension BAS. Application programs also use certain extensions. Lotus 1-2-3 files, for example, may end in WKS or WK1. Table A.2 lists some of the common extensions. You need to be aware of the extensions that DOS uses so that you can choose your own extensions without conflicting with these predefined extensions.

Table A.2
Common Extensions for File Names

Common Extensions Used by DOS

Extension	*Use*
COM	A Command program (DOS command)
EXE	An Executable program (software)
BAS	A BASIC language program
BAT	A Batch command file (a type of DOS file)
SYS	A file that contains System information

Other Conventions Used by Software

Extension	*Use*
TXT	A TEXT file (standard ASCII)
DBF	A dBASE database file
WKS	A Lotus 1-2-3 spreadsheet file
PRN	A Lotus print-to-disk file

Using Global File Characters

One major reason for selecting similar names for related files is that you then have the ability to manipulate those files simultaneously as a group. If the files are named similarly, DOS (and Norton) commands enable you to refer to more than one file by using *wild cards* or *global file characters*. These global file characters are the asterisk (*) and the question mark (?). Like a wild card in a poker game, you can substitute the * and ? for any characters—the asterisk for any number of characters, and the question mark for any one character.

If you want to copy all your data files from one disk to another, for example, you must tell DOS which files to copy. Suppose that your files are named JAN, FEB, MAR, and so on, through DEC. To copy all 12 of these files would require 12 commands, each specifying one file to copy. If the files were named JAN.DAT, FEB.DAT, MAR.DAT, and so on through DEC.DAT, however, you could copy all the files by using the single file specification *.DAT. This specifies files with the extension DAT, regardless of the file name.

Because the ? wild card replaces only one character, the specification ???.DAT substitutes for up to three characters in a file name. This file specification selects J.DAT, JA.DAT, and JAN.DAT, but not JANU.DAT or JANUARY.DAT. The wild card specification *.* matches all files—all file names and all extensions. This appendix gives you specific examples of using wild cards as it introduces DOS commands. Wild cards are extensively used also in Norton commands.

Issuing DOS Commands

DOS, in the form of PC DOS and MS-DOS—the common disk operating systems for the IBM and compatible family of computers—is similar to a language. DOS performs management functions on the PC, but not until you instruct it to do so. You, the user, are the one who typically gives those instructions in the form of a DOS command. A DOS command usually is a word (often a verb) that tells DOS what you want it to do. Sometimes the command is followed by one or more words that clarify which task the command is to perform. These parameters are called *options* or *switches*. The command CLS (Clear Screen), for example, tells DOS to blank out the screen. The CLS command requires no other parameters. On the other hand, the command COPY requires that you also specify *what* to copy. Therefore, you must include additional information in the command.

When the DOS prompt is visible on the computer screen, the operating system is waiting for you to type a DOS command. The DOS prompt usually is a letter (A, B, C, and so on) followed by the > symbol. The following prompt, for example, means that DOS is waiting for instructions and that drive A is the logged-in drive or the default drive:

```
A>
```

If DOS needs to look on disk for some information, it automatically looks on the default drive unless you direct the system to look elsewhere. If you are using a hard disk system, the default drive is usually C, and the prompt is

```
C>
```

This prompt specifies that you currently are logged into drive C. To change drives, type the drive letter followed by a colon and then press Enter.

DOS consists of a number of commands, which are categorized into two types: internal and external commands. *Internal DOS commands* are copied into the computer's memory when DOS is loaded as you boot the computer. These commands stay in memory until you turn off the computer, and you may use the commands whenever the DOS prompt appears on-screen. Internal commands covered in this appendix include ATTRIB, CD, CLS, COPY, DEL, DIR, ERASE, FIND, MD, PATH, PROMPT, RD, RENAME, and TYPE.

If you stored every DOS command in memory, however, not enough memory would be left for application programs. Some DOS commands, therefore, are not copied into the computer's memory at boot time but are stored on disk in a file until they are needed. These *external DOS commands* on disk usually are identified by the COM extension. The FORMAT command, for example, is stored on the DOS diskette as the file FORMAT.COM. If you use an external command, it must be available on disk. After you enter the FORMAT command, for example, DOS looks on the default (logged-in) disk to find the file FORMAT.COM. If the file is not found, the following message appears on-screen:

```
Bad command or file name
```

This error message tells you that the command you requested was not found on disk. External commands covered in this appendix include BACKUP, CHKDSK, DISKCOPY, FORMAT, PRINT, RECOVER, RESTORE, and TREE. See "Working with Directory Path Names," later in this appendix, to learn how to access external DOS commands.

Norton commands are much like DOS external commands. Each command constitutes a program that resides on disk until you enter the command name at the DOS prompt. Then the program is entered into memory and run.

To enter a DOS command, type it at the DOS prompt and press Enter. To use the DIR command to display a list of the files located in the default directory, for example, type

```
DIR
```

and press Enter. To command DOS to display a directory of a disk other than the default disk, you must add more information to the DIR command. To display a directory of the files on the diskette in drive A, for example, use this command:

```
DIR A:
```

Reviewing Some Commonly Used DOS Commands

Although dozens of DOS commands are available, this introduction to DOS is limited to the commonly used commands that you refer to or may need in order to understand the information in this book. This appendix covers selected options and switches for each command. For a more complete list of command parameters, consult your DOS manual.

Note: In the syntax descriptions of the DOS commands, items enclosed in [brackets] are options. Items that appear in *italics* are command variables. You should replace the *filespec* variable with a real file specification when you enter the command at the DOS prompt.

ATTRIB

The ATTRIB command lists or sets the read-only and archive attributes of files. You cannot write to, change, or erase a file that is read-only. The *read-only attribute* protects the file from accidental or unauthorized change. The *archive attribute* indicates whether the file has been backed up. The archive attribute is used for some backup procedures. The ATTRIB command is available on DOS Version 3.0 or higher. The syntax of the command is

ATTRIB [+/−R][+/−A]*filespec*[/S]

A +R sets the file or files indicated in the *filespec* to read-only. A −R sets the read-only attribute off. A +A sets files to archived, and a −A sets the archive attribute off. When you back up a file by using a backup procedure, the archive attribute setting is switched on, indicating to the system that the file has been backed up.

If you use the /S switch, the files in all subdirectories that match the *filespec* also are affected. If you do not use the +/−R or +/−A option, ATTRIB lists file names that match the *filespec* and reports the current archive and read-only settings for those files.

Check Disk (CHKDSK)

The CHKDSK command enables you to examine a diskette or hard disk to determine how much space is being used and whether the disk has any problems. CHKDSK, for example, may detect such problems as lost clusters in files on disk. CHKDSK summarizes the amount of available memory on disk and also reports the amount of RAM available to the computer. CHKDSK is an external DOS command, and uses this syntax:

CHKDSK [*d:*][/F]

where *d:* specifies the diskette or hard disk to check. To check the disk in drive B, for example, use this command:

CHKDSK B:

The /F switch tells CHKDSK to attempt to fix any problems found with the file allocation table. If you do not use the /F switch, CHKDSK still tells you how much space would be fixed if the /F switch had been used, but it does not fix the problems. A better approach than using CHKDSK is to use the Norton Disk Doctor (NDD) to find and solve these kinds of disk problems. For more information on NDD, see Chapter 4, "Recovering Files with Norton Utilities."

Clear Screen (CLS)

The CLS command clears the display screen. No options or switches are available. The syntax is simply

CLS

COPY

The COPY command is one of the most powerful and frequently used DOS commands. The COPY command copies one or more files to another disk or to the same disk under a new name. The syntax is

COPY [*d:*]*filespec* [*d:*][*filespec*]

A more easily remembered syntax is

COPY *source destination*

To copy the file named REPORT.TXT from the current default disk (A) to disk C, for example, use this command:

COPY REPORT.TXT C:REPORT.TXT

The source in this command is the file REPORT.TXT, and the destination is C:REPORT.TXT. Note that you do not have to specify a drive letter if the file is on the default drive. Also, you can omit the name of the destination file if it is the same as the source file. Therefore, the following command from the A> prompt performs the same copy performed by the preceding command:

COPY REPORT.TXT C:

The source file does not have to be on the default drive. You can copy files located on a drive other than the default to another drive simply by including the drive specification in both the source and destination file names. You also can change the name of a file during a copy. Suppose that the default drive is C and you want to copy a file from drive A to drive B and rename the file at the same time. Use this command:

COPY A:REPORT.TXT B:RPT.TXT

Another way to use the COPY command is to copy a file on the same disk to a different file name. To make a duplicate copy of the file REPORT.TXT and call the duplicate copy REPORT.DUP, for example, you can use this command:

COPY REPORT.TXT REPORT.DUP

Attempting to copy a file to itself results in an error. The following command produces an error message:

COPY REPORT.TXT REPORT.TXT

You also can copy multiple files simultaneously, using the global file characters. To copy all your DAT files from the default drive C to drive A, for example, use this command:

COPY *.DAT A:

DIR

The DIR command displays names of files on disk, the file sizes, and the dates and times the files were created. The syntax of the DIR command is

DIR [*d:*][*filespec*] [/P][/W]

The minimum version of the command is

DIR

The DIR command gives you a list of all the files contained on the default drive.

To list files located on another drive, specify the drive letter. To obtain a listing of files on drive B, for example, use this command:

DIR B:

If you include a file specification in the command, DIR lists only those files that match the specification. To view a directory of only the files with DAT extensions, for example, use this command:

DIR *.DAT

To list all files beginning with the letter R, type

DIR R*.*

The switches in the DIR command are /P and /W. The /P switch instructs DOS to pause after a screenful of files is displayed. If more than 22 files are contained in a directory, the files usually scroll off screen during a directory listing. With the /P switch, the first 22 files are listed, and the following message appears at the bottom of the screen:

```
Strike a key when ready...
```

After you press a key, the next 22 files are displayed. This process continues until all files are listed.

The /W switch stands for *wide listing*. In this version of the list, only the file names appear, with several file names listed on each line. This format enables you to display more file names on one screen.

You can combine the DIR command's options and switches. The following command, for example, lists all the files on drive B with a DAT extension, in wide format:

DIR B:*.DAT /W

DISKCOPY

Many times you may want to make an exact copy of a diskette. In fact, when you get new software, you always should copy all the original disks and then use copies rather than originals in your work. You use the DISKCOPY command to copy the contents of an entire diskette from one disk to another of equal size. The syntax is

DISKCOPY *d1: d2:*

whose *d1:* is the source diskette, and *d2:* is the destination diskette. To copy the disk in drive A to the disk in drive B, for example, use the command

DISKCOPY A: B:

If the destination disk is not formatted, the DISKCOPY procedure formats the disk. DISKCOPY makes an exact copy of a diskette. Therefore, if the source or destination diskette contains any bad sectors, the DISKCOPY procedure may not work. Also, both source and destination diskettes must be of the same size. You cannot use the DISKCOPY command to copy from the hard disk to a floppy, for example, because the hard disk is a different size than the floppy diskette.

If you are using a system with only one floppy disk drive, you can still perform a DISKCOPY procedure. From the A> prompt, use this command:

DISKCOPY A: B:

DOS prompts you to insert the source diskette into the drive; then the system prompts you to place the destination diskette in the drive. You may have to swap diskettes several times during each DISKCOPY procedure.

ERASE and DEL

The ERASE and DEL commands remove files from the disk. These commands are identical and use the same syntax:

ERASE [*d:*][*filespec*]

or

DEL [*d:*][*filespec*]

Paying attention to what is on your disk and how much space you have used is essential. A common problem when using a computer is running out of space on disk. The ERASE and DEL commands are available to remove unneeded files from disk and to free up that space for use by other files. You can use these commands, like most DOS commands, on a single file or on multiple files, using the global file characters. To erase the single file named REQUEST.LET, for example, type

```
ERASE REQUEST.LET
```

or

```
DEL REQUEST.LET
```

To erase all files with the extension DAT, use

```
ERASE *.DAT
```

To erase *all* files, use

```
ERASE *.*
```

After you enter the ERASE command, DOS prompts you with the question `Are you sure (Y/N)?`. DOS is offering you a chance to change your mind before it erases everything on your disk.

Warning: Be very sure that you know what you are doing when you enter the ERASE command. Check to make sure that you are logged into the correct disk drive and directory. (If you accidentally erase a file, however, you can recover it with the Norton Quick Unerase command. See Chapter 4, "Recovering Files with Norton Utilities," for more information.)

FDISK

The FDISK command prepares your hard disk (fixed disk) to be formatted. Usually you need to execute this command only once—when you first get a new computer. Occasionally, you may need to start over by using the FDISK command again. The FDISK command begins a program that prompts you with questions about how you want to set up your hard disk.

Warning: If you use FDISK on a hard disk, all information on that disk may be lost. Use FDISK only when you are sure you want to start from scratch on the disk. Refer to your DOS manual for details.

FIND

The FIND command (also called a *filter*) searches for a string of characters within a file or files and lists each line in the file that contains text matching the string. The FIND command can help you look for a file that contains particular information. The syntax of the FIND command is

FIND *string* [*filespec*] [*filespec*] [*filespec*]...

To determine whether the string "1990 BUDGET" is in the files REPORT.1, REPORT.2, and REPORT.3, for example, use this command:

FIND "1990 REPORT" REPORT.1 REPORT.2 REPORT.3

The results of a find may look like this:

```
---------REPORT.1
---------REPORT.2
THE 1990 REPORT ON SILVER PRICES
---------REPORT.3
```

In this example, the phrase "1990 REPORT" was found only in the file named REPORT.2. The line (or lines) that contain the phrase is listed below the name of the file being searched. The other files had no finds associated with them.

The Norton Text Search (TS) command is a powerful alternative to the DOS FIND command. See Chapter 6, "Managing the Resources of Your Computer," for more information.

FORMAT

The FORMAT command prepares diskettes (and hard disks) for use. After you purchase diskettes, you cannot simply put them into the disk drive and use them. You must first format them. Formatting specifies how information is to be stored on disk. The FORMAT procedure also analyzes the entire disk for any defective tracks and prepares the disk to accept DOS files. The syntax of the FORMAT command is

FORMAT [*d:*][/*switches*]

Suppose that you are using a computer with a hard disk drive, and you are logged into drive C. The simplest command to format a new diskette in drive A is

FORMAT A:

After you enter the FORMAT command, DOS responds with the message

```
Insert new diskette for drive A:
and strike ENTER when ready:
```

This prompt gives you a chance to back out of the command if you discover that you do not want to format that diskette. If you want to cancel the command at this point, press Ctrl-Break.

Warning: You can destroy all information on a diskette or hard disk drive by using the FORMAT command incorrectly. If you do not enter the name of the drive to format, for example, the FORMAT command was the default drive. Thus, if you enter the following command from the C> prompt, DOS assumes that you want to format the hard disk drive C:

FORMAT

Be careful not to do this (unless you *want* to erase everything on your hard disk)!

The FORMAT command has a number of switches. Only the two most common ones—/V and /S—are described here. The /V switch enables you to give a volume name to the disk being formatted. To format a disk on drive A and give it a volume label, use this command:

FORMAT A:/V

DOS prompts you with the message

```
Volume label (11 characters, ENTER for none)?
```

You then can type your volume name at the prompt (you can use up to 11 characters). You may want to name your diskettes as a way of uniquely identifying them.

The /S switch causes the FORMAT procedure to create a system disk—one that contains the files necessary to boot the computer. To format the disk in drive A with a label and the system files, type

FORMAT A:/S/V

The Norton Safe Format (SFORMAT) command is a safer, faster alternative to the DOS FORMAT command. For more information, see Chapter 3, "Protecting Your Files with Norton Utilities."

PRINT

The PRINT command enables you to print the contents of a text file to the printer. The syntax is

PRINT [*d:*]*filespec* [/T]

To print a file in drive B called EXAMPLE.TXT to the line printer, for example, enter the command

PRINT B:EXAMPLE.TXT

The computer responds with the prompt

```
Name of list device(PRN):
```

Press Enter to print the file to the standard print device (PRN = Printer), or enter another device name such as LPT1 or LPT2 (parallel ports), or COM1 or COM2 (serial ports).

You can queue several files to print at once by entering several PRINT commands; DOS remembers each of the files and prints them in the order of the PRINT commands. If you decide that you want to stop the print job, reenter the command with the /T switch. To terminate the current print job, for example, enter the command

PRINT /T

This command terminates all print jobs in the print queue. A cancellation message is displayed, the page in the printer is advanced to the top of the form, and the printer's buzzer sounds.

RECOVER

The RECOVER command recovers files that have been damaged in some way. You can misuse this command easily, so you should consider using the Disk Tools command instead. For more information, see Chapter 4, "Recovering Files with Norton Utilities."

RENAME

The RENAME command changes the name of a file on disk. Suppose that you save a file named REPORT with your word processor, but you misspell the file name by typing *repotr*. When you are back in DOS, the easiest way to correct the problem is with the RENAME command. The syntax of the RENAME command is

RENAME [*d:*]*filespec1 filespec2*

Notice that the command REN is an acceptable abbreviation of the RENAME command. Basically, the RENAME command has the following form:

RENAME *oldname newname*

where *oldname* is the current name of a file, and *newname* is the name you want the file to have. You must include a space between the oldname and newname specifications. To rename the file REQUEST.LET as REQUEST.TXT, for example, use this command:

RENAME REQUEST.LET REQUEST.TXT

You can use wild-card characters to rename a group of related files. To rename the files JAN.DAT, FEB.DAT, and so on, through DEC.DAT on drive A to the new names JAN.OLD, FEB.OLD, and so on, through DEC.OLD, use this command from the A> prompt:

RENAME *.DAT *.OLD

You cannot rename a file to a file name that currently exists on that disk. If you try this, you see the error message `Duplicate file name` or `File not found`. Also, note that RENAME is not a COPY command, which means that you cannot rename a file from one disk drive to another. The following command, for example, does not work:

RENAME A:REQUEST.LET B:REQUEST.LET

If you attempt to use this command, the error message `Invalid parameter` appears.

SYS

The SYS command transfers system files from a bootable disk to another disk. The syntax of the SYS command is

SYS *d:*

where *d:* is the drive name of the disk where you want to place the system files.

The system files are hidden files. You cannot access them by using the normal COPY command, nor do they appear when you issue a DIR command. You must place the system files at a certain spot on disk, so unless you formatted a disk by using the /B switch, SYS cannot transfer a copy of the system files to the disk. The Norton Disk Doctor's Disk Tools' Make a Disk Bootable option, however, enables you to transfer system files to a disk that has not been prepared to accept them.

TYPE

The TYPE command prints the contents of a file to the screen. The syntax of the TYPE command is

TYPE [*d:*]*filespec*

To display the contents of the EXAMPLE.TXT file located on drive B, for example, use the command

TYPE B:EXAMPLE.TXT

The file to be printed should be a text file. If you attempt to use TYPE to print the contents of a file that is not an ASCII file, the result probably will be a series of meaningless characters on-screen.

Managing a Hard Disk with DOS Commands

Many microcomputers being sold today include a hard disk storage device. A *hard disk* (also called a *fixed disk*) is a permanent disk that usually is housed in the computer and is capable of storing many times the amount of information that a single floppy diskette can hold. The size of most hard disks is measured in megabytes (M), or millions of bytes. A 30M hard disk can store 30 million characters of information.

Using a computer with a hard disk creates several challenges. The fact that a hard disk can store more information can be an advantage as well as a disadvantage. A hard disk relieves you from having to keep up with a mile-high stack of floppy diskettes, but it requires more planned organization. Managing more than 1,000 files stored on a hard disk can be a huge task. When you enter a DIR command, the information could take several minutes to scroll by.

You can solve this dilemma by dividing the hard disk into several directories, each of which contains related information. One directory may contain all the DOS files. Another directory may contain word processing files. Yet another directory may contain database files. Each directory functions almost like a separate diskette.

DOS has a particular way to set up directories. When you format a disk (including a floppy diskette), the format procedure automatically creates one directory, called the *root directory*. You can create other directories to branch off the root, thus building a directory tree. You must choose which directories to create, and you must develop the philosophy behind the structure. Figure A.1 shows one possible directory tree. This tree is organized by task. The top directory is the original or root directory. Branching off are directories (or subdirectories) that contain the task-oriented partitions of DOS, Word Processing, Database, and Spreadsheet.

Fig. A.1 A directory structure.

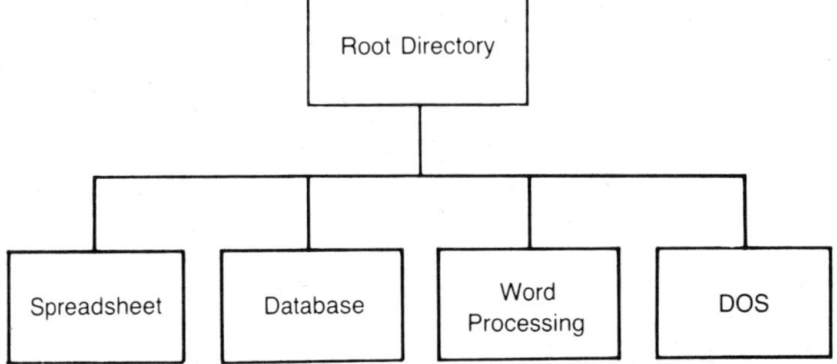

Creating directories according to a planned directory tree can be helpful and can make your work more efficient. You can move from branch to branch according to the tasks you want to complete. If you are doing word processing, for example, you can move to the word processing directory, which gives you access to all your word processing files. Working from this directory also separates you from the unrelated files in other directories. If you are in the word processing directory and enter the command DIR, for example, you get a list of files in that directory.

How do you create a directory? How do you move from one directory to another? How do you get rid of a directory? These questions are answered by a series of DOS commands, which enable you to create, use, and remove directories as needed. Table A.3 lists the commands you use to perform these tasks.

Before learning how to use the DOS commands to manage your hard disk, you should understand how the names of the directories are related to file specifications. You can use the Norton Utilities and Norton Commander NCD (Norton Change Directory) program instead of the DOS commands. This program provides a graphic interface to make creating, changing, and removing directories more intuitive. It also has additional capabilities, such as renaming directories.

Table A.3
Managing Directories with DOS

Command Name	*Abbreviation*	*Effect*
MKDIR	MD	Makes a directory
CHDIR	CD	Changes directories
RMDIR	RD	Removes a directory

Working with Directory Path Names

Each directory has a name. The root directory always is designated as the \ directory, but you assign your own names to the directories you create to branch off the root directory. A directory name can include up to eight characters (see "Specifying Files Names," earlier in this appendix, for more information on restrictions that apply to file names).

When referring to a directory name, most people use the entire path name. A directory's *path name* describes the path DOS can take through the directory tree structure to find the directory. The WP directory branching off the root directory usually is referred to as \WP. The directory named LETTERS branching off the WP directory is specified by the path name \WP\LETTERS. Thus, a backslash (\) is used for two purposes:

- The first backslash (\) specifies the root directory.
- A backslash (\) also is used to separate the names of subdirectories.

A directory path becomes a part of the file specification of any file in that directory. The path appears between the drive specification and the file name and always contains a beginning and an ending backslash.

In general, a complete file specification consists of the following:

d:\path\filename.ext

which represents a drive name, a path, a file name, a period, and an extension.

The complete file specification for a file named MYFILE.TXT on drive C in the \WP directory, for example, would be

C:\WP\MYFILE.TXT

Creating New Directories—The MD Command

You use the DOS MKDIR command, often abbreviated as MD, to make a new directory. The syntax of the command is

MD *path*

or

MKDIR *path*

The following command creates a directory named \WP on drive C:

MD \WP

The new \WP directory branches directly off the root directory. To make a directory named LETTERS that branches off \WP, use this command:

MD \WP\LETTERS

Changing Directories—The CD Command

Every hard disk has one or more directories, beginning with the root directory. The CHDIR command (or CD, in its abbreviated form) changes from the current directory to another directory on the same disk drive. While in a particular directory, you can enter commands such as DIR or RENAME that apply only to the files in the current directory. The syntax of the CD command is

CD *path*

or

CHDIR *path*

To change to the directory named \WP, enter the command

CD \WP

To go back to your root directory, enter the command

CD \

Using the CD command, you can move from any directory to any other directory by entering the command and the complete path of the directory to which you want to change.

Removing Empty Directories— The RD Command

Sometimes you need to remove a directory from the hard disk to make room for other, more important files. You use the RMDIR (RD) command for that purpose. You cannot remove a directory that contains any user files, however, so you must erase or move all files in the directory first. The syntax of the RD command is

RD *path*

or

RMDIR *path*

To remove the directory named \MYDIR, for example, use this command:

RD \MYDIR

Listing Directories— The TREE Command

When your hard disk contains a number of directories, you may want to view a list of which directories are available. The DOS command to perform that task is TREE. The TREE command displays a listing of all the directories on the specified drive. The syntax is

TREE [*d:*]

To see which directories are on your entire disk, enter the command

TREE

Beginning with DOS Version 4.0, the TREE command creates a graphic display of directory names, making it easier for you to see the structure and paths.

Giving Paths to Programs— The PATH Command

At this point, you are undoubtedly familiar with the concept of the path as part of a file specification. PATH also is a DOS command. The PATH command tells DOS where to look for programs that are not in the current directory. Many application programs require you to know how to create or modify a PATH command. The syntax for the PATH command is

PATH [*path*];[*path*];[*path*]...

The TREE command, for example, requires that the file TREE.COM be on disk. Under normal circumstances, if you enter TREE in the \WP directory, you get the message `Bad command or file name`, because the TREE.COM command file is not in the \WP directory and DOS cannot find and execute the command. To avoid having to keep copies of all programs in all directories, you can tell the computer where to find programs when they are requested in a directory in which they do not reside. This function is the responsibility of the PATH command. The PATH command gives the computer a priority list of directories for searching for a particular program. The PATH command causes DOS to search for only three kinds of files: COM (command), BAT (batch), and EXE (program) files.

A common directory setup includes a directory named \DOS. The \DOS directory generally contains all the DOS files, including all external DOS commands. You also may have a \NORTON directory that contains all the Norton commands. The PATH command

PATH C:\;C:\DOS;C:\NORTON

tells DOS that if a command is given in any directory and the command is not found in that directory, DOS should look first in the root directory (specified in the PATH command as C:\). If the command is not found there, DOS should look in the next directory listed in the PATH command—the C:\DOS directory. Finally, if the command still has not been found, DOS should look in the C:\NORTON directory. When the command TREE is given in the \WP directory, therefore, the command file TREE.COM is found in the \DOS directory, and the command is successful. Notice that each directory name in the PATH command is separated from the preceding directory name by a semicolon (;).

When a PATH command is given, it remains in effect until you reboot the computer or turn it off. Therefore, you usually enter the command only once each time you boot the computer. As you learn in this appendix's description of the AUTOEXEC.BAT file, you can automate the entry of the PATH command.

Controlling the DOS Prompt—The PROMPT Command

When switching from directory to directory, you often may have difficulty keeping track of which directory you are in. One way to solve this problem is to customize the DOS prompt, which is normally C> on a hard disk, by using the PROMPT command. The syntax of this command is

PROMPT [*prompt commands*]

The various prompt commands are listed in table A.4. Each command must be preceded by a $. Any text following the PROMPT command that is not preceded by a $ is displayed literally.

Table A.4
PROMPT $ Commands

<table>
<tr><th>Command</th><th>Result</th></tr>
<tr><td>B</td><td>The | character</td></tr>
<tr><td>D</td><td>The system date</td></tr>
<tr><td>E</td><td>The Escape character</td></tr>
<tr><td>G</td><td>The > sign</td></tr>
<tr><td>H</td><td>The Backspace character</td></tr>
<tr><td>L</td><td>The < sign</td></tr>
<tr><td>N</td><td>The default drive letter</td></tr>
<tr><td>P</td><td>The current path</td></tr>
<tr><td>Q</td><td>The = character</td></tr>
<tr><td>T</td><td>The system time</td></tr>
<tr><td>V</td><td>The version of DOS</td></tr>
<tr><td>_</td><td>Carriage return, line feed</td></tr>
</table>

Entering the DOS command

PROMPT PG

causes the DOS prompt to include the path as a part of the prompt. The $P is the prompt command for the path, and the $G is the prompt command for the greater-than sign. Thus, the prompt (while you are in the root directory) becomes

C:\>

The \ between the C: and the > tells you that you are in the root directory. If you enter the command CD \DOS, the prompt becomes

C:\DOS>

This prompt indicates that you are currently in the DOS directory.

The PROMPT command offers a variety of ways to customize the DOS prompt. You can display any text by including it in the PROMPT command without a preceding $. You can use a command like this to display a unique prompt:

```
PROMPT This computer belongs to Bill!$_$P$G
```

The text "This computer belongs to Bill!" is output literally. The $_ command (a dollar sign and an underline) tells PROMPT to perform a carriage return and a line feed, which means that the cursor moves to the next line. On the next line is the prompt specified by the PG prompt commands. Thus, when you are logged into the root directory, this prompt appears:

```
This Computer Belongs to Bill!
C:\>
```

Using Batch and System Files

A BAT file extension indicates that a file is a *batch file*—a file containing several DOS commands that you want to execute in a particular order. A system file often is designated by the SYS extension. A common system file that you need to know about is CONFIG.SYS, which tells the computer certain information about how to operate.

Creating Batch Files

If you have a series of DOS commands that you perform repetitively, you can create a file that contains those commands and have DOS execute all the commands in sequence. Suppose that you often use these two commands:

```
PATH C:\;C:\DOS;C:\WP;C:\DB
PROMPT $P$G
```

You can place those two commands in a file, such as one named BEGIN.BAT. Then, rather than remembering exactly how to type these commands each time you need them, you can type the batch file command *begin*. With this command, you tell DOS to execute the two commands contained in the batch file BEGIN.BAT.

You have several ways to create this kind of file. The most common method is to use a file editor. A simple file editor named EDLIN is included as a part of DOS and is described in this appendix's section on "Using the DOS EDLIN Line Editor Program." Most word processing programs also have the capability to create batch files. The following steps describe an optional way to create a batch file without using a text editor:

1. Enter the following command, which tells DOS that you will be entering (copying) information from the CONSOLE and that the information is to be placed in the file named BEGIN.BAT:

   ```
   COPY CON BEGIN.BAT
   ```

2. Enter the commands that you want to include in the batch file. You may want to enter these commands, for example:

   ```
   PATH \;\DOS;\WP;\DB
   PROMPT $P$G
   ```

   Note that you see no DOS prompt.

3. End this procedure by pressing the F6 function key or Ctrl-Z. The lines you typed now are stored in the file called BEGIN.BAT.

Creating and Using an AUTOEXEC.BAT File

DOS looks for a special batch file called AUTOEXEC.BAT each time you boot the computer. If you want a series of commands to execute each time you boot the computer, you should place them in the AUTOEXEC.BAT file. If you always want the PATH and PROMPT commands to be activated when the computer is booted, rename the BEGIN.BAT file AUTOEXEC.BAT. Then, whenever you boot your computer, your path is set up, and your prompt is customized automatically. These two commands are frequently included in the AUTOEXEC.BAT file.

Creating and Using a CONFIG.SYS File

Another file that DOS looks for each time you boot the computer is CONFIG.SYS. Like the AUTOEXEC.BAT file, CONFIG.SYS is not a required file. If you do have a CONFIG.SYS file in your root directory, however, DOS looks in the file to see how you want the computer configured. You rarely have to decide for yourself what goes into the CONFIG.SYS file, because the software you install usually has instructions about its requirements for the file. DOS, for example, usually enables software to communicate with eight files at once on disk. This number sounds like a great many files, but some complicated programs such as dBASE III need more access to the disk than what DOS usually provides. Therefore, the dBASE III installation manual tells you to place the following lines in your CONFIG.SYS file:

```
FILES = 20
BUFFERS = 15
```

These commands allow more files and more disk buffers than would usually be available. These lines are the two most common settings in the CONFIG.SYS file. Other items that you can set in this file include the following:

Item	*Effect*
COUNTRY	Specifies which country you are in (this has to do with how dates are displayed, for example).
DEVICE	Specifies certain kinds of input and output devices such as monitors, plotters, memory disks, and so on.
LASTDRIVE	Specifies the maximum number of disk drives on your computer (normal setting is E).

You can create the CONFIG.SYS file with a word processor (using Text File mode), the Edlin editor, the Norton Commander editor (F4), or the COPY CON command, as described for batch files.

Remember that DOS executes the AUTOEXEC.BAT and CONFIG.SYS files at boot time. If you change one of these files, you then must reboot the computer to have DOS act on the information in the files.

Using the DOS Edlin Line Editor Program

Edlin is a simple text editor program that comes with DOS. A *text editor* is a program that you can use to create and edit files. The name Edlin comes from the words "line editor." A *line editor* is a program that enables you to add or edit text on only one line at a time. Modern word processors are known as full-screen editors because you can move the cursor to any part of the screen and add or edit text.

Edlin creates standard text files that usually contain no special character codes—only keyboard characters. You also may hear or read about these files being called DOS files or ASCII files. Many word processors (such as WordStar and WordPerfect) place special codes or characters in the file, which may make the files unreadable or uneditable by Edlin—and as batch files or other types of command files. Some word processors have options to save a file as a text file. If your word processor does not create text files, Edlin is a simple alternative to use for creating and editing short text files such as AUTOEXEC.BAT or CONFIG.SYS.

Creating and Editing Files with Edlin

To begin the Edlin program from the DOS prompt, enter the command

EDLIN *filename*

where *filename* is the name of the file you want to create or edit. The filename optionally can include a path and drive name.

If the file name you specify is not currently a file, Edlin responds with the message

```
New file
*
```

This message tells you that you are creating a new file. To enter information into this new file, you must enter an I at the * prompt, which indicates that you want to insert information. After you enter the I command and press Enter, Edlin responds with this prompt:

```
1*:
```

You now can enter information in Line 1. After you type the information and press Enter (note that Edlin has no wordwrap like a word processor does), Edlin responds with the prompt

```
2*:
```

This prompt indicates that you are now entering Line 2. Edlin continues to give you new line numbers until you end the input sequence by pressing Ctrl-Break. After you press Ctrl-Break, Edlin returns to the * prompt without a line number. To exit Edlin and save the information to a file, press E and then Enter.

If you want to edit an existing file, you need to know how to tell Edlin what you want to do to the file. Edlin commands have their own particular syntax (see the following section).

Understanding Edlin Command Syntax

Most Edlin commands consist of a single letter. The letter L, for example, represents the List Lines command. In Edlin, at the * on-screen prompt, you often enter a command by first specifying a range of lines and then typing the letter of the command you want to use. To list Lines 5 through 25, for example, you enter this command:

```
5,25L
```

To refer to a range of lines in Edlin, you enter the first line number, a comma, and the last line number. If you need to refer to Lines 5 through 25, for example, you use the range 5,25. To refer to a single line number, use that line number alone or as the first and last line numbers separated by a comma. To refer to Line 5, you could use the single number 5 or the range 5,5. On many commands, you must refer to a range of lines to use. Otherwise, the command will work only on *one* line or on a default number of lines (for the P and L commands).

Some commands do not require a range. If you enter the L command without a range, the command lists 22 lines to the screen, beginning with the current line being referenced. A range also may consist of relative numbers. The following command lists 10 lines before the current line, the current line, and 10 lines after the current line:

```
-10,+10L
```

The current line usually is the last line edited. When you list the lines in a file (using the L command), an asterisk precedes the current line number. The line number (#) means the line after the last line in the file. The line number . (period) specifies the current line number. You can use the number sign or period instead of an actual number when entering a line range.

In many commands, if you do not specify a line or range of lines, Edlin uses the current line. In a range of lines, if the first line number is omitted, it is assumed to be the current line. The command to list the lines from the current line through line 20, for example, is

```
,20L
```

Like DOS commands, Edlin commands may be followed by parameters. The Search Text command (S), for example, must be followed by the text for which you want to search. Suppose that you want to search for the text "Cedar Hill" in Lines 20 through 100. Use this command:

```
20,100SCedar Hill
```

Using the Edlin Commands

This section includes an alphabetical list of Edlin commands with descriptions and examples of their uses. The following conventions apply to the Edlin commands described in this section:

[]	Indicates optional parameters.
n	Indicates the number of lines to use.
line	Indicates a line number, range, or relative line numbers.
string	Indicates a group of characters (used only in the Search Text and Replace Text commands).

Append Lines (A)

You use the Append Lines command when you are editing a very large file. Not all of the files can reside in memory at one time. Usually, you use Append Lines (A) after you use the Write Lines (W) command to write some of the lines in memory. First, you write some lines to memory to make some room in memory, and then you use the A command to append new lines to those remaining in memory. The syntax of this command is

[*n*]A

where *n* is the number of lines to append. If *n* is missing, A adds as many lines as possible to memory. The memory of Edlin is limited to 64K, even if you have more memory on your computer.

Copy Lines (C)

You use the Copy Lines command to make duplicates of lines. You can duplicate Lines 4 through 6 and place a copy of these lines at Line 20, for example. The syntax of the Copy Lines command is

[*line*],[*line*],*line*[,*count*]C

The first two *line* parameters represent the range of lines to copy FROM. The third *line* parameter is the line to copy TO. The *count* parameter indicates how many copies to make. To copy Lines 4 through 6 to Line 20, for example, use the command

4,6,20C

This command inserts one copy of Lines 4 through 6. To insert three copies, one right after the other, at Line 20, use this command:

4,6,20,3C

Delete Lines (D)

This command is used to delete lines. The syntax of the D command is

[*line*][,*line*]D

To delete Lines 5 through 7 in a file, for example, use this command:

5,7D

If you do not include line numbers, the current line is deleted. When lines are deleted, Edlin renumbers the lines in a file. If you delete Lines 4 and 5, for example, Line 6 becomes Line 4, and so on.

Edit Line

This command is not represented by a letter. You access the Edit Line command by entering the number of the line you want to edit. To edit Line 10, for example, simply type *10* at the * prompt. When you edit a line, that line is echoed to the screen, and the cursor is placed on a blank, numbered line directly under the line to edit. If you are editing Line 2 of a file, for example, you see something like this:

```
2: Its fleece was white as snow
2:_
```

You then can edit the line by retyping the information or by changing selected information in the line. Commands you can use to edit this line follow:

Key	*Effect*
F2	Moves to a specific letter
F3 or →	Moves to the end of the line
Del	Deletes characters
Ins	Inserts characters

The screen displays only the characters from the beginning of the line to the cursor position. If you press F2 and then press W, the cursor moves to the first "w" in the line. The screen then looks like this:

```
2: Its fleece was white as snow
2: Its fleece _
```

If you begin typing at this point, you simultaneously will be erasing the rest of the line. To insert new text at this point, press Ins and then type the new text.

You do not see the result of pressing Del or Ins until you use the F3 or right-arrow key to move to the end of the line to view the entire line. If the cursor is positioned at the first "w," for example, and you press Del four times and then press the F3 key, the lines look like this:

```
2: Its fleece was white as snow
2: Its fleece white as snow
```

After you press Enter, you return to the * prompt.

The text "was" has been deleted. Similarly, if you edit Line 2 again, place the cursor at the "w" in "white," press Ins, type *was*, and press F3, you see

```
2: Its fleece was white as snow
2: Its fleece was white as snow
```

End Edit (E)

You use the End Edit command to exit the Edlin editor and save the contents of the file to disk. The End Edit command has no parameters.

If you edit an existing file, the old file is renamed FILENAME.BAK. If you edit an existing file named MARY.TXT, make changes, and then exit, for example, your original file MARY.TXT is saved on disk under the name MARY.BAK, and the newly edited file is named MARY.TXT. The backup file enables you to recover from accidental changes to your file. Only one BAK file is maintained, however. If you edit a file 20 times, only the 19th version is stored in the BAK file.

Insert Lines (I)

This command tells Edlin that you want to enter Insert mode. In this mode, Edlin provides you with a line number prompt where you can enter text. The syntax for this command is

[*line*]I

The *line* parameter is the number of the line immediately before which you want to insert text. Suppose that you are editing a file that is 20 lines long and you want to insert information between Lines 9 and 10. Enter this command:

```
10I
```

Edlin gives you a `10:` prompt at which you can enter information on a new Line 10. After you press Enter, you get an `11:` prompt, and so on until you press Ctrl-Break. If you enter two lines, all the old lines (10, 11, and so on) are pushed back in the file two lines. The old Line 10 becomes Line 12, the old Line 11 becomes Line 13, and so on.

List Lines (L)

You use this command to list lines to the screen. The syntax of the command is

[*line*][,*line*]L

The first *line* parameter is the number of the first line you want to list, and the second *line* parameter is the number of the last line in the range you want to list. If you do not include any line numbers, L lists the 11 lines before the current line, the current file, and the 11 lines after the current line (23 lines in all).

Move Lines (M)

You use this command to move lines. The syntax of the command is

[*line*],[*line*],*line*M

When lines are moved, they are removed from one area and placed in another. The first two *line* parameters represent the range of lines to move, and the third *line* parameter indicates the destination line number. For example, to move Lines 4 through 6 to Line 10, enter the command

```
4,6,10L
```

After a move, Edlin renumbers all affected lines.

Page (P)

The Page (P) command is similar to the List Lines command. The syntax of Page is

[*line*][,*line*]P

If no line numbers are included, the P command lists the next 23 lines. After you enter a P command, the last line listed becomes the current line. Thus, you can use repeated P commands to page through the file. In DOS Version 4.0 and higher, if 23 lines cannot be listed to the screen, you see a `Continue (Y/N):` prompt after a screenful of information has been listed. If you press Y to answer Yes, the remainder of the 23 lines are displayed on-screen. In older versions of DOS, the 23 lines are listed, even if some scroll off screen.

Quit Edit (Q)

You use the Quit Edit command to end Edlin *without* saving any of the changes made in the file. Use this command only when you do not want your changes to be preserved. The original file remains intact and unchanged.

Replace Text (R)

This command replaces a string of characters with another string of characters. The syntax for the Replace Text command is

[*line*][,*line*][?]R[*string*][<F6>*string*]

Suppose that you want to change the text "Dallas" to "Houston" in Lines 1 through 999 of a file. You can use this command:

1,999RDallas<F6>Houston

The <F6> indicates that you press the F6 function key. If you include the ? parameter, Edlin displays the potential replacement and prompts you with `O.K.?`, which asks whether you want to accept that replacement. Press Y to make the replacement or press N to skip the replacement. If you omit the ?, all possible replacements within the line range occur automatically. If you leave off the range, the replacement takes place from the current line down through the file.

Search Text (S)

You use this command to search for text within the file you are editing currently. The syntax for the Search Text command is

[*line*][,*line*][?]S[*string*]

To search for the first occurrence of the text "Dallas" in Lines 20 through 100, for example, you use the command

```
20,100SDallas
```

This command displays the line that contains text matching the search string. By repeating the command S with no parameters, you can have Edlin look for the next occurrence of the same search string. If you use the ? parameter, Edlin displays a line that contains a match and prompts you with `O.K.?`. If you press N, the search continues to the next match. If you press Y, the search stops. If you omit the range, the search begins with the current line and progresses down through the file.

Transfer Lines (T)

With this command, you can transfer lines from a file on disk into the file in memory (the one you currently are editing). The syntax of this command is

[*line*]T*filespec*

The *line* parameter indicates the number of the line before which you want to place the new lines, and *filespec* is the name of the file to transfer into memory. To transfer the file DUCK.TXT into memory at Line 10, for example, use the command

```
10TDUCK.TXT
```

Write Lines (W)

This command writes a specified number of lines from memory to disk. The syntax of the command is

[*n*]W

where *n* is the number of lines to write. The W command is most useful when you are editing a large file and want to free up some memory. If you write some lines out to disk memory, those lines cannot be edited during that edit session. If your file is 2,000 lines long, for example, Edlin probably will not be able to get all lines in memory at once. Suppose that only the first 1,400 lines come into memory when you use Edlin to edit this file. After editing the file, you can use the W command to write out the first 700 lines, leaving 700 still in memory. (You then cannot edit any of the first 700 lines.) If you want to edit lines past line 1,400, use the A command to append lines from disk into memory. When you exit Edlin, the file is put back together.

Creating and Modifying an AUTOEXEC.BAT File with Edlin

To illustrate how you can use Edlin to create a file, the following example provides step-by-step instructions for creating and modifying a simple AUTOEXEC.BAT file that contains these two lines:

```
PROMPT $P$G
PATH C:\;C:\DOS;C:\NORTON
```

You can generalize the steps to create other files. To create this AUTOEXEC.BAT file, follow these steps:

1. Begin the Edlin program with the command

   ```
   EDLIN AUTOEXEC.BAT
   ```

   If this file is new, you see the message

   ```
   New File
   *
   ```

2. To place Edlin in Insert mode, press I to issue the Insert Lines command. You see the prompt

   ```
   1:_
   ```

   Edlin now is waiting for you to enter information.

3. Type

   ```
   PROMPT $P$G
   ```

   and press Enter.

4. On Line 2, type

   ```
   PATH C:\;C:\DOS;C:\NORTON
   ```

   and press Enter.

5. To end the insert process, press Ctrl-Break. Edlin returns you to the * prompt.

6. To list the contents of the file to the screen, enter the L (List Lines) command at the * prompt. You should see these two lines:

   ```
   1:PROMPT $P$G
    *2:PATH C:\;C:\DOS;C:\NORTON
   ```

   Note that an * appears before Line 2. This asterisk indicates that Line 2 is the current line.

7. To exit the file and place it on disk, enter the command E (End Edit) at the * prompt. You then return to the DOS prompt.

Suppose that you then decide that you want to add to the file another line containing the Norton command FR/SAVE. Follow these steps:

1. At the DOS prompt, enter the command

   EDLIN AUTOEXEC.BAT

   This time, Edlin responds with the message

   ```
   End of Input File
   *
   ```

   You can list the contents of the file by using the L command.

2. To insert a line beginning at Line 3, enter the command 3I at the * prompt.

3. Enter the command line FR/SAVE and press Enter. Edlin responds with a prompt for Line 4.

4. End the insert procedure by pressing Ctrl-Break.

5. Use the E (End Edit) command to end Edlin. You then return to the DOS prompt.

Using DOS To Back Up Your Hard Disk

Another important feature of DOS is its capability to back up the information on your hard disk.

You easily can destroy data on a diskette or hard disk. In fact, sometime during your use of the computer, you are likely to lose some data. If you are careful, you will experience such a loss only rarely, and if you have a backup procedure, you should be able to recover from the loss with a minimum of grief. Although Norton Utilities can help you recover information in a number of ways, keeping backup copies of your work still is a good idea.

One of the simplest ways to back up your information is to make multiple copies of everything you do. If you are writing a paper, for example, be sure to keep at least two copies, each on a separate disk. If your original copy is on a hard disk, copy the file to a floppy each time you finish working on the file. Also, save your work often. Never work on a document for hours without making copies. If the electricity goes off or the computer has problems, you easily can lose an entire day's work. How often you should save your work is determined by how much time you are willing to lose. If you do not mind potentially losing an hour's worth of work, save and back up your work every hour.

Besides backing up a single file (which you can do easily with the COPY command), you also can take advantage of a DOS procedure for backing up an entire hard disk: the BACKUP command.

Using the BACKUP Command

The most common way to back up a hard disk is to copy it to floppy diskettes. The DOS BACKUP command enables you to copy files from the hard disk to any number of floppy diskettes. You can copy the entire disk or just portions of it to diskettes. You may need 30 or more diskettes to back up an entire disk. The syntax of the BACKUP command is

BACKUP *source destination* [*/switches*]

The simplest form of the BACKUP command is

BACKUP C: A:

This command tells DOS to back up all files on drive C to floppy diskettes in drive A. After you issue the command, the computer prompts you to insert Disk #1 into drive A. Information is copied to the diskette until it is full, and then you are prompted to insert Disk #2 into the drive. This procedure is repeated until all the files are backed up onto the diskettes. Note, however, that this form of the command backs up only the files from the currently active directory.

If you are using DOS Version 3.2 or earlier, all backup diskettes first must be formatted. Unfortunately, this requirement means that you must have some idea of how many diskettes will be required for the backup. To back up a 10M hard disk to 360K floppy diskettes, you need 28 diskettes (10,000,000/360,000 = 27.7). Starting with DOS 3.3, you do not need to format diskettes to use for backup. The procedure formats the disks during the backup (if you used the /F switch).

You usually have no reason to back up copies of executable programs from the hard disk, because you should have those programs on their original floppy diskettes, which you could reload in a crisis. What you do want to back up are the files containing your work. To back up specific files, you can enter the names of those files by using global file characters.

Suppose that you name all your data files with a DAT extension, and you want to back up all those files. Use this command:

```
BACKUP C:*.DAT A:
```

This command backs up DAT files only in the currently active subdirectory. To back up all directories, make sure that your file specification begins with the root directory (\) and add the /S switch to the command, as in

```
BACKUP C:\*.DAT A:/S
```

To back up all files in all directories and all subdirectories, use this command:

```
BACKUP C:\ A:/S
```

The switches available for the BACKUP command are listed in table A.5.

Table A.5
Switches for the DOS BACKUP Command

Switch	*Effect*
/S	Backs up all subdirectories, starting with the specified or current directory.
/D:*mm-dd-yy*	Backs up all files modified on or after a specified date.
/A	Adds more files to a set of already backed-up files.
/M	Backs up files that have been modified since the last backup.
/F	Tells Backup to format disks used in the backup if they have not been formatted.
/T:*time*	Backs up all files modified at or after the specified time (hh:mm:ss).

Using the RESTORE Command

If you need to use one or more of the files that you have backed up with the DOS BACKUP command, you must use the RESTORE command to copy these files from the backup diskettes back to the hard disk. The syntax of this command is

RESTORE *source destination* [/*switches*]

An example of the RESTORE command is

RESTORE A: C:/S

This command restores all files from floppies in disk A (source) to the fixed disk C (destination), including all subdirectories (/S). Other options for the RESTORE command are listed in your DOS manual. One that is particularly helpful is the /P or PROMPT switch. When you use this switch, the computer prompts you before restoring a file and enables you to choose the files to restore.

Creating a Disaster Recovery Plan

You should set up a procedure to back up your hard disk—or portions of it—regularly. Here is an example of a good procedure:

1. After initially loading your hard disk, back up the entire hard disk twice.

2. Back up the entire disk daily, using the /M and /A switches.

3. Back up the entire disk once a week. Place the weekly backup in a secure area, away from the office, or have someone take the backup diskettes home.

This procedure results in two backups: one weekly backup stored away from the office in case of an emergency (such as a fire or flood), and one "working" backup at the office to be used daily.

Keep a copy of this book and the Norton Utilities program handy in case a disk accidentally is formatted. See Chapters 3 and 4 on how to prepare for and recover from a potential disk-related disaster.

Because backups take up so much diskette space, you should keep your hard disk clear of unneeded files. Unneeded files on a disk can clutter the directories, limit the amount of disk space for other uses, and prolong the backup procedure. Another good idea, along with the backup procedure, is to set aside time once a week or so to erase any unneeded files from the hard disk, or to copy them to floppies on a semipermanent basis.

Alternatives to the BACKUP command are available. Commercially available programs such as Norton Backup and Fastback provide a quicker way to back up your hard disk. Also, backup devices such as tape drives and optical disk drives enable you to back up an entire hard disk to a single tape or disk in a few minutes.

B

Comparing DOS and Norton Utilities Commands

This appendix contains an alphabetical list of frequently used DOS commands and their descriptions. Each DOS command is compared with a similar Norton Utilities command. In most cases, the Norton commands have advantages over the DOS commands. These advantages are described briefly, and examples of the DOS and its corresponding Norton commands are given. For more information on the available options and switches for each Norton command, consult the alphabetical list of Norton Utilities commands in Chapter 7.

ATTRIB vs. FILEFIND

ATTRIB displays or sets Read-only and Archive attributes for a file.

Example: To set files to Read-only, enter the command

```
ATTRIB +R *.TXT
```

To display the current attributes for all *.TXT files, enter the command

```
ATTRIB *.TXT
```

FILEFIND enables you to set all four attributes, including Read-only, Archive, Hidden, and System. The FA command also can display a directory of files and attributes. It can clear all attributes at once with the /CLEAR switch.

Example: To set all files with the *.TXT extension to read-only (including files in subdirectories), enter the command

```
FILEFIND *.TXT /R+
```

CHDIR or CD vs. NCD

CHDIR enables you to change to another directory.

Example: To change to the \WP\LETTERS directory, enter the command

```
CD \WP\LETTERS
```

Norton Change Directory (NCD) enables you to use only a partial name (when it is unique) to change directories. You can use the NCD command in command-line or in interactive mode. In interactive mode, you can switch to a directory by moving the cursor to the directory name as displayed in a tree diagram.

Example: To change to the directory named \WP\LETTERS, enter the command

```
NCD LET
```

CHKDSK vs. NDD

CHKDSK enables you to check your disk for errors and report the status.

Example: To test a disk and attempt to fix any logical problems in the directory or file allocation table, enter the command

```
CHKDSK A:/F
```

Norton Disk Doctor (NDD) searches the disk for bad sectors and attempts to correct both physical and logical problems. You also can use NDD in interactive mode.

Example: To test the partition table, boot record, root directory, and lost clusters, enter the command

```
NDD/QUICK
```

DATE vs. NCC

The DOS DATE command enables you to set the system date for your computer. This often will not change the internal clock in the counter, however, so that when you reboot, you have to reset the date again. To permanently reset the date, you must use the Setup command on some computers.

Example: To reset the date, type

```
DATE 10-24-91
```

The Norton Control Center (NCC) Time and Date option enables you to reset the system date. For many computers, this also will reset the internal clock.

DEL or ERASE vs. WIPEINFO

DEL or ERASE deletes one or more files.

Example: To delete files with the BAT extension in the default directory, enter the command

```
DEL *.BAT
```

Note: These files could be unerased by the Norton Quick Unerase command.

WIPEINFO erases files so that they cannot be recovered—not even by Norton unerase operations. Optionally, WIPEINFO can mimic the DOS ERASE command to erase files so that they *can* be unerased. WIPEINFO has the advantage of being able to erase files across subdirectories.

Example: To wipe out all files with the BAT extension in the current directory and all subdirectories, enter the command

```
WIPEINFO *.BAT/S
```

DIR vs. FILEFIND

DIR lists selected file names to the screen.

Example: To display all files with the BAT extension, enter the command

```
DIR *.BAT
```

FILEFIND enables you to display selected file names in a list box, of files within a directory, or on the entire hard disk. FILEFIND also lists file attributes, which are not listed with the DIR command.

Example: To list all files on the disk that match the specification, including those in subdirectories, enter the command

```
FILEFIND *.BAT
```

FIND vs. FILEFIND

FIND enables you to find and report the existence of specified text in selected files. You must explicitly list all the files you want to be searched—no global characters are allowed in the search file names.

Example: To list to the screen any lines in the REPORT.DOC file that contain the string "text," type

```
FIND "text" REPORT.DOC
```

FILEFIND enables you to search files in subdirectories and to search erased spaces on the disk for the specified search string. You can make a search case-sensitive.

Example: To search all files having the DOC extension in the current directory and subdirectories or the character string specified by "text," enter the command

```
FILEFIND *.DOC "text"
```

FORMAT vs. SFORMAT

FORMAT prepares a disk to store files.

Example: To format and place a label on the disk in drive A, enter the command

```
FORMAT A:/V
```

Safe Format (SFORMAT) formats disks. The SFORMAT command has several safety features not available in the DOS FORMAT command. For example, SFORMAT saves format information in case the format is an accident. This feature enables you to unformat the disk with the Norton Utilities Unformat command. Safe Format provides several format modes, including Safe Format, the normal DOS FORMAT, Quick Format, and Complete Format (for floppy diskettes). The Quick Format mode simply places a new system area on an already formatted disk—effectively erasing all directories and files on disk. Complete Format reformats bad sectors on a diskette. You can run Safe Format also in interactive mode and choose options from menus rather than remembering command-line switches.

Example: To format and place the label MYDISK on the disk in drive A, enter the command

```
SFORMAT A: /V:MYDISK
```

MKDIR or MD vs. NCD

MKDIR makes a directory.

Example: To make a subdirectory named LETTERS in the WP directory, enter the command

```
MD \WP\LETTERS
```

Norton Change Directory (NCD), when used with the MD option, makes a directory. This command also updates the NCD directory file, which gives you quicker access to directories when you later use the NCD command in interactive mode. In interactive mode, you can add a directory by "pointing" to the directory name on-screen and pressing F7 (Mkdir). Also, the NCD command has a Rename option, which enables you to rename a directory. DOS has no equivalent command.

Example: To make a subdirectory named LETTERS in the WP directory and update the NCD directory file, enter the command

```
NCD MD \WP\LETTERS
```

MODE vs. NCC

MODE specifies communications port settings.

Example: To set up the communication port number 1 as 1200 baud, type

```
MODE COM1 BAUD=1200
```

Norton Command Center (NCC), when used with the Serial Ports option, enables you to set up the parameters of a serial port interactively by choosing options from a menu.

RECOVER vs. DISKTOOL

RECOVER tries to reclaim files with defective sectors or recovers a disk with defective sectors. This command is dangerous because the slightest misuse can be devastating. Files are often renamed to machine-generated names, and perfectly good files can be lost easily. Do not use this command unless you know exactly what you are doing.

Norton's DISKTOOL, when used with RECOVER, attempts to reclaim files and directories that have been renamed and removed by the DOS RECOVER command. Rather than use RECOVER to reclaim files, use the NDD command in interactive mode and choose the Diagnose option or the DISKTOOL command's Revive a Defective Diskette option.

RMDIR or RD vs. NCD

RMDIR or RD removes a directory.

Example: To remove the \WP directory, enter the command

```
RD \WP
```

Norton Change Directory (NCD), when used with the RD option, removes a directory. This command also updates the NCD directory file. You also can run NCD in interactive mode, where you can remove a directory by pointing to the directory name on a graphic tree and pressing F8 (Delete).

Example: To remove the \WP directory, enter the command

```
NCD RD \WP
```

SYS vs. DISKTOOL

SYS places system files (but not the COMMAND.COM file) on disk, if the disk was prepared to receive system files when the disk was originally formatted.

Example: To place the system files on disk C, enter the command

```
SYS C:
```

DISKTOOL, when used with the Make a Disk Bootable option, places the system files on a disk even if it was not prepared to do so when it was formatted. This option also copies the COMMAND.COM file to the disk to make it bootable.

TIME vs. NCC

TIME enables you to set the system time on your computer. For many versions of the PC, however, this time setting does not reset the internal clock, so when you reboot, your time setting may have gone away. To set the internal clock, you may have to use the Setup command.

Example: To set the system time, type

```
TIME 10:40
```

The Norton Control Center's (NCC's) Date and Time option enables you to set the system time. For many computers, this also will set the internal clock.

TREE vs. NCD

TREE displays information about directories on disk. Beginning with DOS 4.0, this command displays directories in a graphic tree structure.

Example: To display directory names for the entire disk, enter the command

```
TREE \
```

Norton Change Directory (NCD), in interactive mode, displays directories in a tree structure and enables you to point to directory names on-screen and choose to add, rename, delete, or change the directories.

VOL vs. NCD

VOL displays the volume label for a disk.

Example: To display the name given to the diskette in drive B when it was formatted, enter the command

```
VOL B:
```

The Norton Change Directory (NCD) command enables you to change a volume label. In interactive mode, the option is on the Disk pull-down menu.

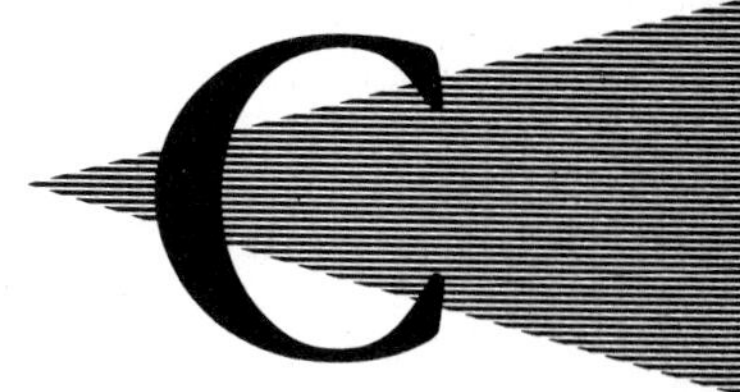

Installation Procedures

This appendix covers installation procedures for Norton Utilities 5.0, Norton Commander 3.0, and Norton Backup 1.1. You learn how to install these programs on a hard disk-based system. You also learn how to create an emergency floppy disk with Norton Utilities.

Installing Norton Utilities 5.0

Norton Advanced Utilities comes with six 5 1/4-inch, 360K diskettes or two 3 1/2-inch, 720K diskettes. You will use the diskettes appropriate for your computer. If your floppy disk A is a 720K or 1.44M, 3 1/2-inch disk drive, use the 3 1/2-inch diskettes. If your disk A is a 360K drive or a 1.2M disk drive, use the 5 1/4-inch disks.

Norton Utilities 5.0 takes about 2.5M of disk space. Because one of Norton Utilities' primary functions is to enable you to manage your hard disk better, you probably will not install the full system on a floppy disk machine. Therefore, these installation instructions assume that you will be installing the full program on a hard disk. It is a good idea to have some of the utility programs available on floppy disk, however. After you learn how to install Norton Utilities on your hard disk, you will learn how to create a floppy disk containing a selection of the utilities.

Installing the Full Norton Utilities 5.0 on a Hard Disk

To install Norton Utilities 5.0 on your hard disk, follow these steps:

1. Turn on your computer and boot it in the usual way. End any programs that are started automatically (such as a menu), so that you are at the DOS prompt (usually a C> prompt on a hard disk).

2. Change the DOS prompt to drive A by entering the command

   ```
   A:
   ```

   Your prompt should be A> or A:>, or an equivalent prompt.

3. Insert the Norton Utilities installation disk into drive A.

4. Many times after a manual is printed, errors are found in the manual or there is some new information that you need to know. On the installation disk, the file READ.ME contains last-minute notes about the program. You may print this file with the command

   ```
   COPY READ.ME LPT1:
   ```

   This command assumes that you have a printer installed on printer port 1. If you do not have a printer, use the type command to examine this file on-screen. Type

   ```
   TYPE READ.ME
   ```

   to examine the contents of the READ.ME file. You also can examine this file by using the Norton Commander Editor or View option, or you can use your word processor to view the contents of the file.

5. To begin the installation procedure for Norton Utilities, enter the command

   ```
   INSTALL
   ```

   The first screen that appears is a warning screen. This screen warns you not to install the utilities if your disk has been formatted accidentally or if you want to unerase some files that are still on your hard disk. You need to perform these commands from a floppy disk. Refer to the next section on creating a floppy disk with Norton commands. To cancel the installation procedure, press R to return to DOS or point to the Return to DOS box with your mouse pointer and click. To continue with installation, press Enter or C. Alternatively, point to the Continue box with the mouse and click.

6. The next screen that appears gives you a summary of how the installation process will take place (see fig. C.1). The installation procedure does the following:

   - Copies Norton Utilities files to your hard disk.
   - Enables you to place certain Norton Utilities commands in your AUTOEXEC.BAT and CONFIG.SYS files.
   - Enables you to set the configuration of your computer (screen colors, mouse, graphics).

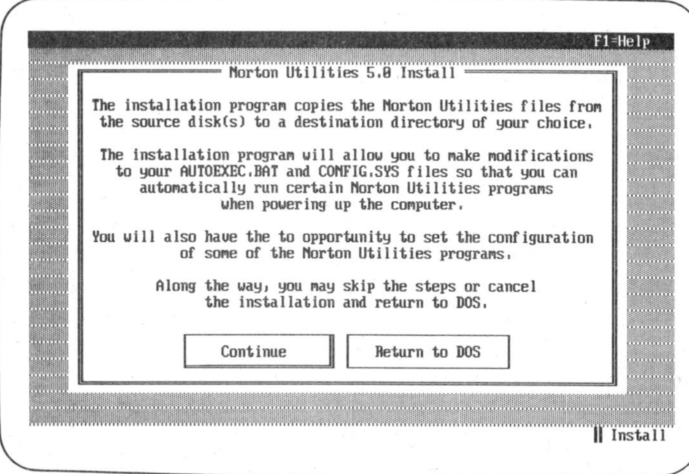

Fig. C.1* *The Norton Utilities 5.0 Install screen.

7. After you select Continue on the initial install screen, you see the screen shown in figure C.2. From this screen, you can choose New Install or Reconfigure. If this is your first time to install Norton Utilities 5.0, choose New Install. After you install the program, you can use the install program to reconfigure some of the choices you made during the original installation by choosing the Reconfigure option.

8. After you choose New Install, you see a screen similar to the one shown in figure C.3. From this screen, you can choose Full Install or Partial Install. Usually, you will choose a Full Install. If you do not have much space on disk, or you want to install only one or a few Norton programs, choose Partial Install.

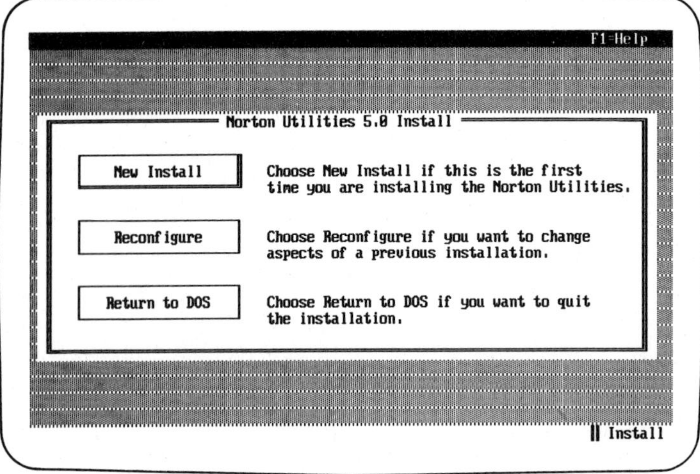

Fig. C.2 ***Choosing New Install or Reconfigure from the Norton Utilities menu.***

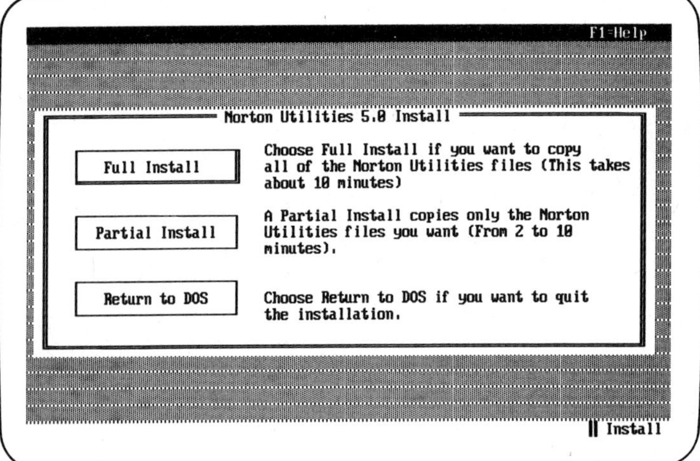

Fig. C.3 ***Choosing Full Install or Partial Install from the Norton Utilities menu.***

9. After you choose Full Install, a prompt appears asking you to

    `Select the drive to install from`

    (see fig. C.4). A list of available drives appears. Press the letter of the drive containing the installation disk, such as A.

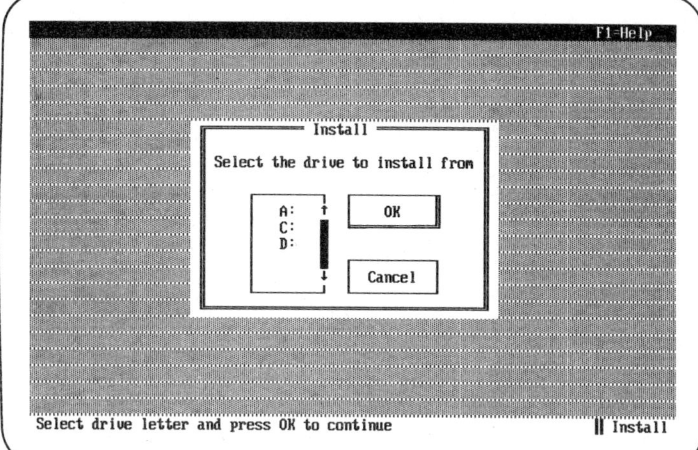

Fig. C.4 ***Using the Norton Utilities menu to choose the disk drive to install from.***

10. The Install program now searches for an existing copy of Norton Utilities on disk. If you have an old copy, you are given a chance to delete the old copy or to back it up to some other location on disk. The default location for Norton Utilities to be installed is C:\NORTON. If you want to accept this location, press Enter to continue the installation. You optionally may change the destination by pressing the Backspace key to delete the C:\NORTON location on-screen, and enter a new location (see figure C.5). After specifying the directory name, press Enter to continue. You then are instructed to insert Disk #1 into the drive, then Disk #2, and so on, until all files are copied from the diskettes to the hard disk. If you insert the wrong disk into the drive, you get a message like the one in figure C.6.

11. After all files are copied, the install program asks if you want to replace the DOS version of the FORMAT command with Norton's Safe Format. Using the Safe Format (SFORMAT) command instead of the DOS FORMAT command gives you added data-protection features (see fig. C.7). Choose Continue to perform this replacement.

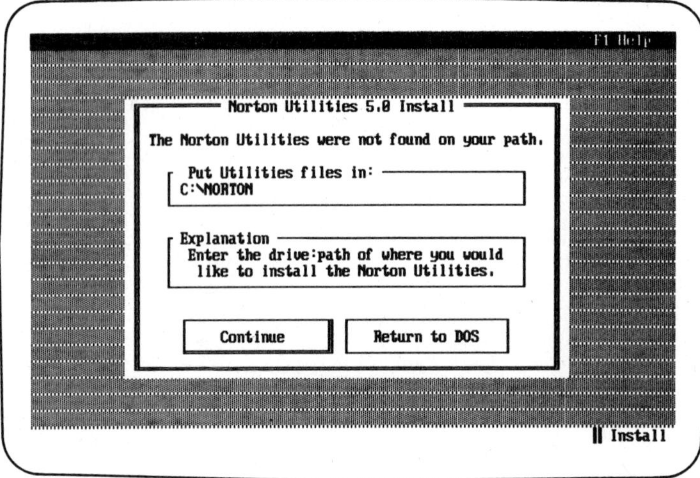

Fig. C.5 ***Using the Norton Utilities menu to choose the disk drive and directory to install to.***

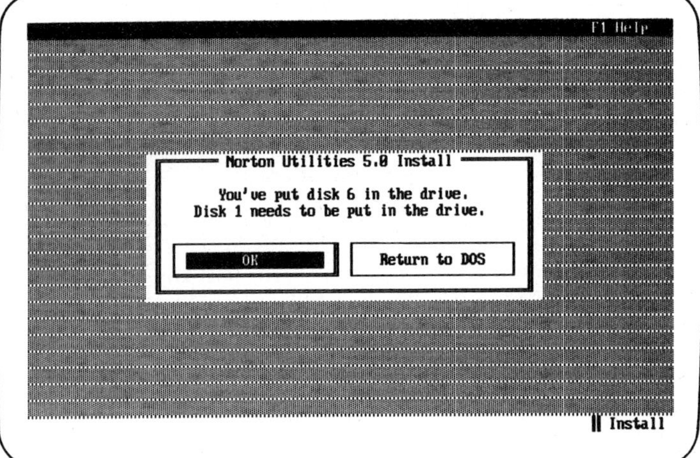

Fig. C.6 ***Norton Utilities warns you that the wrong disk has been inserted.***

12. After the FORMAT program has been replaced, you see the screen shown in figure C.8. This screen contains several options about the configuration of the program and your hardware. Each time you choose one of these options, another menu screen appears. After you select options from this menu, you return to the Configuration menu. The Configuration menu gives you the following options:

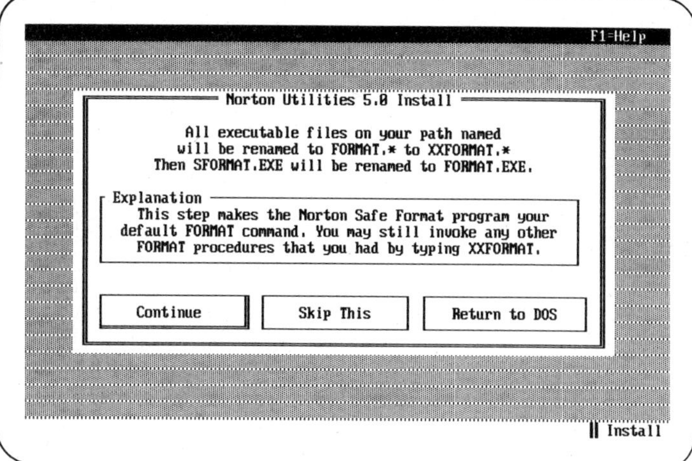

Fig. C.7
The Norton Utilities option replaces the FORMAT command with the Norton Safe Format command.

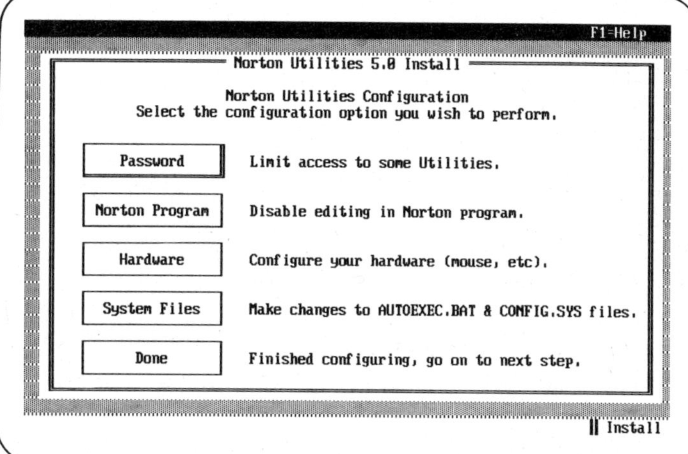

Fig. C.8
The Norton Utilities Configuration menu.

- *Password:* Enables you to prevent persons from using certain commands unless they first enter a password. If you choose the Password option, you see a screen similar to the one shown in figure C.9. This screen lists 14 commands that you can protect by password. Use the arrow keys to highlight the check box in front of each option you want to choose, and then press the space bar to select or deselect an option (an X or checkmark appears when you select an option, and disappears when you deselect an option). Alternatively, point to an option with your mouse and click to select or deselect an option. If you do not know of any reason to password-protect any programs, deselect all of these options and then exit this screen. After you choose all of the programs to password-protect, press Enter to choose OK to lock in your selections.

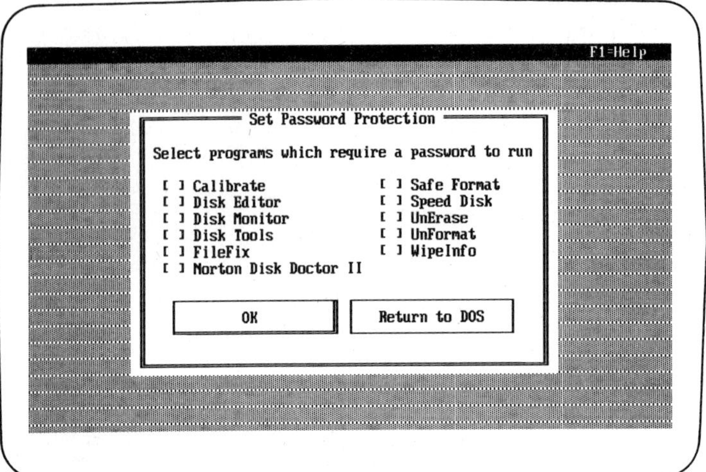

Fig. C.9 The Norton Utilities Set Password Protection screen.

- *Norton Program:* Enables you to choose Disable Editing or Enable Editing. The Disable Editing option means that you cannot add or change the options in the Norton menu. Enable Editing enables you to add, delete, or change options in the menu. If you do not know what to choose, choose Enable.

- *Hardware:* Enables you decide how Norton Utilities will appear on your computer screen (see figure C.10). Use the arrow keys or your mouse to move from option to option. Press the space bar to select or deselect options (or use your mouse). Norton will determine which kind of computer you are using, and the default options on this menu will reflect the options you probably would want to choose. Choose Save to accept the default options, or make changes and then choose Save. If you have made some selections but want to revert to the default options, choose the Cancel option.

- *System Files:* Enables you to make changes to your AUTOEXEC.BAT and CONFIG.SYS files.

- *Done:* Enables you to move to the next step.

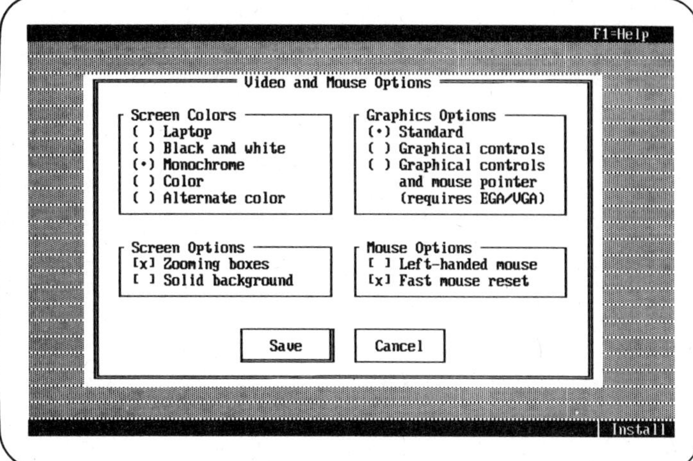

***Fig. C.10* The Norton Utilities Video and Mouse Options screen.**

After you select all of the options you want from the four Configuration menus, choose the Done option.

13. After you finish setting the configuration, you can choose to have Norton Utilities make changes to your AUTOEXEC.BAT and CONFIG.SYS files. These changes enable certain Norton programs to begin each time you boot your computer.

    After you first begin to use Norton, you probably should skip using some of these programs until you understand what they do and how they work. Also, these programs may take up part of your RAM memory so that large application programs may not work. When you decide which programs to use, you can come back to this installation option by choosing the Reconfigure option on the initial Install menu. In the following list, certain options are recommended for first time installation. Skip the other options until you understand the full impact of what these options do.

    The changes that you can enable Norton to make to your AUTOEXEC.BAT file follow:

    - Add the NORTON directory to your PATH statement. This is recommended.
    - Add the NU environment variable. This is recommended.
    - Automatically load the TSR programs Disk Monitor and File Save. Skip this option for first-time installation.

- Automatically run the IMAGE program each time you boot. This is recommended.
- Automatically run the NDD /Quick command each time you boot. Skip this option for first time installation.

After you choose your options, a copy of your AUTOEXEC.BAT file appears on-screen. From this screen, you can save the changes you made, discard the changes, or move a command to a different line in the file.

The changes that you can enable Norton to make to your CONFIG.SYS file follow:

- Install Fast Cache, Small Cache, or No Cache. Skip this option for first-time installation.
- Install an encryption device. Skip this option for first-time installation.

After you choose your options, a copy of your CONFIG.SYS file appears on-screen. From this screen, you can save the changes you made, discard them, or move a command to a different line in the file.

This completes the installation procedure on a hard disk. You now can use Norton Utilities from any directory by entering the name of a Norton command or by typing *norton* to begin the Norton menu program.

Installing a Partial Norton Utilities Program on a Floppy Disk

There are several reasons for creating a Norton Utilities disk with a few selected files on disk:

- You have not yet installed Norton Utilities and you want to use Unerase to unerase files or directories.
- Your hard disk has been formatted accidentally, and you want to try to recover it.
- You want to prepare a disk to help recover from future problems associated with the disk. These problems could include an accidental format of your hard disk, a hard disk that no longer will boot, and other problems that may make the version of Norton Utilities on the hard disk unusable. The use of the Norton commands mentioned here are covered in Chapters 3 through 7 of this book.

To prepare a floppy disk for these uses, perform the following procedures:

1. Format a blank floppy disk by using the System option. To format a disk in drive A, for example, you use the command

   FORMAT A:/S

2. Copy the following programs from the Norton Utilities disks to the floppy disk:

UNFORMAT.EXE	Unformats a hard disk.
UNERASE.EXE	Recovers erased files and directories.
NDD.EXE	Diagnoses problems with a disk and makes a disk bootable again (Norton Disk Doctor).

You also should copy to the floppy disk two other files that may come in handy for recovering information on your hard disk: your AUTOEXEC.BAT and CONFIG.SYS files.

Keep this floppy diskette stored in a convenient location in case you need to use this disk to recover information on your hard disk.

Installing Norton Commander 3.0

The Norton Commander 3.0 package comes with two 5 1/4-inch, 360K diskettes and one 3 1/2-inch, 720K diskette. Obviously, you need to use the diskettes appropriate to your computer. If your drive A is a 720K or a 1.44M, 3 1/2-inch disk drive, use the 3 1/2-inch diskette. If your drive A is a 360K or a 1.2M disk drive, use the 5 1/4-inch diskettes.

Norton Commander takes about 850 bytes of disk space. Because one of the Commander's primary functions is to enable you to manage your hard disk better, you probably would not install the program on a floppy-based machine. Therefore, these installation instructions assume that you are installing Norton Commander on a hard disk system.

To install Norton Commander 3.0, follow these steps:

1. Turn on your computer and boot it normally. Exit any programs that are started automatically (such as a menu) so that you are at the DOS prompt (usually a C prompt on a hard disk).

2. Change the DOS prompt to the A drive by entering the command

   A:

   Your prompt should be A>, A:\>, or an equivalent prompt.

3. Place the installation disk into drive A.

   For 5 1/4-inch drives, insert the first 5 1/4-inch Commander disk (Disk #1) into drive A.

   For 3 1/2-inch drives, insert the 3 1/2-inch Commander disk into drive A.

Tip: After a manual is printed, errors often are found in the manual, or some new information is discovered that you need to know. Commander has two files on disk that contain this type of information. The file INREAD.ME contains helpful information about what to do if the installation process does not work. The file READ.ME contains "last-minute notes" about the program. You can print these files with this command:

   COPY *.ME LPT1:

This command assumes that you have a printer installed on Printer Port 1. If you do not have a printer, use the TYPE command to examine these files on-screen. To examine the contents of the INREAD.ME file, enter

   TYPE INREAD.ME

To examine the contents of the READ.ME file, enter

   TYPE READ.ME

4. To begin the installation process, type the following command and press Enter:

   INSTALL

5. You are first prompted to

   ```
   Select drive to install Norton Commander from
   ```

   A list of drives is given, such as A:, B:, and so on. Type the letter of the drive containing the installation disk.

6. You see a screen similar to the one in figure C.11, which summarizes the installation process.

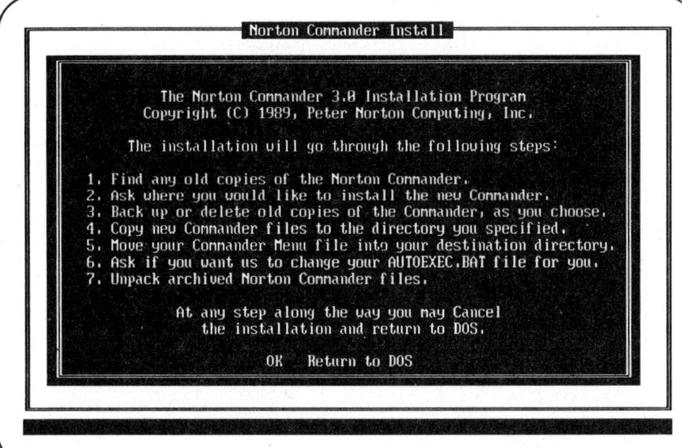

Fig. C.11
The Norton Commander Install screen.

At the bottom of the screen are two options: OK and Return to DOS. OK is highlighted. To continue with installation, press Enter. To return to DOS, press R.

7. The Install program next looks at your disk to see whether a current copy of Norton Commander is installed in a directory named \NC. If you have an old copy, you are given a chance to delete the old copy or back it up to some other location on disk.

8. You then are asked to enter the name of the disk and directory to which Commander should be copied (see fig. C.12). The default location for Commander to be installed is C:\NC. If you accept this location, press Enter to continue the installation. You optionally can change the destination by pressing the Backspace key to delete the destination and entering a new location.

9. After you select the location, the installation program prompts you once more before the copy begins—to give you a chance to return to DOS and cancel installation.

10. The Install program asks whether you want the path to the Commander directory placed in the PATH statement of your AUTOEXEC.BAT file (see fig. C.13). If you are installing Commander for the first time, you normally will choose OK. If you already have a path to the Commander's directory, you can press S to skip this part of the installation.

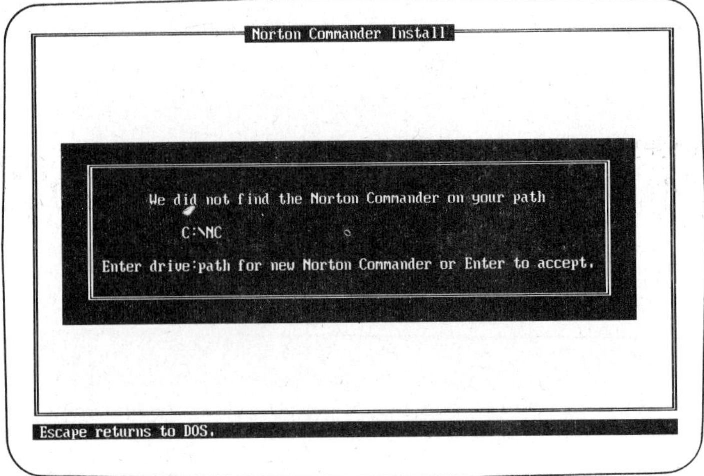

Fig. C.12
Specifying the Norton Commander directory.

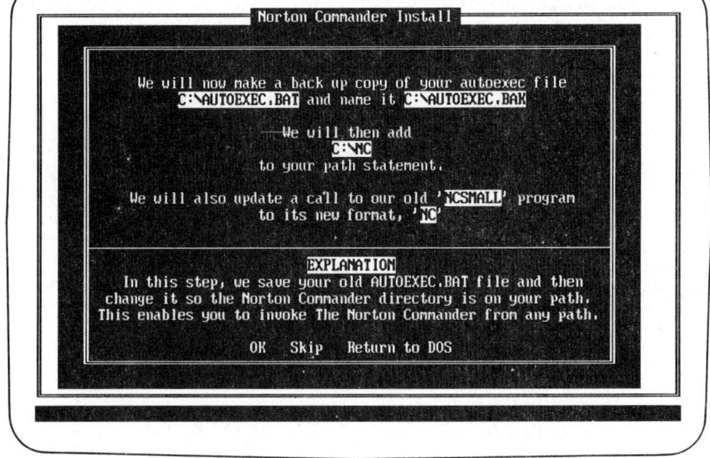

Fig. C.13
The Norton Commander Install AUTOEXEC.BAT prompt.

After all the files are copied to disk, the installation is complete. To begin Norton Commander, you enter the following command at the DOS prompt:

NC

If you want Commander to be run each time you boot your computer, you can place the NC command as the last line in your AUTOEXEC.BAT file. See Appendix A for an explanation of the AUTOEXEC.BAT file and how to edit it.

Installing Norton Backup 1.1

The Norton Backup 1.1 program comes with a 3 1/2-inch diskette and two 5 1/4-inch diskettes. If you are using a computer with a 3 1/2-inch disk (720K or 1.44M), you will use the single 3 1/2-inch disk to install the program. If you are using a computer with a 5 1/4-inch disk (360K or 1.2M), you will use both disks to install the program.

The Backup program requires that you have two blank diskettes to test the program. Therefore, be sure you have these handy when you begin the installation. If you have 3 1/2-inch and 5 1/4-inch disk drives, you can use either size for the test.

The Norton Backup installation program performs several tasks:

- Copies necessary files to your hard disk.
- Modifies your AUTOEXEC.BAT file to place the Norton Backup directory in your PATH command.
- Examines your computer setup to determine which disks your computer contains and which disks may be used as backups.
- Runs several tests on your computer to determine the most efficient way to perform the backup. These tests deal with the speed of your computer and your disks.

To install Norton Backup, place Disk #1 (or the single 3 1/2-inch disk) into drive A. Make the DOS default drive A by entering the command:

```
A:
```

From the DOS prompt, enter the command:

```
INSTALL
```

The Install program asks you a series of questions about your computer. Usually, the best choice is to choose the default settings offered, unless you have a reason to change them. You may change settings later from the Norton Backup program.

After you choose your basic options, the installation procedure runs a series of tests. You will need two blank diskettes to complete these tests. If your computer fails either of these tests, Norton Backup attempts to reset its options to compensate for the problem.

After you install Norton Backup, it is a good idea to back up all or a portion of your hard disk, and then restore it to verify that the program is installed and is working correctly.

After Norton Backup has been installed, begin the program by entering the command

```
NBACKUP
```

at the DOS prompt.

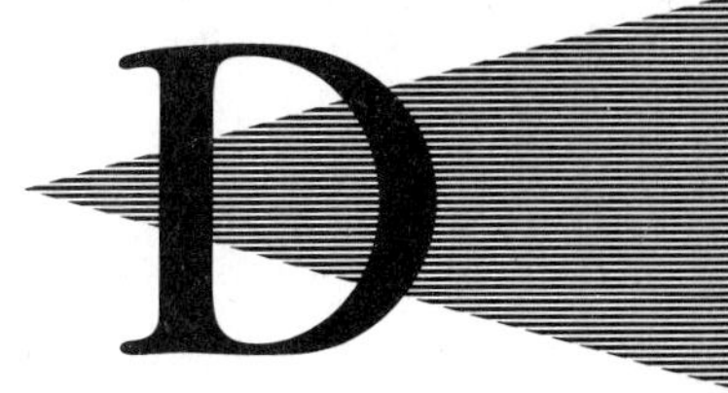

Dealing with Disk-Related Problems

Norton Utilities Version 5.0 provides a number of commands that help you fix disk problems that cannot be solved with DOS commands alone. Many disk problems are caused by bad spots developing on the magnetic surface of a disk. The magnetic signal on the disk gradually weakens until DOS cannot read the information. Other problems are caused by a disk getting almost full and files becoming so fragmented that DOS loses track of critical information. If these problems begin to appear, you may experience difficulties, ranging from the inability to read one file to the inability to access your entire hard disk.

The first part of this appendix describes some common problems and suggests how you can use Norton Utilities commands to diagnose and solve these problems. Sometimes, however, a disk may be irreparable with these methods. You may have to perform a low-level format on the hard disk, which is explained later in this appendix.

Another problem is computer sabotage. The information on your computer may be damaged by a computer virus or by the deliberate act of an individual. For information on handling these types of problems, see "Dealing with Viruses," later in this appendix. For suggestions on how to respond to common DOS error messages, see the final section, "Responding to DOS Error Messages."

Diagnosing and Fixing Disk Problems

This section presents several common disk problems and gives you suggestions for solving them with Norton Utilities and other commands.

Your Computer No Longer Boots from the Hard Disk

If your computer has booted from the hard disk in the past but now will not, you must boot from a floppy diskette in drive A, using a disk that contains DOS. Make sure that the disk contains the same version of DOS that is on the hard disk.

One situation that can cause this problem is if you no longer have the correct COMMAND.COM file in your hard disk root directory. After you boot your computer, examine your hard disk's root directory to determine whether it contains the correct COMMAND.COM—you should be able to tell from its date. If it does not match the date and size on the original DOS disk, copy the correct COMMAND.COM onto the hard disk and try booting again.

If the COMMAND.COM file is okay, your system files may have become corrupted. You can use the DOS SYS command to transfer a fresh copy of the system files to the hard disk. Better yet, use the Norton Disk Tool's Make a Disk Bootable option. This option places COMMAND.COM and the system files on your disk. If this approach does not work, your hard disk may be damaged physically—take it in for repair.

Tip: You should keep a floppy disk handy that contains the files necessary to boot your computer in case your computer becomes unbootable from the hard disk. This floppy disk should be formatted with the system (/S FORMAT option); it should contain the DOS programs FDISK and DEBUG; and it should contain the Norton programs DISKTOOL, NDD, and the files AUTOEXEC.BAT and CONFIG.SYS. Also include any device drivers (mouse driver, plotter, and so on).

Your Hard Disk Does Not Format as a System Disk

The hard disk, like a floppy diskette, uses track 0 to store system information. If that track is bad on a hard disk, the DOS FORMAT command will not create a bootable hard disk. Several possibilities exist for recovering from this problem. After booting from a floppy diskette in drive A, use the Norton Disk Doctor to diagnose the hard disk and attempt to fix the problem. If that approach does not work, you may need to perform a low-level format of the disk. If the disk contains valuable information, you need to use a nondestructive program such as HFORMAT or Spinrite, or Norton's Calibrate command. See "Performing a Low-Level Format," later in this appendix, for more information.

You Get Errors Trying To Copy a Diskette with DISKCOPY

If you use the DOS DISKCOPY command to copy a disk, you may get read errors or write errors, or both. Read errors are associated with reading information from the source disk. Write errors are associated with writing information to the destination disk. If a bad or unreadable spot exists on the source disk, it causes the read error. Similarly, if a bad or unreadable spot exists on the destination disk, it causes a write error. If you get a write error, change to another destination diskette.

The read error is of most concern because it occurs on the disk that contains the original information. If you get a read error, examine the source disk by using Norton Disk Doctor II. NDD will tell you if the read error is in an area that contains a file. If this type of problem is found on disk, NDD will attempt to correct the file problem by moving the file to another, safer part of the disk.

Performing a Low-Level Format of a Hard Disk

When hard disks are manufactured, they contain random magnetic information. To make the disk usable, the manufacturer of the hard disk drive or disk controller performs a low-level format on the hard disk. This format is much more thorough than the procedure performed by DOS FORMAT. A low-level format prepares the surface of the hard disk to receive a DOS format and checks the surface to detect bad spots.

Occasionally, a working hard disk develops problems that cannot be corrected except by a low-level disk format. Some machines have low-level format programs built into their ROM software. Using the DOS DEBUG program, you can tell the program to begin operating. This low-level format usually is a completely destructive format, however, and other, non-destructive low-level format programs are available. Some examples of non-destructive, low-level format programs are HFORMAT (part of HTEST from Paul Mace Software), SpinRite from Gibson Research, and the Calibrate program in Norton Utilities 5.0. By using one of these low-level format procedures, you may be able to recover some information from the disk.

To use the machine's built-in program to perform a low-level format (which is destructive to data currently on the disk), follow these instructions:

1. Boot the computer, using the original DOS disk in drive A.
2. Begin the DEBUG program, which is located on the DOS disk, by typing the command *debug*.
3. A – prompt should appear on-screen. At this prompt, enter the message

   G=C800:5

   and press Enter. If nothing happens within a minute or two, your machine probably does not have a built-in low-level format program. You must reboot the computer and use a program such as HFORMAT.
4. If a low-level format program does exist in ROM, another prompt appears. At this prompt, enter an interleave number, which controls your hard disk access time. The interleave determines how much information is read from the disk on each pass. You should choose an interleave number from 3 to 6. On most AT-type computers, enter an interleave of 3. On most PC- or XT-type computers, enter an interleave of 6. If your PC-type computer is a turbo, you may be able to choose a lower interleave than 6 and therefore make your disk access faster. If you choose a suboptimum interleave, however, your disk access will be too slow. If, after performing the low-level format and some tests (such as the System Information SYSINFO command), you feel

that your disk access is too slow, try a higher interleave number. Running the Calibrate command will give you the best interleave ratio for your disk. Using Calibrate, you can change the interleave without having to redo the destructive low-level format.

The low-level format may take several hours to perform. After it finishes, you need to run the DOS FDISK command before formatting the disk.

Dealing with Viruses and Sabotage

At some time, you may become the unfortunate victim of deliberate computer-information destruction. Someone may sabotage your information by destroying, changing, or erasing information on your computer disk. Or, your computer may become infected by some type of computer virus program. Virus programs have been known to come from normal commercial software (rarely), from pirated software, and from demos that appear in the mail. Some virus programs are nondestructive and simply give you a message (and a scare). Other virus programs may attempt to destroy all data on your disk.

You can take a few precautions to lessen your chance of being sabotaged. First, load software only from reputable sources, and limit others' access to your computer. Also, set the attributes on important files to read-only. These files should at least include the COMMAND.COM, AUTOEXEC.BAT, and CONFIG.SYS files in your root directory. Compare the size of your copy of COMMAND.COM on your hard disk to the copy on your original DOS diskette. If the sizes differ, your COMMAND.COM may be infected.

Another important step in being prepared for data destruction is having current backups of your computer's information. You particularly may want to keep a backup disk of the files in your root directory. Also, keep a current copy of your original DOS disk and a copy of Norton Utilities handy.

Virus programs continue to get more complicated and destructive. Depending on the nature of the attack, you may not be able to recover any information. If your computer's disk has been compromised by a virus or sabotage, however, Norton Utilities offers *some* hope of recovery. The following paragraphs offer possible solutions to various problems arising from virus programs or sabotage.

Your Files Have Been Erased

Use the Norton Unerase command to recover erased files. Do this before you write new information to your disk.

Your Files and Directories Have Been Erased

Use the Norton Unerase command to recover each directory and any associated files that have been erased.

Your System Files Have Been Altered

Virus programs often attempt to change the COMMAND.COM file or other system files. If you suspect a virus, compare the date and time of the COMMAND.COM file in your hard disk's root directory with the original (or backup) copy of COMMAND.COM. If you notice any difference, replace the infected file on the hard disk.

To replace not only COMMAND.COM but also the other system files, boot your computer from a copy of your original DOS disk in drive A. Use the Norton Disk Tools' Make a Disk Bootable option to copy a fresh version of the system to the hard disk. If your problem was caused by a virus program, examine your hard disk to find and remove that program. Until you are sure that you have corrected the problem, quarantine all files from this computer and the floppy you used to reboot the computer—do not distribute any files (particularly program files) from the computer or floppy to any other computer.

Your AUTOEXEC.BAT File Has Been Altered

If you discover that your AUTOEXEC.BAT file has been changed, try to determine when and why the change was made. Some software installation programs change this file and the CONFIG.SYS file as part of the installation process. Some virus programs, however, may change the AUTOEXEC.BAT file in order to run a destructive program or a counter program that will eventually release a destructive virus. A *counter program* counts the number of times your computer is booted or a program is run, and then activates on a preset count. You should examine your AUTOEXEC.BAT and CONFIG.SYS files and understand the reason for each command. If you notice a suspicious command, replace the old AUTOEXEC.BAT with your backup copy, or delete the unknown command. If AUTOEXEC.BAT calls an unknown program, determine where the program is and what it does. Remove the program from your computer if you do not know its purpose. A well-publicized virus that was sent to hundreds of persons in the guise of a demo program used a command in the AUTOEXEC.BAT file to trigger its main counting mechanism.

A Hidden File or Directory Appears on Your Hard Disk

Some legitimate programs create hidden files or directories on disk as part of a file-protection scheme. Some virus programs, however, also create hidden files and directories in which destructive programs may reside. Using the Norton Control Center (NCC) command, you can see any hidden directories that reside on your disk. If you notice one directory that looks suspicious, investigate. Also, using the Norton File Find command, you can discover any hidden files on disk. Again, if you do not know why the files are there, investigate to find out whether a legitimate program placed them there or whether they were created from an unknown source. If you suspect sabotage, be sure to keep copies of all important files on backup disks until you are sure that the danger is past.

Everything on Your Hard Disk Has Been Erased

If your disk looks like it has been erased completely or formatted, you have several options:

- Boot your computer from the original DOS disk and then use the Norton Unerase command to see whether any directories and files can be saved. Some attacks have been known to rename files and directories. You may have to examine recovered information file-by-file to determine what the information is.

- If the disk was formatted, you can try to unformat the disk by using the Unformat command. If you recently ran the Image command, the recovery will be easier.

- Virus attacks are becoming smarter and more destructive. Having backups of your files is important because some attacks completely destroy data. For these problems, recovering your information from backup diskettes is the only solution.

Responding to DOS Error Messages

This section contains information about what to do if you encounter DOS error messages. Not all possible DOS error messages are covered, but the ones mentioned represent the most commonly seen disk-oriented messages.

`Abort, Retry, Ignore, Fail?`

This message may appear if you attempt to read or write something to a disk, printer, or another device. If a disk is bad or not properly in the disk drive, for example, DOS displays this error message. You have four choices for responding to the prompt: press A to abort, R to retry, I to ignore, or F to fail. The meanings of these options follow:

Option	*Effect*
Abort	Cancels the procedure.
Retry	Tries the procedure again.
Ignore	Ignores the error and proceeds. During a copy, for example, Ignore tells the copy to continue, but the resulting file may have missing information that could not be copied correctly.
Fail	Skips the problem, and DOS tries to continue with the procedure. If the problem is the incapability to access a disk drive, you may be prompted to enter a new current disk drive name. (Fail is similar to Ignore.)

The `Abort, Retry, Ignore, Fail?` message may appear for disk- or other device-related problems.

Disk-Related Problems and Solutions

Sometimes if you choose Retry, DOS can read or write to the disk on the second or third try. Even if this approach works, however, you may need to correct the problem by running the Norton Disk Doctor (NDD) to fix files, or Speed Disk to unfragment files.

If the problem is with a floppy diskette, verify that your disk is properly in the disk drive. Make sure that the disk is not upside-down, for example, and that the disk drive door is shut.

Sometimes the magnetic media in the disk jacket gets stuck because of a jacket flaw or because the media is out of alignment. Remove the diskette from the drive and tap the disk on its side to attempt to loosen it up, being careful not to touch the magnetic media. Place the disk back in the drive and try again.

You should be sure that the disk is formatted and that it is formatted so that it can be read on the disk drive you are using. If you are using a 360K drive, for example, and have inserted a disk originally formatted as a 1.2M disk, it cannot be read in that drive.

If you cannot readily solve the problem, choose the Abort option and examine the disk by using the Norton System Information (SYSINFO) or NDD command.

If you are convinced that the disk is formatted properly for this drive, but DOS is still having trouble reading a file, try to correct the problem by using the Norton Disk Doctor (NDD) command.

Problems Caused by Other Devices

Make sure that your printer is turned on, and that it is on-line. Correct any problems and select Retry.

Also make sure that a cable is attached properly to the device. Correct any problems and select Retry.

DOS may be trying to communicate with some other device that is not turned on or is not attached properly. If so, choose Abort and correct the problem.

If DOS is attempting to communicate through a COM port, make sure that it is set up correctly. You can use the DOS MODE command or the Norton Control Center (NCC) to set up a communications (serial) port. Abort the current procedure and fix the problem.

Access Denied

This message may appear if you attempt to change (write to) a file that has its attribute setting as read-only. You can change this setting with the DOS ATTRIB command or with the Norton File Find command. Make sure that you want to change this file before removing the read-only status.

`Access denied` also may appear if you attempt to use a subdirectory as a file, such as trying to edit the subdirectory.

Bad Command or File Name

This message appears if you enter a command at the DOS prompt that DOS does not recognize—for example, if you misspell the command. If you see this message, first check your spelling.

Another possibility is that you entered a correct command but were not in the proper directory or did not have your PATH command set up to find the command in its directory. Correct your PATH command (usually in your AUTOEXEC.BAT file), or change directories by using the DOS CD command or the Norton Change Directory (NCD) command.

Bad or Missing Command Interpreter

This message usually appears if the file COMMAND.COM is not on the boot disk or if DOS has a problem reading this file. If you attempted to boot from a floppy diskette, perhaps it was not a boot disk. If you were booting from a hard disk, you need to correct the problem by re-booting from drive A with a correct version of DOS and then fixing the problem on your hard disk. You may have to copy COMMAND.COM back to the hard disk's root directory. If your hard disk still has problems, you may need to use the Norton Disk Doctor (NDD).

Cannot Find System Files

This message appears if DOS cannot find the hidden system files required to boot the computer. You cannot make a disk bootable simply by placing the COMMAND.COM file on it. You must use the DOS SYS command or Norton Disk Tools' Make a Disk Bootable option to place these hidden files on a disk.

Cannot Read File Allocation Table

This message may occur if you use the DOS RECOVER command. Rather than use this DOS command, use the Norton Disk Doctor (NDD) to attempt to recover damaged files. If you already have used RECOVER, use Norton Disk Tools to recover from the RECOVER command.

Data Error

This message usually means that a disk has a bad spot and DOS is trying to read or write to that spot. You can attempt to locate and correct this problem by using the Norton Disk Doctor (NDD) command.

Drive Not Ready Reading/ Writing Device

This message can occur if the drive door is not fully closed. Check to see that your diskette is inserted properly in the drive and that the drive door is fully closed. The problem also may be caused by a defective drive. If so, you need to get a qualified technician to correct the problem.

Error in Loading Operating System

This message may appear if DOS is unable to find the proper system information while attempting to boot the system. Turn off your computer and try again. You may need to boot the computer from a DOS diskette in drive A and then correct the problem by writing a fresh copy of the system files to disk by using the DOS SYS command. Alternatively, use the Norton Disk Tools' Make a Disk Bootable option to correct the problem.

Error Writing Fixed Disk

This message may be caused by DOS's incapability to write system start-up information to a disk. Use the Norton Disk Doctor (NDD) command to analyze and correct the problem. If the problem persists, attempt to copy as much information from this disk as possible. You may need to boot from a floppy diskette in drive A. You also may need to perform a low-level format of the disk. See "Performing a Low-Level Format on a Hard Disk," earlier in this appendix.

Error Writing Partition Table

This message may appear during the FORMAT procedure and may be caused by a hardware problem or a physically damaged disk. Probably, the boot record at the beginning of the disk cannot be read or written. A possible solution is to reformat the boot record. You can use Norton Disk Doctor (NDD) to attempt to fix your disk and recover information. However, you may need to replace your disk, get a technician to correct the hardware problem, or perform a low-level format on your disk. For more information, see "Performing a Low-Level Format on a Hard Disk."

File Allocation Table Bad

If this message appears, somehow DOS has lost information about where files are stored. This information normally is kept in the file allocation table (FAT). Two versions of the FAT usually reside on disk. By using the Norton Disk Doctor's Diagnose Disk option, you may be able to recover information from the duplicate FAT.

File Cannot Be Copied to Itself

This message occurs if you omit a required destination when using the COPY command. For example, the command

```
COPY MYFILE.TXT
```

produces this error message because DOS does not enable the file, if it exists, to be written to itself.

File Creation Error

This message occurs if DOS is unable to write a file to a directory. The directory or disk may be full. Use the DIR command to list files and see how much space is available on disk. If the directory or disk is full, you can delete unnecessary files to make room for the file. This error message also can occur if you attempt to write to a read-only file. If you want to write to a file that has the read-only attribute set, you need to change the file's attribute (use the DOS ATTRIB command or Norton's File Find command) or save the file under another name.

Also, the disk may be physically damaged, and DOS may have tried to write the file to a bad spot on the disk. You can verify whether there are bad spots on the disk by running the Norton NDD command. NDD will mark bad spots so that they will not be used to store files.

File Not Found

You get this message if you attempt to access a file that is not in the current directory or is not in the directory of the specified path. You may have misspelled the file name or included an incorrect path. You can use the File Find command to locate the file in another directory. If you still get this message, the file space on the disk may be damaged. You then should try to reclaim the file with Norton Disk Doctor's Diagnose Disk option.

General Failure

This message is displayed if DOS cannot figure out why a problem has occurred. In this case, you may have to do your own fishing for the culprit. If you are attempting to access a disk in a drive, you may want to make sure that the disk is readable. For example, are you attempting to access a 1.2M, 5 1/4-inch disk in a 360K drive, or a 1.44M, 3 1/2-inch disk in a 720K drive? Also, check to see that your diskette is inserted correctly in the disk drive and that the disk drive door is closed all the way. The problem also can be caused by a damaged disk or disk drive. Try the disk in another disk drive or use Norton Disk Doctor to attempt to read the diskette.

Incorrect DOS Version

This message occurs if you attempt to use a DOS external command from a version of DOS other than the one under which the machine was booted—for example, you attempt to use the PRINT command (PRINT.COM) for DOS 3.3 when the machine was booted with DOS 4.0. You should make sure that all your DOS commands on disk are from the same version of DOS. To find out which version of DOS you are using, enter the VER command at the DOS prompt.

Incorrect (or Invalid) Number of Parameters

This message appears if you enter a DOS command with the wrong number of parameters. Check your DOS command syntax and reenter the command.

Insufficient Disk Space

This message appears if you attempt to write a file to a disk that is full or that does not have enough free space to hold the file. To correct the problem, erase unneeded files and retry. You also can use the File Find command to see whether there is enough space on a destination disk to receive one or more files.

Invalid Drive Specification (or Invalid Drive or File Name)

This message appears if you use a drive specification that does not exist. If you use drive D in a DOS command when you have no drive D, for example, DOS gives you this error message.

Invalid Partition Table

This message occurs if DOS attempts to boot the computer from your hard disk and finds something wrong with the computer's partition information. This information should be on your disk at track 0. If this area is bad, you can use Norton Disk Doctor from Disk Tools to diagnose and recover the information for you.

Invalid Path, Not Directory, or Directory Not Empty

This message appears if you attempt to remove a directory that contains files or that does not exist. If you want to remove an existing directory, you must first erase all files and subdirectories contained in that directory.

Memory Allocation Error

This message appears if a program you are running overwrites the area in the computer's memory that stores important DOS information, or if not enough memory is available to load portions of DOS. This command may freeze your computer and cause you to have to reboot. A possible solution to this problem is to lower the number of buffers and/or device drivers specified in your CONFIG.SYS file or to remove some memory-resident (stay-resident, pop-up) programs.

Missing Operating System

You get this message if DOS attempts to boot the computer from a disk that the system thinks is a bootable disk, yet some or all of the system information is missing. To correct the problem, you can reformat the disk with DOS (copy all files first) or use the Norton Disk Doctor's Make a Disk Bootable option. With Norton, none of the files on disk are removed, so you do not have to back up the disk first.

Non-System Disk

This message occurs if you attempt to boot from a disk that does not contain the full DOS system or that has damaged system disks. If you are using a hard disk system, make sure that you do not have a disk in drive A, because the computer then attempts to boot from that disk. If your disk should be bootable but is not, you can attempt to fix the disk by using Norton Disk Doctor's Make a Disk Bootable option.

No Room for System on Destination Disk

This message occurs if you attempt to use the DOS SYS command to place a copy of the system files on a disk, but the disk has not been prepared during the format procedure to receive those files. To make the disk bootable with DOS, you should copy all files from the disk and then reformat the disk with the /S option. The Norton Disk Doctor's Make a Disk Bootable option can create a bootable disk without destroying files, even on a disk that was not formatted to be a system disk.

Not Ready

This message appears if DOS attempts to read or write information to a device and cannot. This problem may occur because the disk drive door or knob is not closed completely, the disk is not formatted, the printer is not turned on or is not on-line, or another device is not ready to receive information. Investigate, correct the problem, and try again.

If a drive becomes overheated, it may produce the `Not ready` message. Check to see whether the computer is getting proper ventilation. (You may need to vacuum the vents around the edges of the computer.) Also, if your computer has an exhaust fan, make sure that it is working properly. Turn off the computer and let the disk cool down. If the problem continues, see a technician for further diagnosis.

Probable Non-DOS Disk

This message occurs during a CHKDSK command if DOS has problems reading the FAT or the disk media descriptor. This problem may occur particularly on a hard disk larger than 32M that is partitioned into several drives. You usually can fix the problem by running the Norton Disk Doctor's Diagnose Disk procedure.

Read Fault Error

This message appears if DOS is unable to read information from a disk. The disk may be seated improperly in the drive, or the drive door may not be closed properly. You probably will get the `Abort, Retry, or Fail` message also. Abort the procedure and reseat the disk. To reseat the disk, take the diskette out of the drive and tap the disk on its side to loosen it up. On a 5 1/4-inch disk, you carefully can place two fingers in the center hole and move the disk in the cover to loosen the disk. Place the diskette back into the drive and close the drive door. If other disks work in the drive, but this one cannot be read, try the Norton Disk Tools' Revive a Defective Diskette option.

Required Parameter Missing

This message occurs if you enter a DOS command with an invalid number of parameters. Check your DOS command syntax and reenter the command.

Sector Not Found

This message may occur as a result of DOS attempting to read or write something to a disk when the sector on the disk cannot be accessed. You probably will see the `Abort, Retry, Ignore or Fail` message also. Abort the current command.

If the problem occurs with a floppy diskette, try to read the information in another drive. Copy all the files you can from the disk. Use the Norton Disk Doctor to find and mark bad spots on the disk. Also try the Norton Disk Tools' Revive a Defective Diskette option. Reformat the floppy or discard it.

If the problem occurs with a hard disk, use the Norton Disk Doctor command to find and mark the bad sectors. If the problem persists on the hard disk, you need to back up all possible files and then perform a low-level format on the disk. For more information, see "Performing a Low-Level Format of a Hard Disk," earlier in the appendix.

Seek Error

This message appears if DOS is unable to find the track on disk that is needed to read or write information to the disk. You also get an `Abort, Retry, Ignore, or Fail` message. Choose to abort the process.

If this message appears while you are trying to access a floppy diskette, take the disk out, tap it on its side, and reinsert it correctly in the drive. If the problem continues, attempt to fix the problem with Norton Disk Tools' Revive a Defective Diskette option. Copy all possible information from the disk and then discard the disk or reformat and reuse it.

If the problem occurs when you are trying to access a hard disk, attempt to copy as much information off the disk as possible. You may try to use the Norton Disk Edit command to edit the bad sectors back to health. After you have recovered as much information as possible, perform a low-level format on the hard disk. For more information, see "Performing a Low-Level Format on a Hard Disk," earlier in the appendix.

Too Many Parameters

This message occurs if you enter a DOS command with an invalid number of parameters. Check your DOS command syntax and reenter the command.

Top Level Process Aborted, Cannot Continue

This message appears if a DOS command failed when trying to access the disk. Reboot and run the Norton Disk Doctor (NDD) procedure to locate and attempt to fix any bad sectors.

Write Protect Error

This message may appear if you attempt to write information to a disk that is write-protected. On a 5 1/4-inch diskette, you set write protection by placing a piece of tape over the notch on the side of the diskette. A 3 1/2-inch diskette is write-protected when you move the write-protect tab so that an open hole appears in the corner of the disk. Before removing write protection, make sure that you want to change information on the disk.

ASCII and Extended ASCII Codes

A computer file consists of a series of codes that are stored on disk. The codes in a file represent text characters, program commands, and other computer codes. All information is stored on disk in *binary code*—a series of 0s and 1s. These 0s and 1s are called *bits*. Generally, information is used in packets of eight bits, which is called a *byte*. The capital letter A, for example, is stored in a file as the following byte (a pattern of 0s and 1s):

01000001

Numbers in the binary numbering system can be converted to a more well-known numbering system—the decimal system—which consists of 10 numbers (0 through 9). The decimal equivalent of the binary number for the letter A is 65. Another numbering system that is used in computing is the hexadecimal numbering system, which consists of 16 numbers (0 through 9 and A through F). The capital letter A is represented by the hexadecimal (Hex) number 41.

If you count the number of possible byte patterns that can be represented from 00000000 to 11111111 (00000001, 00000010, and so on), you will discover that 256 patterns are possible—256 different characters, including letters, numbers, and symbols can be repeated. Decimal representations of a byte can be numbered from 0 to 255, for example, and hexadecimal representations of bytes can be represented as 00 through FF (FF = 255 in decimal).

These 256 byte patterns (which represent characters) have specific meanings on the PC. The first 128 codes are called *ASCII codes*, pronounced ASK-KEY (American Standard Code for Information Interchange). The remaining 128 characters are called *extended ASCII codes*. One reason you need to know something about ASCII codes is so that you can recognize their functions in files. Although the most commonly seen ASCII characters are the normal keyboard characters, other ASCII characters play important roles in the contents of computer files.

The first 32 ASCII codes (0 to 31 in decimal format) have special meanings related generally to communications and to controlling devices such as printers. The ASCII character 12 (0C in HEX), for example, is the form-feed character. If you see this character in a text file, it usually means that when you print the file, the character performs a form feed on the printer at that point. The control character 12 also is known as Ctrl-L or ^L. (L is the twelfth character of the alphabet, and you press Ctrl-L to get the ASCII code on-screen).

Another ASCII character that was mentioned in this book is character number 229 (Hex E5), which is printed as the Greek character sigma (Σ). In the directory area on disk, erased files and directories have each had the first character in their names replaced with ASCII character 229. Because the Norton Utilities Diskedit program usually represents the contents of a file in hexadecimal format, you may need to look for the E5 character to locate erased file names.

Tables E.1, E.2, and E.3 list ASCII characters, including their on-screen character representation, decimal value, and hexadecimal value. Table E.1 also lists the meanings of the ASCII characters and the keystrokes to obtain those characters. The ^ before a letter means to press the Ctrl key. Therefore, ^L means that you must hold down the Ctrl key and press the L key.

Table E.1
Standard and Extended ASCII Codes
Control Characters (0 to 31 decimal)

On-screen Character	*Decimal Code*	*Hexadecimal Code*	*Meaning*	*Keystroke*
	0	0	NUL (null)	^@
☺	1	1	SOH (start-of-header)	^A

On-screen Character	*Decimal Code*	*Hexadecimal Code*	*Meaning*	*Keystroke*
●	2	2	STX (start-of-transmission)	^B
♥	3	3	ETX (end-of-transmission)	^C
♦	4	4	EOT (end-of-text)	^D
♣	5	5	ENQ (enquiry)	^E
♠	6	6	ACK (acknowledge)	^F
•	7	7	BEL (bell)	^G
◘	8	8	BS (backspace)	^H
○	9	9	HT (horizontal tab)	^I
◙	10	A	LF (line feed)	^J
♂	11	B	VT (vertical tab)	^K
♀	12	C	FF (form feed)	^L
♪	13	D	CR (carriage return)	^M
♫	14	E	SO (shift out)	^N
☼	15	F	SI (shift in)	^O
►	16	10	DLE (data link escape)	^P
◄	17	11	DC1 (X-ON)	^Q
↕	18	12	DC2 (tape)	^R
‼	19	13	DC3 (X-OFF)	^S
¶	20	14	DC4 (no tape)	^T

Table E.1 *continued*

On-screen Character	*Decimal Code*	*Hexadecimal Code*	*Meaning*	*Keystroke*
§	21	15	NAK (negative acknowledge)	^U
▬	22	16	SYN (synchronize)	^V
↨	23	17	ETB (end-of-transmission block)	^W
↑	24	18	CAN (cancel)	^X
↓	25	19	EM (end of medium)	^Y
→	26	1A	SUB (substitute)	^Z
←	27	1B	ESC (escape)	^[
∟	28	1C	FS (file separator)	^\
↔	29	1D	GS (group separator)	^]
▲	30	1E	RS (record separator)	^^
▼	31	1F	US (unit separator)	^_

Table E.2
Standard and Extended ASCII Codes
ASCII Keyboard Characters (32 to 127 decimal)

On-screen Character	*Decimal Code*	*Hexadecimal Code*
	32	20
!	33	21
"	34	22
#	35	23
$	36	24

On-screen Character	*Decimal Code*	*Hexadecimal Code*
%	37	25
&	38	26
'	39	27
(	40	28
)	41	29
*	42	2A
+	43	2B
,	44	2C
–	45	2D
.	46	2E
/	47	2F
0	48	30
1	49	31
2	50	32
3	51	33
4	52	34
5	53	35
6	54	36
7	55	37
8	56	38
9	57	39
:	58	3A
;	59	3B
<	60	3C
=	61	3D
>	62	3E
?	63	3F
@	64	40
A	65	41
B	66	42
C	67	43
D	68	44
E	69	45
F	70	46
G	71	47
H	72	48
I	73	49
J	74	4A
K	75	4B
L	76	4C

Table E.2 *continued*

On-screen Character	*Decimal Code*	*Hexadecimal Code*
M	77	4D
N	78	4E
O	79	4F
P	80	50
Q	81	51
R	82	52
S	83	53
T	84	54
U	85	55
V	86	56
W	87	57
X	88	58
Y	89	59
Z	90	5A
[	91	5B
\	92	5C
]	93	5D
^	94	5E
—	95	5F
'	96	60
a	97	61
b	98	62
c	99	63
d	100	64
e	101	65
f	102	66
g	103	67
h	104	68
i	105	69
j	106	6A
k	107	6B
l	108	6C
m	109	6D
n	110	6E
o	111	6F
p	112	70
q	113	71
r	114	72

On-screen Character	*Decimal Code*	*Hexadecimal Code*
s	115	73
t	116	74
u	117	75
v	118	76
w	119	77
x	120	78
y	121	79
z	122	7A
{	123	7B
|	124	7C
}	125	7D
~	126	7E
Δ	127	7F

Table E.3
Standard and Extended ASCII Codes
Extended ASCII codes (128 to 255 decimal)

On-screen Character	*Decimal Code*	*Hexadecimal Code*
Ç	128	80
ü	129	81
é	130	82
â	131	83
ä	132	84
à	133	85
å	134	86
ç	135	87
ê	136	88
ë	137	89
è	138	8A
ï	139	8B

Table E.3 *continued*

On-screen Character	*Decimal Code*	*Hexadecimal Code*
î	140	8C
ì	141	8D
Ä	142	8E
Å	143	8F
É	144	90
æ	145	91
Æ	146	92
ô	147	93
ö	148	94
ò	149	95
û	150	96
ù	151	97
ÿ	152	98
Ö	153	99
Ü	154	9A
¢	155	9B
£	156	9C
¥	157	9D
₧	158	9E
ƒ	159	9F
á	160	A0
í	161	A1
ó	162	A2
ú	163	A3
ñ	164	A4
Ñ	165	A5
ª	166	A6
º	167	A7
¿	168	A8
⌐	169	A9
¬	170	AA
½	171	AB
¼	172	AC
¡	173	AD
«	174	AE
»	175	AF
░	176	B0
▒	177	B1
▓	178	B2
│	179	B3

On-screen Character	*Decimal Code*	*Hexadecimal Code*
┤	180	B4
╡	181	B5
╢	182	B6
╖	183	B7
╕	184	B8
╣	185	B9
║	186	BA
╗	187	BB
╝	188	BC
╜	189	BD
╛	190	BE
┐	191	BF
└	192	C0
┴	193	C1
┬	194	C2
├	195	C3
─	196	C4
┼	197	C5
╞	198	C6
╟	199	C7
╚	200	C8
╔	201	C9
╩	202	CA
╦	203	CB
╠	204	CC
═	205	CD
╬	206	CE
╧	207	CF
╨	208	D0
╤	209	D1
╥	210	D2
╙	211	D3
╘	212	D4
╒	213	D5
╓	214	D6
╫	215	D7
╪	216	D8
┘	217	D9
┌	218	DA

Table E.3 *continued*

On-screen Character	*Decimal Code*	*Hexadecimal Code*
█	219	DB
▄	220	DC
▌	221	DD
▐	222	DE
▀	223	DF
α	224	E0
β	225	E1
Γ	226	E2
π	227	E3
Σ	228	E4
σ	229	E5
µ	230	E6
τ	231	E7
Φ	232	E8
Θ	233	E9
Ω	234	EA
δ	235	EB
∞	236	EC
φ	237	ED
∈	238	EE
∩	239	EF
≡	240	F0
±	241	F1
≥	242	F2
≤	243	F3
⌠	244	F4
⌡	245	F5
÷	246	F6
≈	247	F7
°	248	F8
•	249	F9
·	250	FA
√	251	FB
ⁿ	252	FC
²	253	FD
■	254	FE
	255	FF

Index

C

D

E

F

G

H

O

P

Q

R

S

T

U

V

W

Computer Books From Que Mean PC Performance!

Spreadsheets

1-2-3 Database Techniques $24.95
1-2-3 Graphics Techniques $24.95
1-2-3 Macro Library, 3rd Edition $39.95
1-2-3 Release 2.2 Business Applications $39.95
1-2-3 Release 2.2 Quick Reference $ 7.95
1-2-3 Release 2.2 QuickStart $19.95
1-2-3 Release 2.2 Workbook and Disk $29.95
1-2-3 Release 3 Business Applications $39.95
1-2-3 Release 3 Quick Reference $ 7.95
1-2-3 Release 3 QuickStart $19.95
1-2-3 Release 3 Workbook and Disk $29.95
1-2-3 Tips, Tricks, and Traps, 3rd Edition $22.95
Excel Business Applications: IBM Version $39.95
Excel Quick Reference $ 7.95
Excel QuickStart $19.95
Excel Tips, Tricks, and Traps $22.95
Using 1-2-3, Special Edition $26.95
Using 1-2-3 Release 2.2, Special Edition $26.95
Using 1-2-3 Release 3 $27.95
Using Excel: IBM Version $24.95
Using Lotus Spreadsheet for DeskMate $19.95
Using Quattro Pro $24.95
Using SuperCalc5, 2nd Edition $24.95

Databases

dBASE III Plus Handbook, 2nd Edition $24.95
dBASE III Plus Tips, Tricks, and Traps $22.95
dBASE III Plus Workbook and Disk $29.95
dBASE IV Applications Library, 2nd Edition $39.95
dBASE IV Handbook, 3rd Edition $23.95
dBASE IV Programming Techniques $24.95
dBASE IV QueCards $21.95
dBASE IV Quick Reference $ 7.95
dBASE IV QuickStart $19.95
dBASE IV Tips, Tricks,and Traps, 2nd Edition $21.95
dBASE IV Workbook and Disk $29.95
R:BASE User's Guide, 3rd Edition $22.95
Using Clipper $24.95
Using DataEase $22.95
Using dBASE IV $24.95
Using FoxPro $26.95
Using Paradox 3 $24.95
Using Reflex, 2nd Edition $22.95
Using SQL $24.95

Business Applications

Introduction to Business Software $14.95
Introduction to Personal Computers $19.95
Lotus Add-in Toolkit Guide $22.95
Norton Utilities Quick Reference $ 7.95
PC Tools Quick Reference, 2nd Edition $ 7.95
Q&A Quick Reference $ 7.95
Que's Computer User's Dictionary $9.95
Que's Wizard Book $ 9.95
Smart Tips, Tricks, and Traps $24.95
Using Computers in Business $22.95
Using DacEasy, 2nd Edition $22.95
Using Dollars and Sense: IBM Version, 2nd Edition $19.95
Using Enable/OA $24.95
Using Harvard Project Manager $24.95
Using Lotus Magellan $21.95
Using Managing Your Money, 2nd Edition $19.95
Using Microsoft Works: IBM Version $22.95
Using Norton Utilities $24.95
Using PC Tools Deluxe $24.95
Using Peachtree $22.95
Using PFS: First Choice $22.95
Using PROCOMM PLUS $19.95
Using Q&A, 2nd Edition $23.95
Using Quicken $19.95
Using Smart $22.95
Using SmartWare II $24.95
Using Symphony, Special Edition $29.95

CAD

AutoCAD Advanced Techniques $34.95
AutoCAD Quick Reference $ 7.95
AutoCAD Sourcebook $24.95
Using AutoCAD, 2nd Edition $24.95
Using Generic CADD $24.95

Word Processing

DisplayWrite QuickStart $19.95
Microsoft Word 5 Quick Reference $ 7.95
Microsoft Word 5 Tips, Tricks, and Traps: IBM Version $22.95
Using DisplayWrite 4, 2nd Edition $22.95
Using Microsoft Word 5: IBM Version $22.95
Using MultiMate $22.95
Using Professional Write $19.95
Using Word for Windows $22.95
Using WordPerfect, 3rd Edition $21.95
Using WordPerfect 5 $24.95
Using WordPerfect 5.1, Special Edition $24.95
Using WordStar, 2nd Edition $21.95
WordPerfect QueCards $21.95
WordPerfect Quick Reference $ 7.95
WordPerfect QuickStart $21.95
WordPerfect Tips, Tricks, and Traps, 2nd Edition $22.95
WordPerfect 5 Workbook and Disk $29.95
WordPerfect 5.1 Quick Reference $ 7.95
WordPerfect 5.1 QuickStart $19.95
WordPerfect 5.1 Tips, Tricks, and Traps $22.95
WordPerfect 5.1 Workbook and Disk $29.95

Hardware/Systems

DOS Power Techniques $29.95
DOS Tips, Tricks, and Traps $22.95
DOS Workbook and Disk, 2nd Edition $29.95
Hard Disk Quick Reference $ 7.95
MS-DOS Quick Reference $ 7.95
MS-DOS QuickStart $21.95
MS-DOS User's Guide, Special Edition $29.95
Networking Personal Computers, 3rd Edition $22.95
The Printer Bible $24.95
Que's Guide to Data Recovery $24.95
Understanding UNIX, 2nd Edition $21.95
Upgrading and Repairing PCs $27.95
Using DOS $22.95
Using Microsoft Windows 3, 2nd Edition $22.95
Using Novell NetWare $24.95
Using OS/2 $24.95
Using PC DOS, 3rd Edition $24.95
Using UNIX $24.95
Using Your Hard Disk $29.95
Windows 3 Quick Reference $ 7.95

Desktop Publishing/Graphics

Harvard Graphics Quick Reference $ 7.95
Using Animator $24.95
Using Harvard Graphics $24.95
Using Freelance Plus $24.95
Using PageMaker: IBM Version, 2nd Edition $24.95
Using PFS: First Publisher $22.95
Using Ventura Publisher, 2nd Edition $24.95
Ventura Publisher Tips, Tricks, and Traps, $24.95

Macintosh/Apple II

AppleWorks QuickStart $19.95
The Big Mac Book $27.95
Excel QuickStart $19.95
Excel Tips, Tricks, and Traps $22.95
Que's Macintosh Multimedia Handbook $22.95
Using AppleWorks, 3rd Edition $21.95
Using AppleWorks GS $21.95
Using Dollars and Sense: Macintosh Version $19.95
Using Excel: Macintosh Version $24.95
Using FileMaker $24.95
Using MacroMind Director $29.95
Using MacWrite $22.95
Using Microsoft Word 4: Macintosh Version $22.95
Using Microsoft Works: Macintosh Version, 2nd Edition $22.95
Using PageMaker: Macintosh Version $24.95

Programming/Technical

Assembly Language Quick Reference $ 7.95
C Programmer's Toolkit $39.95
C Programming Guide, 3rd Edition $24.95
C Quick Reference $ 7.95
DOS and BIOS Functions Quick Reference $ 7.95
DOS Programmer's Reference, 2nd Edition $27.95
Oracle Programmer's Guide $24.95
Power Graphics Programming $24.95
QuickBASIC Advanced Techniques $22.95
QuickBASIC Programmer's Toolkit $39.95
QuickBASIC Quick Reference $ 7.95
QuickPascal Programming $22.95
SQL Programmer's Guide $29.95
Turbo C Programming $22.95
Turbo Pascal Advanced Techniques $22.95
Turbo Pascal Programmer's Toolkit $39.95
Turbo Pascal Quick Reference $ 7.95
UNIX Programmer's Quick Reference $ 7.95
Using Assembly Language, 2nd Edition $26.95
Using BASIC $19.95
Using C $27.95
Using QuickBASIC 4 $22.95
Using Turbo Pascal $22.95

For More Information,
Call Toll Free!

1-800-428-5331

All prices and titles subject to change without notice. Non-U.S. prices may be higher. Printed in the U.S.A.